One Damned Island After Another
The Saga of the Seventh Air Force in World War Two

Clive Howard
&
Joe Whitley

TABLE OF CONTENTS

PREFACE

Three years after the attack on pearl harbor, when the Seventh Air Force had molded victory from defeat, Corporal Earl Nelson, a newspaper reporter in civilian life, wrote an editorial which put into passionate words what many Pacific air force men had been thinking for a long time.

The editorial, called "Heroes Don't Win Wars," was published in Brief Magazine, the official Seventh Air Force weekly magazine for which Nelson was a combat correspondent.

Nelson's editorial got off to a rather surprising start — surprising because it survived both Army and Navy censorship — by criticizing bitterly the newspapers, magazines, radio, and even Brief Magazine, for their coverage of the war. The press and radio, Nelson complained, were printing and broadcasting only the fantastic exploits of men who wore medals. The public heroes.

"Why don't they talk about the guy who is just a soldier?" Nelson demanded. "Why doesn't anybody ever mention the poor bastard who got dragged into the Army, got stuck out here on one of these God-forsaken holes, and is doing nothing but his job?

"Ninety — or maybe ninety-nine percent of the guys in the Army never had anything happen to them.

"Take, for example, a guy I know named Chuck who was on KP today. Nothing ever happened to him. He doesn't even get into trouble.

"What does he do all day? He drives a truck. He goes back and forth over the island one hundred miles a day. He goes to a movie at night; probably a very bad and very old movie which he has already seen four of five times. He goes back to his tent and writes a gushy letter to some babe who has probably thrown him over a year ago. He lies in his slit trench at night during air raids. He goes on KP about every fifth day.

"He sure as hell isn't going to get any medals or citations. He won't kill any Japs or knock down any Zeros. He won't do a damned thing to get his name in the papers. He won't even get a promotion.

"There are a lot of guys like Chuck. Most of the guys out here on the islands are like Chuck.

"Don't you think," Nelson asked, "that those guys would like to see their names in print, saying that they're fighting the war too?

"Don't you think a mechanic down on the flight line believes what he is doing is just as important as what the pilot or the gunner is doing?

"Heroes don't win wars; they just get their names in the papers.

"The guys who win wars are the guys who lug reams of paper around, or open thousands of cans of C rations, or clean hundreds of pots and pans, or grease jeeps, or dig latrines, or do any of a thousand jobs that nobody ever heard of, except the poor bastard who has to do them.

"The guys who are just serial numbers. The guys who say 'Yes Sir' like automatons. The guys whose jobs have become so regulated and monotonous that they can do them while their minds are 10,000 miles away.

"They are the real heroes of this war. They are the guys who are winning this war — if it is really being won."

Few correspondents, GI or civilian, could have signed their names to such an editorial without drawing sharp criticism from both sides. Nelson's kind of hero, chary of Stateside and rear echelon observers who flew quick, comfortable tours of the Pacific and then made positive, all-embracing and usually asinine statements about what the average GI was thinking, would have rejected most self-appointed spokesmen. The pilots and gunners could have rendered Nelson's editorial pointless by challenging the authority of a man who had not experienced combat flying.

Nelson was a veteran of both kinds of war. In almost four years of Pacific soldiering, Nelson lived on forty-two islands. Probably that is a record. As a combat correspondent, and before that as a bored soldier who flew combat missions for a break in tedium, Nelson flew fifteen missions, one of them a B-29 strike over Japan.

The editorial, when it reached the Seventh's island outposts, caused a mild sensation and resulted in a heavy flow of letters to Brief. There were letters from average GI's saying they had clipped the editorial and mailed it home. There were a few letters from pilots saying they would gladly swap the privileges of rank and the hazards of one minute over an enemy target for three years of comparative safety as file clerks.

There were many letters from pilots and gunners giving overfull credit for the bombs they had dropped on enemy targets and the bullets they had fired into enemy aircraft, to the men nobody ever mentioned.

The pilots, the gunners, the navigators, the bombardiers, and combat aircrewmen who fought the enemy in the air from Pearl Harbor to Tokyo have had the Pacific victory dedicated to them in headlines, in military decorations, in public demonstrations which have taken many forms in many places.

But to the end of the war, and to this very day, nobody has found a way to tell the story of the men — the ninety or ninety-nine percent of men to whom nothing ever happened.

The men who sat, day after endless day, on the scorched griddles of Pacific sand, where a soldier could, in ten minutes, walk to the end of his world. On the atolls where the only release from a monotony deadlier than enemy bombs was a man's diminishing ability to imagine himself somewhere else.

This narrative has attempted to show as much as possible the part they played in winning the war against Japan. But somehow, neither prose, nor poetry, nor photographs adequately tell their story.

To those men, then, this book is dedicated.

To the hungry men ... the thirsty men ... the lonely men. The forgotten men.

ACKNOWLEDGMENTS

This narrative of the combat history of the Seventh Air Force from Pearl Harbor to the end of the war against Japan is the result of the war and peace-time work of many people. Civilians and soldiers, reporters, photographers and historians, the living and the dead, who collected the facts in photographs and texts, of the Pacific air war — to them should go much of the credit for the final production of this work:

To Colonel Hans C. Adamson, whose foresight was responsible for the AAF program to record faithfully and accurately the deeds of the men and women of the AAF in World War II. He overcame countless serious problems to put his plan into operation-chief of which was the twenty-seven days he spent in an open life-raft in the Pacific with Captain Eddie Rickenbacker and six crewmen of a downed Flying Fortress.

To Lucien Hubbard, motion picture writer and producer, and Jack Kirkland, playwright and producer, who, forsaking commercial commitments, journeyed through the Pacific during the war as civilian representatives of the Personnel Narratives Division. But for their painstaking interviews with Air Forces survivors of Pearl Harbor and the men who participated in the early air actions at Wake, Midway, Guadalcanal, and in the Gilberts and Marshals, the human experiences of more than two years of the Seventh's history would have remained forever buried in cold and colorless operational statistics.

To the combat reporters and photographers of the Seventh, who at great personal risk and in complete anonymity, recorded with camera and typewriter the Seventh's war in the air and on the ground, should go full credit:

To combat reporters Bob Fredericks, Francis Merrigan, Tom Hall, Bill Cunningham, Howard Eaton, and Lee Bastajian.

To Ray Brennan, an editor of the Chicago Times and officer in charge of the Seventh's combat correspondents, whose aggressive spirit helped his men overcome their enlisted status and do a professional job of reporting from the places where things were happening.

To Lawrence Swift, a combat correspondent shot down and killed over Guam while reporting B-25 action during the Marianas campaign.

To combat photographers Fred Shelton, Henry B. Krash, Hulbert Burroughs, Carlos Elmer, Clyde Henderson, John Miller, Louis J. Zacharias, and the cameramen of the Seventh Air Force Combat Camera Unit and Documentary Photography Section.

And to the staff reporters and photographers of Brief Magazine, who toiled in many places and in temperatures from 120 in the shade — on the few damned islands where there was any shade — to 20 degrees below zero in enemy stratosphere, to give the men of the Seventh a weekly magazine.

To Roger Angell, Associate Editor, to Assistant Editors Bob Speer and Richard L. Dugan, to Reporters Bob Price, Alan Hartman, William Groppenbacher, Earl Nelson, Zander Hollander and Romeo Dingle; to Brief Photographers Paul Friend, Lyle Strain, John Modzelewski, Diego de Artega, Harold Klee, and Soon Oak Lee.

To Colonel Wilfred J. Paul, Colonel Clanton W. Williams and their staff at the AAF Historical Archives, Gravelly Point, Virginia.

And to Roosevelt Der Tatevasion, Production and Research Director for the Personnel Narratives Division, and the staff of men and women who spent endless hours searching countless records in the AAF Historical Archives for facts and figures documenting this narrative. To Israel Horowitz, Murray Green, Herbert Rosen, Robert Neprud, Bernard Seigle, Estelle R. Schoenholtz, Florence Barsky and Isabel McCollester, assistants.

CLIVE HOWARD
JOE WHITLEY

CHAPTER I: A QUIET SUNDAY MORNING

At sunset, on the evening of December 6, 1941, a formation of Flying Fortresses soared out over San Francisco, wheeled slowly like giant birds and gradually settled on a course straight across the Pacific toward far-flung Manila; first stop, Hawaii.

Some six thousand miles of sky flecked with clouds and sea specked with islands bridge the space between California and the Philippines. The rock and coral and jungle buttresses of this vast and invisible structure lie so far apart that a long-range bomber on an island-to-island flight, even with miraculous navigation and no headwinds, was scraping the bottom of its fuel tanks when it landed.

But the longest gap of all is between San Francisco and Honolulu, 2,392 miles, with not a rock, not so much as a coral reef, to mar one of the greatest stretches of unbroken blue water on the earth.

The B-17's were airborne more than twelve hours when the fingers of dawn ripped through the cellophane of night. The bomber crews peered eagerly through the clouds scudding beneath them for a sight of land. There was nothing but the tumbling horizon. Far to the west, Oahu, like its sister islands, was still wrapped in darkness and silent in slumber.

Yet, even at this early hour, some men on the island were awake and active. One of these was an engineer in a Honolulu broadcasting station who, throughout the night, had been playing records of Hawaiian music to provide a homing beam for the incoming bombers.

Another was Colonel William E. Farthing, base commander at Hickam Field. It was a new thing in December, 1941 — this mass flight of giant land planes across two thousand miles of black ocean between sunset in California and sunrise in Hawaii; new enough to keep a busy, worried base commander awake most of the night and to send him down to the control tower before full daylight, just to see the big ships come in.

It was a few minutes past five when Colonel Farthing stepped from his quarters into the morning freshness. Except for the eternal mists rolling along the towering Koolau Range, the sky was cloudless. A soft wind stirred the palm leaves. The Colonel thought never in the Islands had he seen a dawn so beautiful as this one promised to be.

It was Sunday, the seventh day of December, 1941.

On a lonely hill called Opana, high above the lush green table of land that rises in gentle terraces to the Koolau Ridge, two young soldiers rubbed their eyes and yawned sleepily. The luminous dial of the alarm clock in their tent showed it to be 3:45 a.m. Except for the mynah birds, scolding from the bushes, they were the only evidence of life in that vast panorama of sea and land.

But to Technician Third Class Joe Lockard and Private George Elliott, nothing was beautiful. They had, to their way of thinking, one of the worst jobs in the Army.

They had slept the night, as they had slept every other night for the past three months, in a tent beside a paneled Army truck containing the instrument known technically as an SCR 270-B Radio Direction Finder. Before the first faint flush of dawn, the two men were grumbling through the business of the day, which was to probe a wide area of the sea with radio waves sent out from their finder. The theory was that, up to a certain distance, if the radio waves encountered anything that shouldn't have been there — like a Jap battleship say — they would bounce back again and make a disturbance called a "pip" on a screen called an oscilloscope. At five other widely separated spots on the island, other grumbling members of the Signal Aircraft Company — Hawaii, went about similar duties.

Nobody in Hawaii knew much about SCR 270-B. On Thanksgiving day, an alert had been called and, by superhuman efforts, all six stations had been kept in continuous operation until December 3. Then, as men grumbled and parts began to break down, it was decided to man all stations from an hour before daylight to an hour after sunrise, from four o'clock to seven o'clock. That made it just perfect for griping.

Shortly before six o'clock, Private Elliott walked over to Lockard who was staring into the oscilloscope.

"Any pips today?" he asked brightly.

Lockard stared at him sourly. No pips today. No pips yesterday. Not a single pip, in fact, in the three months Lockard had spent sweating out the oscilloscope.

By now, full daylight had come, and the few people who were abroad to see the sun, as it burst brilliantly through the swirling Hawaiian mists, met more than their number of stragglers coming in from leave. Military duties had been cut to a minimum consistent with the alert. It was the first Sunday after payday and Honolulu was a good liberty town.

The minute hand of the clock on the wall of the Hickam Control Tower stood at exactly forty-five minutes after five when Colonel Farthing came up the stairs at a lively clip. Besides the regular crew, Colonel Cheney L. Bertholf, adjutant general of the Hawaiian Air Forces, was in the lookout post this particular morning.

"Morning! Cheney," Farthing exclaimed. "What's the matter? Couldn't you sleep either?"

"No, Bill. I wanted to see them come in, too. They should be in around eight-thirty," Bertholf said.

An Army sedan which bore the markings of the base hospital moved down the hangar line and pulled up near the tower. Inside was Captain Anthony D'Alfonso, medical officer of the day. "This will do," he said, yawning. "Got the guns loaded?"

The driver, an enlisted man, reported the guns ready for use.

The "guns" were flit guns. It was the duty of the medical officer of the day to spray incoming planes against insect pests. D'Alfonso, too, was waiting for the Fortresses. He settled back luxuriously against the sedan cushions for a nap until the bombers came.

It was exactly seven o'clock when, on Opana Hill, Lockard and Elliott banked shut the last panel door of their radar truck, turned the last key and looked around for the truck that was to take them down the mountain and to breakfast. No truck. They looked down the narrow, rutted road that they and other members of the signal company had built with their hands and sweat on Thanksgiving Day. Still no truck in sight. Therefore, no breakfast.

Lockard swore. "Of all the stinking jobs in this man's Army —" He turned back toward the radar truck.

"Hey," Elliot exclaimed. "Where you going?"

"I'm supposed to give you training, ain't I?" Lockard growled over his shoulder. "Well, dammit, here's your chance."

It was two minutes after seven by the time the generator had turned up to operating efficiency. Lockard peered into the 6-inch cathode ray which forms the oscilloscope. He couldn't believe what he saw.

For the first time in three months of waiting and watching, something was happening. A "pip" jumped up, so big it seemed to hit him right in the eye.

"George!" Lockard yelled. "Hey, George! Lookit here!"

Elliott came running in from outside. He didn't know much; he didn't have to. There it was. A baby would have dropped his bottle and reached for that shadowy image shooting up and down.

"What is it?" he gasped.

"What do you think it is, coming in at a hundred and fifty miles an hour — a fleet of milk wagons? It's planes, lots of 'em.

"Mark!" Lockard commanded.

Elliott ran for a sheet of transparent paper and placed it over the map which lay beside Lockard.

"Mark! Time, 7:02. Miles 136. That's where I caught it first."

Elliott make quick notations on the transparent paper.

"Joe, what d'ya s'pose they are, those planes?"

"How should I know? Navy planes, maybe — off a carrier."

Lockard reached for the telephone. It wasn't, as he knew, his business to worry about what caused the disturbance. In the language of the soldier, whoever was looking into the 'scope when a pip occurred would know that something was happening and would telephone a place over at Fort Shafter called the Information Center, and something would be done about it by somebody else.

Lockard jiggled the hook of the telephone furiously. No one answered and he took another look into the 'scope.

"Mark! 7:04. 132.

"7:04. 132."

Lockard banged the receiver hook up and down. "By God!" He bellowed, "Somebody's got to answer. "Joe! Joe McDonald!" he yelled into the mouthpiece. "Joe! Joe McDonald."

Sweat greased the palm of Lockard's hand and the telephone slid almost from his grasp. "Joe!" he shouted. "Joe McDonald!" Then, as the instrument on the other end clicked into life, Lockard sighed with relief: "Is that you, Joe?"

"Yeah, this is McDonald," an unexcited voice came back over the telephone.

"Joe, it's Joe Lockard! Lockard, at Opana! I gotta get someone at the Information Center. It's important."

"There ain't nobody there," McDonald's voice came calm and unconcerned. "They closed at seven."

"Listen Joe," Lockard pleaded, "I got to talk to an officer. I may get in trouble for this. Be a pal. Grab somebody. Anybody! Any officer at all!"

There was a silence while Lockard and Elliott watched the 'scope, fascinated. The pip continued to flare violently up and down, the intervals lessening as whatever caused it to appear sped closer and closer toward the station.

Suddenly, the telephone came to life, a new voice, crisp and authoritative, cut in: "This is Lieutenant Tyler, the watch officer."

"Sir," said Lockard in a rush, "this is Opana SCR. A large fleet of planes appeared on the 'scope, time 7:02, miles 136, azimuth zero to 10 degrees. They have been coming toward this station ever since. At 7:04, our last reading, they were at 132.

"7:04. 132."

There was a long silence, then: "I see."

Lockard and Elliott waited tensely.

Then the voice again. "Okay. It's okay. That's all."

The Hickam Field Control Tower rose about fifty feet above the ground and from this height the crew had a broad view of Pearl Harbor and the channel which swept down past Fort Kamehameha to the sea, now clearly visible in the morning light.

Colonel Farthing was standing against the tower window, idly scanning the sky with a pair of binoculars. He swung the glasses momentarily over into Pearl Harbor and picked up the dark outlines which crowded the water — more battleships, cruisers and destroyers than, in his fifteen months at Hickam, he had ever seen in Pearl Harbor. The Colonel's glasses moved out to sea and paused, on a freighter, dark against the water, which crept in from the direction of Barber's Point. The glasses moved over the horizon, then swung abruptly back to the freighter.

"Hello, what's that?"

"What?" asked Bertholf.

"That freighter. She got her landing gear swung outboard and there's a destroyer heading for her, blinking her lights. What's she saying?"

"W — h — o?" spelled out a radio operator of the tower crew. "The destroyer's blinker is saying 'W — h — o.'"

"That's funny," said Farthing, watching through the glasses. "That destroyer is rushing in as though she meant business."

At their radar truck near the tip of the island, Lockard and Elliott plotted the incoming flight until, twenty-two miles out, they lost it in the permanent "echo" of their own radio. Until then, the radar showed the planes speeding directly toward them, straight as bullets truly aimed.

At 7:30 exactly, the truck came to take them down to breakfast. As Lockard and Elliott hurriedly shut up shop again, the planes they had been plotting must have passed directly over their heads, high in the air. They neither saw nor heard them.

At 7:55, from their eyrie high in the control tower, Colonel Farthing and Colonel Bertholf saw a long thin line of planes approaching from Kauai way.

Navy peashooters? Marine planes? Farthing was startled out of his first observation by the sharp dart-like plunge of the line toward Pearl Harbor.

"Damned realistic maneuvers! Wonder what the Marines are doing to the Navy so early today?"

Farthing was following them with his binoculars. They weren't Marine planes. Nor Navy. Nor Army. These were single-engined with fixed undercarriages!

A short, thick, black object fell from the first plane. Another.

Bombs!

The plane zoomed and two orange-red disks flashed in the glare of the morning sun.

"Japs."

The word was drowned in the roar as the first bomb exploded the battleship Arizona.

CHAPTER II: RED SUNS ON THEIR WINGS

In the brief moment when men felt the paralyzing impact of the first bomb; when they heard the first staccato bursts of machine guns; when they saw for the first time the flame and smoke of burning buildings, crumbling planes and sinking ships; in the brief moment when the first dead sprawled in lifeless chunks and the first wounded stared at their own welling blood with dazed surprise — in that quick, terrible second, eyes did not believe what they saw, ears did not believe what they heard and men's minds were unable to translate the sight and sound and smell, on earth and in the sky, into the simple, solid fact that This Was War!

BREAKFAST HAD JUST STARTED IN HICKAM'S BIG CONSOLIDATED Barracks, built to house three thousand, when the first explosion was heard.

Frank Rom, a private first class, ran to the window, expecting to see a plane that had crashed. Instead, he saw planes streaking by with red suns on their wings.

"Japs!" he screamed. "Japs!"

"Pipe Down! Wise guy!"

The chorus of jeers was interrupted by a bomb that crashed through the roof. Trays, dishes, food — and men — spattered in all directions.

Captain D'Alfonso, cat-napping in his car on the hangar line, did not hear the first explosion. His driver had dozed off, too. They were yanked from sleep by the sound of many engines overhead.

"Here come our babies," D'Alfonso said. "Let's go shoot 'em as they land."

The driver reached for the flit guns, handed one to the medical officer and they stepped out onto the runway. Those impotent spray guns, with their charges of insect-spraying liquid, were the only guns ready for the Japs when they came.

Colonel Farthing clattered down the narrow control tower steps with one thought in mind": to disperse Hickam's complement of fifty-seven bomber planes, massed at the seaward end of the strip. There they were — parked wingtip to wingtip. Drop a bomb on them, sweep them with machine-gun fire, and they would collapse like tenpins falling before a bowling ball. It was as simple as that!

In the Bachelor Officers' Quarters of the Fifth Bombardment Group, Lieutenant Carl E. Forsyth was listening to an argument about whether Japan would attack America without warning, when he heard one big explosion, followed by another. He decided they were the big 16-inch guns at Fort Kamehameha.

"There'll be a third," he said to himself.

There was. And so close it shook the building. Forsyth ran to the end of the corridor. He saw a dense column of smoke shooting up from the hangar line. A plane streaked through the smoke and dove on the repair shop of the Hawaiian Air Depot, the biggest machine shop for the Army Air Forces in the entire Pacific.

"The whole depot seemed to jump into the air as I looked at it," Forsyth said.

A section of the roof sailed through the air like a blown leaf. The depot burst into flames.

The bomb that exploded the repair shop came from a line of planes which Colonel Farthing, running now across the open expanse runway, saw coming in from the northwest. The planes swung out to sea, losing altitude, flew back over Hickam and dove across the bows of ships in Pearl Harbor, bombing as they went. Like the dive-bombers in the first long thin line Farthing had seen, they came back to Hickam, bombing and strafing moving objects and parked planes.

They reached the parked bombers ahead of Colonel Farthing. Finally, a formation of Jap bombers came in from the southwest toward objectives so specific that they, as Colonel Farthing expressed it, "seemed to have the names of their targets written on the bombs."

Unopposed, they cruised down Hickam's double line of steel and concrete hangars and, with infuriating deliberation, lobbed their bombs through the broad roofs. Some of them veered slightly out of formation and darted toward the big concrete barracks.

Their bombs went through sidewalls, through the great gaps in the concrete made by the attackers who had preceded them; even through open windows, bringing more death and destruction to the five-story building which — even as the echo of the first bomb explosion still rumbled through the dormitories and corridors — had become a mass of writhing, panic-driven humanity.

The broad staircases bulged with a tide of screaming men fighting their way down to the lower floors. Other men, believing that safety lay on the open roofs, fought and clawed against the tide and were swept out of sight. Men, some of them naked, ran headlong from the building into the storm of bullets and shrapnel.

In the mess hall, thirty-two cooks and kitchen men had stayed at their posts through the sound and fury of exploding bombs. They were busy making sandwiches (which they knew would be needed that day), when the second wave of bombers struck. Bombs started hitting near by.

Some of the cooks and kitchen help headed for the huge ice-boxes and crowded into them in the unfortunate belief that they would find protection there. Then came a direct hit, which turned the mess hall into a shambles.

The iceboxes were split open like eggshells. The concussion, rather than direct bomb wounds, killed the men huddled inside.

Master Sergeant Theodore B. Harman, the mess sergeant, was on his way into the bakery when he saw a great, blue flash. He was blown through a window and, the next he knew, was "coming to" on the ground outside. His head ached with the terrific, ringing clatter that hundreds of steel trays made when the bomb blasts hurled them against the steel rafters. There were about two thousand trays in all, and Harman said the weird sound they made whirling through the air was worse than the explosion of the bomb.

Lieutenant Forsyth, a mild-looking, slight young man, his mind still on the pre-attack argument about whether Japan would strike without warning, ran through the streets of Hickam Field toward the hangar of the Headquarters Squadron, Fifth Bombardment Group, of which he was adjutant. Several times he dodged Japs strafing the north end of the officers' quarters area. Above him, torpedo planes circled lazily over Pearl Harbor. The fire house, as Forsyth ran past it, was a mass of flames. The big repair hangar at the Hawaiian Air Depot was a blazing hulk.

But with all this, nothing seemed real, nothing seemed true and final, until — as he turned in toward his hangar — a soldier ran up, yelling:

"Dixon! Where's Dixon? Dixon!"

Forsyth noticed a man lying beside a truck.

"Is that Dixon?" he asked.

With the soldier, he ran over to the truck. The man lying there was dead and not recognizable. Forsyth opened the dead man's bloody shirt and found his identification tags. It was Dixon.

The soldier collapsed over the body of his friend, crying bitterly. And for the first time that morning, the full, terrible impact of the word War settled on Lieutenant Forsyth.

Gradually the shock and panic and mob paralysis gave way to order and action. Older, cooler heads took charge. Young, unafraid leaders emerged from the chaos. Non-coms plunged into the terrible maelstrom of humanity in the barracks.

"Disperse! Disperse!" they commanded. "Don't gang up!"

Ernest E. Field, acting first sergeant of an AAF ground defense company, was one of the first to recover. At the height of the attack, he ran through the barracks buildings to break up clusters of men who had huddled together.

Under the mess hall, already a shambles, he found forty men huddled together. Field knew that a single direct hit would kill them all.

"Get out and scatter!" he ordered.

Young, frightened, and feeling the instinctive human impulse of safety in numbers, none of them made a move. Silently they sat, not defiantly, but in a daze. Field yanked his .45 out of its holster, released the safety. He pointed the gun into the crowd.

"Now, dammit, scatter!"

The boys scattered. Among those who dashed for safety were a quick-thinking GI who stuffed himself into the steel chamber of a steam roller on the Hickam Hospital lawn; another who dove head first into a metal garbage can so that only his legs thrashed the air; two men who dove under a small truck and who found themselves, a few seconds later, looking at nothing but broad daylight and a skyful of Japs — someone with a better idea had jumped aboard the truck and driven it off to safety; and the panting, out-of-breath corporal who said that he was not afraid and that he was not running — but observed, grinning, that he "passed a heap of fellows who were."

One unidentified lieutenant hauled the heavy iron cover of a manhole off, just outside the mess hall door. He wasted no time arguing, but tripped man after man as they ran out the door and pushed them into the manhole. A bomb struck and blew the lieutenant and the manhole cover to oblivion. But every man he helped into the hole was saved.

And gradually, there grew among the men — the unarmed and unprepared men — the will to fight back, to kill, if they could, the men killing them; to stop, if they could, the holocaust of airplanes, ammunition, gasoline, oil.

Few weapons were at hand. What guns there were, were locked in racks at unit headquarters. The men who reached the racks first had no keys; so they broke the locks with axes or tore down casings with their bare hands. Most of them had never been taught how to assemble the guns, how to mount them, how to shoot them in the peacetime army. And yet, through some sort of miracle, they learned.

They stood their ground, these men. They did the best they could with what little they had. Their best was a pitiful little but their deeds form a great and moving story — the bloody chronicle of the AAF in the battle of Pearl Harbor.

Corporal Charles H. Young wears a Silver Star as a sequel to that Sunday morning. He was in the barracks when the attack began.

"I don't know how I got out of the barracks, or how I got to the Base armament school," he said. "There was a machine gun there; it was in three pieces."

Private Edward Finn, a buddy of Young's, helped him lug the gun out to the baseball diamond. Somehow, they got it together.

"A fellow who came along showed us how to start the ammunition belt in it. When I pulled the trigger it started going."

More accurately, the gun "started going" at Japanese planes which roared back and forth over the ball diamond on shuttle runs between Hickam and Pearl Harbor. One of the Japs, who was making a low-level run at the big barracks, was caught in a spray of bullets from the chattering gun and dropped his bomb harmlessly in center field of the ball park.

Sergeant Stanley A. McLeod, of the 19th Transport Squadron — a Regular Army soldier with two years in on his second hitch — was one of several men who took guns and ran across the open parade ground to the center, where other men were stacking ammunition.

McLeod and the men with him were still loading their guns when several Japanese planes dove in from various directions. The other men ran for the nearest palm trees. They saw McLeod crouching on the parade ground, firing his submachine gun at a plane 150 feet over his head. The other planes dove on McLeod, and the men hiding behind the palm trees broke and ran for better shelter. While they were still running, they heard a terrific blast and, looking back, saw a great crater, and debris climbing into the sky about twenty-five feet from where, seconds before, McLeod had been firing. That was the end of McLeod.

Still another man from the 19th Transport Squadron died that day with a machine gun in his hands. Staff Sergeant Doyle Kimmey, a flight engineer from Texas, got a submachine gun from the squadron supply room. Taking cover under a small truck, he began firing at the low-flying planes which were bombing and strafing the area.

Private Gustave R. Feldman, armed only with a 45 automatic pistol, crouched under the truck with Kimmey. Three Jap planes dove on the parade grounds in front of them.

"That .45 of yours is no good here," Kimmey told the private when the first wave had passed over. "No sense risking your neck."

The private, following the non-com's instructions, ran across the street and burrowed under the Post Exchange building. In the midst of the attack he saw Kimmey's gun cease fire, out of ammunition. As he watched, Kimmey emerged from under the truck, ran out into the open and picked up an abandoned submachine gun and several clips of ammunition. He reached the truck safely, ducked under it, reloaded and resumed firing. The Thompson continued its stuttering fire until a direct hit blew the truck into a thousand pieces — the tough sergeant with it.

Not all the names of the men who died heroes that morning were preserved out of the chaos. Not all these names could be listed anyhow, in a chronicle of this sort. The names of the men, for instance, in Second Lieutenant Ansel B. Vaughn's battery of machine guns, spotted there in the open sun of the parade grounds. The names of eight men in two crews cut down by the Japanese guns; the names of the men — the untrained and unprepared men — who ran forward and took their places.

Lieutenant Vaughn was assigned to command the five little machine guns on tripods set up on the parade grounds. The boy who was trying to fire one of the guns was unfamiliar with it and was having his troubles.

"Here, let me show you," said Vaughn, and got into the harness. He had just stepped away from the gun again, and the gunner had settled into the harness, when a diving plane swung a spray of bullets, cutting down every man in the gun's crew and that of the gun next to it.

Only the lieutenant survived.

Not all of the attackers got back to the ships which had launched them. During one attack, a Jap dove on the gun manned by Staff Sergeant Charles R. (Chuck) Middaugh, heavyweight boxing champion and a football star of the Seventh Corps Area. The sergeant stood fast and followed through with the .30 caliber machine gun. He grunted with satisfaction as he saw smoke trail from the plane. The wounded Jap banked over Pearl Harbor and wobbled off crazily toward the ocean, apparently out of control.

Middaugh was wounded a little later, but stuck to his gun through the attack.

Improvised machine-gun mounts were common that day. One enlisted man dragged a typewriter desk out of a hangar, opened it and placed a .30 caliber machine gun where the typewriter belonged. The drawers he filled with belts of ammunition.

Most of the men at the guns were green, their fire erratic. But the curtain of bullets thrown up by that impromptu battery of guns, spotted in the open on the parade grounds, on the ball diamond, on the lawn in front of the barracks, in the places where the bombs and bullets were thickest, caused more than one Jap to waver from his course.

No men on Oahu displayed more courage that Sunday than the soldiers who, after the first attack, ran to the hangar line to halt, if they could, the spreading destruction. Forty per cent of the men in Hickam's fire house had been killed during the first attack; most of the fire-fighting equipment was smashed beyond use. So the clerks and crew chiefs, the desk officers and pilots — and even the men set free from the guard house after the first bomb struck — worked in as deadly peril as was to be found anywhere on the island that morning.

While airplane tanks exploded in the flame and heat of the hangar infernos, they lugged out cases of ammunition from stacks that were already burning. While explosions that would have blown their soot-blackened bodies into eternity were only seconds away, they pushed and pulled bombers and fighters to safety. They unloaded dynamite and fully-fused cannon shells while bombs exploded around them, while rifle and machine-gun ammunition banged away like deadly firecrackers in burning boxes.

Lieutenant Forsyth — the argument about whether Japan would or would not attack without warning completely forgotten now — joined a group of men inside a burning hangar. An old B-12, useless as an aircraft, had been bombed and set afire. They tried to get the old plane outside the hangar so that the flames would not spread to a B-17 and a B-18 parked next to it.

"The big hangar doors had been sprung by the concussion. We tried tractors, trucks, and our bare hands," Forsyth said, "but we couldn't open them. While we were heaving away, somebody yelled: 'Here they come again!'

"This time it was high-level bombers," Forsyth said. "We stood outside the hangar door watching them with our jaws hanging, until we saw the bombs leaving them.

"Then, in a flash, there just wasn't anybody standing there at all."

Forsyth darted back into the hangar and ran for the supply room, which was in a lean-to at the side of the main hangar. Before he arrived, there was a tremendous explosion. A bomb had come directly through the hole in the roof made by the first one. The concussion snuffed out the fire of the B-12 in a flash. Forsyth was blown twenty feet back against the sprung hangar door.

He got to his feet and started for the supply room again. He made it just as a dive-bomber blew in the outside wall of the lean-to. Forsyth had managed to squirm under two steel desks and remained there until the attackers had passed.

Most of the officers and men in the hangar had been killed. One lieutenant had his leg completely blown off. A water main in front of the demolished fire house had been ripped open by a bomb and water was rushing out in a torrent. The wounded lieutenant was lying half in and half out of the water and his leg was floating away as Forsyth got to him.

"I grabbed the leg and hauled it ashore, then tightened my belt as a tourniquet around the man's stump and sent the man and his leg to the hospital together in a truck," Forsyth said. "I don't know why I grabbed the leg. I guess I had some sort of confused idea they could do something with it at the hospital."

Wounded men were all around.

The Consolidated barracks across the street had been hit again and men were staggering out upon the lawn. The whole expanse, an acre or so, looked like one mass of writhing, struggling humanity. Some were half in and half out of the water, and others, less badly hurt, were dragging them out.

Mingled with the outcries of the wounded was the insistent wail of an automobile horn which had apparently been jammed down by concussion. Someone ran out during the lull and smashed the blaring horn with a rock.

Many men said it was the most nerve-wracking sound heard during the whole attack.

One of those wounded by the bombers which had driven Lieutenant Forsyth under the steel desks, was Corporal Herbert J. Roseman, who — according to the custom of many peacetime soldiers — had spent the night of December 6 standing at the bar of the Royal Hawaiian Hotel dressed in a maroon tuxedo. Roseman survived the first attack on the barracks and ran to the hangar line, where he joined a group trying to pull a medium bomber out of a burning hangar. A bomb exploded on the roof and Roseman was pinned under the falling wreckage. Six men who had been pushing the bomber with him were killed instantly.

The wing of the plane crushed Roseman's chest, snapping two ribs. A footlocker, which he fell next to and which stopped the fall of twisted steel girders, gave Roseman a few inches of clearance. Thirty minutes later, a rescue party got to him and laid him out outside the hangar to wait for an ambulance.

Helpless to move, he saw a Jap plane flash overhead and heard a bomb explode. A piece of shrapnel laid open two inches of his scalp. Another Jap strafer put a .31 caliber bullet in his arm.

Roseman was lifted into the ambulance — a command car with the rear seats torn out — and another soldier was laid beside him. As they rounded the parade ground, Roseman caught a glimpse of a soldier running toward a gun standing on a tripod. Strafers cut the man down in his tracks. Roseman turned to say something to the man beside him. As the other soldier replied, his face was riddled with bullets. The same burst gave Roseman his fourth wound, this time in the leg.

At the peak of the attack, the loudspeaker in the Hickam Control Tower suddenly crackled into life, and above the sound of Japanese engines and Japanese bombs and bullets, the men in the tower heard an American voice calmly ask for landing instructions.

The B-17's, almost forgotten during the first chaotic quarter-hour of the war, had arrived from the mainland. There were fourteen Fortresses in the formation, now arriving singly and at ten-minute intervals, over Oahu. They were in command of Major Truman H. Landon — later a general — one of the best bomber pilots in the world.

Forty miles from the coast of Oahu, Landon had brought his bomber down through the overcast — right in the middle of a flight of nine dive-bombers, headed north. Landon, who at first thought the bombers friendly, was surprised to see them making runs at him.

"Hell, they're Japs!" shouted Cadet-Bombardier Erwin F. Cihack.

The B-17 was doing around 230 miles an hour. The Japs were doing around 170 in old-style, fixed-undercarriage planes. Landon pulled the control column back into his lap and climbed easily out of range. The bombers were unarmed.

At a last minute conference between Major Landon and General Arnold, it had been decided that the guns would be mounted and ammunition would be checked out in Hawaii for the flight to the Philippines. Between California and Hickam, the longest leg of the flight, gasoline was more important than guns and ammunition. As it was, many of the bombers were scraping the bottom of their tanks when they arrived over Oahu. A minor miscalculation in navigation had carried them a hundred miles off course, which accounts for Landon's approach from the north instead of east.

The first B-17 to arrive over Hickam came in on a downwind approach. Captain Gordon Blake, base operations officer, had taken charge of traffic control. Because he had a poor radio voice, he relayed orders through a towerman. Blake saw the bomber coming in with the wind at its back and told the pilot, Lieutenant Bruce Allen, to make another turn and come in upwind.

Allen, with too little gas to make the turn, managed to make the landing anyhow, but burned out the brakes and tires trying to bring the bomber to a stop.

At the same time, another plane, making the conventional upwind approach, came in. The plane's wheels had almost touched the ground when Blake shouted: "Tell him to goose his engines up and get the hell out of here; there's a Jap on his tail."

The man at the mike shouted a warning, but it was too late.

Colonel Farthing, directing the dispersal of salvageable aircraft on the runway, witnessed the tragedy.

Farthing saw the bomber settle on the runway. Over the heavy burbling of its four engines, he heard the high-pitched hum of a diving fighter. The Jap was hurtling down on the Fortress in an almost vertical dive. Farthing saw red darts spurting from the guns in the Jap's wings, and heard the heavy, hollow sound of the cannon in the Jap's nose.

The Fortress collapsed on the runway and broke in two. Flames roared up from broken gas tanks and Farthing saw men running from the plane. Most of them ran to the left, but two men, one of whom was Flight Surgeon William R. Shick, ran to the right. Shick was hit and later died.

In his eagerness to destroy the bomber, the Jap flew into trouble. Farthing saw him shoot toward the ground and prayed he would crash. The Jap hit the ground, bent his prop and smashed in his fuselage, but somehow managed to regain the air and flew away.

The Jap plane was so close to Colonel Farthing, and the scene so vivid, that he read and remembered the last three digits of the number on the plane — 197. A Jap plane with a number ending in 197 was later found on the slopes of Koolau ridge.

The pilot of another of the incoming B-17's was Captain Frank P. Bostrom, who later flew General MacArthur out of the Philippines. Passing Diamond Head, Oahu's famous landfall, he broke radio silence and called Hickam.

"Land west to east," came the level-voiced instructions from the tower, with no hint of what was happening.

Bostrom flew on serenely into pattern. It wasn't until he was close enough to see the columns of smoke that he realized something was wrong. Then the anti-aircraft batteries around Pearl Harbor cut loose and shrapnel began to burst around the plane. The gunners were taking no chances.

Bostrom banked sharply upward and ducked into a projecting cloud-bank to think it over. He milled around in the cloud for about fifteen minutes and then, with gas running dangerously low, called Hickam again. He was told to stay away.

Six Jap fighters jumped Bostrom's big bomber as he turned to circle the island again. The fuselage was pierced in many places and two engines were shot out. But the Fortress stayed in the air and Bostrom called the tower to say he would try a landing on a fairway at Kuhuka Golf Course. Captain Blake, remembering the course as nothing more than a not-yet-reformed cow pasture, advised the pilot against it. But Bostrom put his wheels down and got away with it.

Another B-17, failing to get in at Hickam, landed at Bellows Field on the eastern side of the island. The pilot, Lieutenant Robert Richards, saved the lives of everyone aboard — including two men wounded by gunfire over Hickam — by landing downwind on a 2600-foot fighter strip.

Still another plane landed at Wheeler Field, northwest of Hickam and almost in the center of the island. The bomber raced into the landing with six Japs on its tail, all spewing bullets as fast as their guns could fire. Miraculously, bomber and crew made it intact.

Meanwhile, the rest of the B-17's were landing at Hickam. As Captain Blake brought them in, he directed them to disperse on the other side of the field, shoving their noses into the brush as far as possible.

One pilot, Lieutenant Karl T. Barthlemess, after fighting his bomber to a halt in the bushes on the far side of the field, still did not know that he had flown into a war.

"Hot Ziggity, these maneuvers are realistic," he said as he came across the hangar line. "Who's got a cigarette?" He was lighting the cigarette when a piece of shrapnel whistled past his ear and embedded itself in the concrete wall of a hangar.

Sometime during the first hour of the attack, Sergeant Max Butterfield suddenly remembered an argument he had had on his way to breakfast that morning with Staff Sergeant Charles M. Judd, his pal.

Charlie Judd believed the Japs had a lousy air force, and he had a magazine article to prove it. If the Jap air force was no good — like the magazine article said — how in the hell could they ever attack us, Charlie wanted to know.

After the first attack, Butterfield ran back into the barracks, wondering what Charlie Judd thought about the Jap air force now.

Charlie was stretched out on his bunk, the same way he had been when he stopped Max on his way to breakfast. Only, Charlie was dead. There was a Jap bullet in his head.

Still clutched in the dead man's hand was the September, 1941, issue of Aviation Magazine, opened to an article called "Japanese Air Power."

Charlie Judd, a few minutes before seven o'clock on Sunday morning, December 7, had been reading it aloud to Max:

"Isolated from her Axis fellow aggressors. . . her air force of low offensive strength . . . Japan, if engaged in a great air war, would crumble like a house of cards."

CHAPTER III: "I NEVER WAS SO SCARED"

FROM TEN THOUSAND FEET IN THE AIR THE ISLAND OF OAHU LOOKS like a sagging old shoe with its toe pointed eastward toward the California mainland. Pearl Harbor and Hickam Field are the arch between the toe and the heel.

Twelve miles inland from Pearl Harbor, on a north-by-west course, is Wheeler Field. Eight miles up the toe of the shoe, at about the base of the instep, is Bellows Field. On the north shore, near the Opana radio station which logged the approach of the Japanese planes, is a grassy runway laid along the edge of the surf, a little-used emergency landing field called Haleiwa.

Wheeler, Bellows, and Haleiwa, all fighter bases, were the AAF's first line of defense on the morning of December 7. Bellows and Haleiwa were remote fields with a few flimsy, temporary buildings used mainly for gunnery training. What aircraft they had were obsolete and useless for military action.

Wheeler Field, headquarters of the Hawaiian Air Force fighter wing, was a sprawling, fully developed air base with a glistening, concrete runway bordered on one side by a line of vast steel hangars.

At Wheeler that Sunday morning were seventy-five shiny, new Curtiss P-40 Kittyhawk fighter planes parked so close to each other that a man climbing onto the plane at the head of the line could have walked to the last plane without once dropping to the runway.

At the Officers' Club on Wheeler that Sunday morning, there had been a poker game following a dance. Among the players were two young fighter pilots, Lieutenants George Welch and Ken Taylor, both temporarily assigned to Haleiwa.

As the sun rose, the two pilots were discussing whether to go to bed or drive to Haleiwa for a swim, when the matter was decided for them. Between twenty and thirty dive-bombers came in, one after the other, over the Wheeler hangar line. Welch and Taylor ran outside for a better view.

They were staring open-mouthed at the planes, and Welch was trying to remember what the orange-red circles on the planes meant when the Japs broke formation and began a series of wild, erratic strafing runs with no regard to possible collision.

One of the planes, flying less than two hundred feet off the ground, came straight at Welch and Taylor. They began to run when they saw the bullets chipping asphalt from the road in front of them and made the inside of the club just as bullets splintered the door.

There was a telephone in the center of the room, attached to a long cord. Welch grabbed the phone.

While Welch was trying to rouse Haleiwa and Taylor was hanging over his shoulder, the Japs machine-gunned the Officers' Club. As a Jap came in on one side, the two fliers ran along the corridor away from them, Welch still holding the phone. Shots spattered from the other direction, and the man ran back again as far as the phone cord would reach.

Finally Haleiwa answered. Yes, they had seen planes coming in from the sea — about seventy-five of them. Haleiwa thought they were Navy planes.

No, nothing had happened since.

"They're Japs," Welch yelled, "and they're pasting hell out of Wheeler. Load two of die P-40's — mine and Taylor's."

They hopped into Taylor's car. Bombs were exploding near by, and there was the sound of machine guns overhead; such traffic as was moving when they raced toward the Wheeler gate was erratic indeed.

At every explosion or burst of machine-gun bullets, some vehicles veered right, others spun off to the left, and still other intrepid drivers stepped on the gas and pursued a hell-bent-for-leather course straight ahead. Taylor, one part of his mind still dwelling on peace, wondered if the cops would try to stop him as he careened over the eight-mile stretch of winding road between Wheeler and Haleiwa. He made it in less than ten minutes.

As the car skidded to a stop on the grassy runway at Haleiwa, ground crewmen jumped from the cockpits of two P-40's whose propellers were already turning over. Welch and Taylor scrambled in and were soon airborne. Overhead there was a broken overcast at about 3,000 feet for which the fliers were to be thankful several times that day.

"There's one," said Taylor over the radio. "Big as a pullman car. Let's take it."

They turned toward the plane and were about to cut loose when Welch recognized it as a B-17 which had already been shot at by everything else on the island.

Over Wheeler, Welch and Taylor found no sign of the Japs except the black smoke billowing from bombed hangars and the broad sheet of flame standing into the sky from a long, narrow swath of concrete which had been the parking area for seventy-five brand new fighter planes.

The attack on Wheeler had lasted fifteen minutes. And in that quarter-hour, Wheeler Field's fighter strength, the AAF's first line of defense in Hawaii, was virtually made impotent.

With throttles wide open, Welch and Taylor sped toward Barber's Point. They saw nothing but the dense pall of black smoke drifting above the stricken ships in Pearl Harbor.

Looking down on Ewa, the Marine Air Base, they saw fifteen or twenty dive-bombers gliding in a tight circle. Every few seconds, one of the bombers would pitch out of the circle and dart down over the airstrip. There would be a wink of fire, a mushroom of white smoke, then a mounting blaze and a growing column of black smoke.

Side by side, Welch and Taylor streaked down the sky, breaking into the Jap formation like an express train plowing into a funeral procession.

Welch pressed his gun button and saw flame and smoke and flying debris where, a second before, there had been an airplane with orange-red circles on its wings. Taylor, with the detached, surprised sensation of a witness at a bad accident, saw a Japanese plane in front of him coming apart in the air and noticed that his hand was on his own gun release.

The first Japs they hit never saw anything. The others tried to fire back from their hand-operated rear guns but missed the streaking P-40's, which in level flight were much faster than the Jap dive-bombers with the fixed undercarriages.

Taylor, as he chandelled out of the first pass, saw a Jap bomber running toward the sea.

"I let him have a short burst — I don't think I fired more than fifteen rounds," he said. "As he flamed he went into the most perfect slow roll I've ever seen. All I could see was his wheels sticking out of the smoke, and fire spurting from the ship. He hit the surf right off the beach."

Meanwhile, Welch was in trouble. While he was lining up one Jap in his gunsights, another moved up on him unnoticed. The rear gunner poured a stream of incendiaries into Welch's cockpit.

Smoke enveloped the P-40, and the pilot, thinking he was on fire, pulled up into the overcast. He considered bailing out and thought better of it; the Japs would probably strafe him.

Welch gave his ship the rudder and found it still working. The smoke, which came from an incendiary bullet lodged in the baggage compartment behind the pilot, seemed to thin out; so he came down through the overcast and looked around.

He noticed a plane headed north toward the sea. He figured it was Taylor and tried to catch up, but as he began to overtake the speeding plane, he saw it was another Jap bomber. He closed in behind the Jap and shot him into the sea.

The Japs were scattered in all directions now. Most of them headed toward the open sea.

Taylor, after he had shot down his first Jap, climbed for altitude and spotted another dive-bomber escaping to the sea.

"I pulled up behind him fast and came so close that I could have thrown a rock at him. My first burst killed the rear gunner. I kept firing and smoke started to pour from the Jap. He veered off and began to lose altitude fast."

Welch and Taylor were armed only with .30 caliber machine guns. One of Welch's four guns was jammed, the incendiary still smoked from his baggage compartment, and both planes were nearly out of fuel. But they sped out to sea in pursuit of the Japs.

"I never was so scared in all my life," Welch said afterward. "Once, when we were pretty far out to sea, J called to Ken: 'Hey, what the hell are we doing out here anyway? Let's get back before we really run into something.'"

Wheeler Field, when the pilots came back to refuel and re-arm, was a complete wreck. Smoke and flame belched from buildings and planes. In an effort to save some of the planes, ground-crew personnel had dragged them out to the runway.

"We had a hell of a time landing in that mess," Taylor said.

As soon as the pilots got their ships off the runway, they began yelling for more ammunition. They were told there was none, but Taylor remembered that there were 1,000,000 rounds stored in the 6th Squadron hangar, which now was an inferno. Two mechanics — whose names Taylor and Welch could not remember later — dashed into the hail of exploding bullets and came out dragging cartridge belts and ammunition boxes. While they were loading, and Welch stood by nervously dragging at a cigarette, Major "Wild Bill" Morgan, commanding officer of the 18th Fighter Group, told the pilots to put their planes in a revetment.

The unexpected reprieve came as the pilots were almost ready to take off. They grinned sourly at the crewmen loading the planes and shrugged. An order was an order. Just as they were ready to comply, a crewman loading one of Taylor's guns looked down the runway and yelled, "Look out! Here they come again!"

There were fifteen Jap bombers coming in from the direction of Hickam Field, flying low and in string formation.

Welch and Taylor made a quick decision. It would be suicidal, they knew, to try to taxi the planes to the revetments. It would be equally suicidal to remain where they were. There was only one place to go — up. And fast!

Welch was the first to get off. Taylor, as he saw Welch leave the ground, and as the Japs grew bigger and bigger, gave his engine the gun. As his plane lurched forward, boxes of ammunition flew from its wings; it rolled over dollies, crushed boxes and brushed aside debris. Finally, it gained the runway and roared into the air. He was flying head on into the Japs when he left the ground, which probably saved his life.

"I started firing at them just as my wheels left the ground," he said. "I came out of a chandelle right in the middle of the Japs, sitting smack on the tail of one of them."

Taylor pressed the trigger but felt only the weak recoil of one .30 caliber — the only gun in his ship the crew had had time to load before the Japs came back. The Jap swung into evasive action to shake his pursuer. He made a tight turn and then nosed up into a steep climb. For a fraction of a second, he was poised squarely in Taylor's gunsight. Taylor fired and, next he knew, bullets were splattering his own plane. One smashed through the canopy, hit Taylor's arm and went on to hit the trim tab, where it exploded. Taylor was climbing toward the overcast, hoping he could duck inside it before the Jap cut him to pieces when the firing behind him abruptly ceased. He looked back and saw the Jap ablaze and careening toward the ground.

Welch, who had spotted his friend's predicament, came over and picked the Jap off his tail with one burst, getting in return a series of bursts which put holes in his prop, Prestone cooler, and fuselage. When the coast was clear Taylor, who was bleeding from the wound in his arm, landed. Welch, in spite of the bullet holes in his plane, flew back to Ewa and knocked down another Jap. Out of ammunition again, he landed at Haleiwa. Welch got into the air once more that day. His wingman was Lieutenant John Dains, flying an obsolete P-36.

By that time, everything that moved in the sky was a target, and the air, as Welch and Dains crossed the island, was muddy with anti-aircraft bursts. As the two fighters sped over Schofield Barracks at 1,000 feet, every gun on the post let go. Dains crashed and was killed. Welch got out of the barrage and sped toward Pearl Harbor. There he received another burst from the Navy. He escaped to sea and decided to call it a day. Coming in to Wheeler, he sneaked along the Waianae Hills and finally dodged into a landing without drawing fire.

At Wheeler, a caprice of war allowed a number of planes to get into the air during the attack. In burning, the new P-40's threw a protective screen of black smoke over the obsolete P-36's belonging to the 46th squadron. The old planes were towed across the field and out of harm's way under cover of the smoke.

From there, as soon as they could be made ready, the P-36's were sent into the air. Lieutenants Lewis M. Sanders, P. M. Thacker, Gordon H. Sterling, and Philip M. Rasmussen were in the first flight. Circling Diamond Head at 8,000 feet, they saw Japanese airplanes strafing Bellows Field.

With Sanders leading the group, they moved into the Jap strafers. Sterling maneuvered to the tail of one Jap, but just then another Jap got on his tail; Sanders in turn got on the tail of the second enemy ship. Sterling shot down his Jap but was in turn shot down by the Jap behind him. Sanders then got the Jap who had shot Sterling down. In the general mix-up, Rasmussen got one and a pilot known only as "Available" Brown, who had joined the melee in an old P-36, shot down another Jap.

During the attack the pilots of the P-40's left planeless at Wheeler commandeered cars and raced for Bellows Field which, because of its obscure location, had escaped major damage. As fast as the few P-40's and P-36's on the field were armed and made ready, attempts were made to get them into the air.

The first, a P-40 with Lieutenant George Whiteman at the controls, was taxiing to the takeoff when six Japs dived on it. Whiteman cleared the ground, but as he was climbing from the runway, one of the Japs got on his tail. He went into a vertical bank and was probably the first American pilot during the war to attempt a turn inside a Zero. He paid with his life in learning something that many other Americans learned later in the same, hard way: it couldn't be done.

Lieutenant Hans Christdanson climbed into the cockpit of the next plane on the line. He was moving toward the takeoff when a Jap dove low. The P-40 continued its slow, eccentric course, crossed the runway and plunged into the brush on the other side of the field, its whirling propeller slicing through the underbrush. A dead man was at the controls.

Lieutenant Samuel W. Bishop tried it next. He got into the air and over the ocean before he was shot down. Bishop was lucky — he survived the crash and swam ashore.

The attack ended before the other planes could get into the air.

Seven gallant American pilots got their gunsights on Japanese planes that morning. They shot down eleven of the enemy. Welch accounted for four of them, and Taylor two.

Eleven enemy aircraft divided among seven pilots would, even in the future days when American pilots were ranging the Japanese homeland in the best fighter aircraft in the world, have been considered a remarkable average. Accounting for the elements of inadequate training, obsolete airplanes and guns, and complete tactical surprise, it is all the more remarkable.

More than anything else, it is a fair indication of what might have happened if Hawaii's fighter aircraft had been deployed, armed, and alerted for attack, instead of massed together and drained of fuel and ammunition as a caution against sabotage.

And if only somebody at Fort Shafter had done something about the "pip" that Private Lockard saw racing up and down the oscilloscope on Opana Hill on a quiet Sunday morning in December!

CHAPTER IV: MONDAY IN PARADISE

IT WAS MONDAY, DECEMBER 8, 1941, AND AS COLD AS IT EVER GETS in Paradise.

The wind-driven rain beat through the streets of Hickam and slashed at the runways of Wheeler, Bellows, and the other airfields and encampments on the islands of Hawaii. It whipped at the ragged edges of shattered debris and drenched the spirits of the men left to defend the skeleton of a stricken giant.

Soldiers huddled in tents, wet, weary, and defeated. Hospitals numbered their wounded in long rows and the dead were unburied. And in the few areas which were unmarked by bombs and fire the odor of ginger blossoms was mingled with the stench of death.

The great ships in the harbor either lay on their sides, cracked and bleeding, or had given up the ghost and with great sighs had sunk to the bottom of the channel.

Aircraft, no longer fit to fly, stood riddled and torn on blasted strips or spread their charred remains in gutted hangars.

Men of great stature and bravery, men of calm judgment, looked into the future and found it was black as the clouds scudding down the slopes of the Pali.

Those who escaped the first blow waited for the final pay-off.

This was the Japanese interpretation of the rules of international warfare. While their diplomats had talked brotherhood of man in Washington, their warlords had struck!

Coming in from various directions, starting at 7:55 o'clock, small units of Japanese planes had attacked Pearl Harbor, Hickam, Wheeler, the Marine field at Ewa, and Ft. Kamehameha.

These points were all within a radius of twenty miles, with Pearl Harbor, roughly, in the center. At about the same time another group had hit the Kaneohe Naval Air Station about seventeen air miles northeast of Pearl Harbor. Then these same planes, apparently as an afterthought, had attacked Bellows Field about seventeen miles across the island on the east.

Within the brief span of two hours, the Jap planes had accomplished their mission and departed, leaving behind them a blood-streaked and flame-seared swath of destruction.

According to most observers there were three periods of attack, each lasting about thirty minutes, between 7:55 and 9:30. In the first, Ewa, Ford Island, Pearl Harbor, Hickam, Wheeler Field, and Kaneohe were struck. The second period was devoted chiefly to Hickam, and the third concentrated on Pearl Harbor, Hickam, Wheeler, and Bellows. Each attack was made in a series of waves, or successive blows. The brief duration of the attack did not allow for refueling and rearming the attacking Japanese planes.

Possibly twenty dive-bombers were in that first "long thin line" that Colonel Farthing saw plunging down on Pearl Harbor. The explosions caused by their bombs, particularly the terrific blast that sank the battleship Arizona , were the sounds that awakened Hickam Field shortly before the strafing of that field began.

At the same time, or so soon afterward that it seemed part of the same attack, some half dozen planes from the direction of Ft. Kamehameha had bombed the second line of Hickam hangars.

Then the Jap planes finally disappeared in the mist and mystery that closed in on the shattered dream islands.

Before the ending of the war with Japan, we could only estimate the number of enemy aircraft and naval vessels used during these operations. A Japanese answer was received in an interview with Captain Fuchida Mitsuo on November 28, 1945. Captain Mitsuo, of the Japanese Imperial Navy, was air group commander stationed on the carrier Akagi during the attack.

Captain Mitsuo said that a total of 360 planes and 30 surface craft were used against us that Sunday morning.

In the first wave, 190 planes were launched against Oahu including 50 high-level and 40 torpedo-bomber Kates; 50 dive-bombing Vals; and 50 Zekes (fighters). The second wave of 170 planes included 50 high-level Kate bombers, 80 dive-bomber Vals, and 40 Zekes, according to Captain Mitsuo.

Surface craft, Captain Mitsuo said, included the battleships Hiyei and Kirishima, the carriers Akagi, Kaga, Soryu, Hiryu, Shokaku, and Zuikaku, the heavy cruiser Tone Chikuma, the light cruiser Nagara, and twenty large-type destroyers.

Enemy losses, he stated, included 29 planes, of which nine were lost in the first wave and 20 in the second.

On the morning of the attack, according to later reports of the Roberts Commission, we had only 221 combat planes on Oahu. Of these 102 were out of commission, many of them being overhauled in preparation for transportation to the Philippines. Of the 72 bombers, 33 were out of commission and of the 149 pursuit planes, 69 were being repaired. The only bombers available for real missions were 6 B-17's and 10 A-20's.

The box score was unbelievable. The Japs destroyed 8 B-17's, 22 B-18's, 7 A-2o's, 62 P-40 B's, 10 P-40 Cs, 23 P-36's, and 9 P-26's.

I4I out Of 22 1.

General Martin, on December 16, revealed that total AAF casualties included 163 killed in action, 336 wounded and 43 missing. Hickam Field lost 121 dead, 274 wounded, and 37 missing. At Wheeler Field, 37 were killed, 53 were wounded, and 6 were missing. Bellows lost 5 in dead and 9 wounded.

The enemy had come, inflicted a crushing blow, and departed. But they would come back. It was inevitable. There it lay — Oahu — the pride of the Pacific. A gem for the taking. Reach down, pick it up, gather it in as another bright gem in the spreading light of the rising sun.

It seemed as terrible as that. Hawaii was lost!

When the enemy acted — as act they surely must — when they came back in their battleships and their landing craft, in their planes and their barges — what was to stop them? Our Navy? Glance at blasted Pearl Harbor and gutted Kaneohe. Our Air Force? Count the planes unable to leave the ground and consider the pathetic might of those few that could.

The coastal defenses and anti-aircraft were still there — what there was of them — but how long could they remain effective under the poundings of an unchallenged fleet and the attack of a triumphant air arm?

The men of calm judgment and the frantic service wives alike looked at the sky and the sea and waited for the blow to fall.

Then, suddenly, these men of calm judgment weren't so calm. The attack had stunned — they went through all the reflex and sometimes heroic motions of soldiers under fire, but they were stunned.

Throughout the night, even while they worked, they weighed and worried and consorted with despair. But as the morning broke and the rain fell and the wreckage of their fortress lay about them, something suddenly clicked and permeated through their hearts and guts.

Anger!

This new-found fury spread through the ranks, generals and privates and admirals and gobs alike. And when more than a hundred thousand fighting men suddenly become aroused at the same time — seething with anger and still remaining calm — when all this happens at once, something is sure to break loose.

It did!

Without realizing it, the Japs set off the explosion that had not been part of the plot. Many Americans, on that Monday morning, found themselves sore as hell. And Hawaii, helpless in its defeat, was already on its way back!

The road back started in Alimanu Crater on Oahu that day.

It had been the long-time plan, in case of an enemy attack, for headquarters of all key arms of the service — air, ground, and artillery — to be moved to the Crater where documents, plans, and personnel would be safe from bombing or naval gunfire. So here, in tunnels carved 200 feet into the belly of a hill, was established new headquarters of the Hawaiian Department.

Walls and ceilings had been concreted but not the floors, and dust hung thick on the fetid air. Desks of the men who had to plan the defense of the islands and the American mainland, as well as work out the millions of details, were strung along in rows deep in the tunnels without regard to rank. There were no air-conditioning units working and for a time there was no electricity; fluttering light from oil lamps guided their hands.

At one of the dusty desks in the Crater sat Major General Frederick Martin, commanding officer of the Hawaiian Air Force, which was soon to become the Seventh Air Force. Ill, weary, and heart-broken, he pondered desperately the unescapable questions:

How did it happen? Where did he err? What could he do now?

Through all the anxious weeks of the deepening Japanese-American crisis all possibilities had been examined and weighed. There were two methods by which the enemy might strike: internal sabotage or external attack.

Because 65 per cent of Hawaii's foreign-born population were Japanese and an overwhelming percentage of island-born citizens were of Japanese ancestry — many of whom still retained strong ties with the homeland — it was thought that any attack would come from internal sabotage.

It was impossible to guard the planes against both threats — at least not with the resources which were at hand at the time.

To guard against sabotage and make the most of a limited number of troops, it is necessary to park planes as closely as they can be jammed together in an open spot and put armed men around them. Guns are dismounted, ammunition removed, and tanks drained.

Against external attack, planes are scattered and placed under cover, so that if a raiding force slips through, it can only destroy them one by one. As a safeguard the planes are armed, fueled and made ready for an immediate takeoff so that they can meet the enemy in the air.

The Hawaiian military establishment had gambled on the black. The red came up. They had backed the wrong color on the wheel of chance.

But the General wasn't looking for excuses or making explanations. There was too much to be done. His air force was shattered. Hangars and repair ships at Hickam and Wheeler had been destroyed or badly damaged — they must be repaired or raised from the dust.

And he must have fighting planes in shape to meet the new attack when it came. Would the Japs give him time? Could he make it?

Overnight the unbelievable happened — within a week, a miracle.

Out at Wheeler Field a chunky, jolly little man surveyed the shambles and said quietly:

"Well, boys, looks like our turn at bat."

It was Colonel William J. Flood, then commanding officer of the field.

By the night of December 7, fifteen planes were in the air at Wheeler. Two days later forty-five were flying — repaired from parts salvaged from wrecked fighters and a graveyard of aircraft awaiting repair. Before replacements arrived from the mainland toward the end of the month, eighty ships of one kind or other were usable at Wheeler alone.

These figures are not official. They come from the memories of men who had dodged bullets, worked, sweated, sworn, and got results. They had little time for tabulations. The Roberts Commission report listed thirty-five planes of all types as taking off from Wheeler that first day. But the number isn't important. What is important is that a shattered air force became a fighting air force in a matter of hours when the books said that it couldn't be done.

And General Martin, surveying these miracles, said: "God, give me more Floods!"

Master Sergeant Everest Waid, shop superintendent of Base Engineering at Wheeler, had practically no assembly crews available when the Japs struck, his men having been assigned to ground defense against sabotage before the attack.

At last, however, he found enough men to form seven crews.

"No one slept for a week," he said, "and everything that could be made to fly was patched and put into the air. This included P-26's with a few guns but no armor which could be used for patrol. But it was the P-40's on which we concentrated. They really looked good."

After starting the production rolling at Wheeler and giving his original crews a night's rest after that harrowing week, Waid took his hard-driving crews to Hickam to assemble a shipment of Curtiss P-40's which had been en route from the mainland at the time of the attack.

"For about two weeks after the attack both ground crews and pilots accomplished fantastic things," Waid said. "Then, suddenly, there was the inevitable letdown. Nerves started to crack and things began to happen. My men began making mistakes; that would have never happened a month before. The pilots, who had been on constant, wearing patrols, never complaining and bringing their planes back home in good shape, also felt the letdown.

"One day a flyer with a perfect record forgot to lower his wheels on landing and came in on his belly, ripping his P-40 to bits. And even while we were hauling it in, three more planes, one after the other, made the same error. The pilots walked away from the wrecks like men in a fog. They hadn't any idea how they made such crazy mistakes. They weren't even aware themselves that their nerves had cracked."

The going was tough at Hickam, too, where the destruction was much greater. Here, where the bombers were kept, was the Hawaiian Air Depot, which made history with its time-clock modifications.

Colonel Kingston E. Tibbets, deputy chief of staff for services of the Seventh and commanding officer of the Seventh Air Service Command, was a major then.

"The first repair completed at Hickam was the tail section of a P-40 which had been hit during the attack. This was completed by 11:00 on the morning of December 8. The Depot went on two twelve-hour shifts with a seven-day week. In a short time we had repaired and put in the air some ninety pursuit and other type planes. Many looked like patchwork quilts, but they flew.

"With so much of our materials destroyed and our machinery beaten up we were fortunate to be doing so well. We'd repair a plane, give it such tests as we could on the ground, and then one of the pilots would take it up and pray it held together. Fortunately they all did!

"We concentrated on getting the damaged P-40's into the air immediately after the attack, but later had to check and test new ones as they arrived from the mainland. After the first of the year we began to receive P-39's in crates. We turned out an average of ten a day and they were flown to Wheeler.

"Although our emphasis was on fighters at this time we didn't neglect the big B-17's. They were flown over from the United States and we could keep only a few for our use. We worked them over and then watched them head for the southwest Pacific where, higher headquarters said, they were needed worse than they were in the Central Pacific at the moment.

"Those that were left took an awful beating, flying 2,000-mile patrols constantly. They required first, second, and third echelon maintenance half the time.

"In February the first shipment of civilian workers from the mainland arrived to work at the Depot, and soon afterwards another group arrived. Most of the men were all right and we owe them a lot," he said.

Colonel Tibbets was awarded the Legion of Merit for "exceptionally meritorious service."

The Depot was too close to Pearl Harbor to be safe from the next Jap attack. So the Army built a highly integrated depot in a secret location, much of it underground and the remainder widely dispersed in canyons and camouflaged.

Acres of working space, properly illuminated and air conditioned, with power to run the machines supplied by emergency as well as regular sources, were cut out of the deep earth, safe from all bombing or shell fire.

It was a tremendous undertaking, but under the spur of the expected attack it was accomplished with remarkable swiftness. Tunnels were dug in hillsides and all command posts, ammunition centers, and much of the gas supply were stored underground.

Even today, records and maps of these installations, their capacities and purposes are closely guarded secrets.

On December 18, General Martin was transferred to the mainland (where, a few months later he was to be retired because of bad health) and the Hawaiian Air Force came under the command of Major General

Clarence L. Tinker. Since the overall strategic plan of the moment was only to fortify, prepare, and hold the Islands, the burden of detecting and striking the first blows against any invader lay with the air arm.

Thus the Hawaiian Air Force, of necessity, became a tactical air force. For purposes of command, the old 14th Pursuit Wing, composed of fighter planes, was redesignated the Hawaiian Interceptor Command under Brigadier General Howard C. Davidson.

At Hickam Field, during the attack, General Davidson had grabbed a piece of fire equipment from a wounded soldier and finished the job of saving a burning plane. The rangy, broad-shouldered Texan had been everywhere on the flying line that morning, personally directing the extinguishing of fires, the dispersal of planes and dispatching pursuit planes to strike back at the enemy. He received a Legion of Merit for that work, and later became one of the finest tacticians of the war as Commanding General of the Tenth Air Force in Burma.

For the time being, the old 18th Bombardment Wing retained its designation until February of 1942 when a complete redesignation of the Air Corps units in the Hawaiian area was effected. At this time, the Hawaiian Air Force became the Seventh Air Force, the 18th Bombardment Wing became the VII Bomber Command, and the Hawaiian Interceptor Command became the VII Interceptor Command, later, in May, to be redesignated the VII Fighter Command.

It was as the Seventh Air Force that this group made history.

Now, with the shops at Wheeler groaning with an emergency speed-up, with the hangars at Hickam and the Hawaiian Air Depot spurred to a war-time schedule, and with the arrival of some new aircraft from the mainland, the gaunt outline of an air force began to emerge.

CHAPTER V: "DEFEND! DEFEND!"

THE JAPS WERE RETURNING. GET READY — GET READY!

Guam had been occupied on December 10 and Wake had fallen on December 23. The Gilberts were occupied on December 27. Enemy submarines prowled the waters of Paradise, and on December 15 one of them boldly shelled the islands of Maui and Lanai, southeast of Oahu.

Hawaii was being surrounded by an ominous ring of steel! And the pilots teamed with crew chiefs and mechanics and worked day and night to build airplanes from the wreckage, hoping they could meet the enemy in the air instead of on the ground.

Civilians — old men and young men, the banker and the fisherman, the brown, the yellow, and the white — stood guard on lonely beaches at night and prayed that when the enemy returned they could find the courage to put up a good fight.

The women of the island — the wives and mothers of service men, the women who lived in tidy tropical houses in the hills, shivered in their beds at the sound of musketry in the night and the distant, hollow calls of nervous guards who shot first and then challenged shadows that moved in the darkness.

The Japs were coming!

The enemy agents hidden in the hills believed it and worked frantically at their tiny radios, hoping to send enough vital information that would enable Japanese invaders to reach them before they were captured by searching American patrols.

The generals and admirals felt it and acted. They started a twenty-four-hour-a-day race to build a defense from the ruins.

Radar and air-field construction received top priority on Oahu. But construction wasn't the only answer — destruction was necessary. Pencils moved across maps, and the bull-dozers and dynamite that were being used to construct new fields on outer Hawaiian islands were turned into weapons to destroy them — lest these fields be used by an invading enemy.

From the twisted wrecks of American battleships on the bottom of littered Pearl Harbor, Admiral Nimitz salvaged guns to add to the Island's scant artillery and anti-aircraft defenses.

Dummy planes were built and distributed around the various airfields, masking our pitiful scarcity of planes and intending to confuse any returning enemy raiders. Dummy flying fields were laid out, complete with buildings. With these, our fighter pilots also had training targets with which to learn strafing and dive-bombing.

Defense!

On January 1, General Tinker had available only 202 fighter planes, seventy-eight bombers and seven observation craft.

Of the bombers, forty-two were B-17's and the other thirty-six were B-18's and A-20's — the latter two types unreliable for the long patrol and reconnaissance schedule. Of the fighters 138 were P-40's, twenty-four were P-39's and forty were P-36's and Second-line miscellaneous craft. The observation planes, assigned to the 86th Observation Squadron, were obsolete.

And not all this pitiful handful of planes were always available. Many were frequently grounded for repair and maintenance. It was a never-ending schedule of patrols that extended 800 miles to sea, which meant that — with the outgoing trip, the dog-leg turn, and the return flight — crews were in the air from twelve to fourteen hours, all over water.

Water, water, water. Men came to grow grim at the thought of it. It wasn't like a hop across the English Channel. It was vast expanses of heaving ocean without a landmark. But it provided invaluable training for green pilots who were later to carry out an offensive against the enemy in the largest water theater in the world.

The main assignment of the overworked pilots was to search out any approaching fleet which was too far out to be picked up by radar. But they were always alert for the prowling enemy submarines that infested the waters.

On December 18, six B-18's, several hundred miles out, spotted an oil slick. It was bombed and enlarged to three times its former size, leading the crews to believe they had nailed their first pig boat.

Then again, six days later, three A-20's and a B-18 flew a mission against enemy submarines reported in the Kaulakahi Channel between the islands of Kauai and Niihau, slightly northwest of Oahu. The craft were spotted, bombs dropped, and although they seemed to hit the targets there was no official confirmation of the kills.

But official confirmation was secondary to men who played watchdog for the Islands. Service women and children were being evacuated to the mainland, and flyers shuddered at the thoughts of torpedoes crashing into these crowded ships.

Defend! Defend!

And General Emmons eliminated any plan that did not bear directly on this.

Radar aircraft warning service, which had proved itself the morning of the attack even though its warning had been ignored, was placed under the VII Interceptor Command. This group, which became the VII Fighter Command, also took over the 53rd Coast Artillery Brigade (an anti-aircraft outfit), and all shore-based Navy and Marine aircraft, thus co-ordinating several important defense branches. Later the VII Fighter Command took on the training of fighter pilots for the Fifth and Thirteenth Air Forces at forward bases.

We made one tragic mistake at Pearl Harbor because there was no efficient central headquarters to receive the reports from the radar stations around the Islands. Steps were taken to see that this didn't happen again.

While a mammoth tunnel was being prepared at Ft. Shafter, operations were underway at "Robert," the code name for an old barn in the signal area adjacent to Ft. Shafter. Here, on a huge board, the course of any craft in the vicinity of the Islands was plotted from information called in by outlying posts. Exact charts were kept and there was a shift of soldiers on duty twenty-four hours a day. But the men available were too few, and many able men were needed for combat.

General Davidson, of the Fighter Command, was entrusted with the responsibilities of this growing organization and, faced by a critical manpower shortage, solved his problem by an appeal to the women of the Islands.

Through the Red Cross he contacted Mrs. Roger Williams, Mrs. John Howard, and Mrs. H. A. Walker, life-long Island citizens. He explained the need for help in this vital project.

Requirements were stiff. Women were required to be between twenty and thirty-four, free of family obligations to live at Ft. Shafter, able to pass Army physicals and A-2 intelligence examinations, and to be available twenty-four hours a day if necessary.

The number of available Island women fell short of those needed, so special waivers were granted Army, Navy, and Marine wives slated for evacuation. After two weeks of training, the women, who were to be known as the Women's Air Raid Defense, replaced a group of enlisted men.

Brigadier General Ernest (Mickey) Moore (later head of the VII Fighter Command), then a colonel in charge of the Hawaiian Air Force A-1 Personnel, recalls the beginning of this project.

"We had a bad winter that year. The WARD stayed in that old barn from January until the following May, when they were transferred to the modern quarters in the tunnel. Their working quarters were drafty and damp and they slopped around in boots and overcoats when they went to their quarters and to eat. But there was little sickness, no slacking duties, and no complaints.

"Their overall strength finally reached 146, and they did a tremendous job all during the war," General Moore said.

There is an ancient Hawaiian proverb that says: "I kahiki ka ua, ako e ka hale," which means "While the rain is still far off, thatch your house." An unthatched house awaited the Jap when he struck Pearl Harbor. Now, Oahu worked in frenzied haste to prepare for the rain.

By day Honolulu, once the sleepy Mecca of a million honey-mooners and wanderers of the earth, swarmed with activity. Machine shops roared and shipyards burst with activity. Streets of the city teemed with uniforms of every branch of service as men rushed against time.

Bronzed beach boys, who recently basked in the sun at Waikiki Beach and rode surfboards in on the curling breakers, now worked at the Hawaiian Air Depot.

By night bellowing, bustling Honolulu became a city of the dead. The streets were deserted, save for armed patrols and a few others on official business who moved like ghosts in the darkness.

At Kaimuki and Waikiki, Wahiawa, and Waianae, at Mokapuu Point and the Kolekole pass, and a hundred other points with soft-voweled names, barbed wire and guns studded the tropical foliage. From the Nuuanu Pali, where King Kamehameha I stood, in 1795, and surveyed his domain after his conquest of Oahu, there was nothing but the darkness that rode the winds from the mountains. On lonely beaches where men watched the sea and the sky there was no sound but the sand-muffled footsteps of sentries and the cry of the Aukuu, the night-fishing heron.

During the first few months after the Japs struck, there were less than three hundred officers and four thousand men to perform the duties of a fighter command in this critical theater, as well as to train and send twenty-five pilots a month to the two man-hungry Air Forces fighting in the South and Southwest Pacific. Men were arriving daily from the mainland but they were, mostly, untrained. Men who were inducted on one day and on a ship the next. Fighter pilots untrained at flying over water with no landmarks to guide them. Gunners who had never before touched a machine gun.

Necessity often made for strange and untrained bedfellows. Such as, for instance, the prisoner serving a stretch in the guardhouse of a pre-attack attempt to stow-away in a ship back to the mainland. After the attack he was pressed into service as a cook and three weeks later was made a tail gunner, so hard up were the Air Forces for flight crews. The stories that most cooks were picked because they were former truck drivers or plumbers are legion. But this was a case where tradition was reversed. "He was a damn good gunner, too," his old mess sergeant remembers. "Made pie of quite a few Japs, he did."

Colonel W. S. Steele, of the VII Fighter Command training and operations, remembered these early days vividly. He was then Captain Steele of Wheeler Field.

"Most of the pilots assigned us from the mainland had less than ten hours instruction on the P-40 when they were rushed to Oahu," he said. "Normally, they required sixty to seventy additional hours training, usually spread over a period of six weeks.

"The first five hours were a transitory check out. They were drilled in formation flying, acrobatics, and gunnery. I think we did a good job, for our pilots — all of them did not stay in the Pacific — made records all over the world." Major Francis S. Gabreski, European ace, and Lieutenant John McNicol, later killed when he led the first flight of P-38's from Africa to Italy, were two of them.

Also in the training program that prepared the island for defense, was anti-aircraft practice. Planes trailing long canvas sleeve targets moved over the islands, and the night was made hideous by the gun batteries blasting away as blinding searchlights blazed from the hills. It was like a giant fireworks exhibit at a fair, but with the ominous threat of things to come. Such as Jap bombers.

Flying these target planes took high courage, for gun crews were still learning. Some tow craft disappeared, never to be heard of again. But, through it all, the flyers kept the sense of humor that made it possible for men of the Seventh to beat death and the deadly monotony of the atoll circuit — the loneliest theater in the world. Such as, for instance, the pilot who suddenly found flak bursting all around his plane instead of the target he was pulling. He said nothing until a double burst exploded directly in front of him. Then he growled back at his radio man: "Hey, tell those bastards I'm pulling this damned rag, not pushing it!"

And now, after back-breaking effort and heartbreaking disappointments, the threat of an enemy return could be met without undue fear and trembling. An attack would not have been welcomed. But neither would it have caught Paradise unprepared a second time.

Out of a shambles, out of defeat and alarm, we had gained stature and strength. Even the little islands to the south and southwest — the Line Islands, the Phoenix, the Ellices, and the Fijis — the outpost islands, essential in the great military migration to the battlegrounds of the Pacific and our outer perimeter for defense and eventual attack — even these tiny atolls and islets flexed their muscles and found them growing strong!

CHAPTER VI: A MISSION FOR MORALE

THE CREW CHIEFS AND THE PILOTS, THE MECHANICS AND THE civilians who manned the machine shops, were working, working, working against time, lack of equipment, and the ring that was closing in on three sides of Hawaii.

Fast dwindling stocks of new materials were used sparingly, and ingenious workers scraped the bottom of scrap heaps for materials to patch damaged planes.

And as they worked they looked anxiously toward the east for reinforcements they were afraid wouldn't come, and to the sea and the sky in the west for the Jap ships and planes they were afraid would come at any minute.

The responsibility for this gigantic defense task was on the broad shoulders of General Tinker, one-eighth Indian and a raw-boned man of vision and tireless energy. And while 99 per cent of his mind was occupied with this assignment, one per cent was distracted by a nagging idea that wouldn't let him rest.

A mission against Wake Island!

This idea was born when General Tinker heard the details of the heroic fall of Wake Island on December 23. And it may have been the start of an idea that led him to his death six months later — for his grim interest in Wake never waned and the island seemed to attract him like a loadstar.

Wake, defended by a garrison of four hundred Marines under Major James P. S. Devereaux, a little island sheltering sixty-three Naval personnel and approximately 1,200 civilians, had held out from December 8 (when the first enemy planes appeared), until December 23.

The Japanese, with overwhelming troop superiority and backed by battleships, carriers, and planes, finally landed at 1:30 o'clock in the morning. American troops had faced the landing barges with hand grenades, and, before they surrendered, had killed 3,700 Japs while losing only ninety-six killed. A ratio of thirty-nine to one!

These things General Tinker remembered as he headed for the Crater headquarters for a meeting with General Emmons to propose the first American offensive strike of the Central Pacific.

In the darkness of the catacombs, the generals unrolled a dusty map.

Facing them was the spearhead of Jap power. Tarawa, Jaluit, Wotje, and Eniwetok in the Marshalls — southwest of Hawaii and a direct threat to Oahu and Johnston Island.

Now Wake, which was only 1,029 miles from our Midway outpost, was another link in the chain. Was it to be used as a springboard for an attack on Midway and Hawaii?

It was reasonable strategy for an enemy possessing Japan's advantages. They had planes and pilots tested and sharp from years of aggression in China. They had a fleet. Most of ours was on the bottom of Pearl Harbor. Their bases virtually surrounded us — and any of these bases might be a springboard for an Hawaiian invasion. They might come at any time and from one or several directions.

If we knew what was now happening on Wake Island we might be better prepared. If we knew how much and what type of air power was being concentrated there . . . If we knew whether or not units of the powerful Japanese Navy were lurking near the island . . .

General Tinker and General Emmons reasoned and planned and hoped. They knew that bombing Wake at the moment would be a pleasant but unpractical gesture. But a photographing mission would mean securing information badly needed.

Photographs would answer many questions, but sitting at a desk in the dusty catacombs General Tinker and General Emmons argued the handicaps of such a mission.

Getting these pictures meant a round trip flight of 4,340 miles, staging through Midway. It meant pin-point navigation because the leg between Midway and Wake is unmarked by as much as a flick of an island landmark, and there would be no radio beam to guide planes in to the target.

And Wake had been in Jap hands for a week.

There was importance even beyond the taking of pictures on this mission. This would be the first strike-back in the Central Pacific theater against the enemy. A feeble blow, perhaps, but General Tinker knew that men of the Air Forces would use it as a yardstick for future action.

It had to be successful.

General Tinker picked his crew carefully. Lieutenant Cecil Faulkner, a steady, tested, brilliant veteran of thousands of miles of over-water flying was chosen as pilot. Faulkner was known to be resourceful, calm, and yet daring. And the General knew that it would take daring as well as skill to complete successfully the mission in the old B-17D they were planning to use.

Second Lieutenant Heitzmann, chosen as navigator, was also seasoned in that particular rugged and exhausting type of open-sea flying. He had made several practice navigational missions to Wake before it had fallen, and had learned, as all later navigators must learn, that dead-reckoning was absolutely essential in flying these vast, unmarked distances.

Master Sergeant S. L. Jennings drew the photography assignment. During the pre-war Japanese-American crisis he had been scheduled to go to Wake for a secret photography mission over the Jap-mandated islands in the Carolines. The war had cancelled this assignment. Now he was scheduled to photograph Wake itself.

"It was with a terrific feeling of suspense that we took off from Hickam Field on January 1, 1942," Heitzmann recalled. "It wasn't so much fear of the enemy as it was not knowing what to expect. We had no idea what sort of opposition we would encounter. We had no information as to what sort of weather we could expect, and storms can come up in a hurry in this theater.

"Then, for me, there was the feeling of terrific responsibility for the navigation. It wasn't so bad on the first leg, for northwest from Oahu there is a little help in landmarks. Nihoa Island, a small barren rock that looks like a black crescent with the points turning upward. Necker Island, a dragon-shaped mass of lava. The bare islets of the French Frigate Shoal. I watched them pass underneath with relief, for they were valuable check-points in the emptiness of the oceans."

The old B-17 swung around and hit the runway at Midway without incident. There was a welcome, rest, and an opportunity to relax. The crew drank coffee as black as the sky and chain-smoked cigarettes, watching the smoke scudding off into the darkness.

Three o'clock in the morning of January 2 was the hour for the takeoff. The crew was torn between an apprehensive dread of the unknown and the uneasy desire to "get it over with."

They knew that this flight would take them 1,029 miles southwest into nothingness. They were one unescorted plane against an enemy that had destroyed everything they had touched. They knew that General Tinker and their buddies were "sweating out" this mission.

This was the first offensive strike. Morale and hopes of thousands of men, as well as a chance to secure vital information that might save Hawaii, would be in their hands.

And there was nothing but darkness, mystery, and vast stretches of water between their objectives. For check-points they had vagrant whales and gooney-birds!

"We had made this trip before the war, but this was entirely different," Heitzmann said. "Then, there had been no pressure. There had been a radio beam for a check. Now, there was only silence, emptiness, and a terrific feeling of being completely alone. We knew we were going in in broad daylight. We didn't know what would hit us but we did know that we were asking for it."

They were due over Wake at about 11 o'clock in the morning, but hit strong headwinds. Faulkner watched the gas gauge drop down and down. The scheduled eight hours passed and there wasn't a sight of land. The wind increased and the four engines drank more gas in their labors.

Heitzmann frantically checked and re-checked his instruments. Twelve o'clock — nothing.

"Finally, at one o'clock in the afternoon, we spotted the island," Jennings recalled. "It is a broken ring of coral built on the peak of a submerged volcanic island. There it lay — white, bare, and treeless.

"Expecting every moment to be deluged with flak and enemy fighter planes and wondering as to the adequacy of our armor and few guns against such opposition, I focused my K3B manually-operated camera and made fifteen exposures as we circled the island at 18,000 feet.

"We were amazed when there was no flak nor attack by enemy fighter planes."

When they headed back the fuel indicators showed that there was only two-thirds of the gasoline necessary to reach Midway!

Then, with the crew huddled around the flight deck watching the dropping gas gauge, the murderous return trip began.

"Most pilots would have turned back when we hit the headwinds on the outward trip," Heitzmann said, "but not Faulkner. That guy simply wouldn't quit. He knew how much was riding on our shoulders.

"All of us thought of the odds against us if we had to make a sea landing in enemy dominated territory. I felt terrific pressure because navigation must be zero-perfect if we were to have a chance."

Jennings had finished his picture assignment but wondered if the film would ever be delivered.

"We could only sit and pray we'd make it," the photographer said. "Fortunately the wind kept up, and this time it was an ally instead of an enemy. We caught it on our tail and saw the airspeed indicator go up to ground speed of 250 miles an hour.

"Heitzmann was sweating over his navigation table and time seemed endless as the ocean. At last, on the horizon, we saw the speck that was Midway. It was the most welcome sight we had ever seen!"

Faulkner nursed the old B-17 in with fifteen minutes' gas supply left.

When the weary B-17 rolled to a stop on the runway the crew were deluged by back-thumping crewmen who had sweated out the trip.

"Hell, you guys were gone so long we thought you'd decided to go to Japan to photograph the Emperor's Palace," a crew chief quipped.

But there was no time for celebrations or even for rest. General Tinker was waiting for the pictures. After an hour for refueling, the crew headed for Hickam to deliver nine pictures that told Army authorities the things they wanted to know about Wake.

This pioneer crew also delivered a fine laboratory of experience to pass on to future flyers, and a great morale shot-in-the-arm for the Air Forces.

There were Distinguished Flying Crosses passed out in Oahu for this mission — a trail blazer for the type that finally blasted Hirohito's hatchet men out of this war.

Back on Oahu the men who faced the sea and the unknown might of the enemy found new hope and confidence from this mission.

From Hawaii American crews faced, in the Central Pacific, the largest water theater in the world. It was sixteen million square miles — five times the size of the United States.

Against such handicaps it was inevitable that all crews who made these early long distance flights would not come through as well as did Lieutenant Faulkner's crew. Even an ordinary 2,000-mile patrol flight was a bid for destruction, for at that time aids to navigation and radar were still in their infancy.

There were mishaps and misadventures, some with happy endings and some without. Facing the sea was a terrible ordeal anywhere in this theater, even when there was a well-integrated plan which included the zoning of submarines and rescue planes later in the war.

In the early stages luck was more of a factor than planning.

But some, like Lieutenant Earl B. Cooper and his B-17 crew of eight, were among those who went down at sea and lived to fight again.

Lieutenant Cooper and his crew took off from Hickam Field on December 26 on a reconnaissance flight. For hours they flew westward and anxiously scanned the empty Pacific for the mighty Japanese Navy that was thought to be lurking near by.

Then they headed back for Oahu and, with night coming on they realized that they were lost!

"We flew about in blackness for hours. There was nothing on the horizon but sea and more sea. I cut down the gasoline as much as possible but the gauge kept dropping lower and lower.

"Finally, I saw there was no hope of reaching land. We had all had instructions about what to do when ditching became necessary, but the instruction always seemed useless, for one always pictures such things as happening to someone else.

"Now here we were facing it alone and at night. We had no idea where we were. I searched my brain frantically to remember all the instructions we'd had. But most of it was dim and forgotten.

"I told the crew to prepare for a crash landing. Then I feathered the props and headed down for sea. Holding the nose up I eased her down while the crew braced themselves for the jolt.

"The water came up to meet us and fortunately we were able to land without injuring any of the crew.

"Suddenly the water was all around us and we were swimming away from the sinking plane. We could find only one two-man life raft at first and all of us were forced to crowd on and around it. It was shipping water heavily from the weight. Luckily, another raft broke loose from the plane and came to the surface. Four of the fellows swam over to it.

"Our only provisions were two canteens of three-weeks-old coffee. Not a promising start for a fight against the Pacific Ocean!

"During the next two days we sighted several Navy patrol planes. Each time one would appear on the horizon we'd wave frantically and fire our Very signal pistols. There is, I'm sure, no more desolate feeling possible than watching a potential rescue plane fly by with no indication that they have seen your wild signals.

"As you watch it get farther and farther away your cheers change to curses and you wish the hell he'd fall into the sea.

"At the end of the third day we were almost without hope. We saw no more planes and figured we had drifted out of patrol range.

"The monotony is deadly when you are crowded on a small raft. You do all sorts of things to help pass the time and get your mind off your hopeless situation.

"We added up all the money in the crowd. It amounted to some $600 and we figured all the ways in which we could spend that much money if we were on land," Lieutenant Cooper recalled.

Hunger and thirst were acute. Then a gooney bird, one of those crazy creatures that infest Midway, flew over. Private D. C. McCord, radio operator, shot him with his .45 and the bird fell on the raft. The hungry men tore the bird apart and inside him found a newly swallowed fish. The fish and fowl made a solid, if unepicurean meal.

"By the fourth day it seemed we had been lost a thousand years," Lieutenant Cooper said. "Our eyes were strained and red from looking at the sky. Then someone yelled: 'There's a plane.'

"Again we waved and fired signal pistols. We thought he was going to pass us by but at last he circled. It was one of the famous Navy 'Dumbo' planes. None of us shall ever forget it as long as we live. Then we were picked up and returned to Oahu. It was like coming back from the dead!"

Exhausted and hungry, but otherwise unharmed, they soon returned to a schedule of flying the long stretches of greedy sea from which they had escaped.

These Navy flying boats, the lumbering but extremely effective PBM's, PB2Y's and PB2B's, operating all over the Pacific, saved the lives of hundreds of flyers as they saved Lieutenant Cooper and his men.

Later there were other rescues and the increase in flying activities justified an increase in the size of the rescue service. More boats were acquired and the site of the Honolulu Yacht Club at the Ala Aloana Basin was chosen as a new base, with sub-bases at various points around the island of Oahu as well as Hilo, Hawaii, and Waimoa, Kauai.

General Tinker and General Emmons were not overlooking anything that could be done to safeguard the lives of their harddriven flying crews — they were too precious and too few.

CHAPTER VII: THE ATOLL CIRCUIT

TO THE SOUTH AND THE SOUTHWEST OF HAWAII ARE SCORES OF low sandy atolls. Some rise only a few feet above the sea and are so narrow that a man can stand on the beach and throw a chunk of coral into the ocean on the other side.

They are, mostly, as gaunt and white as gull-picked whale skeletons, and on some the glare of the sun is unbroken by a single tree. These groups include the Ellice, Phoenix, Union, and Line Islands.

Baker and Canton, Nanomea and Christmas and Funafuti — pinpoints of coral reefs and white sand in infinitesimal lost island chains — they were bird sanctuaries and weather stations. Before the war these names were known to few except men of the sea and restless adventurers who follow the sun.

Now, the names that had meant nothing suddenly became as important as Gibraltar and Suez.

These spits of sand in the sun became our outer defense perimeter and were to be the first stepping stones in the seven-league strides of the Seventh Air Force on the road west and north.

In the beginning, however, they were potential Japanese stepping stones to Hawaii, California, and the world.

The great Japanese offensive was moving like a runaway bulldozer. "Too little and too late" became a familiar headline over the stories written by war correspondents in the Pacific.

The enemy drive moved from Formosa to the Dutch East Indies on through New Guinea to the Solomons, the Philippines, the Marianas, the Marshalls, the Gilberts, and Wake.

These conquests made it possible for the enemy practically to choose the strategy with which this part of the war would be fought. With these bases they could quickly concentrate even short-range fighter planes at any point for either offense or defense.

Against this integrated power we were forced to fly the longest missions of any theater of war. Early strikes averaged 2,431 miles (more than four times the distance from London to Berlin), and were flown without fighter escort and entirely over water.

And the enemy possessed more than hastily prepared defenses.

The Carolines, Marshalls, and their islands in the Marianas, had been given to Japan as mandated possessions for token participation against Germany in World War I. There had been a provision that these bases were not to be fortified.

The Japs had ignored their promises and had been secretly building military bases on the islands for years. By the time of the attack these outposts were bristling arsenals. With the occupation of the Gilberts, the enemy held a dagger pointed straight at the heart of Hawaii and the mainland. Many military authorities felt it would be virtually impossible to break this steel ring with orthodox navy and ground forces.

The Air Forces had a terrible and fateful responsibility. From Jap-occupied Tarawa in the Gilberts, it is only 462 miles to Nanomea, in the Ellice group. From Tarawa to Baker it is only 643 miles.

Invasion seemed imminent.

Airfields in these outposts were vital for defense and for keeping supply lines to the south and southwest open. Fortunately, we didn't have to start from scratch in this great undertaking. As early as 1936, practical air officers realized that we were heading toward war in the Pacific. They knew of the Japanese secret fortification projects in the mandated islands. But officially our hands were tied; so the Army decided to match guile with guile.

Robert Campbell, an engineer in the Civil Aeronautics Authority, came in 1936 to Honolulu to become C.A.A. Engineer for the Pacific Ocean Area. Campbell, a sturdy, chunky man with a weather-beaten face and quick smile, had lived planes and airfields for twenty-five years. In the 1930's he had, in six days, built an airstrip on tiny Howland Island (in the Phoenix group) for the ill-fated flight in which Amelia Earhart was lost. These experiences now paid off in the Pacific.

On his arrival in Honolulu he was instructed to make a survey of Canton, Christmas, Johnston, Palmyra, the Ellices, the Phoenix, and other small islands, "for the C.A.A.," to determine which of them were best suited for airfields for land-based planes. The object, it was said, was to determine if such fields could be used "commercially."

This "commercial" angle was one of subterfuge. The project was backed by the Army and Navy.

With nice regard for proprieties, these surveys were duly forwarded to proper civil authorities in Washington. They were also turned over to Air Force Headquarters in Hawaii.

The direction of prevailing winds was noted so that runways could be constructed accordingly; the kind of equipment necessary for the work (which varied on most islands) was listed and slowly acquired; the handicaps of supply and individual difficulties of construction were noted and methods devised to overcome them; the approximate length of time to build each airfield under local conditions and difficulties was estimated and allowed for.

It was a tedious, wearing job, but at last it was accomplished, and when the information was needed we had only to check these plans, re-examine them for error, and go into action.

In October, 1941, Campbell resigned from the C.A.A. and went to work for the Callahan Construction Company, the chief contractor employed by the Army to build the airports for which Campbell had previously planned and surveyed.

Up to that time, American airmen had been delivering Boeing B-17's to Mac Arthur in the Philippines by flying incredible stretches of ocean over a northerly route. With war approaching, officials in the War Department believed that this route would be closed immediately; so the Army set about preparing runways for heavy bombardment craft on Canton, Christmas, New Caledonia, the Fijis, and Australia.

In November, 1941, expeditions were organized in Honolulu for work on Canton and Christmas Islands. Four Navy vessels took 208 military and civilian personnel to Canton, together with a large quantity of supplies.

Canton, the largest and most northerly of the Phoenix group, is 1,600 miles from Oahu. It is a narrow strip of desert island ranging from one hundred to five hundred yards wide. There is no fresh water. It was covered with pig weed and cow trees, a stubby kind of withered oak, and was inhabited by millions of rats. Pan American Airways had built a Clipper base there a few months earlier, but it was a small one and occupied only a tiny piece of the coast.

One lone cocoanut palm, a tree which became a familiar landmark to weary pilots who flew the vast ocean stretches, stood out against the southern sky.

The 804th Engineers and civilian contractors were in charge of the work of transforming Canton into a military airfield. Anticipating trouble —

which developed all too soon — the 804th proceeded to its task fully equipped with defensive weapons and ammunition.

By request, the Navy sent a destroyer to Canton to stand by, and a defense detachment of Marines was also dispatched. The Canton Marines manned five-inch guns and batteries of anti-aircraft guns.

The Engineers ran into difficulties from the start but surmounted them one by one. At Canton there was the problem of fresh water supply, the island being flat and arid. All stills available in Hawaii were purchased from a bankrupt brewery and a bankrupt distillery and used for distilling water.

Empty gasoline drums and 500-gallon fuel tanks were used to ship 70,000 gallons of fresh water to Canton.

On Canton, Campbell was in charge of the civilian crews.

"Our first group of 150 civilian workers were a game, crack crew who had volunteered for the job and knew their business," the engineer said.

"Without them we would have been lost. But it was different with the next group of 150 workers who were sent to us from Los Angeles just before the Pearl Harbor attack. I don't know what they expected, but they seemed to have the idea they were going to work on one of those legendary Pacific paradise islands, and when they saw how we were living they raised hell.

"For a while I thought I would have a mutiny on my hands. We were sleeping in tents and sitting on benches, when we had time to sit, and the food was prepared sort of hit or miss in our own field kitchens. It was not too good, but these civilian workers apparently expected the impossible. Most of them were lazy and some were yellow as well. On December 7, when we got word of the Jap attack on Oahu, fifty or sixty of them took to the brush and we never saw them again until we left the island on December 14 by order of the Navy.

"The work on Canton was killing, particularly in getting heavy bulldozers and graders ashore. We were working against time, too. Our stuff was on a Navy ship and they wanted to get out of there, believing the Japs would strike at any minute.

"There is no natural harbor at Canton so we had to build temporary docks," Campbell continued. "These were washed out by several storms which hit us, leaving us without any means of landing equipment. So, we decided to blast through the coral reef leading into the lagoon which was protected from the storms. We blasted through all right, but even that didn't end our problem because the channel could only be used at high tide.

"To offset this, we would load a pineapple barge with whatever it would hold, bring it through the channel and into the lagoon at high tide. When the barge got close to the shore we would throw heavy planks from the sides to the revetments built on shore and then work like fury to get the barge unloaded before the tide went out.

"We used other ways of beating the time element, too. We devised a method of tying lumber onto rafts and dumping them over the side of the supply ship, letting the tide carry them ashore. We did the same thing with gasoline drums. The tide would carry the stuff in and we would pull it up on land when the tide went out.

"Once we got our bulldozers and carry-alls ashore, the actual work of building runways was easier. Places like Canton and Christmas have a varying depth of topsoil — in the case of Canton very thin — and once this is scraped off there is a good coral base which makes a fine strip even without asphalt coating. When such a strip is graded, watered, and rolled with heavy equipment you have a serviceable runway.

"This use of coral was a trick the Japs never seemed to understand, or perhaps they lacked the heavy equipment to take advantage of it," Campbell said.

"By using coral bases we were able, when necessary, to slap down strips in a matter of days, making it possible to move in fighters and bombers on islands where, by all the rules, if we had to transport basic material, such as concrete, we would have been held up for months."

When the Japs struck at Pearl Harbor, Campbell had unloaded the heavy equipment, built a road from the lagoon dock to the airport site and had started work on the east-west runway.

A week later, all civilians were ordered off Canton, and he rounded up the deserters and loaded all civilians on a Navy supply ship bound for Samoa, which lay 969 miles to the south.

The assignment of defending the island and completing the airstrip was left to the small military detachment. Two weeks later, the Air Forces Engineers and enlisted men had carved an airfield out of the coral, and the first link in the long chain was forged.

This was the beginning of the "Atoll circuit" — the first stage of sweating out the war in the bitter loneliness of the Central Pacific where men were marked for life by the monotony of nothingness.

This was the first of what men of the Seventh Air Force were to call "One Damned Island After Another" — the empty bases to which flyers returned after spanning the vast, empty stretches of ocean — the melancholy homes where mechanics contracted atoll sickness that was almost more than they could bear.

One by one, aviation engineers constructed the island airfields that were to serve as ferrying flights to the Southwest Pacific, as bases for patrol and reconnaissance, and at long last as springboards for the conquest of the Central Pacific.

Transport — patrol — attack! Could more important functions be imagined? General Flood smiled sardonically when he recalled: "The Army told us we would never go farther than five hundred miles from Hawaii, so why construct airfields?"

So completely did the Army change its official mind, however, that not only did the aviation engineers construct the chain of airfields described, but constructed a complete substitute rear route in case the Japs took Canton, the Fijis, or Samoa!

This route, starting in Hawaii, extended through Palmyra or Christmas and on 1,156 miles southwest to Bora Bora in the Society Islands. From there it extended 481 miles west to Aitutakai in the Cook Islands and another 885 miles southwest to Tongatabu in the Tonga Islands. From there the route led either to New Zealand, 1,067 miles southwest, or to New Caledonia, 1,087 miles west, and thence to Australia.

This was a longer but perfectly feasible route, for even fighter planes could be ferried across with the use of extra gas tanks. As things turned out, it was never necessary to use this route, but it was a comfortable backstop for our logistics-burdened Air Force.

Work on other islands, such as Christmas, was also going on. Christmas Island, in the Line group, is 1,161 miles due south of Hawaii. The name has a holiday sound, and the island looks like a profile of Jimmy Durante wearing a flying officer's cap.

A great coral spit, reminiscent of the comedian's nose, juts into Southwest Point. There is a receding chin and skinny neck of coastline that extends southwest.

But the group of 120 civilian workmen and eighty soldiers, who left Oahu on November 14, 1941, felt little comedy or Yuletide spirit in the mood of the island.

The Bay of Wrecks on the east coast, for years a coral-jutted death trap for ships, seemed more typical of the atmosphere when they landed.

On Christmas Island there are scrubby trees and cocoanut palms, salt water lakes and marshes — and little fresh water.

Lieutenant Colonel Lloyd L. Rail of Galesville, Wisconsin, was in charge of the detail that sailed from Pearl Harbor. A thousand-ton barge was chartered and loaded with lumber, construction material, gasoline, and oil. A railroad crane was mounted on another barge.

"Getting the bulldozers and crane ashore was tough sledding," Colonel Rail said. "It was hot as hell and we had to hoard our water because the U.S.S. Haleakala had been able to bring only 20,000 gallons. The ship, however, was equipped with evaporators of thirty tons daily capacity and after we were able to secure containers it stood by and filled them with fresh water.

"By December 5 we were set up and had started to work. The topsoil on Christmas was deeper than Canton's, but underneath was the same fine coral base."

When the Japs struck two days later, Colonel Rail's work — unlike Campbell's on Canton — wasn't interrupted by the desertion of some of his civilian workers.

"Not only did our civilians go all out to step up the building job, but they volunteered for defense of the island against the expected invasion by the Japs. They put in a staggering amount of work and an extra three hours each day for three weeks drilling with the soldiers.

"Three weeks later, when we received a few military reinforcements, they were reluctant to give up their roles as soldiers.

"If the Japs had hit us then, however, they would hardly have been bothered by the resistance, as willing and brave as the soldiers and workers were. Our total armament was exactly four machine guns, one hundred rifles and five pistols!"

At Funafuti (in the Ellice group and 645 miles southwest of Canton), an early Marine base with a seaplane airport, another landing strip was cut. Funafuti is a little over six miles long and from fifty to seven hundred yards wide.

Nanomea, in the Ellice chain and 252 miles north of Funafuti, yielded a staging base and the Campbell-prepared landing strip built for Amelia Earhart on tiny Howland Island was repaired to the extent that it served as an emergency landing strip.

Baker, in the Phoenix group and virtually in the backyard of the Jap-held Gilberts, was carved and scraped until it gave us a field large enough to receive B-17's and B-24's. Scattered herbs, grass, and low shrubs did little to break the eternal glare of the sun and relieve the weary soldier's atoll fever on this former bird sanctuary.

Our occupation and work on Baker was one of the best-kept secrets of the Central Pacific. Jap reconnaissance planes, which might have penetrated the defense screen, were shot down and it is doubtful if they ever discovered we were there. In spite of the island's proximity to the Gilberts it was never bombed, although the Japs did attack our installations on other islands further away.

Brigadier General Robert W. Douglass, who later became Commanding General of the Seventh AAF, paid tribute to the aviation engineers who were responsible for the work. This tribute could fit most of the men who built those early bases.

"In spite of having to overcome the obstacles involved in landing the necessary equipment on an island with an entirely inadequate harbor, an airstrip was built and the first plane landed on it within six days," he said. "The strip could have been used for an emergency landing within three days."

All this construction was done under the very noses of the Japanese, but either their reconnaissance was bad or their attitude was one of cocky indifference. If it was the latter, they were more stupid than would appear likely. If they did not know of the construction, it was undoubtedly because of the secrecy which screened the work of the engineers. This secrecy, on occasion, was completely effective.

Base-building began to pay off when Lieutenant Colonel Sweeney came to Canton on January 17, 1942, with five B-17's, to begin submarine patrol over ocean routes followed by our Navy craft.

Sweeney had left Hickam Field the day before with six planes, but on landing at Palmyra in heavy rain Lieutenant Robert Sullivan's plane hit short of the runway, tearing off the tail section below the vertical fin. The other five planes made the landing but had their troubles. The rain had cut visibility in the immediate vicinity of the island, and the aircraft had literally to feel their way in. Colonel Sweeney barely avoided a crack-up.

Homing by radio compass signals transmitted by Palmyra was impossible because of strong static interference, and although the plane passed within a mile at five hundred feet, it was impossible to see the island. The ground station used radar, and at last brought Sweeney and his crew to safety.

This flight was typical of most of those early days. Danger was a constant companion and Death a persistent co-pilot. The myriad mechanical perfections which were later to reduce operational losses to a minimum were not yet developed.

Leaving Palmyra, the five B-17's winged southwest toward Canton with still more misadventure awaiting. They arrived at night during a storm. Two came in satisfactorily on dead reckoning and two others passed the island. They had requested homing signals from the Pan American station located there, but had not received them. The fifth plane became definitely lost.

Colonel Sweeney was steaming with rage. Immediately on landing he hurried to the Pan American station across the lagoon from the landing strip to demand the reason why no homing signals had been dispatched. There is no record of exactly what was said, or how Sweeney said it, but it must have been a very stormy moment, more than matching the squalls in the heavens.

Sweeney's report of the incident says only: "The radio operator on duty was shortly and properly instructed, and the fifth airplane soon picked up the signals and effected a safe landing."

Facilities at Canton were very limited and gassing was done by hand from fifty-gallon drums. Nor was the gasoline itself satisfactory. It was dirty, watered, and full of metal corrosives. Nevertheless, the anti-submarine patrol was maintained.

On one trip, the plane which had so nearly been lost on arrival at Canton had sighted two submarines off Hull Island, located a few miles southwest of Canton. One of the subs had been bombed with doubtful results.

The following day two of the fortresses were sent to that sector and reported another contact with an undersea boat. Results were again doubtful, but the Japs were learning that we were fighting back and had a dangerous weapon.

Trouble dogged the Canton group. On January 19, while returning from a search mission, Captain George Blakey made a hazardous cross-wind landing, from which the crew walked away, but two propellers and the undercarriage were damaged. There were no spare parts on the islands; so Sweeney sent Lieutenant Francis Seeburger back to Palmyra to remove two props and the landing gear from the damaged B-17 there. On taking off for the return trip Seeburger's plane blew a cylinder head. A head was removed from Sullivan's now well-cannibalized plane and Seeburger returned to Canton with the replacement parts, and within six hours Captain Blakey's plane was in the air again.

Two flights were made to Nandi, in the Fijis, on one of which a submarine was sighted and bombed with doubtful results. On the second, Colonel Sweeney made a side trip to Nausoris, a New Zealand-operated field fifteen miles from Suva.

On January 30, the five planes returned to Hickam and Colonel Sweeney made his report, which placed particular emphasis on the necessity of perfect dead reckoning navigation — a recommendation hardly to be wondered at in view of the dangers on the assignment.

Brigadier General Willis H. Hale, then Commanding General of the VII Bomber Command, in his comment to Headquarters said:

"There is one step towards the improvement of navigation which cannot be made by the VII Bomber Command, but should be made by higher headquarters. One particular difficulty is the newly assigned navigators' reluctance to accept the need for absolute precision in dead reckoning. A large majority of the navigators now assigned to the tactical units are graduates of the Pan American School, Coral Gables, Florida. That school does not teach dead reckoning, nor does it stress the importance of this type of navigation."

All this meant that early navigators on these long hops were learning the hard way. Fortunately for many of them, their pilots were seasoned dead reckoning flyers and frequently took over and brought their ships safely through. The smart navigator thus received crack training under actual conditions. Furthermore, at Hickam the Seventh Air Force didn't relax with its complaint to Headquarters, but started a school of its own, where navigators from the mainland were given added instruction.

In March, a force of 1,100 infantrymen were put aboard the Army Transport President Taylor, together with supplies and equipment for an Air Base force which was to follow, and an ill-fated journey began. The ship arrived at Canton where it struck a reef and cracked open. Fortunately there was no loss of life, but 80 per cent of the supplies and equipment were lost or ruined.

The Air Base force, which arrived on the U.S.S. Haleakala soon afterward, joined the infantrymen in a frantic effort at salvage. During this time General Tinker arrived on an inspection tour.

"Every activity at Canton had been adversely affected by the grounding of the President Taylor" General Tinker said. "When the ship went aground equipment was damaged by oil and salt water. Unloading of the craft was also complicated by the necessity of working in water-filled holds,

"I believe that most of the low morale attributed to Canton arose from this dirty job. However, the fact that these men worked from twelve to fifteen hours a day diving into holds filled with oil and salt water indicates high, rather than low morale."

Probably General Tinker's judgment of morale was sound at the time, but if so there was a violent change before many weary, routine months passed. Master Sergeant Roy W. Freeman, in charge of the Air Base Force, who was later commissioned for his work at Canton, painted a grimmer picture.

"While the engineers, with Hawaiian labor, extended the runway and built another one, the Air Base men built bunkers, salvaged what supplies they could, and set up shops, mess halls, barracks, and other installations," Freeman said. About a third of the island was occupied. The Pan American Headquarters was on one side of the island, which was merely a narrow ring of land curving around the lagoon. The remainder of the island was segregated with heavy mine fields and barbed wire.

"Before we pulled out late in 1942, Canton was a young fortress, with plenty of big guns set up and ranges pre-determined. It was armed for repelling almost any invasion. But in those early days we had only a couple of six-inch guns without sights, four anti-aircraft guns, and a few rifles, side arms and a small radar installation salvaged from the wrecked transport. We would not have exactly welcomed a visit from the Japs.

"That single palm tree was a wonderful help. Until we could rig up a tower, it was the only elevation on the island. We built a platform close up under its spreading fronds and from there sentinels scanned the sea with glasses. Our radio antenna extended to its crest.

"We were short on food and were working deadly hours. The men lost from ten to fifty pounds each during the first six months. Morale really stank. The setup was enough to make a man go nuts, and many did. We heard that about three hundred men on the island at this time were returned to Hawaii, but I can't be sure for there were only a few in our outfit who couldn't take it.

"Besides the constant threat of invasion there was the terrible loneliness and monotony. The food was terrible and the heat so terrific that even some of the Hawaiian boys were sent to the hospital for sunburn. There were almost no facilities for recreation. It was months before we had movies. Swimming was strictly forbidden. There was sense to this, of course, because coral cuts made dangerous wounds and the water was full of tropical fish which would attack any living thing. There were no boats for fishing."

Furthermore, Sergeant Freeman pointed out, there were no women on the island — white or native. In fact, only two women were seen during the first six months. One was an Army nurse, desperately ill, who was transported through on a plane from the South Pacific, and the other the wife of a RAF pilot named McDonald, who flew her and his two children out of Australia to Canada while doing a ferrying job.

Fortunately the Medical Corps was thoroughly competent. They developed a complete hospital setup underground, which would have been invaluable in case of Jap attack. Not that the little island escaped attack completely. Submarines shelled the installations several times, causing some damage, and in 1942 the island was bombed four or five times.

The situation was so critical during those first six months that no records were kept, except those for daily gasoline consumption. Temporary records of crews and passengers of planes stopping there were retained only until the planes reached the next stop. Then the records were destroyed, because, in the event of capture, records would have furnished the Japs a perfect picture of traffic through the station and thus inform them of what reinforcements had gone to the islands "down under."

But regardless of the tension, the danger, the sweat and tears, and monotony, despite the fact that in ten minutes a man could walk to the end of his world and find only sea and sand and coral for comfort, the work went on at Canton and Christmas and other island stepping stones. And where there had been wilderness or swamplands or cocoanut groves there were now airfields, and the Air Transport Command had bases for delivering their precious cargo and priceless planes.

The Seventh Air Force, which had come into being on February 5, 1942, was going through the illness of infancy. It had risen from the old Hawaiian Air Department and out of the chaos and the ruins of Hickam and Wheeler and Bellows. And perhaps no other air force in any theater was born to face so much with so little.

It was like a cripple fighting an elephant with a willow wand. But as it struck out it grew stronger, and the base builders were providing stepping stones for vital patrol, reconnaissance, and ferrying of supplies.

However, while the construction of island outposts may have been gratifying, and the far-visioned few may have recognized in them points for an eventual offensive, no wave of confidence swept the Pacific. The Japs were well entrenched and strong. They were hurling legions of men and mountains of materials into the Southwest Pacific and at any moment might turn east again.

Panic had gone from Hawaii, but not concern over another possible enemy attack. Nerves had calmed, but fear had not departed. Although it had shed its feeling of hysteria, the same old overtones were in the air:

"The Japs are coming — get ready, get ready!"

And now, at last, they were returning. It was early in May of 1942 — and the first traces of the gigantic conflict which was to test the strength of our preparation against the Jap's vaunted power cast a shadow over the vast Pacific. Forces were being gathered which would meet to shape the history of the world. The cards were dealt, the blue chips were down.

The first great battle of the Central Pacific was brewing!

CHAPTER VIII: THE BATTLE OF MIDWAY

SOMEBODY IN TOKYO SENT TO SOMEBODY SOMEWHERE ELSE IN the Japanese Empire the detailed plan, in secret code, of the next blow to be struck at the United States. Somebody sitting before a short wave radio at Pearl Harbor was listening. Somebody else methodically decoded the secret message.

One day the Hawaiian sky was full of harmlessly patrolling B-17's. The next day these same planes were on the ground; mechanics swarmed over them, checking engines and controls, testing bomb releases, hunting flaws in the intricate wiring systems, checking and double-checking the machine guns and bombsights. They were being made ready for a fight.

Now, finally, we knew where the Japs were going to strike.

The target was Midway. Then, probably, Hawaii. Then — well, there was the California mainland. It might not follow, of course. But it could. It could happen if Midway fell. It could happen if Midway, then Hawaii, became their outposts instead of ours.

The intercepted communication revealing the Jap plan to attack Midway with an invasion force, supported by a tremendous task force, was not specific as to date. June 1 seemed likely, although any time up to June 5 seemed probable.

This information fell into our hands about the middle of May.

It could have been a deliberately contrived misdirection to send what little fleet we had, and the few combat aircraft we had, on an 1100-mile wild goose chase while the Jap fleet and landing force struck instead at almost undefended Hawaii.

Or it could have been that the Japanese did not know we had cracked their secret military code.

The Army and Navy decided to gamble. The payoff, if they could intercept the Japanese fleet at Midway, was too great to overlook. The gamble worked. The Battle of Midway was a Navy show, essentially. But the Seventh Air Force did its share. It slugged and tortured and harassed the enemy, striking, tearing, delaying, throwing plans off schedule. It made its kills, and it took its losses, and it produced its heroes.

The Navy minimized but did not deny its aid. It could not, very well, in view of the record.

The men who had been flying the B-17's on patrol since the start of the war — a wearing, monotonous, griping routine which left their nerves ragged and their morale low — were pleased but perplexed when the order came through on May 18 putting them on ground alert. The B-i8's took up their work as best they could. This limited the distances from the Island which could be patrolled and was further proof of the risks involved in the great gamble.

The alerted B-17 crews began to sense action. They were eager, but they were apprehensive.

Were they ready for combat?

For four long months, from December 7 until April 1, the long-range bombers had been doing nothing but patrol. Except for an occasional bomb dropped on what they suspected was an enemy submarine, bombardiers had no training. Gunners had found no targets.

On April 1, 25 per cent of the planes of VII Bomber Command were made available for combat. This helped somewhat, but the simple and tragic truth is that the crews were not ready.

Then, on May 20, the period of alert expanded to one of action and the next day six planes of the 431st, two from the 31st and one from the 72nd squadron were flown to Midway. The 1400-air-mile flight was completed without mishap. Lt. Col. Walter Sweeney was commanding and under him were such experienced men as Cecil Faulkner, Bob Sullivan, Bob Andrews, Paul Payne — men with reputations as sound as the great planes they flew.

At Midway, with practically no rest after the long flight from Oahu, the nine crews were immediately thrown into patrol. Another day went by, and still another, the brutal, long-range patrols continuing without cessation — with the flight crews, pilots included, doing their own servicing. In two days before the actual beginning of hostilities, combat crews flew approximately thirty hours each, in addition to accomplishing their own maintenance.

Colonel Sweeney protested to the Midway commander that his men couldn't keep it up, that if the crews were thrown into combat on top of the gruelling patrol flights, their chances for survival would be lessened.

The Midway commander, tense with genuine alarm, refused to relieve the crews. Sweeney and his crews carried on. Still no Japs.

Then, suddenly, when the men were draining the last reservoirs of their strength, it happened. A Navy search plane, on the morning of June 3, radioed to Midway that an enemy surface force was approaching from the west.

Shortly before noon, Colonel Sweeney called his men about him. The eight pilots besides himself who were to take part in the first strike from Midway were Gregory and Woodbury, who were to accompany Sweeney in the first element; Tokarz, Sullivan, and Payne, who made up the second; Faulkner, Steedman, and Andrews, who comprised the third. There were no more seasoned over-water fliers in the world than these nine and when they roared into the air from Eastern Island on Midway atoll, they were as qualified as any man could be to undertake the difficult job of locating and bombing the invading force.

The laconic intelligence report reads this way: "Late in the afternoon, at a distance of 570 miles south of west of Midway, interception of the Japanese force was effected."

What no report could adequately say and no man could fittingly express is the impact, on the American fliers, of the first startling sight of the Japanese task force as it broke into view.

Sweeney turned to his co-pilot, Everett Wessman. "Good God," he said, "look at 'em!"

Wessman saw, on the placid blue surface of the ocean, the rigid, precise outlines of ships sailing in battle formation; ships which stood squarely into the sparkling, lacy wakes of ships ahead of them — a pattern stretching beyond the horizon and unbroken except for the sweeping curlicues of escort vessels circling the fringes of the formation.

It was a staggering force even for that period, estimated to number forty-five ships, including five battleships or big cruisers, a number of destroyers and auxiliary ships and transports.

Sweeney switched the interplane radio onto "command," and gave instructions. "Element two go in at 10,000 feet, element three at 12,000." He was taking his own flight in over the Japanese fleet at 8,000 feet.

As Sweeney led his flight into the bomb run over the Jap force, every gun below them opened up. The darting red spurts flashing on and off looked to one crew member, "like a Times Square electric sign gone haywire."

Each plane in the first element dropped 600-pound bombs, their targets being either a battleship or a heavy cruiser — it was impossible to say which, since flak crashing around the planes made observation difficult.

It was believed that one hit, possibly two, with near misses on the port side, were scored by the first element.

Tokarz, Sullivan, and Payne, in the second element at 10,000 feet, fared somewhat better. Two hits were scored on a battleship or heavy cruiser, setting fire to the target. Two of Paul Payne's 600-pounders failed to release on the first run, so he swung his plane back over the objective, picked out a fat transport and let go. At least one of the bombs hit its mark, for the transport was seen to be burning as Payne wheeled around and started for home.

Faulkner, Steedman and Andrews scored with one near miss on a transport. Faulkner and Andrews dropped their load of four 600-pound bombs each, but Steedman's electrical release system failed to operate and only one projectile was sent on its way.

As the nine planes winged homeward individually, after breaking formation to avoid anti-aircraft fire, Sweeney circled out of range and looked back. Both the heavy battlewagon and the transport were out of column, appeared motionless and, as the flight leader described it, "huge clouds of dark smoke mushroomed above them."

Strike one for the B-17's. The weary, flight-drunk crews flew home, landing at night at Eastern Island, hoping to snatch a few hours sleep.

They needed that rest. But they got precious little of it.

While Sweeney's planes were on their first mission, six B-17's from the 42nd Squadron, under Lieutenant Colonel Brooke Allen, arrived from Barking Sands.

Allen had been ordered to the scene too quickly to take on more than a few maintenance men and spare parts. The new plane crews pitched in with the old to help the overworked mechanics service the fifteen fortresses now on the little field.

Sweeney, Faulkner, Tokarz and the other six pilots of that first mission spent most of the night describing to the newcomers their first experience under fire.

"They are pretty good, those Japs; keep your wits about you," Sweeney advised. "Watch them at the bomb release line. That is where they hit hardest. Break quick when your bombs are away. Their fire was consistently trailing us, but they must have learned something today too."

June 4, the second day of the Battle of Midway, was the longest day of the war for many of the air and ground crews on the island.

It was the day the Seventh Air Force hit the Jap fleet the hardest, the day it took most of its losses. It began before dawn with Fortresses taking off into the first streak of light and ended long after dark with pilots guiding their crippled planes onto the runway by the light of burning oil dumps.

For the nine crews under Colonel Sweeney, the days began while it was still dark, when an operations officer shook them out of their exhausted sleep and herded them to the runway so the Fortresses could be airborne and away from the island in case the Japs unleashed an attack timed with the first light of dawn.

In all, fourteen Fortresses got away from the island before dawn. Sweeney's nine planes were joined by five from Colonel Allen's squadron. Paul Williams, Richard Eberenz, Carl Wuertele, and Hugh Grundman were the pilots in Allen's flight. Mechanical trouble had grounded the sixth plane in Allen's squadron.

Rendezvous for the fourteen Fortresses was at Kure Island, west and south of Midway, from where they were ordered to proceed west to attack the same body of ships bombed the previous day. En route — Allen remembered it as being about a hundred miles out — a message was received, uncoded and succinct, directing the planes to change course and attack another enemy task force which was approaching Midway from almost due north and was within 145 miles of the Island.

This second task force was made up of four carriers and escorting ships, ranging from the Japs' great battle-wagons to myriads of destroyers. It was the dagger to be plunged into the heart of the defending force. The carrier planes were to slash down the Navy and Army Air Forces on the island, rake gun emplacements, and prepare the way for the invasion of assault troops which were approaching on the transports of the task force previously attacked and steaming from the west and south.

There was no time to lose. The new Jap force was already cutting down those 145 miles to Midway. Even as the message crackled over the radio, the Jap planes undoubtedly had already been launched from their carriers.

"They're probably knocking hell out of Midway right now," Bob Andrews told his co-pilot, Paul Willis.

They were.

Staff Sergeant Joseph Soler, one of the ground crew men who had been flown hurriedly to the scene of battle, was working over the grounded B-17 from Allen's flight when the alert sounded.

Soler was running toward a slit trench when the Japs came in. "It looked like hundreds of them," he said. "They came in low and we could see they weren't going to bomb the runway itself — apparently they were saving it for their own use after the invasion. But they hit everything else on the island."

Soler arrived at his slit trench just behind a gooney bird, one of the crazy flying creatures which infest Midway by the thousands. They stand about two feet high, with a wingspread of about four feet, and have the comedy instincts of a panda. As Sergeant Soler found out, they can be pretty tough on occasion.

"The Japs were lacing the field with machine guns, so I picked up that gooney and tossed him the hell out of there."

Soler dived into the slit trench.

"Whereupon," Soler continued, "that damned gooney jumps in on top of me and beats the bejesus out of me with his wings."

Over on the other side of the runway, Captain Joseph E. Walthers, a flight surgeon, had been helping the Marines set up machine guns when the alert sounded. He had moved about fifty yards in the direction of the hospital when the anti-aircraft opened up.

"I ducked into a slit trench, but I was so dumb and scared I picked one right beside the supply shack which they were trying to get."

There were ninety fighters in the attack on Eastern Island, with another ninety giving the business to Sand Island, across the lagoon.

"After they got their bombs away," Walther continued, "the Japs began strafing. They were so low I saw a Marine kill one of the pilots with his automatic rifle. The plane crashed in the lagoon.

"I don't know how long it lasted — it seemed like two hours or more — but finally the planes left. We figured they were just going back to their carriers to reload and then attack us again."

"That is apparently what they tried to do — and that is where we won the battle of Midway. Their carriers were destroyed while they were knocking hell out of us."

In effect, that is what did happen. While the fighters and bombers were attacking Midway, the Navy, the Marines, and the Seventh Army Air Force were pounding the Jap carriers. But certainly all the fighters and dive bombers were not at Midway, and it was not by any means as cut-and-dried as the flight surgeon made it sound.

There was opposition above the carriers — and plenty of it.

The flight of fourteen Flying Fortresses, in command of Sweeney and Allen, flying now at 20,000 feet so they could search wide areas of the sea, were en route to the stiffest fighter and anti-aircraft opposition of the whole battle.

And four other Seventh Air Force planes, faster, smaller than the big bombers, now in flight and destined to find the target first, were to test the opposition over the carriers and find it so strong that only two were able to return to base. And they were little more than flying pieces of junk when they crash-landed on the island.

The planes were B-26's. The B-26 Martin is a twin-engine medium bomber, fast, sturdy, and with a reserve of power. Their flight from Midway was the final test of an experiment that had been months in the making.

The Seventh Air Force had long believed that the Army would need torpedo bombers if the Japs came back to Hawaii and had experimented with the old A-20's. But the A-20 wasn't enough airplane to carry a 2,000-pound torpedo. Then, in the spring, a flight of B-26's arrived in Hawaii. Four of them were turned over to Colonel Bert Lewis and Albert Boyd at the Hawaiian Air Depot.

The work of converting medium bombers into torpedo bombers was a problem in aircraft modification and was proceeding with fitting deliberation when the alert came for the Battle of Midway.

Then the job was pressed home. The torpedos were too big for the plane's bomb-bays; so a metal sling was invented and fixed to the bomber's belly. In flight, the plane looked as though it was carrying a huge log. Another device, also invented for the experiment, was supposed to release the explosive at the exact right moment in the torpedo run.

The Navy, an old hand at torpedo-bombing, gave the pilots icked for the Midway assignment a quick orientation in what is perhaps the boldest and most suicidal form of aerial warfare.

Four B-26's took off in a swirl of coral dust from Midway that morning. Two came back.

Captain James F. Collins, Jr., was one of the surviving pilots.

"We sighted the enemy force at five minutes after 7:00 in the morning," he said. "Our formation turned slightly to the left, then sharply to the right in order to avoid the ack-ack of the surface vessels."

"We were going through heavy fire at 700 feet when six Zeroes came at us head-on. We dove down to 200 feet off the water; most of their fire passed over us."

It was at this point that Collins lost sight of his Number 2 and 3 wingmen, Lieutenant Herbert C. Mayes and Lieutenant William S. Watson. Collins turned his plane again to the right and started his torpedo run from about 20 degrees off the carrier's bow.

"We released our torpedo 800 yards from the carrier at about 220 feet and at 210 miles per hour."

Collins saw the carrier's long wake standing almost at right angles to the big ship as it squirmed in the ocean to avoid the torpedo.

"Just after release I could see my No. 4 ship (Lieutenant Muri's), slightly under us and to the left, making his attack. His navigator said our torpedo hit the water cleanly and when last seen was making a true run toward the carrier."

In a fight like that you don't stick around to watch your own or the other fellow's torpedo run its course. Lieutenant Muri's ship was at that moment pressing home its attack. Muri, a calm young man, was able to locate some of the guns firing at him.

"The anti-aircraft I saw was coming from one battleship, three cruisers, several destroyers, and two aircraft carriers. I judged there were fifty Zeroes working on us at the same time."

Just as the plane swung into its attack, the belly gunner, Corporal Frank Melo wormed his way up to the flight deck, blood streaming from a bullet wound over his left eye, and reported that the ship was on fire and the other two gunners had been hit. Melo asked the co-pilot, Lieutenant Pren Moore, to come back and help him move the tail gunner, Private Earl Ashley, who was badly hurt and pinned behind his gun.

"We were right on the carrier then and everything had to wait," Moore said later. "Muri continued right on, boring into that rain of fire and to hell with how we came out."

Muri's torpedo was released 450 yards slightly ahead of the carrier, 150 feet off the water. He turned directly into the carrier, sped across it and gave his engines full throttle to out-fly the swarm of Zeroes crowding him.

Moore got out of his co-pilot's seat and ran to the tail. "A tracer had set fire to a cushion and that had to be handled first before the whole plane blew up," he recalled. "I got it out, but found it a lot harder than it sounds to throw something that large out of a plane window."

Ashley, the tail gunner, was so badly wounded that he could not be moved from his gun.

"I propped him up as best I could," Moore said. "He was suffering intensely, but he was conscious. He even helped me load the gun. I gave him some sulfanilamide and went to work on the Jap fighters."

The turret gunner, Sergeant John Gojoj, was hit around the face but continued to fire at the Zeroes diving on the fleeing bomber.

For fifteen or twenty minutes, the fighters pressed home their attacks against the two bombers. Finally, the B-26's flew inside an overcast, shook off the last Zero and turned toward home, little more than flying pieces of junk.

It was a miracle that the two planes remained together until they reached Midway, where they both crash landed. The planes were never flown again. Ground crewmen who hauled the broken skeletons from the runway found fifty bullet holes in the leakproof tank of one of the bombers.

The other two B-26's were shot down during the attack. One of them was observed to have launched its torpedo just before it cartwheeled into the sea.

At 7:30 in the morning, twenty-five minutes after the B-26's located the Jap fleet and at about the time when they were shaking off the last Zero, the formation of fourteen Fortresses arrived at 20,000 feet over the same objective. They skirted the fleet and flew for thirty minutes, trailing long sleeves of vapor, before the real objectives — the carriers — broke the cloud coverage under which they had been circling, and were open to bombing.

Sweeney said there were two carriers; Allen said there were four. The simple explanation is that from 20,000 feet in the air, with anti-aircraft crashing around your plane and fighters racing at you above and below, there is slight capacity for a calm count of the ant-like surface vessels squirming in the ocean miles below.

Sweeney led his flight to the right, Allen to the left. Each plane was loaded with eight 500-pound bombs, and there wasn't a single instance of a hang-up on any of them, although several individual runs had to be made to effect release. Tactics called for pattern bombing as the most effective method of getting hits on such minute and difficult targets.

Captain Faulkner, leader of the third element of three planes in Sweeney's flight, reported that one hit was scored on the port bow of a carrier, possibly other hits on the starboard bow and five near misses by his element. Faulkner's plane was attacked by four Zeroes on the return flight, one of which hit his No. 4 engine, disabling it. But they got one of the Zeroes.

The lead element — Sweeney, Gregory, and Woodbury, scored one hit on the stern of a carrier. The second element — Tokarz, Sullivan, and Payne — observed no hits, but one Zero was shot down.

Colonel Allen, Lieutenant Eberenz, and Lieutenant Williams, making up another element, believed they got one hit and two near misses on a carrier, while Captain Wuertele and Lieutenant Grundman, in a flight of two, claimed one hit, one possible, and one near miss.

Scarred and torn, the fourteen great planes lumbered back to Midway to lick their wounds, refuel and, if possible, take to the air again. But for some of them this was not to be possible, for there wasn't much of a landing field left. Jagged chips of coral and splintered shells littered the runway and the tires of four of the incoming Fortresses were ripped to shreds.

The field was clear of Japs at the moment, but they were expected back, and the weary combat crews had to help ground crews get the planes ready to go back into the air. The aqua system for automatic fuel pumping had been bombed out and gasoline had to be dumped in by hand or at best with the aid of small put-puts which a few planes carried.

Less than two hours later, when an alert was sounded, seven of the B-17's got into the air, many of them hurriedly patched up with parts from ships too wrecked for combat. Again, Sweeney and Allen led the flights. Two of Allen's flight, which had been slower getting away because of bad tires, missed the rendezvous at Kure Island but tagged along after the mission when the lead flight of five was ordered back to the same objective they had bombed in the morning.

It was a beautiful, cloudless afternoon with visibility unlimited, so the five planes climbed to an altitude of 25,000 feet for better search vision. At the bearing they were given, they sighted a burning carrier and a burning capital ship, but they saved their bomb loads for an undamaged carrier, if there was one around, and continued their search. Then, as Colonel

Sweeney put it, "not finding a conditioned carrier, and because sunset was approaching, decision was made to attack a heavy cruiser."

The hard-hit enemy fleet was by this time "deployed and weaving," but conditions on the bombing run were excellent and the pattern bombing of the five planes resulted in one hit on the cruiser, one possible and two near misses. When planes turned for home, a heavy cloud of smoke was seen issuing from the cruiser, which immediately lost speed. But the attack had not been without cost. At the bomb release line, an anti-aircraft shell burst near the wing of Woodbury's plane, damaging it severely, and Gregory's ship was also hit.

The other two planes, flown by Wuertele and Grundman, arrived just as Allen, Sweeney, and their flights were pulling away. Both made two runs each at 10,000 feet in dropping their sixteen 500-pound bombs. They scored one hit and two near misses on a battleship, and believed they got two hits on the burning carrier which Sweeney and Allen had elected to ignore.

The seven planes returned to Midway at sundown and rejoined as sorry a lot of B-17's as were ever gathered together. Only three ships of Allen's command were fit for further combat; none of Sweeney's were. Wings, fuselages, and bomb-bay doors were damaged, engines were not performing — and the men were dead on their feet. Sweeney's men had had one more day of fighting than Allen's outfit, as well as two days of patrol, and many of them would have been greater liabilities than assets if they attempted more combat. Some of them had gone ninety-six hours without sleep.

Lieutenant Walter Heitzmann, who had been with Captain Faulkner on the first reconnaissance mission over Wake the previous December 31, was still Faulkner's navigator through the Battle of Midway.

"Between flying search patrols and combat missions, we did not have our shoes off for five days," he said later in discussing the battle.

So, it was time for Colonel Sweeney and his weary crews to climb into such planes as could fly, but were unfit for combat, and get back to Hickam. It was not as if they were abandoning Colonel Allen to his fate, however, for that same night Major George Blakey had led a flight of six B-17's of the 23rd Squadron from Hickam to Midway.

Major Blakey's flight had not flown directly from field to field. With only half a bomb load and bomb-bay tank, the six planes were ordered from Hawaii to the scene of battle, flying some 170 miles beyond Midway to deliver their attack. Pilots in this flight, besides Blakey, were Ernest Manierre, Francis Seeburger, Narce Whitaker, Jack Whidden, and Otto Haney.

It was Blakey's first crack at the Japs, and he elected to fling his element literally into their teeth. He led the attack at 3,700 feet — practically ground-level for a four-engined bomber.

As Sergeant George Scherba, belly-gunner in Blakey's lead plane, described it later, "The sun was on the horizon when we turned in toward the carrier, we got the sun on our backs and came in low, so damn low they could see our teeth.

"But the Japs couldn't get it into their heads to shorten the range, thank God. Their shots seemed to be breaking above and behind us. I saw a heavy cruiser immediately under us, on a direct line with the carrier we were after.

"I opened up on the cruiser. My guns started at the stern and went over the whole length of it. I don't think anybody ever figured on a B-17 strafing, it is a little big for that kind of horsing around, but I was doing it.

"The cruiser seemed to suck the tracers right into its deck. All the time the Japs were shooting at us and it was a funny feeling looking into their gun barrels.

"My only thought was, 'I hope I don't get it between the eyes.'"

The element cleared the cruiser and hit the carrier. They dropped seven bombs. Two were near-misses which sent towering geysers up over the carrier's rail. One was a direct hit.

"When we saw that bomb hit the carrier you could have heard us yell clear back to Hickam," Lieutenant Herb Henckell, copilot for Blakey, said later.

The crews were still yelling when the Zeroes met the element. One of them flipped out of a cloud and, with the sun at his back, plunged down on Blakey's ship.

"It is a funny feeling when that first fighter makes his pass and you know he is not kidding," Henckell said later. "Your stomach lets go."

A stream of tracers swung across the sky and splashed squarely on the fuselage of the diving Zero. There was a red ball of flame, brighter than the setting sun, and then pieces of an airplane, unidentifiable pieces, drifted down into the sea.

"But when you see that happen," Henckell said, "when you see the Jap blow up — that is something else again."

In the running Zero-Fortress battle that followed Blakey's low-level attack, the gunners in his element, facing their first live targets, shot down four of the attacking Zeroes.

The second element of Blakey's flight, led by Captain Whitaker, also came in low at 3,700 feet. One of the five bombs they dropped hit a destroyer. Lieutenant Haney's bombardier, Sergeant Henry Earnest, probably because of the excitement of a first battle, failed to release his bombs on signal of the lead bombardier in Whitaker's plane, Corporal Floyd Blair.

The Zeroes were crowding this element, too, and while the gunners knocked down two of them, the Fortresses did not get away untouched. The port wing of Jack Whidden's plane was hit by an exploding shell and the number one engine was shot out. Whitaker's ship was hit by shrapnel, as were several others to a lesser degree.

Twilight in the Pacific is of short duration and darkness settled over the ocean as the bombers, their fuel supply almost exhausted from the non-stop flight all the way from Hawaii, groped back toward Midway.

Herb Henckell, co-pilot for Blakey, made the landing at Midway sound funny when he told it, but it was not so funny when it happened.

"We only found Midway that night because an oil fire on the island served as a beacon," he said. "When the wheels touched the ground, I took a deep breath of relief.

"At the end of the runway both starboard engines cut out. Blakey turned to me and yelled: 'What the hell do you think you're doing?'

"'What are you talking about?'

"'The engines — you cut 'm.'

"'Like hell I did!'

"We checked up and found we were out of gas. Five minutes more and we would have been in the drink."

Blakey, after the other ships in his flight were safely in from the long mission, took stock of the situation with Colonel Allen. It was not too encouraging. Whidden's ship was deadlined from further combat and was ordered to clear the field and fumble its way back to Hawaii.

At best, the other planes were in doubtful condition. But by patching here, repairing there, with a mass turning of official heads in some other direction when it seemed advisable, eight planes were scheduled for the next day's fight.

At dawn on the morning of June 5 two flights of four planes each, under Colonel Allen, took to the air on what was to be the last day of battle. At the same time, six more Fortresses left Hawaii for Midway to refuel and load there and enter the final stages of the fight during the late afternoon. This was a flight led by Captain Donald Ridings of the 72nd Squadron and it was to provide the worst B-17 tragedy of the engagement.

Colonel Allen, Major Blakey, and their flights rendezvoused as usual over Kure Island where instructions were received to attack two cruisers reported to be from forty to ninety miles north of Midway. But the weather was overcast, and after searching vainly for a couple of hours, the flights returned to Kure to report and receive further instructions.

These were quick in coming. Two battleships, Midway informed them, had been located by Navy scout planes 150 miles due west.

"We found the battleships and my flight dropped on one, Blakey's on the other," Colonel Allen afterwards reported. "We put a pattern over the battleships and think we got two hits. Midway then thought it had located the original carrier force and we went back to the field for gas and bombs before proceeding. We were helped by Marines. We were delayed in getting oxygen which had to be brought by barge from the other island (Sand) to Eastern. We went back out that afternoon."

Colonel Allen still had his four planes, but Blakey's flight was cut to three. Captain Manierre's ship had developed engine trouble and was temporarily grounded.

"The target was expected to be 280 miles out, traveling at a speed of twelve knots," Allen stated. "There was no sign of carriers when we got to the point of interception, but we found a heavy cruiser steaming back toward Midway. I assumed it to be a decoy and we went on a wide search for 420 miles, but found nothing.

"My navigator took me back to the cruiser and we got the sun at our backs for the bomb run. We dropped a salvo right on the Jap ship with probably one or two hits."

With this attack, Colonel Allen led his planes back to Midway and, as events determined, out of the battle.

There was one final strike of B-17's still to be delivered. This was Captain Ridings' ill-fated flight of five planes which had flown to Midway from Bellows Field on Oahu.

Some four hundred miles at sea, the five ships overtook a heavy cruiser. By that time, the Jap fleet had apparently been so badly beaten that all pretense of formation had been abandoned and it was a case of every ship for itself.

Ridings found even this solitary ship under attack by Navy dive bombers, but he decided to pitch in and help. "My bombs would not go," he said, "so I circled the cruiser at 10,000 feet waiting for the other planes to drop theirs. The cruiser was firing everything she had in anti-aircraft. I judge there were four big antiaircraft guns on each side and three or four pompoms. A tracer or two came up through the formation."

The flight had split up during the attack, and Ridings circled around at 10,000 feet to draw fire while the planes which could release their bombs got in their licks. That was the last he ever saw of his friend, Lieutenant Robert Porter.

Porter, Captain Glenn Kramer and Captain Richard Stepp made a down-sun run on the cruiser. Kramer reported that he scored two hits, but Stepp claimed none. Porter's bomb-bay was open and suddenly the bomb-bay tank, as well as bombs, fell out.

The plane, the City of San Francisco, which had been donated to the Government by the citizens of that city, swerved out of formation. When last seen, it showed no particular signs of distress and Ridings dismissed it from his mind, thinking that Porter would find his own way back to Midway. However, the plane never arrived and no member of the crew was ever found. Presumably it was hit by the murderous ack-ack from the cruiser and crash-landed at sea, sinking before the crew could get out and into life rafts.

The day ended in tragedy for Captain Kramer as well. It was dark before Ridings' plane made landfall at Midway, and they had to be brought in by radar. Kramer was misdirected, and by the time he had been straightened out, his plane was out of gas. He came within fifteen minutes of making the field, but went down at sea.

The radio-gunner, Sergeant Freeborn Durrett, was killed in the landing. The rest of the crew managed to extricate themselves from the wrecked plane and get into life rafts. They spent that night and most of the next day on the open sea and were finally rescued by a PBY. Suffering from various bruises, a few minor injuries, and severe sunburn, they were taken to Midway and evacuated to Hickam by a hospital ship.

Thus, in tragedy, ended the Seventh Air Force's participation in the Battle of Midway. More planes were flown to Midway during the next day or two, and patrol missions were constantly probing the sea, but no more attacks were made and the enemy was not sighted again. Lieutenant Colonel L. C. Coddington led a flight of six B-17's of the 26th Squadron from Hickam to Midway on June 6, and dropped several 1100-pound demolition bombs on what was thought to be a Jap ship. However, the target turned out to be one of the Navy's submarines, which fortunately crash-dived and was untouched.

Reporting on the Seventh's participation in the entire Midway operation, General Howard C. Davidson wrote to General Arnold on June 13:

"A total of fifty-five B-17 plane missions were flown, and 314 five-hundred or six-hundred-pound bombs were dropped from altitudes varying from 3,600 to 25,000 feet. These bombs were dropped on an accumulated total of seven battleships or cruisers, seven aircraft carriers, one destroyer, and two transports.

"Twenty-two direct hits, six probable hits and forty-six near misses were reported.

"Ten Zeroes were shot down and two damaged.

"Two B-17's were lost at sea and two were damaged.

"Four B-26 plane missions were flown with four torpedoes, scoring three hits on two carriers.

"Two B-26's were lost at sea and two made crash landings at Midway, badly damaged.

"Very heavy AA fire was reported throughout."

The Navy, summing up later, was somewhat skeptical of the twenty-two direct hits, and was inclined to doubt that three torpedoes from the Air Force's experimental B-26's hit home, although not specifically denying it. It was more likely, the casual Naval Officer held, that the torpedoes, dropped by inexperienced men, sounded and passed under the carriers.

There was no "official" opinion at the time, but the argument between Navy and Air Force men in the ranks was quick to break out, and it reached an aggressive stage in Honolulu during the following weeks, when pilots of the two forces, celebrating the victory, on occasion backed up their claims with pitched battles of their own.

The argument, of course, was foolish. Officials of both branches of service were quick to point out to their men that this kind of dissension was exactly what the Japanese wanted.

Privately, the men in command of the Seventh Air Force were a little pleased about it. For in it they saw the end of the bitter, defeated, unsure complex which had ridden their men in the weary days after Pearl Harbor;

they saw the beginning of the chip-on-the-shoulder, spit-in-your-eye attitude which told them that the men of the Seventh were ready for their next big engagement — the Battle of the Solomons.

They were to participate in that historical engagement, however, under the leadership of another general, for the Battle of Midway was to cost the Seventh the life of its colorful, beloved Commander, Major General Clarence L. Tinker.

CHAPTER IX: The Lodestar

IT WAS JUNE 6, 1942.

Five men sat around a table in Seventh Headquarters' tent at Midway. Four of them were among the most experienced long-range bomber pilots in the world. The other was a fighter pilot who had turned to bombers for the occasion.

Outside on the runway, flights of B-17's were roaring off in final pursuit of the fleeing, battered Jap fleets. But it is doubtful if the five men heard them. They were too intent on their discussion. A great many lives depended on it — a great, far-reaching plan depended on it.

"Look, Sugar, pay attention. These planes won't fly that slow — not the way they're loaded."

"I got here, didn't I?"

"Sure, but God knows how."

"You're a fighter pilot, Sugar. We know you expect bombers to go slow — but not that slow. You might even have it in your head you can pull them out if they fall away. They don't work that way. Sure as hell you'll wind up in the drink."

"I've flown bombers before."

"So have we. Thousands of hours more than you — but in B-17's. This isn't the same thing. These Liberators have got their own ideas. They will outrange a Fortress. They are tough as steel, but they have their tricks, and one of them is they can't fly at a walk when they're loaded to 65,000 pounds."

"My idea is to fly at the speed which uses up the least amount of gas. It's a long way to Wake."

"Sure — and you've got to nurse your gas. We know that. But half a load left over never did anybody any good at the bottom of the ocean. You weren't doing more than 140 coming here to Midway from Hickam."

"So what? I said before that I got here — or maybe you didn't notice."

"Don't get sore, Sugar. This is for your own good — yours and the General's. We like the guy."

"If I didn't, do you think I would be flying a crate instead of an airplane?"

"Okay. We're together on one thing anyway. So, why take a chance? An airspeed of 160 will get you there and back with plenty of gas to spare. Why ask for trouble?"

"The General wants Liberators out here — I want to make a showing for him."

"You're not going to make a showing by losing your plane."

"All right, all right. Have it your way."

"You mean it?"

"Sure, but I still think you fellows are afraid to take a chance."

The four men glanced at each other. Their voice was a chorus. "You're damn right we are, sonny!"

The meeting broke up. Some of the pilots walked down the runway to inspect the planes — four big, new, squat, powerful Liberators, then known as LB-30's, later, with modifications for combat duty, to be called B-24's. The other pilots went down to the tower to check with operations for the flight from Midway to Wake and return which was scheduled for that night.

The seasoned bomber pilots were Truman Landon, R. L. Waldron, Roger Ramey and Arthur Meehan. The fighter-turned-bomber pilot was Lieutenant "Sugar" Hinton. They all arrived that morning with their crews from Hawaii on the first leg of a mission which, by its far-reaching implications, simply had to be successful.

Their obligation went even farther than that. Major General Clarence Tinker, Commander of the Seventh, was making the trip with them. The mission was his idea — his baby. He was deep in reasons for it — and the men knew they had to see him through. He was a highly respected, warmly liked leader, and their concern over his safety moved them to caution.

Hinton was General Tinker's pilot, as well as his aide, and the seasoned bomber pilots, very openly and frankly, did not like the way Hinton had handled his plane on the flight from Hickam to Midway. And that was only a 1,400 mile hop, or thereabouts! To Wake and return was 2,500 miles or better, and there was not a navigational check point over the whole distance. The mission, in LB-30's, was an experiment and every inch of the way was a potential death trap.

General Tinker had been waiting a long time for this opportunity. He wanted Liberators in his command. He knew he was not going to get many of the B-17's which were rolling off the production lines. They were needed more vitally in other theaters. But this newer type of bomber was not so eagerly sought after. It was anything but a pretty airplane on the ground — it had none of the racy lines of the B-17 — and some trouble had been experienced in flying it, particularly on take-offs.

But Tinker knew they had range — as cargo planes they had proved that — and he believed that their unfavorable reputation was due more to the flying habits of the men at the controls than to any basic flaw in the plane itself. He believed pilots had to be trained to fly the plane in its own way — that was all!

According to the stories which circulated through the Central Pacific area, General Tinker felt that in order to convince General Arnold to give him Liberators he had to do something spectacular with them. But more than that, his own personality leaned toward the spectacular. Part Indian and proud of it, Tinker's dress reflected his colorful tastes; as a squadron leader he had encouraged his pilots to add distinctive identifying insignia to their uniforms. He was lean, hard, eager, and restless, a terrific driving force and as unsparing of himself as he was of others.

When the preparations for the Battle of Midway started, General Tinker conceived the idea of setting the Japs back on their heels by leading a counter-punch bombing attack on Wake. But this was obviously unsound, since the B-17's did not have sufficient range to carry a useful bomb load that distance and return. Moreover, all the Fortresses available would be in demand to defend Midway.

Then, on June 2 or 3, Major Waldron led a flight of four LB-30 bombers from the Mainland to Hickam, and General Tinker saw in them the answer to his prayer. These planes had the range to carry a bomb load to Wake if extra gas tanks were fitted into them — and they were equipped with radar.

Tinker went to General Emmons and asked permission to make the flight and it was promptly given.

The plan called for the four planes to land at Midway, refuel and then take off for Wake, scheduling their departure so that they would arrive over the Jap-held island at dawn.

Tinker, bursting with enthusiasm, turned the supervision of the preparation of the LB-30's to Waldron and the Hawaiian Air Depot, and waited with ill-concealed impatience while the planes were readied. The work could not be done overnight, however. The Battle of Midway ran its course, and it was not until the night of June 5 that the four LB-30's departed for Midway.

Ted Landon flew one plane, Art Meehan a second, Bob Waldron, with Roger Ramey in command, flew a third, and Sugar Hinton with General Tinker piloted the fourth. General Tinker was completely convinced of Hinton's ability to fly the big Liberator. Landon, Meehan, and Waldron spoke to him about the fighter pilot's lack of experience, but Tinker was adamant.

The flight from Hickam to Midway was agony for the big-plane pilots. When the planes reached cruising altitude, Hinton slowed down to a speed which the others felt was too dangerous to maintain with their gas-heavy planes. They proceeded on at a reasonable but safe air speed. Hinton was quite some time in trailing them in, and they sweated out an agonizing period. But at last he landed at Midway safely.

That afternoon came the talk and that night, with Hinton's promise still fresh in their ears, the four planes taxied down the runway on Eastern Island and wheeled into the take-off for the mission to Wake.

There was an overcast at about 6,000 feet and the four planes met above it. Besides carrying a full gas load and a complete crew, each plane carried six 500-pound bombs which had been picked up at Midway. They were loaded to the last ounce.

It was no time to experiment with flying speed. But once again, the bomber pilots saw that Hinton was crowding the plane's capacity to stay aloft. Furthermore, Hinton, who was to lead the flight, got off course immediately.

Nor did he correct his position. Ted Landon later said he was completely dumbfounded when the Tinker plane continued to roam around almost pointlessly. It was a beautiful clear night above the overcast and the planes were clearly visible to the occupants. Dutifully, the three planes trailed

Hinton around the sky, the pilots wondering what was going on, since it was so obvious that they were far off course.

Finally, after about thirty minutes of erratic flying, General Tinker's plane nosed forward into the overcast. It didn't fall off or spin, it simply mushed into the clouds and disappeared. Art Meehan later told General William Flood that he saw a light flash on in the cockpit and then flash off just as the plane entered the overcast, but neither Waldron nor Landon saw it. Meehan also, in looking back on the incident, said he believed the plane may have slid off on its left wing. But he was not sure, and Landon was firm in his recollection that the big craft gave no indication of being out of control.

Ramey flipped his radio onto command and spoke to Landon.

"What do you make of it, Ted?"

"I don't know. Looks as if the General's decided to go on back to Midway for some reason. Maybe engine trouble."

"Should we go on?"

"Guess we had better. He wouldn't like it if we turned back too."

"Okay."

The three remaining planes straightened out their course and the long flight began. It had been the General's hope that he would find Jap cripples from the Midway battle at Wake and mop up on them, and the crews of the three LB-30's wanted to be able to report back to him that the mission was accomplished. So they continued on through the night, hoping that dawn would find them over the target. But when, at last, morning came, there was no sign of land below them. Nor could they find the Island. For some reason, the extraordinary navigation talents of Landon, Meehan, and Waldron had failed them.

General Landon later said: "No amount of talent will help celestial navigation on a flight of four to four and one-half hours without a star shot. The weather out and back on that flight was bad — as bad as our navigation!"

An Australian wing commander was flying with Landon as observer.

"Doesn't look as if we are going to find it," the pilot said.

The wing commander glanced out at the budding daylight and thought of what pigeons they would be for the Japs in bright sunshine.

"I certainly hope we do not," he answered with complete honesty.

Roger Ramey said later that he made a landfall, but if so, he did not tell his pilot, Major Waldron, about it at the time, and Waldron declared he saw nothing; neither did Landon nor Meehan.

At last, with gas running low, the big planes turned around and headed back for Midway. Landon and Meehan jettisoned their bombs, but Ramey decided he could make it back with the extra weight.

As the planes swung over Midway that evening, Landon scanned the runway.

"That's funny," he said.

"What?" the Wing Commander wanted to know.

"I don't see the General's plane."

"Perhaps he has gone on back to Hickam."

"That could be true."

But it was not. No part of the plane was ever seen again. No bodies were found and no life rafts sighted, although Air Force and Navy patrols were doubled in an effort to find the lost men should they have managed to ditch the plane.

Landon reasoned, and his opinion was concurred in by the other pilots on the mission, that Hinton, as he had been warned, was unable to regain flying speed after nosing into the overcast, and the plane simply continued to mush on down until it hit the water with such force and at such an angle that the men inside did not have a chance to ditch it. It probably sank instantly with all on board.

Grief-stricken, the three crews returned to Hickam. But they did not remain inactive long. They were more determined than ever to prove that General Tinker had been right in his judgment of the value of the Liberator in the Pacific.

Twenty days later, on June 26, Landon, Meehan, Waldron, and Ramey were in the air again bound for Wake in the same three planes. This time there was nothing to mar their triumph. Ramey led the flight and at midnight came in over Wake, which was picked up at 8,500 feet by radar through an overcast.

Ramey pushed the nose of his plane down and the three bombers followed, coming out of the overcast at 4,500 feet, and continued on down to 4,000, at which altitude the bomb run was made. In making the run at that altitude, they were following the advice of Colonel Custis, Air Force Ordnance officer at Hickam, who had told them that at 4,000 feet they would be too high for small arms and machine guns to reach them and would be going too fast for heavier weapons to get their range before they were clear.

Colonel Custis was right. All hell burst loose on the island; anti-aircraft and automatic weapons threw up everything they had, but the bullets and shells were either under or above the Liberators. One small flak hole in the left wing flap of Waldron's and Ramey's plane was the only damage sustained. Nor did the Japs get any fighters into the air, although Intelligence had been informed that a big fleet of Zeroes had been assembled at Wake to move on to Midway when it was captured. Apparently, the Japs had not yet installed radar on Wake.

The Liberators were carrying eighteen bombs when they broke through the overcast. All eighteen bombs exploded on the target.

Bombardier Franklin grinned when he recalled the mission.

"We sure messed them up. Runways, hangars, planes on the ground — the works. I never had so much fun. You know, you get so you don't like those bastards."

The three big planes winged proudly back to Midway. For the first time the enemy had been struck — and viciously — on his own home grounds. The Seventh had proved it carried a sting, and — equally gratifying — General Tinker's judgment had been proved sound.

In the months and years that followed, the Liberator became the work-horse of the Army Air Forces in the Pacific.

CHAPTER X: "YOU NEVER HAD IT SO GOOD"

ON JULY 23, 1942, THREE BEAT-UP B-17'S SOARED OUT OF Canton on a photo-reconnaissance mission to Makin, Little Makin, and other islands in the Gilberts, a thousand miles northwest of Canton.

This was no routine mission. The invasion of Guadalcanal was scheduled within two weeks and to divert attention from the Solomons it was decided to send Carlson's Raiders into the Gilberts.

This photo mission was considered so important that Brigadier General William E. Lynd, Commanding General of the VII Bomber Command, was on one of the Flying Fortresses. The flight proved so successful that the island of Makin was chosen for the Marine coup that was to be recorded in Lucien Hubbard's movie "Gung Ho!"

Lieutenant Roy Bright, winner of the Distinguished Flying Cross and the Silver Star, was navigator for General Lynd's plane.

"No one knew what to expect in the way of enemy opposition," Lieutenant Bright said. "We made the outward flight without incident and hit our targets on the nose. There was only light anti-aircraft fire as we circled the islands and took our pictures. We were congratulating ourselves as we headed back to Canton. Then we ran into trouble.

"I was checking my charts when, suddenly, someone yelled that one of our engines had gone out. Captain Philip J. Kuhl, pilot of our plane, feathered the prop. Then, one at a time, an engine in each of the other two planes ceased to function.

"Our gasoline began to run dangerously low. The hours dragged by. Eleven! Twelve! Thirteen! Canton should have been in sight but there was only empty ocean. I checked my charts like mad for a possible navigation error!"

Captain Kuhl ordered everything which could be torn out to be thrown overboard to lighten the weight and conserve the disappearing gasoline. Guns and gun mounts; flak suits; and then the cameras went into the ocean.

"Finally a second engine sputtered and died," Lieutenant Bright said. "It was night and Canton was under strict blackout. I thought about General Tinker lost on the Wake flight and wondered if missions with generals were always ill-fated.

"It looked like the pay-off when we received orders from Captain Kuhl to prepare for a water crash-landing. I checked and saw we had been in the air fourteen and a half hours. Then men braced themselves and waited.

"Then, suddenly, there was a shaft of light in the sky-the most welcome sight I had ever seen. Searchlights on Canton had been turned on. Then we picked up the radar signals from the island.

"But the odds were still against us," Bright said. "Our gas gauge registered empty and all of us realized that we might very easily crash short of the field. We were braced for a crack-up as Kuhl nursed us in. Somehow he made it and landed with the last breath of our flying speed. So little gasoline remained that our plane had to be pulled off the runway to make room for the other two to land."

The planes were aloft fourteen hours and forty-five minutes and a check showed that there was less than ten gallons of gasoline remaining in General Lynd's plane. But the film was delivered and the Marine raid on Makin was set!

To furnish support for the fateful Solomons campaign that was to start us back on the road to Tokyo, the Seventh's 11th Bomb Group was "farmed out" to the Southwest Pacific. There it was scheduled to provide scouting, attack, and air coverage for the offensive forces under Vice Admiral Robert L. Ghormly, of the Navy.

On July 10, 1942, the ground echelon of the Eleventh had sailed from Oahu on the U.S.S. Argoirne for Noumea, New Caledonia, about 3,500 miles southwest.

A week later the air echelon, consisting of the 26th, 42nd, 98th, and 431st squadrons, followed them. The entire group possessed only thirty-five B-17E's.

This group, under the command of colorful then Colonel L. V. G. "Blondy" Saunders (so nicknamed because of his night-black hair and beard), lost little time in getting into action on arriving at Noumea.

The A4arine landing on Guadalcanal was scheduled for August 7 and Rear Admiral John S. McCain, commander of the task force of which the Eleventh was to become a part, instructed Saunders to hit a supply dump at Lunga Point, Guadalcanal, with everything he had.

On July 31 Saunders, staging through Efate in the New Hebrides, personally led a flight of nine B-17's in the first mission of the campaign against the target, some 930 miles northwest of Noumea.

"Out of Efate we ran into a murderous overcast that kept us within five hundred feet of the water," Saunders said. "Flying at that altitude for that distance is a fluttering horror. A sudden down-draft can flip a plane into the sea before you can say Guadalcanal.

"When we were within 120 miles of the target the cloud bank still shut us in but I knew we had to take a chance, so I ordered our formation to ascend and we went into the overcast — not knowing whether or not we'd come out this side of Mars.

"We finally broke out of the soup at 18,000 feet and circled Lunga Point. Ack-ack was heavy but we got our bombs away on the target and returned to our base undamaged."

Although there were many handicaps American flyers had to overcome in the Pacific — distance, enemy air superiority, strongly fortified Jap ground bases — of all the specters that rode the planes on every mission weather was considered the closest ally of Death!

Major Bill Kinney, pilot of the 26th Squadron's famous plane Zero-Six-Zero, had this to say about this foe:

"To the boys flying the Solomons circuit, weather was the worst foe of all. Massive fronts, turbulent and unpredictable, would roll across the Coral Sea without warning, blotting out sky and water. These huge, black tumbleweeds of the air sometimes blacked out whole island chains. You were crazy if you tried to fly into them and you couldn't always fly around or over them. We tried every dodge possible, but sometimes it was no go.

"You'd try to climb over a front and maybe you'd get up to 20,000 feet and still the clouds would be piling up around you. Or you'd go down to sea level and try to hop the waves. But after you'd pushed in under the overcast for a little way your plane would start bobbing and twisting and you'd better damned well get out while you were able!

"You might try skirting the edges and fly a couple of hundred miles off course to get around the front, only to find that it stretched out beyond your range. The Japs never stopped us from making a mission, but the weather often did.

"In those storm heads a B-17 would be blown around like a leaf," he said. "A bomber, flying at 18,000 feet would be caught in a sudden down-draft and come out seconds later at 2,000 feet, going like the devil and 180 degrees off course. We lost more planes to storms than to Zeroes.

"And living conditions on these islands were hardly conducive for satisfactory conditioning, either physically or mentally, for the terrific impending battle against time and the enemy," he said.

When the 98th Squadron arrived at Espiritu Santo, northmost of the New Hebrides Islands, they found a land of mountain peaks, mosquitoes, and no roads nor docks to handle supplies.

"We were forced to unload our gasoline in drums by swimming them in through the surf," Blondy Saunders said. "We had to unload 20,000 gallons a day from a barge, swim it ashore, load it into trucks and then hand-load the fuel into planes.

"Mosquitoes, flies, and gasping heat added to the joy of it all. We had no tents and slept under trees for a week — after working twenty hours a day.

"Cooking was done under a canvas strip with no sides. There was no mess hall and the men ate their heated canned rations standing up and had to wave away swarms of flies before each bite was conveyed to the mouth. Naturally, many bugs went down with the food. It was wonderful for dysentery.

"It was weeks before we received material with which to build a control tower. Our pilots said they ascertained wind direction by spitting out of their cockpits."

Airfields at this time were little more than strips cut out of cocoanut plantations and were thickly covered with dust. The revetments were barely large enough to keep the nose of a B-17 from jutting over the runway.

"It would have been risky for even a bat to make a night landing on Santo Field," Saunders said, "but the Eleventh combat crews flew in where bats feared to flit. There were no lights, and for the pre-dawn take-offs the ground crews set out bottles of oil with strips of paper for wicks. Operations clerks placed a jeep at the end of the runway so the headlights would guide the pilots. Invariably the prop-wash extinguished the bottle flares and the next plane had to wait until the lamps were relighted before they could take off.

"We had plenty of dysentery, but malaria was the biggest threat," he said. "It was difficult to prevent it under such conditions. Quinine lowered flying qualities and we used it only after malaria had been contracted instead of as a preventative. Out of about two thousand men in our group, twenty-five had the fever at the time. This wasn't too bad, but the malaria season was just starting. The best preventative is to keep the mosquitoes away. The insects usually act only at night and the best way to combat them is to protect the personnel with screens or mosquito netting. But these are hot and made sleeping difficult.

"But all the time the men, in spite of these handicaps, were flying 1,500-mile missions as a regular day's grind, dodging ack-ack and blasting at enemy fighters which stung at them in bee-like clusters. Nevertheless, the standard retort to any griping was the ironic G.I. phrase, 'You never had it so good.'"

Each island airbase had its individual peculiarities. Plaines des Gaiacs on the west coast of New Caledonia, 371 miles southwest of Espiritu Santo, was another island of mountains and drab trees.

The field there, constructed by Bob Campbell's men after leaving Canton, was covered with dust which held a metallic content that played hell with plane engines. Saunders reported that because of it a plane was fortunate to get six flying hours from a full load of oil.

But one advantage this island held over the others was its puzzling lack of mosquitoes and malaria. This was considered an oddity as the near-by islands swarmed with the insects.

Like many explorers who, when in doubt, go to the natives, these searchers for the light did the same. The natives shrugged in surprise. Didn't the all-knowing white man know a thing as simple as that? It was the trees — the white-barked gaiacs peculiar to the island and for which the site, Plaines des Gaiacs, was named. Mosquitoes didn't like these trees and stayed away.

Legend? Superstition? The natives were fond of the gaiac; its bark covered their homes; it provided a kind of oil for which medicinal properties were claimed. Perhaps out of gratitude it was also credited with the solution of the mosquito mystery; perhaps there was absolutely no truth in the explanation. But how could you quarrel with them? There were no mosquitoes and malaria at Plaines des Gaiacs — and there were gaiac trees!

On these islands, like most of the others in the Pacific, food presented a major problem in morale. Good food was about all the men could hope for after working and flying long hours and following a routine that never changed.

Canned rations was the unvarying diet provided by the makeshift mess. Men ate canned rations until the very sight of this never changing diet made them ill. But here they were luckier than men on the barren atolls of the Central Pacific. Here, there was an abundance of fresh fruit.

Bananas, large tangerines, papayas, alligator pears, and oranges grew in profusion, and men could make a meal of fruit when they could no longer choke down the monotonous C and K rations.

Day and night, until the invasion of Guadalcanal, the men of the Eleventh pounded at Lunga Point and the airfield which was to become known as Henderson Field, and in general contributed to the business of softening up the enemy. Colonel Saunders thinks it is doubtful if they could have done it as efficiently without this fresh fruit.

It was Saunders' constant hope to fly combat missions of nine bombers, particularly against Jap naval vessels, but from July 31 to November 15, he was able on only six occasions to get flights of more than six planes over objectives. Field conditions, engine failure, weather, errors in navigation — a hundred causes usually stumped his efforts. The planes were always flying at the extreme of their range, so the opportunity for failure was enormous.

Usually he settled for flights of five planes in an inverted V. Invariably six craft were ordered into the air, thus allowing for one failure without disturbing the flight pattern. When all six reached the target the extra trailed the V.

The spread of a bombing pattern from a formation of five planes is not excessive and there is a large opportunity for error on a maneuvering target such as a carrier or battleship. To overcome this, these flights of five had to drop their bombs as low as 7,500 feet and not higher than 13,000, where anti-aircraft fire was accurate and murderous.

Bombing results were good from these altitudes, but it meant the cards were on the table. Adding this to the other hazards of weather, water, distance, navigation, enemy air superiority, flak, and engine failure, the odds were brutal.

But the men of the Eleventh took it. Not because they liked it — they hated every minute of it. But the ironic "You never had it so good" was a bitter tonic that helped them keep a saving sense of humor for the task of helping to retake Guadalcanal which loomed on the horizon.

It was difficult to beat men who could laugh at their plight like that, and the Japs soon learned it. In the seven days of operations preceding D-day on August 7, the Eleventh flew fifty-six striking-force missions. Lunga Point remained the primary target, because of the important supply dumps and personnel concentrations located there. Another target was an uncompleted airfield southeast of the Point. It was necessary to hit this field to prevent the Japanese from completing it and using it as a heavy bombardment field. Tulagi was also hit daily by the B-17's.

Losses during this week were heavy. On one three-plane mission over Lunga Point, Lieutenant Rush E. McDonald circled the field, dropped his bombs on the target and was making his turn when five Zeroes dived on him out of the sun.

"One of the Zeroes was hit and went out of control," Colonel Saunders said. "The burning plane continued on through our formation and hit Lieutenant Rush E. McDonald's B-17 at the No. 3 engine. The bomber immediately exploded and went down in flames. Men in the other two planes saw two parachutes open but the crew was never heard of again."

But these losses only made the men of the Eleventh more determined that their assignment in the impending battle would be successful.

Suddenly, it was the morning of August 7. And the men of the Eleventh were ready!

CHAPTER XI: "THEY THREW THE BOOK AT US"

GUADALCANAL, IN THE SOLOMONS, LIES 558 MILES NORTHWEST of Espiritu Santo and 764 miles northwest of Plaines des Gaiacs. It was occupied by the Japanese on the night of May 2, 1942.

In the Coral Sea battle of May 4-8, which had cost the Japs eleven ships sunk and the United States the carrier Lexington, the Jap time table had been set back two months. It wasn't until July that the enemy had been able to bring a large force into the Solomons. Only about 80 per cent of the scheduled building had been completed when we struck. When we returned on August 7, the victory-happy Japs were astonished — they had no idea that we dared attempt an offensive.

A haze that surrounded the island, concealing our task force as the Navy moved into position, added to the element of surprise. At 6:17 in the morning the big guns of the fleet began to boom as carriers steamed in and launched Navy dive bombers to assist in the attack.

Jap shore installations, batteries, and camps were bombed and strafed and enemy ships were sunk in the harbor. Nine Zeroes equipped with floats, five large patrol seaplanes, and one four-engined bomber were knocked out before they could get into the air, leaving the Japs with no planes available in the Solomons.

The bombardment took place along a fifteen-mile stretch as the Marines prepared to push ashore at Guadalcanal, Florida Island, and Tulagi — the latter two a few miles north of Guadalcanal. At eight o'clock, the landing craft moved in and Combat Group A, under Marine Lieutenant-Colonel L. P. Hunt, landed on Guadalcanal, then rapidly deployed through the cocoanut groves, as tanks and tractors hit the beach and a headquarters was established on the water's edge. The group led by Captain E. J. Crane landed on a Florida promontory overlooking Tulagi, and shortly afterward Colonel Merritt Edson's force landed on a beach at the northwest end of Tulagi.

So perfectly had the operations been carried out that the Japs were caught completely off guard and fled to the hills. American troops found 75-mm. guns along the coast — unmanned.

The lack of opposition to the landings was amazing to those who knew the Japanese. True, the enemy, confused by the surprising offensive, fled to their caves in the hills. But surrender was something that was against the peculiar Japanese philosophy. It was necessary to dig and burn them out of their holes. Thus began a type of warfare that was to make the Pacific the most ruthless combat zone in the world.

On Guadalcanal troops pushed inland without opposition and spent the first night, unopposed by the enemy, in a pouring tropical rain.

On Tulagi, however, it was different. Marines split into two parties and headed toward the town of Tulagi. One group, edging cautiously southeast through a heavily wooded section, ran smack into Japs holed-up in machine-gun emplacements in hillside caves. To get past, it was necessary to send men up the hill under fire and then down a cliff to lob hand grenades into the caves.

The other group, picking their way along the other side of the ridge, took the hill on which stood the former British Residency. Jap snipers were thick, and the Marines encountered the enemy's main line of defense, a ravine filled with pillboxes and dugouts. The Leathernecks were forced to go on the defense and await reinforcements.

Landing parties had also moved in on the islands of Gavatu and Tananbogo, just off Tulagi. Gavatu was attacked about noon by a force under Major Robert H. Williams, and at dusk Tananbogo was attacked for the first time. Gavatu was taken in the afternoon of the first day and Tananbogo the next.

Although all Jap planes in the Solomons were destroyed in the initial attack, Jap aircraft from near-by islands swarmed in to support their bewildered ground troops. About 3:30 in the afternoon on the seventh, twenty-five enemy heavy bombers came in, catching our armada in the middle of the channel. The Japs met a withering stream of ack-ack fire, Navy fighters pitched in and many Jap planes went into the sea. No damage was received by our forces.

At four o'clock that afternoon, ten more Jap dive-bombers roared in and an American destroyer was damaged. At noon the following day, forty-two torpedo bombers came in low, and that night cruiser-launched high altitude bombers, with fighter protection, followed, dropping flares to light their targets. Another American destroyer was hit and the high altitude bombers sunk our transport Nevil. The enemy lost eighteen planes.

From then on the enemy used Mitsubishi 97's, which closely resembled our B-26's but were faster. They usually flew at between 25,000 and 30,000 feet and used 1,000-pound "grass-cutter" bombs.

On the same night, Jap warships joined the attack. They failed to get within range of our fleet, but on the night of the ninth they landed 700 men on Tulagi. The Marines killed 670 of them immediately. Enemy submarines began to appear, surfacing in the harbor and shelling the shore.

By noon of August 10, the five islands invaded by our forces were secured, but the bitter fight for the Solomons had just begun. The Japs were dug in in the hills and refused to surrender. On Tulagi, for instance, there had been 600 in the original force. Of this force, all were eventually killed but one. When asked why he gave up, the Jap shrugged his shoulders and said he had no water and wanted a drink.

And the Jap Navy, still powerful, continued to land fresh, fanatic troops on the islands.

On Guadalcanal the Marines had isolated the Japs in the northeast corner around Cape Esperance and settled down to defend their hard-won territory at any cost. Included in the territory taken by our troops was the airfield near Lunga Point, which was given the name of Henderson Field.

The strip was only about half completed when captured from the Japs. The enemy had brought in around three million dollars worth of equipment in July, including steam rollers, bulldozers, and other supplies, to build up their bases in the Solomons.

They had begun work at each end of the strip and were working toward the center. The Japs, notoriously bad technicians, had done a poor job, and even our own formidable engineering groups found the going hard. Henderson was a second-rate field for many months, although within two weeks half a dozen P-40's, some Marine fighters and thirty-three Navy dive-bombers and fighters were based there.

Our B-17's were unable to move in in force until September, but the victory at Guadalcanal did change the tactics of the 11th Bomb Group. Heretofore, stationary objectives in or near Lunga Point and the uncompleted airstrip had been primary targets. Now search and patrol became the primary mission, with strikes against enemy objectives, particularly surface vessels, undertaken as opportunity arose.

On August 18, Captain Kermit Messerschmitt of Ft. Collins, Colorado, and his crew were plodding home to Santo after a long flight when suddenly they found themselves within range of a huge Japanese four-engine Mavis. Both planes let fly at each other. The Jap lost his No. 3 engine and disappeared into a cloud bank.

Two days later Captain Walter Lucas of Starkville, Mississippi, flying a mission from Santos, met another Mavis.

"The crewmen were having sandwiches and coffee when I spied the Jap, and I yelled to them to get him," Captain Lucas said.

"Our plane was more maneuverable than the Mavis and I came up on him from below and the gunners cut loose. The Jap began to weave from side to side in an effort to bring us within range of his 20-mm. cannon in the tail. I saw what he was trying to do and whipped our plane up broadside to the Mavis.

"Sergeant Vernon Nelson, one of our waist gunners, lowered his sights on the Jap tail gunner and you could see his tracer bullets go in. That knocked out the cannon."

Lucas now pressed home his attack to even closer range. "Captain Lucas handled our B-17 like a fighter plane," Sergeant Nelson said. "First we'd be on one side and then the other. The Jap was trying to get down to the water and he'd side-slip under us. Once our wings were almost tip to tip. It was like formation flying."

For twenty-five minutes the two Gargantuas of the air traded blows. The Mavis, its guns firing wildly, twisted and turned, trying to escape the B-17. Finally Nelson and Technical Sergeant Chester Malizeski, engineer and top-turret gunner, shot out the Jap's No. 4 engine. The American gunners hit the other two engines, starting a fire, and the Mavis went down for a water landing near an island.

"The Jap was taxiing toward shore and shelter when Captain Lucas flew low across his wing," Technical Sergeant Edward Spetch, another gunner said. "I'd been griping because I hadn't had an opportunity to get in any licks, but now I caught him in my sights and gave him hell. The Mavis exploded and burned."

A few days later another Fortress, piloted by Lieutenant James W. Lancaster of Temple, Texas, with Lieutenant Jay Gordon as co-pilot, met another Mavis off Rendova Island.

"Sergeant Rollin Hefferman, Corporal Bernard Cowgill, and Sergeant Hugh Hayward cut loose on him and within three minutes he exploded in the air and went into the sea," Lieutenant Lancaster said.

The Japs didn't like losing Guadalcanal. Their troops back in the brush and caves on the northeast corner of the island held out frantically, first against the Marines and then against the Army troops relieving them. Their Navy was active, tricky, and powerful. Their air force outnumbered ours greatly, and their flyers were out of the top drawer. The month of August, 1942, was plain hell for our armed forces.

On the night of August 23, the Japs made one of their many efforts at reinforcement. A thousand men were landed under cover of darkness. The fact that the Marines led them into a trap and killed 700 of them didn't seem to discourage the Japs, for the next day the 11th Group received a report that an enemy carrier and escort had been sighted 720 miles from Espiritu Santo coming down the "Slot" — that section of ocean lying west and north of Guadalcanal, through which the enemy poured its Truk-based task forces.

To attack at that distance, carrying a heavy bomb load, was a terrific undertaking for the B-17's and the contact report didn't come in until 12:15, making a night return to base necessary. Admiral McCain left the decision to Colonel Saunders. The 11th commander grabbed at the opportunity.

Saunders was able to dispatch seven planes against the Jap force, four of them under Major Allan Seward and three under Major Ernest Manierre.

About 5:30 on the afternoon of August 24, Manierre spotted the Jap force and went in for the attack.

Manierre claimed four direct hits with 500-pound bombs on the second run of his flight over a carrier, and while it was not confirmed, the carrier was still dead in the water early the next morning when a Navy PBY made contact. Manierre's three planes met ten Zeroes and shot down two in running fight following the bombing.

Seward and his flight of four proceeded some sixty miles east of Manierre's and shortly after 6:00 p.m. ran flush into a big task force which included three cruisers, a battleship, four destroyers, and what was believed to be a small carrier. The carrier, of course, drew the priority, and five 300-pound bombs crashed home on that vessel. Later it was believed that it might have been a heavy cruiser, the confusion resulting from the fact that it was growing dark, but there was never any question that the bombs hit the target.

Seward's flight shook off an attacking force of land and water-based Zeroes and shot down five definitely, and probably two more. Then it, too, turned back to Espiritu Santo.

But now luck ran out for the seven planes. Just as the flights were due to land at ten o'clock that night, a violent rainstorm flooded the island. Until that time it was clear with a full moon. Seward decided against the risks of landing at Santo in that kind of a storm and directed his flight to Efate. Low on gas, they nevertheless managed the extra hundred and more miles and landed safely. Manierre decided to come in at Santo regardless of conditions and he and Carl Wuertele, "with God flying the airplanes," as Colonel Saunders put it, skimmed the trees, hit the runway, and at last braked to a safe halt.

But Bob Guenther wasn't that lucky. In the fight with the Zeroes, one engine had been shot out and he had to come in on three. He was coming in rather low, gunned his three motors to get over some trees and hit a little hill at the edge of the field. Five of the crew, including Guenther, were killed.

The rain squall blew over within forty minutes and it was just as well, for three hours later another Navy contact report came to 11th Group headquarters of a third carrier moving in on Guadalcanal with transports. Sweating, praying, and working through the night, Colonel Saunders was able to get eight B-17's off at 5:30 in the morning.

"When we got there, the carrier apparently had received news of the treatment the other two had received and decided to get out," Saunders wrote General Hale on August 26. "We hit two cruisers, set one on fire, and with three direct hits on the other it just broke in two . . . Yesterday was really good hunting as there were task forces all over, going the other way, but no carriers . . . Evidently the Japs changed their tactics from grouping of carriers as at Midway to scattering them over a wide area. It looked as if they attempted to hit Efate and Santo with a carrier each, simultaneous with an attack on and occupation of Guadalcanal."

The Japs changed their tactics about grouping of carriers — as a matter of fact, there were none seen again in that section until the middle of November — but they remained relentless in their determination to re-occupy the Solomons. In this, they adopted a plan which varied so little that the United States forces engaged could almost tell the day of the month by their tactics.

Thus it was that, about two weeks later, around September 12, the 11th Group had planes on bombing missions against a task force which came down the "Slot" as usual in its effort to reinforce the hold-out Jap forces on Guadalcanal. Then again, about two weeks later, on September 25, one of the B-17's of the 98th Squadron, was credited with a direct hit on a Jap cruiser north of Tonolei Harbor, part of a task force bearing down on the Americans.

In the action toward the end of September, at about the time when Henderson Field was able to receive B-17's, ten planes of the 11th Group took off as a striking force to bomb enemy naval vessels contacted south of Bougainville. Four of these planes belonged to the 98th Squadron, and they seemed to have personalities of their own. They were real bunker mates. They were the Skipper, piloted by Major Rasmussen, the Goonie, which stood up under thirty consecutive days of missions, flown by Lieutenant Durbin, Madame X with Lieutenant Cope, and the Blue Goose, with Lieutenant Frank Waskowitz piloting.

The Blue Goose had been asking for it. Conspicuous because of its brilliant blue paint job, it had always drawn more than its share of enemy fire and the skill and daring of the pilot and crew could not offset this self-imposed disadvantage indefinitely.

On the first run over the target, Lieutenant Joseph Todd's bombs failed to release, and Lieutenant Waskowitz turned for another run. As he came in over the target the second time, a direct hit from Jap ack-ack tore a wing from the B-17 and the Blue Goose fluttered into the sea, the entire crew lost.

It was a hard blow for the men of the 11th, for there were so few of them fighting it out together on these far Pacific islands that they all knew each other well and warmly. Also, the crew of the Blue Goose had stamped their presence on the consciousness of the other airmen on the very day of their arrival.

This crew had arrived at Santo while the pioneers were laboring under maddening hardships to keep planes in the air. The food was rough Army staples with no extras; the few tents were leaky; the flies and mosquitoes were unafraid and carnivorous. There wasn't even an imitation of a civilized community within hundreds of miles. Onto this bedraggled island stepped this brash new crew, and surveying the shabby tents bordering a tropical jungle, quipped: "Where's the USO?"

From that day on they were branded the "USO Kids," a name they never lived down and died proudly owning. Besides Pilot Waskowitz and Bombardier Todd, the crew included Lieutenant Clarence L. Marthey, co-pilot, Lieutenant Arthur Piatt, navigator, Sergeant David Dixon, Sergeant J. W. Childers, Sergeant Raymond Joslin, Corporal Henry Nosalik, and

Corporal Robert G. Thomas, radio operators, engineers, and gunners. Childers and Joslin were old hands. They were a part of Major Landon's crew that arrived at Oahu on December 7, 1941.

Writing to General Hale about trials and conditions during this period, Colonel Saunders said: "I hope I have not painted things too drab. The boys have got a real desire to lock with the Japs. They all want to go on striking missions. The morale is surprisingly high considering the conditions, which shows that real punchers will survive tough conditions as long as they have promise of a fight. We have a few laughs, especially when the natives parade across the airdromes each morning to report for work. They always walk in single file as a result of travel through the bush and their only clothing is a G-string with a wrapping of straw."

Substantial reinforcements, in the form of twelve B-17's of the 5th Group's 72 Squadron, came to Colonel Saunders' aid just in time to participate in the September 26 activity, which centered around Tonolei Harbor and Shortland Island, off the southern tip of Bougainville Island. Here the Japs had gathered a strong naval force, and it was a nice target on which the 72nd could cut its teeth. Of the striking force of ten planes, five were from the 72nd Squadron and included several Midway veterans, among them Major Don Ridings and Captain Glenn Kramer, the same Kramer who had had to ditch his airplane the last day of the Midway victory.

Major Ridings' element of three planes scored two direct hits and set fire to a cruiser. Other elements of the flight scored three hits on a large transport and accounted for three of some dozen Zeroes that challenged them. The flight landed at Guadalcanal nine hours after taking off from Santo, the biggest force of B-17's thus far to use Henderson Field.

The boys of the 72nd Squadron that night congratulated themselves on the success of their first mission, but their luck was not to hold. The next morning, five of the 27th's planes at Henderson which were operational took off for the same target — Tonolei and Shortland Island.

Major Ridings led the first element of three planes over the target. They got off their bombs and rode through the anti-aircraft safely. But the second element of two planes, made up of Kramer and Lieutenant Therman Classen, were several miles to the rear and by the time they reached the bomb release point fifteen Zeroes were waiting. The guns from the B-17's blazed and roared and Kramer and Classen resorted to every trick at their command to maneuver away from the attack.

Eventually they brought their planes through, but again, as at Midway, Kramer's crew did not escape injury. Two 20-mm. shells from the Zeroes exploded inside the plane, wounding Navigator Crawford, Bombardier Caird, and Corporal Moody, a gunner. Kramer landed at Guadalcanal to get first-aid treatment for his injured men, but the other planes, with the exception of that flown by Lieutenant Bloch, whose engineer, Sergeant Brozack, was hit, returned to Espiritu Santo.

"The thing that hurt the Guadalcanal situation the worst," said Colonel Saunders, "was the infiltration tactics used by the Jap destroyers coming down and dropping off personnel and supplies. They would shell the place and go back, and by the time they were located they would be out of range of dive and torpedo bombers. By the time the 11th Group's planes, located most of the time at Espiritu Santo 600 miles to the rear, reached there they would be out of range and dispersed."

But on October 12th the Japs, tired of playing hide and seek, sent down a large and determined force of battle-wagons. There were no carriers involved. If the Japs had any of these left in this theater, they were hoarding them . This was an effort to reinforce their troops and at the same time cut our Army, Navy, and Marine air strength to ribbons by shelling their bases at Henderson Field.

There was never any rest for our forces. Regularly at noon the Jap bombers came. There would be eighteen to twenty-four of them flying high in the sun, accompanied by twenty or more Zeroes.

At Henderson Field, tired and hungry crewmen and mechanics would work until the last minute and then sprint for foxholes. In a moment the field would be deserted. A squadron historian wrote:

"On clear days you could see bomb doors open and the bombs drop. Men in foxholes would pull helmet chin-straps tighter, tense their muscles against the earth, and pray.

"Then: Wham! (The first hit.) Wham! (Closer.) WHAM! (Walking right up to your foxhole.) WHAAAMMM! (Oh, Jesus! Oh, God in Heaven!) WH AAA AMMMM! (Oh, Christ!) WHAM! (Thank God, they missed us!) Wham! (The bombs were walking away.) Wham! (They still shook the earth and the dirt trickled in.) Wham! Then it was as quiet as death."

The noon bombing was not the only interruption to work. Occasionally there would be an afternoon bombing or strafing by Zeroes. Sometimes the Japs managed to get field pieces or naval guns ashore and set them up in the hills.

Each night a lone multi-engined bomber, named Washing-Machine Charlie (because of the sound of its engines), would buzz the field — usually between midnight and three o'clock in the morning. Weary men were sent cursing to foxholes, which were frequently gooey with mud.

Frequently, too, a submarine or destroyer, and on several occasions a whole Jap naval force, would anchor off Lunga Point and lob shells into American-held territory.

A squadron historian recorded what it was like at this time:

"A bombing is bad enough because as the big planes drone overhead the whole field seems to shrink to the size of your foxhole and when the bombs begin to swish-swish-swish as they fall, they seem to be aimed right at you. But a bombing usually doesn't last long.

"A shelling, however, is unmitigated, indescribable hell! And it can last for hours. When the shells scream overhead, you cringe, expecting a hit, and when there is a let-up you tremble, knowing that they are getting your range and the next one will be a hit. A. shelling is sheer, abject terror from which you never quite recover!"

The Jap task force, which came down on October 12, hovered in the area several days. The Japs were successful in landing some troops at Kokumbona, but at a terrific price. Many of their transports were sunk and the B-17's, dispatched in the greatest numbers available, bombed installations and troop concentrations. Quite by accident, the 11th Group got a battleship off Cape Esperance on October 14. Misunderstanding the pilot, the bombardier of a B-17 tripped his bombs at the wrong time. The pilot was after a transport, but instead, the 500-pounders struck a battleship. Normally this would have done no more than damage the vessel, but on this occasion it caught fire and when last seen was an inferno.

Still inadequately supplied, their planes battered, and themselves so weary that they slept like dead men when they had the opportunity, the men of the 11th nevertheless continued to slug at the enemy whenever they had the chance, and ceaselessly maintained their gruelling patrols.

Encounters by single B-17's with ten or a dozen land or water-based Zeroes were regular events. On one occasion, Captain Bob Sullivan of the 431st Bomb Squadron, returning from a photographic mission, encountered a formation which his crew estimated must have run as high as fifty Japs. They weren't all fighters, but almost half of them were. Nevertheless, Sullivan escaped unscathed into a cloud bank after shooting down four and probably a fifth. Speaking of the Zero vs. B-17, Colonel Saunders said:

"In our defense against fighters, we shot down at least one out of every four that attacked. While not all of them actually pressed home their attacks, I believe the ratio would probably be about 50 per cent of those that did. Their losses were extremely high."

The air forces of the world were watching the results of this combat high in the heavens over all-but-forgotten islands. As Colonel Saunders and his weary airmen fought battle after battle with fast fighter planes, their experiences were noted and used. The B-17 became the proudest bomber in the skies, and the tricks learned by these first encounters in the Pacific were passed on to other men in other parts of the world. Even modifications of the plane itself came about directly from experiences under these actual combat conditions. It was, in a sense, a testing and experimental period as well as a campaign in the air.

It was a campaign that continued for long, brutal months. The Japs came back in some strength around November 1, following their habitual two-week schedule, and Major James Edmundsen, with a flight of five B-17's, scored on them, claiming a battleship.

The Jap naval attack backed by fighter planes from Buin and other fields, was a staunch one, but it was only a rehearsal for the next one, an all-out attack beginning about November 12, into which the enemy poured everything they had. The Japs seemed to recognize that it was now or never if they were ever to recapture Guadalcanal, so they threw the book at us.

In these big naval encounters, it must be remembered that frequently they were not straight, win-or-lose battles. They were really running fights and thus could begin on one day and continue, at one place or another, for a number of days following.

Thus it was that our far-ranging planes came upon the Japs on November 12 at various points north of Guadalcanal and contact was made. The enemy could not have expected to get to Guadalcanal unobserved, but, rather, depended on the land-based planes at Buin and the water-based Zeroes at Rekata Bay to cover the force, which was made up of battleships, cruisers, destroyers, and many troop transports. One carrier was reported, but it soon disappeared from the scene, fearful of its existence after the mauling other carriers had received from the Navy and Army during previous attacks.

According to the Jap plan — and they were apparently incapable of changing one once it was made — the heavy bombardment force was to proceed to Guadalcanal and by bombardment eliminate all our aircraft there, while the transports continued on to the Jap positions along the Kokumbona River area of Guadalcanal. In order to make the bombardment of Henderson effective, the guns on the ships were, for the most part, loaded with demolition shells and shrapnel and not with armor-piercing missiles. This made them less effective against heavily armored and gunned opposition craft, and to offset this, the Japs either depended on their aircraft, or believed we didn't have sufficient Navy in the area to dare come out to attack.

But we did have the Navy and it did come out. Our cruiser force sailed in and blasted the Jap heavy battle-wagons so wide open in the next two days that they never did reach Guadalcanal. That left our fighter force free to use Henderson Field, and it took, according to Colonel Saunders, only two hours for us to eliminate most of the fighter coverage for the Jap occupational force proceeding to Kokumbona.

This provided a real field day for the TBF's, SBD's and fighters based at Guadalcanal. "You can imagine," said Colonel Saunders, "what a lot of fun the boys had taking care of the Jap ships with practically no air coverage."

The 11th Group's B-17's were still operating for the most part from Espiritu Santo, but there were some at Henderson. Saunders had no specific directive, but was told the importance of the attack and the rest was left to his judgment. He told Admiral McCain he'd fly up the "Slot" at daybreak on the morning of November 13 with everything he could muster, perhaps twenty-eight planes in all, a record number for the campaign.

The bombers began taking off from Santo at 3:30 in the morning in a torrential rainstorm and facing a weather front of unknown proportions. They had absolutely no business being in the air, but every assigned plane got off the field and proceeded either on search as directed or to the assembly point over St. Cristobal, just south of Guadalcanal. Here they were joined by the B-17's from Henderson and divided into three formations. The first formation, under Major Ridings, located a crippled battleship between Guadalcanal and Florida Island. The big ship was still capable of doing 20 knots, so Ridings elected to try to get it, although transports were the primary target. He reasoned that he might not encounter any transports and this was a prize too tempting to pass up.

The bombers lazily turned at 14,000 feet over the vessel, which threw up heavy anti-aircraft fire, and then squared away for the bomb run. At least two, perhaps three or four, hits were true and the battle-wagon wound up going in circles, its steering gear shot out. This was only some forty miles from Guadalcanal, and the flight turned back for Santo, leaving the final destruction of the battleship to the Navy.

The second flight of this striking force claimed hits on two transports and the third flight, as Colonel Saunders put it, "ran into a whole flock of stuff." Many of the Jap vessels sighted were already ablaze, listing or beached, proving the dive and torpedo-bombers were getting in their licks. Another pilot and his crew, on search mission, encountered the only carrier seen in the battle, which was well over a hundred miles northwest of Guadalcanal and running for cover. It was never seen again by the long range search planes.

All except Riding's formation based that night at Henderson, and the next morning, at daylight, Saunders once again mustered his operational planes for search and strike missions, for the Japs still refused to admit they were licked and kept trying.

A flight of nine B-17's came upon the enemy between the New Georgia and Russell Islands. This force consisted of upward of twenty-five vessels of all kinds, four of which were already ablaze, the torpedo planes and dive-bombers from Henderson already having attacked. The Fortresses laid their pattern over a sea full of targets and then returned to Henderson. Other flights found other objectives and dropped their bombs, and then also returned to base.

By November 15, the battle was practically over and the Japs were on the run. They had really been dealt a blow this time — a blow from which they never recovered.

The shores of Guadalcanal were littered with beached vessels, while the sea remained dotted with burning craft. The B-17s made some contacts and fought off several half-hearted efforts on the part of Zeroes, but the fight was out of them. Lieutenant Raphael Bloch reported spotting two heavy cruisers and two destroyers withdrawing from the area under full pressure. Captain Narce Whittaker was attacked by eight Zeroes, but easily fought them off. Thorough, careful men like Darby and Hawes and Thompson, on search missions, returned to base without seeing a trace of the enemy.

Guadalcanal was saved. Nor was it ever threatened again by invasion. The back of their fleet wasn't broken, but the wounds were deep, and the

Jap Navy retreated to their bases to lick them. From here on, it was only a question of time when we would have the strength to move forward. Opinions varied, but the Jap loss in fighting ships and transports was put as high as thirty-nine in the three-day battle.

It was a time when reasonable men would have rested momentarily on their laurels. But these men in the Solomons weren't reasonable. It wasn't in them to relax. Particularly was this true of the crews of the B-17's. Some were sent back to Koumac for a week of rest, but most of them stayed on at Santo and Guadalcanal, constantly searching and probing for the enemy in case he should return, to strike at him in his strongholds.

It was on a mission such as this that the 11th Group's famous leader, Colonel Saunders, was almost lost, and two of the crack pilots of the campaign gave up their lives. Oddly enough, it was the first time that the Fortresses had been given fighter protection, P-38's having arrived in the theater with wing tanks which made the long hauls possible.

Taking off before dawn on November 18 from Guadalcanal as command pilot, with Major Seward flying and Lieutenant Lee as co-pilot, Colonel Saunders led a flight of five planes, and Lieutenant Colonel Brooke Allen, one of six in a raid on the Buin area. Their objective was to sink the Jap transports which had escaped destruction in the attempted landing on Guadalcanal a few days previous, and had been reported in Tonolei harbor.

There was always plenty of opposition from Jap fighters in this area and the bombers welcomed the chance to have the eight P-38's fly cover for them. Instructions to the P-38's that day were to protect the B-17's from the customary quarter frontal attacks, and to do this they were to stay about 4,000 feet above the bombers, keeping 50 per cent of their power in reserve, and were to pick off the Zeroes as they were making their turn for the head-on assault.

But several things messed up the plan. First, the bombers made their run at 12,000 feet, which was too low to get the most efficient protection from the fighters. Then unfortunately, the first flight of five bombers under Saunders, because of mechanical difficulties, failed to release their bombs over the target.

When Saunders' plane failed to release, therefore, it meant the first flight had to go back for a second run. The second flight meanwhile came over the target, released and scored direct hits on a large transport. It then proceeded on its withdrawal, back to its base.

As both first and second flights turned in the same direction after passing over the target, and the P-38's did not receive Saunders' instructions to the first flight to make a second run, the fighters assumed that both flights were withdrawing. Thus when the Jap fighters, which had not been alerted until the bombers were well on their run, reached altitude, the P-38's attacked the first to come up to them chasing them off. The 38's then dropped their wing tanks and returned home, leaving the first flight of bombers to make its second run unescorted.

It was a good run. Saunders' bombs again failed to release, but on orders the other planes dropped theirs. Another transport was hit. But now the Zeroes were all over the five B-17's. As was usual they bore down on the lead plane, that flown by Seward and Lee and commanded by Saunders.

It was almost as if the Japs knew that that Fortress carried the leader whose fame had spread throughout the Solomons. They came in relentlessly, pouring lead into the cockpit. Saunders saw Lieutenant Lee wince and involuntarily grab for his leg.

"You hit, Lieutenant?" he yelled over the roar of the motors and the thunder of the guns.

Lee nodded. "I'll be okay." Then he suddenly pitched forward, hit again, this time in the stomach.

"I unharnessed him and started to pull him out of the co-pilot's seat in order to take his place," Saunders said. "Seward was slapping his controls around, trying to out-maneuver the storming Japs. At last I got Lee on the floor and climbed into his seat.

"Then Seward got it. A bullet went through his heart, killing him instantly. I grabbed the controls and jockeyed the plane into flying position.

"First one, then the second engine in the left wing was shot out. The wing itself became redhot. The plane was beginning to lose altitude rapidly. I was afraid to open the bomb bay doors and jettison the heavy bombs that remained there for fear that we would lose flying speed and stall. I levelled the plane as best I could and tried to get Seward's body out of the first pilot's seat where the trim tabs were located, but Seward was jammed in and the shifting weight as I moved caused the plane to lurch. I jumped back into the co-pilot's seat and levelled the ship again.

"Fortunately, a cloud formation appeared and I headed for it, hoping to reach the comparative safety it afforded before the Jap fighters could slice us to pieces. At last we made it, shaking off the last Zero. Through the cloud formation the bomber continued to lose altitude.

"I was flying by the seat of my pants, as there wasn't an instrument left working in the plane except the clock — and I surer than hell wasn't interested in what time it was."

The bomber came out of the cloud formation still right side up at 500 feet and Saunders brought it in for a water landing. The plane smacked the water, but didn't sink, and the crew was ordered to climb into rubber rafts. They brought Lieutenant Lee with them, but he died in Saunders' arms.

The next day, a Navy PBY, escorted by protective P-38's, picked up the men and took them to Tulagi. From there they were returned to Espiritu Santo.

The month of November saw the 11th Group, now staging almost entirely out of Guadalcanal, spreading its wings over new enemy territory as well as hammering old entrenched Jap positions. The seaplane base at Rekata came in for a steady pounding, as did the airfield at Buka and those at Kehili, Keita, and Munda Point in the New Georgia group. The Buin area was slapped constantly, while the bombers did not neglect their old targets on the Kokumbona River on Guadalcanal itself, Iambeti Village, and targets in the Shortlands.

"We discovered that the Japs were unloading supplies and equipment at Munda," Saunders said, "so we raided it and kept photographing it. Soon what looked suspiciously like a landing field started to develop under a cocoanut grove and grew longer every day. Then one morning the cocoanut trees disappeared and they had a landing field there. A few days later we went up, strafed them, and got twenty-six planes on the ground."

On December 1 Corporal Joseph E. Hartman of Birmingham, Alabama, tail gunner of a B-17 of the 43 1st Squadron took off from Guadalcanal on what started out as a routine search and photographic mission and ended in a story as fantastic as something from the Arabian Nights.

"We took off at 5:30 in the morning and nothing happened until we had started back," Corporal Hartman said. "Near the southern end of Bougainville we were hopped by six Zeroes. One of them dove past our right wing tip and came up on the other side. I got him in my sights and down he went. Another came in from the rear and I cut loose at him and he exploded in mid-air. The other four took off in a hurry.

"We continued eastward, flying at 17,000 feet, and near Choiseul we were intercepted by seven more Zeroes. Six of them circled us but kept out of range. Suddenly the seventh, which was above, came diving out of the clouds — straight at our nose. The Jap dropped four aerial bombs which missed, but instead of peeling off he kept coming.

"There was a grinding crash and everything went black!"

This would have ordinarily been the ending of the story, for the B-17 broke in two, the forward portion bursting into flames, carrying to destruction its pilot, Captain Willis E. Jacobs, Oak Park, Illinois; the co-pilot, Lieutenant Stanley H. Sommers, Galesburg, Illinois; the navigator, Lieutenant William S. Jackimczyk, Northampton, Massachusetts; the bombardier, Lieutenant Clarence R. Johnson, Denver, Colorado; radio operators, Staff Sergeant Eino S. Hamalainen, New York City, and Private First Class Arthur L. Lemar, Pawtucket, Rhode Island; gunners, Sergeant Delos J. Tuffey, Sangerfield, New York; Corporal Ray Lindamood, Marietta, Ohio; and Corporal Clair W. Glover, Gromberg, Montana; and a Navy photographer.

But, like an episode in a movie serial thriller, the tail section carrying Hartman rolled to one side and descended like a glider.

"I struggled back to consciousness with the wind shrieking in my ears," Hartman said. "I was still dazed but suddenly I realized what was happening and opened the escape hatch.

"I struggled with my parachute and became frantic when my heavy winter flying suit prevented fastening of the leg straps. I fumbled for what seemed like hours but all my fingers were thumbs and the ocean was rushing up at me. I decided to go out with only the shoulder straps fastened but when I tried to step out the door the rushing wind smacked me in the face. It was like trying to push through a concrete wall. Finally, however, I was able to get out and jerked at the rip-cord. It opened and the jerk of the chute, without the leg straps to break the shock, knocked me out again. I came to a few feet above the water and managed to slip out of the harness and into the sea."

Hartman landed about 150 yards off shore about 15 miles southeast of the northwest extremity of Choiseul.

"When I hit the water I was pretty badly dazed from the batterings in the plane and parachute. I managed to swim ashore and when I crawled up on the beach I was astonished to find myself completely naked. I still don't remember doing it, but somehow during the swim I had removed all my clothing!

"As I stood shivering on the beach, I wondered what I could possibly do next. I was in enemy territory and without a stitch of clothing, much less any means of getting back to base.

"Suddenly two very black men appeared. I didn't know what to do. I thought of cannibals and stories I'd read when I was a kid. I considered running, for I thought at the very best that they were Jap stooges who would turn me over to the enemy.

"But in my condition I didn't have much choice, so I remained, and discovered that they spoke a little English and seemed anxious to help me.

"They had a canoe and we climbed in and they paddled to a point about five miles north and took me to a village called Polo, a settlement of grass shacks. There they took me to the chief.

"I was still suspicious, but the chief was very friendly and gave me a loin cloth to wear. I had two cuts on my head and he had them cleaned and gave me food.

"The chief dispatched a runner to arrange for me to be moved to a safer place. I remained in Polo for seven days while we waited for his return.

"Finally he came back and the chief organized a party to take me through the jungles to the opposite side of the island.

"I shall never forget that trip. I was barefooted and the natives had no shoes for me. They told me it was only a short trip but it seemed endless. My feet were torn and bleeding and kept swelling. We covered miles but more miles and more forest always loomed ahead. My feet gave me hell, but I was even more concerned as to where we were going. This 'short trip' might be leading me to the Japs or to the cooking pots for all I knew.

"Finally after three days of unadulterated hell we arrived in the village of Tagatora on Tipersacera Mountain. Again I was received like visiting royalty. I remained there for three weeks, living in reasonably clean 'bachelor quarters' and hunting and fishing.

"Curious natives came from miles to see me but I didn't mind, as they were so genuinely friendly. We had plenty of food, including fruit, vegetables, and the meat of birds and flying fox.

"One day, however, we received a warning that Jap detachments were moving in a few miles to the north so the whole village moved into the jungles where we remained for more than a week. Then we received word that it was safe to go back to the village.

"One day the natives brought in a Jap flyer who had bailed out at the southern end of the island. The natives had escorted him through the jungles. The Jap was armed with a pistol but the natives had encouraged him to waste all his ammunition shooting at birds. He wasn't exactly glad to meet me in a receiving line and made himself extremely unpopular with the natives. They gave him a very short trial — native fashion. I trust his journey to his ancestors wasn't too painful, for I owe him a sort of debt, I suppose, since he 'willed' me his pistol and a small Jap flag," Hartman said.

However romantic this whole affair proved to be, Hartman was anxious to escape from this Never-Never Land. It was difficult to stir the easy going natives into action, for they were enjoying his company. But, finally, he was able to persuade them to furnish him sea-going accommodations.

"One night we set out in a huge, unwieldy canoe manned by twenty-one husky paddlers," Hartman said. "We headed for Sassamunga, south of the mountain, and traveling only by night we moved down the south coasts of Choiseul and Santa Isabel Islands.

"It was tedious, risky business because Japs were all about us. If we had been caught I knew that the natives would certainly be murdered for helping me. We hid in the jungles by day and inched along through the shadows at night. Washed-up and abandoned Jap barges were everywhere. Once we spotted a Jap warship off the southern end of Isabel and I thought it was the finish, but somehow they failed to see us.

"Then we really got a break. In the evacuated remains of wharves on that island we found a motor launch. I was amazed to see some of our native crew swarm aboard and, familiar with such mechanical contraptions, start the motor. Then we rode in style to Tulagi."

Corporal Hartman and other members of the 11th played a prominent role in the Solomons campaign. On both land and naval targets they dropped 269,100 pounds of bombs, with nineteen enemy surface vessels of all types sunk and nine damaged.

The 11th destroyed 124 enemy planes and damaged fifty-seven while losing only six bombers to Jap fighters and anti-aircraft, eleven to operational causes, and one for "reasons unknown." Three B-17's were severely damaged during shellings of Henderson Field.

For their role in this action the 11th received the War Department citation, and Colonel Saunders received the Distinguished Service Medal for achievement during this period. He was also promoted to Brigadier General.

On December 6, after the question of jurisdiction of the air groups in the Southern Pacific area had been settled by General Harmon and General Emmons, administration and control of the joint 11th and 5th Groups was taken over by General Harmon, and the two groups ceased to be a part of the Seventh.

The airmen themselves remained in the theater until February and March, 1943, and on March 11 the 11th Group was officially relieved from further duty in the South Pacific. All planes were transferred to the 5th Group, and on March 28 the last personnel of the 11th sailed for Honolulu on the President Polk. If there was a man who wanted to remain in the Solomons he didn't make it known through proper channels.

On their return to Oahu they were reassigned to the Seventh officially and the group was reconstituted as a B-24 group. They were given the choice of remaining there or returning to the mainland for reassignment. Figures speak more loudly than words. Three officers and twenty enlisted men elected to remain in Paradise.

Men of the 11th wrote millions of words in letters dispatched from the Solomons. They might all be summed up in a verse written by an 11th bard whose name has been lost in the whirlpool of time. It was recited in a thousand tents and sung, to the tune of "Casey Jones," in a thousand war weary B-17's by men on endless missions.

TALKING BLUES
Back in Oahu in '42
Eager beavers, me and you.
Guadalcanal — '43
Reluctant dragons, you and me.

Espiritu Santo, Fiji and all.
We're behind it-the big 8-ball.
Lizards, flies, mosquitoes, too,
Corned beef hash and G.L stew.

Eight hundred miles out to sea,
Started to sweat that No. 3;
That goes out, we come down,
Nothing but ocean all around.

Here I sit, tear in my eye,
Tired of living, too young to die,
Going to Auckland pretty soon,
Get me a woman — howl at the moon.

Striking force out to sea,
Sighted transport — him or me?
We made our run, AA got rough,
On the way home, Zeroes got tough.

Pilots can fly, gunners can gun,
Bombardiers busy during the run.
Navigator's got a gun — he shoots too.
Damn co-pilot's got nothing to do.

Up at Buka the other day
Fifteen Zeroes came out to play
Down in the turret, both guns jammed
Started to see that promised land.

Six months of action,
Where's my relief?
Sweating each mission
May end in grief.
Waiting for a ship that never comes in,
Waiting for a chance to go and sin.

If I get back no more I'll roam.
I'll see my woman and stay at home.
Don't give a damn what you people do.
But, boy, my flying days are through!
This tells it all. There is little to be added to the plaintive wail. The air war in the South Pacific wasn't the boys' idea of how to spend a holiday.

CHAPTER XII: "HE WHO FIGHTS AND RUNS AWAY"

IT WAS THE SPRING OF 1943.

There was a grin all over General Willis Hale's face as he leaned back in his chair at Seventh Air Force Headquarters on Hickam Field and talked to his generals, Truman Landon, Robert Douglass, and William Flood.

Hale had just come from General Emmons' office. The Department Commander had given the Air Force General the green light on a project which had originated in Admiral Nimitz' mind and was eagerly applauded by every flying officer in the theater.

The Seventh was going to spread its wings again. That was all that mattered. It mattered a great deal to the generals and the colonels, the sergeants and the privates.

It had been a year and four months since Pearl Harbor; eight months since the Battle of Midway. In the South Pacific, Guadalcanal had been secured. In Europe, the Eighth Air Force had made what was then their deepest penetration into Europe, a B-17 mission to Hamm, beyond the Ruhr Valley, Germany.

In Hawaii, very little had happened.

For one thing, General Tinker's spectacular mission to Wake had effected a change-over from Flying Fortresses to Liberators — not without some personnel difficulties.

The men of the Seventh accepted the change simply as further proof that they were a bastard outfit — foredoomed even to fly airplanes that nobody else wanted. The feeling against the B-24 persisted so strongly that General Hale found it necessary to relieve the Group Commander and one squadron commander of the 90th group; the disparaging statements made by members of the group about the B-24 had reached even General Arnold in Washington.

The bitterness lessened but did not altogether die when, on December 22, Colonel William A. Matheny led a flight of twenty-six Liberators to Wake Island.

The planes went over Wake at altitudes of from 8,000 feet down to 2,500 feet — almost on the deck. The cost to us was two machine gun holes in Matheny's plane.

The mission helped prove the Liberator a worthy tactical aircraft. The griping diminished somewhat.

There was another feature of those early missions which contributed to the low morale of the Seventh. It had to do with the Navy and the war correspondents.

Most of the Pacific correspondents, all of whom had to be accredited to the Navy, worked in Navy press headquarters at Pearl Harbor. There they were handed official Navy communiques along with occasional Seventh AAF strike reports. Somehow, the fact that the Liberators belonged to the Seventh Air Force frequently was left out of final dispatches and, because the Navy often had a report or two about their own search Liberators, the Army missions usually sounded like Navy efforts.

Captain O. W. Turley, Jr., adjutant for the Headquarters Squadron, had a rough time with the problem. Turley was mail censor.

"A big percentage of the letters I had to read were from fellows trying to answer their families' inquiries about just where the Seventh Air Force operated. Our targets were restricted; whatever I could leave in those letters didn't add up to much of an explanation. That didn't help morale a bit."

Once, shortly after Midway, the Seventh had come in for a burst of world acclaim which temporarily heightened the spirits of the men. On January 23, the Seventh attempted the longest mass over-water flight of single engine planes in aircraft history. Twenty-four pilots of the 78th Fighter Squadron took off from Barking Sands on Kauai and sweated their single-fanned P-40KI's over 1,400 miles of water, through severe storms, and landed intact at Midway, many with less than five minutes of fuel supply remaining.

Even as the world acclaimed the flight, another Fighter Squadron, the 73rd, being relieved at Midway, impudently threw the cold water of a repeat performance over the 78th's grueling, hazardous flight. They flew from Midway to Oahu a few days after the 78th Squadron made the pioneer trip, making the whole venture seem — at least to the people who didn't have to make the flight — little more than routine.

Otherwise, nothing had happened in Hawaii. The monotonous patrols continued; the even more monotonous grind of training combat crews for other theaters continued.

So this new plan that brought a broad smile to General Hale's face would mean a lot of things to a lot of men.

It meant a great deal, for instance, to Lieutenant Colonel Dee Rains, commanding officer of the Seventh Air Force Headquarters Squadron. Rains smiled happily as he walked back from the staff meeting at Hale's office to the cluster of two-story wooden barracks buildings near the flight line which housed his squadron.

He was thinking that this was going to help morale. He knew that it mattered little to his men that they had participated by proxy in the Guadalcanal campaign. They felt out of the war, condemned to sit out the duration on a rock in the middle of the Pacific.

Rains, one of the best-liked officers in the Pacific, waved cheerfully at two men who walked down the company street toward him.

"Pretty soon now," he said to himself, "they'll feel a little better about their Air Force."

The two men were Sergeant Don Backer and Private First Class Romeo Dingle. They walked over to a line of soldiers in rumpled khaki uniforms and to the end of the line which extended a hundred yards down the gutter of an asphalt street before it turned abruptly into a short gravel path which led into the mess hall.

Backer bought a copy of the Honolulu Advertiser from a barefooted Hawaiian boy who moved down the chow line. Dingle read the paper over his shoulder.

They fell to reading the story, date-lined from London, of a young fighter pilot named Francis A. Gabreski who had arrived in England for fighter duty with the Eighth Air Force. Gabreski had been at Wheeler Field the morning of December 7.

The Advertiser story played up the fact that Gabreski was one of many pilots in Europe and the South Pacific trained in Hawaii by the Seventh Air Force. It could be supposed that training pilots and gunners for other theaters gave the men of the Seventh a sense of participation in the global war.

They had another way of looking at it.

"You know," Dingle said to his friend Backer, "those guys got it pretty good over there in England. Passes in London, for instance. And beer — even if it is warm beer. Theaters, maybe even night clubs. Subways, too."

Backer, a tall, studious-looking Californian who worked in the Squadron orderly room, squinted up at the incredibly blue Hawaiian sky.

"You know what?" he said. "Sometimes I wish it would rain. I wish it would rain like a sonovabitch."

It rarely rained in Hawaii. There were light squalls sometimes, lasting fifteen minutes or half an hour — "liquid sunshine," the tourist bureaus called it. Mostly, it was always warm in Hawaii. Never hot; never cold.

"I wish it would rain for a week," Backer continued, "all day and all night. I wish it would get cold and miserable for awhile."

As Backer and Dingle talked, there was a double rainbow arched in all its delicate glory against the Koolau Ridge north of Hickam. The two men didn't notice it. They had long since grown tired of double rainbows.

"Liquor's another thing," Dingle said, as the chow line inched forward. "I'll bet those guys get whiskey over there. Scotch, too, maybe."

There was only a little liquor in Hawaii. There was rum, made on the Islands. A man could get a few blazing shots of it by standing in line all afternoon before a place in Honolulu called "Dispenser General."

"Something else they have," Backer said. "White women. I'll bet those English girls are really nice."

Women in Hawaii?

At one point in the Island's military history, there was one woman for every five hundred men. Counting the women who didn't wear shoes. Counting the dark women of mixed racial strain.

They had a gag about those women.

"The longer you're here," they used to say, "the whiter those women get."

It was true, too.

Men like Backer and Dingle called themselves Pineapple Soldiers, reluctant serial numbers in the comic opera Pineapple Army. It was an ironic, bitter classification which they freely applied to themselves, but they swung on transients who used the mocking appellation.

Mostly, the men of the Pineapple Army wanted to go home. But home was the end of the war, and it looked as though this war hadn't even started for them.

They didn't want to fight. What man of normal inclination does? They didn't want to live on the Islands sitting sullenly at thousand-mile intervals in the 6,000-mile stretch of water between Hawaii and Japan.

But if going home meant crawling on their bellies over those islands, one by one, to end the war, that was what they wanted.

No wonder then, that General Hale smiled. No wonder, too, that Douglass and Landon and Flood smiled.

The Seventh was going to hit the Japs in the Gilberts and on Nauru. It went beyond the importance of a succession of quick air blows at the Japs' outer defenses; this mission was a feeler, intended to test the enemy's strength and pave the way for a future all-out attack.

It was late in March when Hale hurried back from Emmons' office with the good news. The hard, quick, powerful jab was scheduled for April; the full-scale war would start in November.

Funafuti, in the Ellice group, had already served as a staging base for reconnaissance flights over the Gilberts. Now it was to be used as a springboard for a test assault.

"We're sending a boatload of supplies to Funafuti early in April," General Hale told his staff commanders. "The planes will go down about April 18."

Lieutenant Colonel Corwin Van Sant and Captain Dan McKeever, in charge of the supply ships, got started shortly after April 1. There were absolutely no Air Force supplies on Funafuti, and while the striking force was to consist of only twenty-four bombers, even this limited number and their crews required a mountain of material.

The main body, under General Hale and General Landon, were to fly down on April 18. An advance party under Colonel Weddington went down on April 12 in an LB-30.

The whole mission was a top-drawer secret, and Weddington's advance plane proceeded with the greatest caution. This plane was to go first to Canton and then on to Funafuti, but in order to cloud the movement completely, it was scheduled out to Hickam for Hilo, on the Island of Hawaii, in an apparently routine check flight from which it was supposed to return to Hickam.

On the ninety mile flight to Hilo, however, the plane lost one engine and its stop there was for a further purpose than secrecy. While the engine was being serviced, the crew, sworn to silence, went into town for a few hours. One of them was Captain John McIlvaine.

Strolling along the main street of Hilo during the afternoon, McIlvaine met a girl he knew. They stopped to talk a minute.

Presently the girl said:

"Say, when are you fellows getting off to Funafuti?"

McIlvaine gulped and shook his head. So much for military secrets.

Perhaps because of this tip-off that the secret was out, Colonel Weddington ordered the plane to return to Hickam as a covering move. The next day it proceeded on to Canton, and then to Funafuti.

On April 18, General Hale led his outfit down. The twenty-four planes and their crews were from the 371st and 372nd squadrons of the 307th Group. Some of them — Lieutenants Jessie Stay, Ernest Carey, Herb Henckell, and Lieutenant Colonels Jay Rutledge, William Holzapfel and L. G. "Snap" Eskridge — were veterans of the early Wake strikes. But there were many green pilots and crews, men like Lieutenant Louis Zamperini, the famous Berlin Olympic miler, bombardier of a B-24.

Nauru, a solitary Jap-held island lying over a thousand miles west and north of Funafuti, was to be the first target. Tarawa, more than 800 miles to the north in the Gilberts, was to be the second. These called for a round trip of more than 2,000 miles with effective bomb loads on one, and something like 1,640 air miles round trip on the other.

The objective on the island of Nauru was the extensive phosphate works which the Japs were operating there. And it is true that the phosphate works were a target. However, the purpose of the mission was broader than that.

It was combat training for green crews; it was a further test of the method of training. It was a morale builder, and it provided experience for the supply services which must function in that general area during the big offensive which was to follow. It would be a way of testing the real strength of the enemy in that section, and if things went right, some important damage might be done.

Twenty-two planes roared off in the night from Funafuti to make the strike against Nauru the morning of April 20. General Hale himself led the mission. The Japs probably had radar on the island because enemy fighters and anti-aircraft were waiting when they got there.

They dropped twenty-eight 1,000-pound and forty-five 500-pound general purpose bombs and forty-five fragmentation clusters, scoring hits on the runway, dispersal areas, and direct strikes on the phosphate works. Oil supplies on the north end of the runway were destroyed and all targets battered viciously.

Because of the location of the targets, the planes' approach had to be in one direction along the shore line, making them wide open for concentrated anti-aircraft attack. The bomb runs were all made below

8,500 feet, a good bid for trouble from anti-aircraft and automatic-weapons fire.

"The men behaved magnificently," General Hale wrote to General Arnold. "They stayed down the groove in order to assure accuracy of bombing, notwithstanding the heavy attacks being made by anti-aircraft and fighters."

Five of our planes were damaged, but they all returned to Funafuti.

Colonel William Holzapfel and Lieutenant Colonel Jay Rutledge, in the Pacific Tramp, not only dropped bombs but went back over the target for a photographic run.

"Good results were shown by the pictures," Colonel Rutledge said later. "Anti-aircraft seemed like a lot at the time, although it wasn't too effective, but the fighters were really aggressive."

One man was killed, and some half dozen others were wounded.

Late that afternoon, the twenty-two bombers proudly returned to base. The Japs weren't so tough, they thought.

But that conviction didn't last long. The crews went to bed early to be ready for the raid on Tarawa the next day with the remaining undamaged planes, numbering around seventeen.

It was a beautiful night on Funafuti. The moon was full. There were very few mosquitoes. Everything was dreamy and quiet. Then, at 3:30 in the morning, the warning siren sounded. At first softly, then in bleating rasps — the same siren that was to go with the Seventh Bomber Command through the Gilberts, the Marshalls and the Marianas.

The Japs were coming!

The moonlight was no longer a thing of beauty but something to fear. In it, the white stone church of the London Missionary Society stood out like a radiant diamond, a brilliant aiming point for enemy bombardiers.

The airmen kept clear of the church, diving under anything that offered shelter. There were a number of holes near the Bomber Command area, dug by the natives to plant cocoanut trees. They measured about five feet across, were about three feet deep, and made adequate foxholes. There weren't nearly enough of them, and the rolling, diving men quickly filled them to overflowing, piling on top of each other like football players on a line plunge. The natives chose the church, a place which had always meant salvation to them.

Then the Japs struck. Their first run damaged the runway and part of the command area, but it wasn't too severe.

Hale, Landon, Holzapfel, and Rutledge didn't take shelter during this first run and were standing on a native concrete abutment near the water's edge when a string of bombs landed near the church. That was enough of that. They hit the beach on all fours and with their helmets dug a three foot ditch in the time it takes to tell about it.

The Japs roared away and brutally took their time as they rendezvoused and prepared for a second run. It was about twenty minutes before they struck again.

This time, they were dead on the target. The natives, clustered together in the church, were certain to be killed. A soldier, risking his life, darted from his place of safety and at the point of a gun drove them out into the cocoanut groves. He had just dispersed them when a bomb smashed into the church.

Many of the airmen had left their impromptu foxholes after the first attack to help the wounded, and were caught in the clear when the second run started. Again they dove for the cocoanut tree holes, sprawling over each other. Three men in a foxhole near the one occupied by Captain McIlvaine were wounded; McIlvaine was hit and Major Charles W. Marsalek, who shared his shallow shelter, was fatally wounded.

Marsalek, an Intelligence Officer and former newspaperman, had been a Navy officer during the last World War. He was older than most of the men on Funafuti and so was one of the last to reach even the sketchy haven of a makeshift foxhole. He jumped on top of McIlvaine just as a bomb exploded nearby. McIlvaine felt the body of the man above him quiver spasmodically.

As the planes passed out of sight, Marsalek said quietly, "This feels like it, boys," and lapsed into unconsciousness. He died next day while being flown to Samoa — a bomb fragment embedded in his back.

In one foxhole, medical technicians found a dead man whose body showed no wounds; he had died from a heart attack. Many men suffered broken ear drums as a result of the concussion.

The Japs hung around for several hours, making perhaps five runs in all before finally quitting the target and heading for home, presumably Tarawa.

During the raid, men had sought any place that suggested safety. Six airmen, including Lieutenant John Schroeder, bombardier for Captain Leslie Scholar, crowded under the body of an old abandoned automobile. Lieutenant Ralph Ortiz, another bombardier (who was killed the following winter over Maloelap), hid at the end of a coral jetty being built out into the ocean. He couldn't swim and as the tide came in he had the choice of risking the Japs or drowning. The Japs went away by the time the water had reached his waist.

There were incidents of comedy. Captain McIlvaine, who had been sleeping in his shorts when the raid started, lost his clothes and ran around in his underwear until someone dug up an outfit for him. Others lost shoes and personal possessions.

The next morning, surveying the wreckage, General Hale asked a sergeant if he could help him in working on one of the planes. Without bothering to look down, the man answered, "Your damned tootin' you can. Get up here and help clear these guns." The General did.

The damage was serious. The Japs had done a good job on a very small target. Two planes were destroyed and a number severely damaged, so that only twelve remained operational for the mission to Tarawa. The idea of a day raid on that island was given up, and it was not until almost midnight that the twelve took off.

Tarawa was struck at about 4 o'clock in the morning. The bombers had flown east of the nearer Gilberts on their way north to avoid Jap coast watchers, and had then flown directly west to the island. The Japs were caught by surprise, and the first elements dropped their bombs and were away before any anti-aircraft fire developed. Colonel Holzapfel led a later element and caught plenty, but only one plane of the twelve was hit.

It was another beautiful moonlight night, only this time the Japs were on the receiving end. Direct hits were scored in the gas storage and barracks area. The airmen felt pleased and avenged as they flew back to Funafuti, arriving well after daylight.

That same afternoon, the mission headed back for Canton and so on to Oahu. It was considered a success in spite of severe losses. General Hale referred to the strike and retirement as the "quickest and farthest retreat in military history."

The night the bombers got back to Hickam, Sergeant Don Backer and Private First Class Romeo Dingle were standing on the fringes of a little knot of men gathered before a bulletin board in the Headquarters Squadron day room. Pinned to the board were copies of the front pages of the Honolulu Advertiser and the Honolulu Star-Bulletin. In an obscure position at the bottom of the page, was a dispatch from London detailing a mass mission by Flying Forts over Germany. In the banner headline and occupying most of the front page, was the story of the strike against the Gilberts. This time, the correspondents remembered that the bombers belonged to the Seventh Air Force.

Dingle thoughtfully studied the bulletin board for a few minutes, then turned to Backer.

"You know," he said, "I never thought of it before — but I wonder what a pass in Tokyo would be like. They got beer up there, I hear. And big buildings like they have at home.

"Come to think of it," he concluded, "they even have subways."

Funafuti was penny-ante stuff compared to what was being tossed on the tables in Europe, but we had learned a lot about the Japs' strength in the Gilberts. More important, we were going back soon — this time to stay.

The night Jap raid on Funafuti will always remain green in the memory of those who endured it. It was the first time our new Air Force had taken a beating on the ground. It was for many the first touch of war.

No wonder Lieutenant Thore Hamrin, a concert pianist before the war, later a B-24 pilot and a veteran of the Gilberts strike, composed the "Ballad of Funafuti" during a long patrol mission out of Oahu a few weeks after his return from "down under."

THE BALLAD OF FUNAFUTI
Draw close as I tell
My tale of hell —
I swear to you it's true.
Let me take you back
To the night attack
On the Island of Funafu.

It had rained just enough
To dampen the ruff
Of the foliage and dimple the sea.
Then the moon came out
And I heard a shout,
"Take cover!" My God, they meant me.

I found my tin hat,
And gas mask at that.
"Put out that goddamned light!"

Most every soul
Had found him a hole,
But others weren't sure they were right.

Then came the drone
Of engines, a tone
I could hear while still in my tent.
The siren's shrill wail
Cut the air like a nail
Driven rustily into cement.

There was firing at first,
A regular burst,
From the guns manned by game Marines.
Then, Christ! what a swish,
It was death's shrieking hiss
From the devil's own greatest of fiends.

One lad named Carey
Arose in such hurry
As had never been seen heretofore.
He is known to most
As the white diving ghost
Who digs ditches and cries, "Nevermore."

Hail the man from New York,
Who cried out his retort
From a stance akin to the "toitle."
"Dis is stuff for de boids,
It gets on me noives
I wish I was home wit me Moitle."

A captain, no less,
Was quite dispossessed
Of all save his shorts and intelligence.
'Though his courage was high,
A bomb that dropped nigh
Missed by chance and God's own benevolence.

And though this sounds droll
That night took its toll.
There was smoke and the stench of the dead.
Screams of men dying,
Like animals crying.
Ground that was stained a bright red.

We buried the dead
And not much was said —
But we loaded our bombs with new ardor.
That night we plastered
The yellow bastard
With thrice the load and much harder.

So you've heard me tell
My tale of Hell.
I swear again it's true.
Of an airman's plight
On a tropical night
On the Island of Funafu.

CHAPTER XIII: OPERATION GALVANIC

GALVANIC!

Late in the summer of 1943 that cryptic word began appearing on a multiplying array of military papers spread on desks of Army and Navy staff officers throughout the Central Pacific.

These papers began as a thin trickle, but the trickle swelled to a stream and the stream to a torrent. "TOP SECRET," warned the red letters at the tops and bottoms of closely-guarded directives.

GALVANIC!

This word was well chosen, for it galvanized the swelling forces of the Central Pacific into fresh life. At first only a few trusted officers in the highest echelons heard the word. Even fewer knew what it meant.

But as the weeks limped by, a whisper echoed down the line: "We're getting ready to move up! We're getting ready to move up!"

And the pilots flying the dreary "recon" missions from Oahu, the supply clerk who cursed the never changing sand and sun of Canton Island, and the cooks on Funafuti who tried to dream up new ways to make spam taste like steak, felt the excitement filter through their lethargy.

Where and when they would strike was still the deepest secret. But even those who knew little of the strategic principles of warfare could guess. The pattern of our bombing and the location of our bases hinted at the Gilberts.

These former British possessions, lying some 2,100 miles southwest of Hawaii, had been occupied by the Japanese on December 27, 1941. Since then we had been gradually edging closer and our heavy bombers had been striking at Tarawa and Makin, from the Ellice Islands to the south, and from Canton to the east.

We had some information about the Gilberts, a chain of sixteen tiny, barren atolls flung along half a thousand miles of white-flecked water. Before the war the British had conducted a desultory copra trade there — all the industry the thin-soiled islands, with their 27,000 brown-skinned Gilbertese, could support.

Tarawa, chief atoll of this group, consists of a chain of long narrow islets located on a reef shaped like a right triangle. The islands are partially wooded with cocoanut trees and covered with dense undergrowth.

On Tarawa the Japanese were known to have an intricate system of ground defenses, with radar eyes to warn of hostile threats. On the nine large islets dotting the twenty-two-mile-long atoll large stores of military supplies were dispersed. From their airfield on Betio Island Jap bombers took off to harass our outpost bases and fighters swarmed up to meet our bombers bound on long missions. Jap seaplanes also operated from Tarawa, and warships anchored in its broad lagoon. Tarawa constituted the chief threat to our positions in the Central Pacific.

Makin, a group of four large islets and several smaller ones, is shaped like a grotesque leg-and-foot skeleton. It had been rebuilt by the Japs after the Carlson raid a year before, and had a seaplane base and an airfield.

Third of the GALVANIC objectives was Apemama, a minor base and evidently lightly fortified. It was expected to give little trouble.

The Seventh Air Force was to be a key player on the team of planes and ships and men that must carry out this first major offensive strike in the Central Pacific. Its primary mission, extending beyond the Gilberts, was outlined as follows:

"To deny the airfields at Tarawa, Makin, Nauru, Mille, Jaluit, and Maloelap for use by enemy aircraft."

These targets fell into three groups: first, Makin and Tarawa, our immediate ground invasion objectives in the Gilberts; second, Nauru, a lonely island about 380 miles west of the Gilberts; and third, Mille, Jaluit, and Maloelap, far to the north in the Marshalls, powerful Jap bases which must be neutralized to protect from counter-attacks from the air.

The Marshall bases, particularly, meant long gruelling missions, but they had to be undertaken to protect the ships and ground forces from enemy ground-based planes.

Jaluit was an important seaplane base and supply center for the entire Gilberts-Marshall area — crowded with military installations and bristling with strong defenses. Mille, with two runways, dispersal areas, hangars, and barracks, was strongly fortified, and Maloelap had a particularly well-developed airbase.

Makin . . . Tarawa . . . Mille . . . Nauru . . . Jaluit . . . Maloelap. Knock them out and keep them out! That was the tremendous job assigned to "Hale's Handful"!

The Navy was in charge of the show, with COMCENPAC — meaning Vice-Admiral Raymond A. Spruance, Commander of the Central Pacific Force — in command. COMAIRCENPAC, the cabalistic designation for Vice Admiral J. H. Hoover, Commander of Aircraft of the Central Pacific Force, was given operational control of the air arm. General Hale was designated as Commander of "Task Group 57.2," in charge of all strike units of land-based planes.

Hale and his aides were responsible for making available highly-trained and efficient air-strike units to COMAIRCENPAC.

The training for the job was one of the biggest items. Still larger was the task of supply.

Not all the planes and men of the Seventh could be thrown into the hopper, however. Always there was the defense of Hawaii to be considered. At no time could we afford to leave this bastion unprotected. We had learned that in one costly lesson.

One heavy, four medium, and seven fighter squadrons were reserved for the Hawaiian area. That left seven heavy, two fighter, and one fighter-bomber squadrons for the Gilberts action. The 11th Bomb Group with four squadrons (the 42nd, 431st, 26th, and 98th), was one of the task force heavy units and the 30th Bomb Group (with the 27th, 38th, 392nd, and 819th) the other.

Most of the veterans of the 11th had been pulled back to the mainland for re-assignment after the Solomons campaign, and almost a complete new team rung in.

This meant a strenuous job of training for the Bomber Command — driving hours on the gunnery ranges on Oahu, practice bombing over long water flights, and schooling of the new navigators, on whose shoulders would rest the lives of the crews.

The commanders of the Seventh knew that their chief enemy was not the Jap but those empty wastes of water and the treacherous skies above. The targets in the Marshalls were so far from our scheduled operating bases that the crews would be making the longest flights attempted in the war up to this time.

Not until October 11, 1943, did the 30th Group arrive on Oahu. This meant that the men had less than six weeks to complete their training before pushing off for the forward area. The crews of the 30th, with more training in the States, were more experienced than the new airmen of the 11th.

The old 45th, which had its baptism of fire at Wheeler Field at the outset of the war, moved down to Baker Island with its P-40 fighter planes in August. There, on the pinpoint of coral which breaks the gap between Canton and the Gilberts, it waited for the big push.

The 46th, which had accounted for three Jap planes over Oahu on the first day of the war, was held at Canton — ready to move its P-39's into the Gilberts as soon as we secured a toe-hold there. The 531st, flying A-24's, was also at Canton, combining training with anti-submarine search and dive-bombing missions.

These were the fighting men and planes. But in order to fulfill their assignment a tremendous machine of supply must be set in motion.

No other job the Seventh had taken on to date had called for such a tremendous marshalling of supplies and equipment. Materials had to be transported over thousands of miles of ocean and delivered on specific beaches. It had to be the right place at the right time — not too soon and not too late.

This was the problem facing the Seventh Air Force Service Command. From a permanently-based defensive force it had to be transformed into a group of highly mobile units, suitable for island-to-island operations — like a garrison soldier uprooted and sent into the field with his pack on his back.

These Air Service Support Squadrons ("ASSRONS") had to be small and compact enough to move onto a tiny atoll already crowded to overflowing with all types of tactical units trying to keep their feet and powder dry. They had to be able to set up overnight, do their all-important job of supplying the fighting units, then be able to pull out instantly when the word came and leapfrog to the next atoll on the long road to Tokyo.

First move in this direction was made in August when the First ASSRONS squadron was formed and its twenty officers and two hundred enlisted men briefed to occupy Baker Island.

A month later the Second ASSRONS came into being. At the proper time it was to occupy the three Gilberts atolls. Its officers and men began training at once. They had to learn not only how to handle supplies, but how to climb down cargo nets and wade ashore from landing barges — for they were to follow assault troops ashore.

Third ASSRONS was then formed to take over the supply job in the Ellice Islands. New units continued to spring into being under the complex and far-seeing plan.

The long supply train, whose engine chugged toward Tarawa while its caboose rattled across the United States, was in motion.

Long before the GALVANIC directives appeared, A-4 Supply had been preparing for this day. Observers had gone into the South and Southwest Pacific to observe action there and study the types of Air Service Units, supplies and equipment needed for atoll operations.

Brigadier General Walter J. Reed, Commanding General of the Service Group, set up his advanced headquarters on Funafuti, and studied the reports of inventories of supplies available in the area. The report was not encouraging. Neither the supply stocks nor the equipment were adequate. Much of the material available was not the correct type for atoll warfare. Much of the vast requirements would have to come from the States.

Now began the battle against Time and Distance. Over all the vast operations hung the deadly importance of keeping the enemy in the dark. Thousands of men had to assist in assembling those supplies. Thousands of girl clerks and civilian workers on docks and railroads were a part of the complex picture.

Somehow the secret of GALVANIC must be kept from them — lest an unguarded word slip, and men die uselessly on distant beaches because the enemy had learned When and Where and How!

Supply representatives were sent to Washington to expedite shipments and make spot decisions to avoid having to message back through channels over the 5,500 miles and risk the possibility of enemy interception.

Soon, by train and truck, troops and supplies were rolling to the San Francisco port of embarkation. An even flow had to be maintained to avoid port congestion. Spotted freight cars, preloaded, were held awaiting call of the Port Regulating Officer.

Elaborate estimates were needed of ship tonnage necessary to move units and supplies to Hawaii and thence down the line to a mysterious destination known only as "TREE."

Throughout October the supply department of H.A.D. worked under the white Hawaiian sun and blazing flood lights, and miniature mountains of crates and bales grew on Honolulu docks. By trailer and flat car and truck they were hauled to dispersal areas all over the island. It was a constant battle to keep these mountains from burying the docks altogether.

There wasn't enough storage space. There weren't enough trucks. Drivers and machines were strained to the breaking point to keep the tide moving. Time was of the essence!

While all this infinity of preparation was going on, the fighting front was not idle. Pilots were flying planes to new bases. Ships were plowing the ocean, carrying ground crews to join them. And from the advanced bases at Funafuti, Nukufetau, Nanumea and Canton, heavily-loaded bombers were lumbering off to carry on the steady softening-up of our objectives.

Back on Oahu, after grinding weeks of training, various units were alerted for movement. On November 1, 1943, at 4 o'clock in the afternoon the U. S. Army Transport President Tyler sailed with personnel of the Seventh Air Force and the Bomber Command, including the 11th Bomber Group with its four squadrons — the 26th, 98th, 42nd, and 431st.

Units of the 30th Group, including the 27th, 38th and 392nd Squadrons, after a month and a half of bewildering preparations, also debarked. All personnel had been assembled at Bellows Field, given hasty amphibious training, and staged for departure while their organizational equipment was being assembled at Hickam.

"This concurrent mixing of phases of development causes tremendous hardships and confusion for all concerned," said Major Howard R. Hayes. "Assembly of troops, training, packing, and staging are separate steps. They cannot be mixed without increasing the normal confusion a hundredfold."

That was but one of the many lessons we learned through mistakes of our first large operation.

A small command section and a radar unit were assigned to accompany the "S Detachment" assault troops headed for Makin.

Later the smaller "Q Detachment," bound for Apemama, and the "R Detachment" for Tarawa were loaded. Divorced from their parent unit, they were setting out on their own.

"S Detachment," the parent unit, found itself aboard with the 165th Infantry. On shipboard, strategy boards met regularly and troops trained daily. The public address system blared out the details of the impending operation which up to that time had been an official secret.

D-Day was set for November 20th!

The rime-table for GALVANIC ran from November 13 to December 6 — D-minus-7 to D-plus-16.

General Hale and his staff arrived at Funafuti from Oahu on November 6 and set up advanced headquarters from which Air Force operations could be directed. All tactical units of Task Group 57.2 were set.

They were disposed at the corners of a great watery triangle. At Funafuti, 714 miles southeast of Tarawa, were the 42nd and 431st bomber squadrons. The 27th and 38th were at Nanomea and the 98th was at Nukufetau.

At Canton the remaining units of heavies, the 26th and 392nd, were stationed along with the 46th and 27th Fighter Squadrons and the 531st Fighter-Bomber Squadron. At Baker Island, at the northern point of the triangle, the 45th Fighter Squadron moved in. Baker was designated for use as a forward base for the staging of Canton-based heavy bombers on the long missions to the Gilberts and Marshalls.

The Seventh Air Force was now poised, ready to strike its first great offensive blow of the war. The weary days of the "Pineapple War" were over. The waiting was past!

GALVANIC!

It was the dawn of November 14, 1943.

GALVANIC!

The great Central Pacific offensive was on!

CHAPTER XIV: "SPITS OF SAND IN THE SUN"

D-DAY IN THE GILBERTS WAS ONLY A WEEK AWAY WHEN THE Seventh Air Force went into all-out action.

Tarawa . . . Makin . . . Apemama . . . knock them out! Wipe out the planes! Hit their gun positions! Wreck that radar!

Mille . . . Jaluit . . . Maloelap, in the Marshalls . . . and Nauru. Get those planes on the ground! Put those airstrips out of commission!

Each enemy plane knocked out was one potential threat less to American task forces that would soon be steaming up to the invasion beaches. Each gun emplacement smashed by our bombs meant the possible saving of scores of lives of American ground forces.

This was a tremendous responsibility for "Hale's Handful" of seven squadrons. "Too much dispersion of effort really to neutralize those bases," worried the planners of the Seventh.

Distance. Infinitesimal targets. The worst weather conditions in any theater of war.

On November 13, the 431st Squadron made their first mission from Funafuti. Nine B-24's, piloted by Captains John R. Risher and Thore Hamrin, Jr., and Lieutenants Nicholas J. Davis, Thomas G. Perry, D. L. Mac Arthur, Ivan N. Osborne, Russel H. Darley, Warren S. Rowe, and Harvey I. Lundy struck Tarawa.

Roaring over the enemy stronghold, at altitudes of from 8,500 to 15,000 feet, they showered aerial installations and enemy barracks with thirty-pound fragmentation bombs. Ninety per cent of the bombs hit the target, and fires and explosions were visible seventy miles from the atoll as the B-24's returned to their base.

On November 14, eleven B-24's of the 26th Squadron took off from Canton and, staging through Baker Island, bombed Mille on the following day.

Ten B-24's of the 431st, piloted by Captain Pierce L. Vieth, Lieutenant Victor P. Malmgren, Captains Risher and Hamrin, and Lieutenants Davis, Perry, MacArthur, Osborne, Darley, Rowe, and Lundy, went into the Marshalls on November 15 to hit Jaluit. Despite turbulent weather, the plane blasted the enemy seaplane base at Emidj, scoring hits with 500-pound bombs on Jap hangars, barracks, and oil storage areas.

The Ducking Duckling, a B-24 of the 38th Squadron, flew a mission against the Jap seaplane base at Jaluit in the Marshalls on November 16.

"We were told we probably wouldn't run into any fighter opposition," said Technical Sergeant William Gates, Greenfield, Massachusetts, flight engineer on the plane.

"After we made our bomb run, however, a couple of dozen float-type Rufes swarmed us. They were fast and maneuverable and one came diving within forty yards of our plane. He was so close I could see the Jap gunner slumped over his guns — someone else had already killed him, I cut loose with my turret guns and the plane went to pieces and fell into the sea.

"It was a long hop with that damned water below you all the time. We had to duck the Gilberts where the Japs had a nasty-habit of shooting hell out of you. By the time we had returned, we had flown about 2,000 miles.

"On another mission against the same target we hit rough weather and came out over the target at 1,200 feet and still going down. Our pilot, Captain Morris Miller, didn't figure we were that close to Jaluit and everyone was surprised and scared as hell when we came in practically sitting on their doorstep.

"There was nothing to do then but let 'em have it. We could see Japs on the ground and, after dropping our bombs, we began strafing like a fighter plane. We got in some helluva good licks, too.

"The Japs were throwing everything in the books at us. Machine-gun and 20-mm. shells hitting the plane sounded like hail on a tin roof. One slug went through a gear box, but we were lucky. Because of the position of the controls at the time, it missed the gears. We were below 300 feet at the moment and if the gears had been hit — well that would have been all, brother!"

Luck always plays a major part in wars. Sometimes it's good and sometimes bad. A few breaks one way or another is the difference between living and dying.

Technical Sergeant Carlyle Elrod, Anderson, Indiana, and his B-24 crew at Nanomea, also were among those who got a good break.

"We were heading for Tarawa when we hit a storm and only two planes got over the target," Sergeant Elrod said. "We got our bombs on the target but eighteen Zeroes ganged us and proceeded to give us a helluva time. They concentrated on our plane and followed us out for two hours. Our group downed eight Zeroes but our plane caught hell. Two of our engines were shot out before the Jap fighters finally turned back. I caught a slug in the hip and all the way back it hurt like fire.

"It was tough sledding with two engines gone. Finally, we were in sight of Nanomea but we didn't quite make it. We made a crash landing on a reef about fifty yards offshore. I had a piece of metal driven through my foot but managed to get to land safely. It was a miracle we weren't all killed, but thanks to the skillful piloting of Captain Jimmy Andrews — plus a good dose of luck — we made it."

On November 17, eleven planes of the 26th Squadron ran into trouble on a mission against Taroa Island in the Maloelap Atoll in the Marshalls. And again the breaks were good.

"Over the target we encountered intense anti-aircraft fire," Lieutenant John J. Lieb, pilot of one of the B-24's, said. "Fifteen to eighteen Zekes swarmed up to meet us, and all hell broke loose.

"Our No. 4 engine was shot out. As I feathered the prop, Technical Sergeant Lewis T. Horton, our chief engineer, called on the interphone to say a fire had started in the waist section of the plane.

"I headed back for Canton. The air was full of enemy fighters diving at us from every direction. Our gunners were unable to leave their posts to fight the fire — they were too busy fighting off enemy planes.

"We saw one Zeke go down in flames. Finally the Japs began to fall back and we gradually outdistanced them but we were still in bad shape. The fire had spread to the tail section of the plane and the control cables were so badly damaged that they were in danger of giving way any minute and sending us spinning into the sea. One engine was out, our gas was low, and Canton seemed a million miles away.

"Sergeant Horton never lost his head. Cans of fruit juice were opened and he passed them around and supervised the dousing of the fire with the juice. Then, with little more than the skin holding the tail section to the fuselage, Horton picked his way back and repaired the damaged cables and I managed to bring her back to base. Horton was awarded a Silver Star for his outstanding courage and skill."

On the same day Veith, Risher, Perry, Davis, Malmgren, and Osborne, of the 431st, shattered runways and barracks, destroyed an oil dump, knocked out a gun battery, damaged Jap planes on the ground, and hit runways and barracks at Tarawa.

Despite the hairline accuracy of the Norden bombsight and rigorous training of the bombardiers who had to hit the smallest targets in any theater, luck was sometimes our best weapon in bombings.

Take the case of Lieutenant Harry Hodge, bombardier of the Ducking Duckling.

"We were over Maloelap and two of our 500-pounders wouldn't release over the target," Lieutenant Hodge said. "Realizing that we were running out of land to bomb, I grabbed the salvo handle and released everything at once. Our ball turret gunner, Wilbert Rightmyer, saw the bombs go all the way in. They missed land completely but hit and sank a 4,000-ton Jap cargo ship offshore."

Luck ran out for Captain Veith on November 19, however. The 431st Squadron hero, on a mission against Tarawa, lost two engines over the target. Although his left shoulder was torn by flying glass from the damaged turret, he managed to nurse his plane back to Nanomea. He circled the field twice, trying to land, but each time was waved off by men in the control tower because the plane just ahead of him had crashed and was burning on the runway.

Lieutenant Maston M. Jacks, Assistant Intelligence Officer who was in the plane as an observer, tells the story:

"Captain Veith tried vainly to gain altitude and come in again, but with two engines shot out by enemy 20-mm. fire the plane would not respond. We headed into the sea about a mile off Nanomea.

"We braced ourselves and the plane hit with a crash that broke the front of the plane off at the instrument panel and sheared the entire greenhouse off the topside of the ship. Somehow I managed to claw my way out of the plane, which was sinking fast. When we checked up we found everyone free except Captain Veith and Sergeant Robert F. Neuman, a gunner.

"Lieutenant Burton L. Moore, the navigator, tried to assist Veith to escape but was ordered by the injured pilot to help Sergeant Neuman instead. Moore helped the gunner free himself from the wreck.

"Meanwhile, Lieutenant Robert N. Stafford, co-pilot, had dived into the cockpit and released two life rafts and we climbed aboard. We were unable to rescue Veith and he went down with the plane.

"We headed for shore but our luck was still bad. As we hit the breakers at a coral shelf about 200 yards from land, our raft was overturned and Technical Sergeant Robert F. Beyler, gunner, disappeared into the sea. His body was washed ashore the next day."

It was November 19 and the invasion of the Gilberts was only two days away. It was of increasing importance that enemy gun positions be knocked out.

Ten B-24's of the 98th Squadron took off from Nukufetau at twenty-eight minutes past midnight to hit Betio Island at Tarawa Atoll.

"We were loaded with 100-pound demolition bombs and scheduled to hit gun positions and foxholes along the south edge of the island between the beach and main runway and gun positions and foxholes along the northwest tip of the island," Major Allen H. Wood, commanding officer and pilot of the lead plane, said.

"At 4:45 in the morning we spotted Tarawa, thirty-five miles away. Fires and thick black smoke, from bombings by formations ahead of us, were billowing up 2,000 feet. We dropped down to 8,000 feet and went over the target in formation. Guns on the ground spurted red flames and then glowed for a minute after each burst. Flak was intense and accurate, bracketing our flight.

"We were particularly careful not to hit airfields and buildings because we knew they would be of use to us in a short time. We also took care to miss the native villages. As we headed home we could see damaged Jap barracks and airfields covered with bomb craters, proof that earlier missions had been successful."

On the trip back Major Wood sat in on a radio conversation that might have had serious implications.

"About an hour out of Nanomea I was surprised to hear the strict radio silence broken," he said. "Flyers of another squadron were carrying on conversation giving positions, their estimated time of arrival, ground speed, and facts pertaining to the mission.

"The conversation included such dialogue as 'Is your frequency on 6210?' 'Are you stopping at first base or going on home?'

"In the middle of the talk a Japanese voice, speaking perfect English, came in on 6210 kilocycles saying: Thank you, Mr. (and he called three pilots' names), for giving information on your bases at Nanomea, Nukufetau and Funafuti — here's to many bombings.'"

Fortunately, however, the Jap air force was being too well pasted to take full advantage of such information.

November 21, 1943. It was D-Day at last — the day towards which all the months of planning and preparation had been leading. But it was more than a mere invasion of a few coral atolls. It was our first giant stride along the road back. It was the beginning of our first all-out, major drive against the enemy in the Central Pacific. Its success or failure would foretell the shape of things to come. Men of the Seventh knew this as they flew their frantic missions against distant targets. Bearded men waiting in the darkness on crowded transport ships knew what it meant as they smoked endless cigarettes and waited to board the landing barges.

Now the great Pacific fleet, resurrected from the graveyard of Pearl Harbor, moved in. Hour after hour they rained fire and shells on the invasion beaches while carrier planes dove and strafed. Far to the north in the Marshalls the great bombers of the Seventh hit the airstrips at Jaluit, at Mille and Maloelap, helping to eliminate the threat of Jap fighter planes.

The Marines of the Second Division waited off the north shore of Betio Island of the Tarawa atoll.

There was little talking as they waited — beachhead war was too new and zero hour too close for conversation. They sat and waited and cursed the never ending monotonous rumble of the guns that jarred a thousand raw nerves.

At last there was silence and hundreds of landing barges, looking like giant water spiders, headed for the beach.

Once-beautiful Tarawa was a scene of devastation, its palm trees shattered and its coral churned by thousands of bombs and shells. Planes of the Seventh had showered the target with 500-pound bombs, and big guns of the fleet had thrown a deadly barrage of 2,000 tons of shells. Carrier planes dropped 800 tons of bombs.

Because of pre-invasion strikes against Jap airfields, we had absolute air supremacy and no more than six enemy planes at a time were seen at Betio.

But what should have been an isle of the dead became a nightmare that resembled an inferno.

The island was a mass of well-placed guns and defensive emplacements. The guns, ranging from 3 to 8-inch caliber, were so well protected by concrete, steel and cocoanut trees that a direct hit was necessary to knock them out.

Reinforced concrete blocks were set into the reefs offshore and double-apron barbed wire fences supported by steel posts covered the reefs and beach. Anti-tank ditches five feet deep and twelve feet wide, with cocoanut logs buried upright in them, were located back of the beachline. Large anti-tank mines, spaced seventy-five feet apart, covered the reef and beach.

Hexagonal steel pill boxes, protected by reinforced concrete, cocoanut palm logs, steel planes, and sand were on all beaches. The five hundred pillboxes were so arranged that when troops fought their way past one they were moving into cross-fire of two inner pillboxes.

The Jap garrison at Betio included 3,500 Imperial Marines and 1,000 Korean laborers, and the latter were forced to assist in the defense of the island. The Japs put up a fanatic defense and all but ten Jap Marines and 140 Koreans refused to surrender and were wiped out. It was necessary to use dynamite, bulldozers, and flame throwers to blast the Nips out of the pillboxes.

At the same time, men of the 165th Infantry, New York's "Fighting 69th" of World War I fame, headed for the west and north shore of Butaritari Island on Makin atoll.

Jap machine guns opened fire when the boats were still 500 yards offshore. Some landing craft ran aground on reefs and men were forced to wade ashore in chest-deep water.

Six LST's loaded with men of the "S" detachment of the Second ASSRONS group, whose task it was to build an airstrip on Makin, were scheduled to land on D-plus-1. They were held offshore until late afternoon. The first boat running into the lagoon nosed into a reef and grounded about 400 feet offshore, with its bow in three or four feet of water in extreme low tide. Several large underwater craters lay in front of it. Guides had to wade ashore to guide the craft in.

Bulldozers chuffed and clattered while bullets still whined across the shattered atoll. Keeping pace with the Infantry, undeterred by the jungle warfare around them, the Aviation Engineers struck out across the shell-torn surface of the island with markers and machines to carve an airstrip out of the Makin cocoanut groves.

Jap snipers, hidden in the fronded tops of the trees, were still firing at every moving object within a thousand yards when the engineers began their labors.

Technical Sergeant Norman D. Hoch, Oklahoma City, Oklahoma, told Sergeant Bill Cunningham, Seventh AAF correspondent, of the first few days on Makin.

"Some of the bombs dropped by the Seventh AAF Liberators left craters 70 feet wide/' Hoch said, "and our bombardiers had been terribly accurate in their aim.

"There were bodies of dead Japs all over the place, but the most peculiar sight I saw was a group of six Jap soldiers who had committed mass suicide in the wreckage of a Jap plane. Two were sitting up and the others sprawled in a heap. Apparently the two had killed the rest and then shot each other."

Hoch said warehouses and other buildings on the island were shattered by bombs and shells and two ammunition dumps were exploded.

"There wasn't a blade of grass left standing near those dumps," he said. "All over the island there were palm trees with their tops blown off and whole groves of trees laid flat.

"Thousands of tons of rice were strewn about and there were also many white Jap Marine leggings scattered around. The natives were making themselves rich — in native terms — on the Jap clothing.

"The warehouses had been loaded with Jap beer, saki, and wine. The assault troops got most of the bottles which escaped the bombing and shelling. After what they went through, however, they deserved it."

The souvenir business was brisk after the fighting stopped. The Infantry had a corner on the market, and prices such as $500 for a Jap Luger were asked and paid. Those fortunate enough to have a Samurai sword were not selling at any price.

"I met one boy who had a sword he was certainly entitled to," he said. "He was a mild, easy-going hillbilly.

"The night after he landed and dug in, a Jap officer jumped into his foxhole and in perfect English said 'I guess I got you, Joe,' and then lunged at the American with that sword. The soldier side-stepped and went into action fast with an old hunting knife. The Jap's body had seventeen stab wounds in it when the carving was over. The hillbilly had the sword."

For the first three days Hoch and his companions heard rifle fire all day. At the end of the third, amphibious troops landed on the opposite end of the island and finished off most of the Japs.

"I saw a dead Jap with a neat looking pin on his lapel and took it, thinking it might be a regimental insignia that would be an interesting souvenir. One of our interpreters laughed when I showed it to him. The Jap inscription on it said: 'Tokyo Follies.' Just an ad for a show, but it was fine irony. It described the whole war!"

Propaganda material was plentiful, including enemy papers with uncomplimentary cartoons of Churchill and Roosevelt.

"One I particularly remembered," Hoch said, "showed Uncle Sam reaching a long arm across the Pacific to grasp the Gilberts and Marshalls. A handsome Jap was swinging a huge sword to cut the arm off."

In four short weeks the ASSRONS engineers solved the problems of unpredictable sink holes, unexpected marshy areas, ground water five feet below the surface of the "floating island," and Jap snipers. Days and nights of non-stop work cut their streamlined schedule even closer.

Meanwhile, our heavy bombers continued their strikes aimed at blocking off all help for the beleaguered Japanese in the Gilberts. Twenty tons of bombs were dropped on Nauru on D-plus-1, harassed Mille on D-plus-2, Taroa Island on Maloelap atoll on D-plus-4. By that time the worst of the fighting on Tarawa was over.

Apemama was occupied on November 22, and on the following day seven planes of the 98th Squadron hit Jaluit. The ships, piloted by Captain Gardiner Cornwell, Bridgeport, West Virginia, and Lieutenants Herbert T. Kurz, Caldwell, New Jersey, Thomas M. Esmond, Bellinger, Texas, Raymond R. Hindersinn, Seekonk, Massachusetts, Alton O. McClesky, Hagerman, New Mexico, Walter P. Jordanek, Chicago, Illinois, and Lewis E. Cartwright, Cornwall, Connecticut, came in on the target at 12:30 at night and released their bombs. Lieutenant Cartwright's plane received a hit in the left wing which severed a fuel line, and Lieutenant Kurz's plane had the hydraulic line shot out.

Cartwright's ship returned safely but Kurz's Liberator, with the hydraulics out, was unable to stop on the runway at Nukufetau. It rolled off the southern end of the strip and about 50 yards into the ocean. None of the crew was injured, however.

On the same day eleven planes of the 26th Squadron hit the Mille airfield and were attacked by twelve enemy fighters. Two Jap planes were shot down, one was probably destroyed, and seven were damaged. All our planes returned safely.

On the shell-torn islands of the Gilberts we began to see the results of Japanese occupation for the first time. In the compound of a native village on Makin we found Monseigneur Octave Terraine, Bishop of all the Gilberts, and his fellow missionaries, Father Peirre Gurchard, Father Marcel Viallon, Brother C. Weber, and Brother H. Englehart, all of the Mission of the Sacred Heart, a French Catholic Society.

Before the war, the priests were stationed on the various Gilbert Islands but were brought to Tarawa when the Japs moved in. From them we received a comprehensive story of the Jap occupation.

Adjacent to their quarters was a stockade in which twenty-two Australian, New Zealand, and English prisoners had been confined. They were mostly civil service workers, teachers and radiomen, captured at the time of the Jap occupation. On October 15, 1942, four unidentified planes suddenly appeared overhead and a ship or submarine was seen off-coast. In the excitement one prisoner escaped from the stockade, ran to the shore and frantically signaled the planes — thinking them friendly. He was shot down on the spot.

Monseigneur Terraine covered his eyes — what followed he could not bear to talk about. The other prisoners were tied to cocoanut trees for two days and then the troops were turned loose on the helpless men.

"Mais oui, tous les vingt-deux!" said Father Viallon, drawing a finger across his throat.

The reason the priests were not also massacred was explained by the Jap naval commander: "You are missionaries and French and to treat you well is good propaganda!"

A week later they were moved to Makin but didn't see the Carlson raiders.

"We were warned by the Japs to stay out of sight," Father Viallon said. "After the raid there were nine Marines left behind. We were told by the natives that two of them were Catholics and wanted to see us. We told the Marines that they should go to Maraki, an island southeast of Makin, where they would be safer, but they were captured and taken to Ponape.

"After this we were not allowed to leave the compound of our yard and were constantly spied upon," he said.

Their jealousy of fellow soldiers and contempt for those of lesser rank was a predominant factor among the Japs, the priests said.

"I couldn't give something to one Jap without another coming to demand the same thing," Father Gurchard said. "One Jap officer had been kind to us so I gave him the last two eggs we had. The next day his superior officer called and demanded some eggs. When he learned we had no more he was very angry that I had shown preference to his junior officer.

"The contempt with which the officer treated the enlisted man is almost incomprehensible. One day a soldier stopped to talk to me and an officer came up and without warning or reason struck him on the head with his riding crop. The soldier bowed deeply, walked backwards five steps, bowed again and left. The officer then started a pleasant conversation as if nothing had happened.

"And it extends all the way down. The enlisted men would not talk to the Korean laborers, nor flyers to Jap Marines. Everything is caste. I believe that if they were not fighting us they would be fighting each other.

"The lash was constantly in use. One Korean — a mass of welts and bruises — came to Father Viallon and said he was a Christian. His commanding officer had discovered it and ordered him beaten every day. He later died," Father Gurchard said.

Jap military propagandists had convinced their soldiers that they would surely be beheaded if they surrendered to our forces. Their papers were full of it.

"And it was not only the uneducated soldier who believed this fantastic propaganda," Father Gurchard said. "One Jap officer, a former exchange student at Columbia University, said the America he once knew was a wonderful place. 'But that has all changed and they are now a nation of blood-thirsty murderers,' he said. When I appealed to his reasoning as an educated man, he said that the Jap newspapers had printed proof of all the atrocities the United States had committed.

"All during this time we saw only one Jap who expressed himself differently. He was a flight surgeon who had studied in America and Germany. 'I know the difference between American and Jap production too well to be deluded,' he said sadly. He was kind to us and had contempt for the military. He was transferred before the American occupation."

The Japs conscripted native labor by going to village chiefs and giving each a quota to fill. If the workers were not produced, the chief was confined and beaten. Natives were forced to work twelve hours a day and received nothing but rations and occasional gifts of money and a few articles of clothing.

"The Gilbertese are better educated and more intelligent than the average Jap," Father Gurchard said. "The Japs published a daily news sheet telling in glowing terms of the destruction of the American fleet, planes, and armies. The natives got a big laugh out of it — they recognized the absurdities of the claims.

"The Jap soldier liked the Gilberts better than the Marshalls — probably because here we had no civilian government and the soldier could simply walk into a native's hut and take what he wanted. The poor Gilbertese dared not do or say anything."

The Japs knew we were coming, the priests said. Early in September they told the missionaries to move to Tanimaiki, an adjoining island, for safety. The priests were there when our carrier attack was launched on September 18-19.

"About three days after the carrier attack a rubber raft with Navy flyers landed on Bikati Island," Bishop Terraine said. "The natives fed them and sent word to us of their presence. Jap food was sent the flyers, but the Japs learned the Navy flyers were there and they were captured. We heard that the Americans were probably lost when the ship on which they were being taken to Ponape was torpedoed."

With the Gilberts secured, the seven-league Seventh was already launching another campaign by a never ending series of strikes against their next objective — the Marshalls.

On November 23, eleven planes of the 26th Squadron pounded Mille. Of the twelve Jap fighters that came up, two were destroyed, seven damaged, and another probably destroyed.

The Navy joined in and carrier planes hit Mille and Jaluit with 191 tons of bombs. The Japs struck back in a night attack on November 25, with their torpedo Kates dropping flares to light their targets.

Two weeks after D-day a Navy task force drove into the Marshalls and battered Kwajalein and Wotje, destroying seventy-two enemy craft, and then withdrew, running a 24-hour gauntlet of attack from angry Jap planes rising from the hornet's nest behind them.

The pace was stepping up.

Even before the books were closed on GALVANIC, our next operation was beginning against the Marshalls — next step on the road to Tokyo. We were losing no time.

On paper, the GALVANIC operation closed December 6 — D-plus-16. The mission of the Seventh had been accomplished at surprisingly low cost.

In the twenty-nine strike missions, 348 sorties had been dispatched and 325 tons of bombs dropped with 67 per cent of the bombs on the pin-point targets.

Anti-aircraft fire had been mostly meager and inaccurate — although the worst was yet to come as we gave the Japs practice. There had been some fanatical interception but we had lost only seven planes — two to anti-aircraft, one to enemy fighters, one for operational causes, and three for "reasons unknown." Only six men had been killed, thirty wounded, and thirty-one missing.

Photo and Intelligence reports showed extensive damage to enemy installations, but Seventh staff officers were not satisfied. So great were the distances flown that bomb loads had to be curtailed so the planes could carry enough gas. Bloody Tarawa had taught the need of carrying larger bombs. Had it not been for the high training and efficiency of our air units, results would have been far less.

More important to the success of the Central Pacific campaign were the lessons in atoll warfare which had been learned from this first major offensive action. The Marines had learned these lessons on the ground at bloody cost. The Navy had learned them on the sea. The Seventh Air Force had learned them in the air. And each was stronger for it.

CHAPTER XV: THE MARSHALLS ARE OURS

AND NOW A NEW PASSWORD ECHOED THROUGH THE STAFF rooms of the Central Pacific Command:

FLINTLOCK!

There were fresh batches of plans and directives red-stamped "TOP SECRET." There was no break in operations, but there was a new D-day on the road to Tokyo toward which all efforts pointed.

Next stop, Kwajalein!

Kwajalein is the largest atoll in the world. Until January 31, when American assault forces landed, it was one of the great Jap bases in the Pacific. Its taking promised to be a bloody job. The Japs had less than two years to fortify Tarawa — and Tarawa was costly to us. They had twenty-four years in the Marshalls.

From an operations standpoint, the burden on the Seventh Air Force in the early stages of FLINTLOCK was somewhat eased. The mechanics of hauling troops from rear to forward areas, of building airstrips and setting up defensive tactics, the tremendous task of deploying fighter and bomber groups, of supplying them with planes, bullets, and bombs for the offensive thrust, had been worked out in the Gilberts. Now, with some of the bugs ironed out, the plans automatically went back into operation. Quietly at first, so as not to tip the Japs to our next objective. But quickly.

D-Day on Kwajalein was set at January 31. Early in November, the Seventh began preparations for a seventy-day air assault which was to begin late that month and end fifteen minutes before the first invasion wave hit the beach.

Aviation engineers, working on airfields at Tarawa, Makin, and Apemama, began working sixteen-hour shifts. The ground echelons — the clerks, typists, and maintenance men — were already on the high seas bound for the Gilberts. They had embarked early in November at Oahu, at Funafuti, and at Canton.

Down from Oahu to Tarawa and Apemama came twenty-five medium bombers of the 820th Bomb Squadron. The planes were two-engine Mitchells, B-25CS bristling with machine guns, some of them mounting a

75-millimeter cannon in the nose. Three other squadrons of the same group were to arrive in mid-January, in time for the last pre-invasion strikes.

On the morning of December 14, the aircraft carrier U.S.S. Nassau arrived off Makin Island, her hangar deck bulging with Army fighter aircraft, P-38Q's of the 46th and 72nd Squadrons and thirteen new A-24 dive-bombers of the 531st Fighter-Bomber Squadron. Three days later, the land planes were successfully catapulted from the Nassau's flight deck. They landed on the strip which the 804th Aviation Engineers were rushing to completion on Butatari Island, Makin.

Tarawa became advance headquarters. It was headquarters also for the Bomber Command and for the 11th Bomber Group, which moved its three operational squadrons up from the Ellices.

All the while our forces were being redeployed for the Marshall campaign, the raids "down the line" continued without cessation. Frequently, while the ground echelon of a bomb group was packing duffle bags and crating equipment for the trip to a new base, the air echelon was planning a mission.

The movement of the 431st Bomb Squadron of the 11th Bomber Group was typical of the smoothness with which FLINTLOCK directives were carried out. While an LST loaded with the squadron's ground personnel moved out of the harbor at Funafuti on the way to Tarawa, six of the squadron's B-24's roared overhead on their way to a target. The air echelon carried out continued operations from Funafuti while the ground personnel sweated out a four-day trip to Tarawa, unloaded the LST and set up rough facilities for a tactical operation. Then the bombers flew up, arriving in the morning and pulling their first mission of the Marshall campaign that night.

Tarawa, Apemama, and Makin Islands in the Gilberts and Nanomea in the Ellices were now our operating bases for the Marshals campaign.

The Marshalls lie northwest of the Gilberts, with about 200 miles of water between Makin, northernmost of the Gilberts, and Mille, southernmost of the Marshalls. There are thirty-three typical coral atolls strung in a double chain and scattered over 150,000 square miles of water. But all the little chunks of coral together contain only 160 square miles of land — half the size of New York City.

Up to and including D-minus-three, the Seventh Air Force, in the concise and matter-of-fact language of the FLINTLOCK directives, was assigned the job of "denying the enemy the use of their air bases, Mille and Jaluit."

And, the directives stated, "to destroy enemy aircraft and air facilities at Maloelap, at Wotje, and at Roi and Kwajalein."

On D-plus-two and thereafter, our mission was "to assist other forces engaged in denying Wotje and Maloelap as air bases to the enemy."

The pattern of warfare in the Central Pacific, which had its beginnings in the Gilberts campaign, took final shape for the Marshall invasion. The primary assignment for the Seventh Air Force was to furnish bomb support of one invasion, while it softened up targets for future invasions and protected the rear and flank of our westward advancing troops from attack by enemy forces on bypassed islands.

In the Gilberts offensive, Mille, Wotje, Jaluit, and Maloelap were secondary targets. Now we would throw everything we had at them as the principal FLINTLOCK targets while we were neutralizing by-passed Nauru and planning still another invasion.

Mille, within fighter-attack distance of Makin, was the site of the largest Jap airfield in the Marshalls. Wotje held two airstrips. Jaluit, the site of administrative headquarters for the Marshalls Islands, held a submarine base and submarine refueling stations. Maloelap, center of the four islands, was strongly defended by Jap fighter aircraft and could quickly be reinforced from other islands. It proved the toughest target in the Marshalls.

The Pathfinders, a B-24 Group which had a bitter kind of pride in the fact that they were the first to fly over most of the Central Pacific targets, first to test the enemy's fighter and anti-aircraft defenses, first to encounter his new weapons, and frequently the first to test our own air-sea rescue facilities in a new patch of ocean, found out just how tough Maloelap was.

Their early missions to Maloelap, which were among the first flown during the FLINTLOCK drive, originated at Canton Island, even before they moved up to the Gilberts. In their first strike at the 32-mile chain of sixty islands which comprise Maloelap Atoll, the Pathfinders flushed between thirty-five and forty interceptors.

Their next raid was a nightmare.

Again, some forty enemy interceptors met the Liberator formation. Flak was more intense, more accurate. In addition, the Pathfinders ran head on into a new weapon — aerial phosphorus bombs. These bizarre bombs were dropped by Jap fighters poised 2,000 feet over the Liberators as they came off the target. Returning crews said they looked and sounded like ack-ack as they exploded around the formation. Then, terrifyingly, the grey

mushrooms burnt into long, white tentacles which drifted down the sky —
phosphorus arms which, crews soon discovered, could envelop a bomber
and send it flaming into the sea.

Two planes failed to return from that mission. Over the target, the B-24's
piloted by Lieutenant Burl W. Justice and Lieutenant Walter A. Ward were
hit simultaneously by machine-gun fire and flak. The No. 3 engines of both
planes caught fire, but both pilots held formation and got their bombs
away.

Just as Ward's plane cleared the atoll, it staggered and fell, bursting in
flames as it went down — but with all guns blazing in a final, grim gesture
of defiance at the Japs following it to the water. A few minutes later,
Justice was forced to take his flaming plane down into a crash landing on
the sea. Zeroes followed it down and strafed the plane murderously as it
sledded into the water.

Every plane that returned from that mission had been hit and suffered
some damage.

It was a tough mission and set the pace for the stormy weeks ahead. In
the opening weeks of December, as the tempo of our raids increased, the
fibre of Japanese resistance stiffened. Anti-aircraft grew more accurate and
more intense. Jap interceptors, wary at first, pressed home their attacks and
began to take an alarming toll in planes and lives.

For the medium bombers, dive-bombers, and fighter planes going into
offensive action for the first time in the Pacific, the Marshalls' targets
sometimes were deceptively easy at first.

The cannon-toting B-25's of the 820th caught the Japs on Mille with
little or no defense against their first flashing attack, which opened with
75-millimeter cannon bursts, continued with .50 caliber nose guns,
climaxed with bombs and concluded with a deadly strafing from the waist,
tail and top turret .50's. They went over Mille doing better than two
hundred miles an hour and flying as close to zero as pilots can fly bombers.

Next time, however, three of the Mitchells were shot down. One crew
was picked up in the water but the others were never found. Another B-25
on the same mission, shot up by Zeroes, managed a crash-landing at
Makin.

One of the epics of the Seventh Air Force is the story of the 40-minute
running battle between a lone crippled Mitchell, flying on one engine, and
39 Jap fighters, which ended with three Japs shot down, five probably
destroyed, and the crew of the B-25 wet but safe.

The B-25, piloted by Lieutenant Allen H. Cobb of Jacksonville, Florida, had flown up on a 10-plane mission to Maloelap. The Jap interceptors were just taking off as the Mitchells arrived. The entire formation made its bomb run, dropping heavy demolition bombs and blasting the base with their cannon. As they crossed the lagoon, they could see the Japanese fighters waiting.

The formation closed up, with Cobb's plane on the right wing. On the first pass, his right engine was shot out. He was unable to feather the prop, and it started windmilling. The plane dropped behind, and Japs ganged the straggler.

In the same flight with Cobb were B-25's piloted by Lieutenants James Blair of East Cleveland, Ohio, and Robert L. Cecil of Globe, Arizona. To protect Cobb, they swung back and flew in such close formation on him that the wings almost touched.

"Except for them," related Lieutenant Bernard J. McKenna of Staten Island, New York, Cobb's navigator, "we never would have had a chance. They saved us a good many rounds of ammunition that we needed later, and gave our gunners a chance to get set while Lieutenant Cobb tried to get the bad engine under control.

"Our hydraulic system must have been hit, for the flaps on the wings started dragging and that slowed us down. But still the plane flew, and we were getting a few of the Japs," he said.

McKenna acted as fire-control officer during the flight, risking his neck in the astroglass — the small glass dome from which celestial observations are made — to call the direction of the successive attacks.

"We just prayed her out of it," he said later. "After it was over, every man on the plane told me he said a prayer of some kind during the flight.

"Each of the gunners got one for sure. One of them crashed so close that the Zero almost hit our tail gunner. Another on the left came in to 150 yards before going to pieces. There were five others that we saw going away in smoke."

Sewn up, down, and crosswise by Jap machine-gun fire, the bomber labored along. One bullet creased the heel of the G.I. shoe worn by Technical Sergeant Oliver S. Koski of Eveleth, Minnesota, radio operator and waist gunner. Another burst took the seat out from under the tail gunner, Staff Sergeant Fred Kirchoff of San Antonio, Texas. But miraculously, not a man was wounded.

Koski, Kirchoff, and the turret gunner, Staff Sergeant A. Young Lester of Atlanta, had been pals during two years of training and combat. The whole team clicked that day, firing 3,700 rounds without a single stoppage or a jammed shell.

"It's strange what excitement does to the sense of the passage of time," Lieutenant McKenna said. "I remember looking at my watch five times, and each time it said ten minutes to one. Then it seemed like only a short time until we were out of ammunition.

"After we had used every scrap of it, even single rounds that had fallen on the floor, the gunners used showmanship. Sergeant Lester kept swinging his turret around and pointing his guns. The others kept pointing theirs too, to make the Japs think we were holding our fire for a sure target."

Five minutes after the last cartridge had been fired, the Japs ran out of ammunition too.

"That last Jap to come in — from 1 o'clock as usual — ran out when he was half way through his pass," said McKenna. "And I've never seen anything go away as fast as he did. I looked up and the line of Zeroes on that side was gone. So was the other.

"We had nothing to worry about — except drowning and the gas supply. We were about 75 or 80 miles away from Makin when Lieutenant Cobb passed the word to get ready to ditch.

"Still on the one engine," continued McKenna, "Cobb got the plane up to about 500 feet, and started the glide down. The first bump came when we hit a swell, and that was bad enough. Then there was a tremendous crash when we really hit the water. It seemed awfully solid.

"The escape hatch was open, and Sergeant Kirchoff, who had come up to the flight deck for the crash, was thrown through it and landed about 20 feet in front of the plane. The flight deck filled with water immediately, and we all scrambled out.

"Our life raft inflated perfectly. That was just another of the day's miracles. How it had escaped being shot full of holes no one knows.

"We had just time enough to look the plane over before she sank. We estimated that there were at least 300 bullet holes in her.

"We were all bumped around in landing, and got some cuts and bruises, but none of them was serious. You do strange things, though, in an emergency like that. Lieutenant Cobb was dazed and brought along a seat cushion when we got out, and Sergeant Koski turned up with a book he hadn't finished reading." McKenna grinned.

The book was "Lost Horizon."

All of the crew had come out safely. Luck stayed with them. Soon they were spotted by American fighter planes, which took turns flying cover over them until, three hours after the ditching, a Navy crash boat picked them up.

That night came the pay-off.

Safe back at their Makin base, the men tuned in on "Tokyo Rose," the Japanese woman newscaster whose inside dope on recent events was sometimes startlingly accurate. They heard her say, in substance:

"American medium bombers today attempted a raid on our base at Alaloelap, but were driven off after inflicting minor damage. The gallant pilots of the Purple Heart Squadron and the Imperial Navy successfully engaged the big formation and shot down one of the enemy bombers in flames. All of the crew perished."

"Pinch me, pal," said Lieutenant Conrad W. Opperman, Cobb's co-pilot, "I must be dead after all."

Intelligence officers briefing crews for the FLINTLOCK operation had a standard way of closing out each session.

"And don't forget," the briefing officer would say as the men scrambled to their feet and started for their airplanes, "shipping has first priority over all other targets."

"Shipping — don't forget!"

Captain James E. Brown, a B-25 pilot, is a very literal-minded young man. Momentarily alone over Wotje one afternoon, Brown spotted three enemy freighters in the lagoon. He didn't forget.

That evening Brown walked into the interrogation shack on Makin trailing a Japanese flag.

Brown had sunk one ship, damaged the other two. He flew so low in his daredevil strike that the fuselage of his plane grazed the mast of a freighter. When he landed after the strike, the crew found the Japanese ship's ensign caught in the fuselage!

A 4,000-ton freighter, one destroyer, one 150-foot Jap sloop, and assorted smaller craft were the shipping bag of one B-25 formation which all but cleaned out the lagoon at Taroa Island on Maloelap early one evening.

Major Sol Willis, group operations officer and later executive officer, led the flight in a B-25 called the Coral Princess, and did most of the damage. Willis had pulled his plane up to 125 feet after clearing the island on a strafing run. The additional altitude revealed two 125-foot ships at the south shore of the island. The ships began pouring out streams of bullets at the Mitchells, which was a mistake.

Willis crossed the freighter at attack speed, releasing a 500-pound bomb which landed dead on target and, as the tail gunner, Staff Sergeant Floyd M. Hooper happily reported, "blew the damn ship right out of the water."

A few seconds later, the formation spotted a destroyer and another freighter. Willis, with two wingmen, wheeled toward the target while another flight took the freighter. Ack-ack had been heavy on the first run; now the destroyer, freighter, and every gun on the island opened up on the B-25's. Thousands of tracers curved through the sky and water spouts climbed up after the attackers as the destroyer's big guns fired down the lagoon. Land-based guns from Taroa poured bullets and shells after the planes.

The Coral Princess leaped ahead, shuddering under the recoil of her .75 as the navigator, Lieutenant Gust. J. Yandala, slammed home shell after shell. The lead flight was still a thousand yards from the destroyer when the warship's guns suddenly ceased firing. Willis released a 500-pound bomb and turned sharply toward the sea to out-run the long lines of tracers spewing up from a tiny island on the other side of the lagoon.

"We hit that damned destroyer solid," said Sergeant Joe McDonough, top turret gunner. "There were about thirty Japs running around on the far side of the deck and jumping into the ocean."

McDonough, who had a choice mezzanine seat for the attack on the freighter as well as the strike made by his own flight, reported sure hits.

"The bombs landed right on her decks," he said. "For awhile, I thought they were duds, they delayed so long. Then — blooey! — there was a hell of an explosion. The last I saw of that freighter there was just the bow and stern sticking up."

The Mitchells all but stole the FLINTLOCK show from the Liberators and dive-bombers of the Seventh. They flew 300 sorties, dropping 91 per cent of their bombs on target. They lost sixteen planes, seven to ack-ack, six to interceptors, two to operational accidents, one "unknown." Against that record, they claimed seventeen Jap planes shot down, thirteen probables in the air and, on the ground, thirty-two damaged, twenty-two certains, three probables, and ten more damaged.

And that does not begin to tell the story of the havoc wrought on Jap installations, shipping, and personnel.

On December 18, in the third week of the air assault, the fighters and dive-bombers which had come ashore at Makin from the deck of the Nassau, got into action over Mille. Like the B-25's which found Maloelap easy on their first mission, they caught Mille by surprise.

Lieutenant Frank A. Tinker, reported missing on a later mission, was in one of the lead dive-bombers.

"We took off at nine-thirty in the morning," he said later, "with a flight of P-38's arrowing defensively around us as we went up to Mille.

"The Japs didn't get our range until we had peeled out and started our dive on the target. A few tracers streaked by, but rather wide of the mark. Our gunners saw anti-aircraft explosions just over our tails and to the sides."

The first fighter and dive-bomber attack by the Seventh was an auspicious first. A few planes were hit, none seriously. When the dive-bombers picked up their fighter escort on the other side of Mille and started home, the target area was obscured by a cloud of smoke, indicating that ammunition stores had been exploded.

But, just as the B-25's had found Maloelap tough on their second strike, tougher on their third, the dive-bombers saw opposition over Mille stiffen and grow more deadly with each mission. They lost four of their thirteen A-24's during the FLINTLOCK operation and could only balance their losses against the satisfying fact that they were helping soften up a target which had the singular and unhappy distinction of receiving the heaviest concentration of bombs of any target in any theater up to this time — including Berlin and Cassino. Before the mile-square spit of sand joined the limbo of bombed-out targets, it was hit with more than 1,000 tons of bombs.

Part of the bomb load pumped on Mille was delivered in an extremely unorthodox manner.

It started the day Lieutenant Benjamin C. Warren, a pilot and engineering officer of the "Sky Riders" Fighter Squadron, came home from one mission complaining: "When the weather is bad over Mille, all you can do is spit. Strafing is out. Dammit, I want to hit something!"

He talked it over with Staff Sergeant Jonas Orrell, a mechanic. Orrell went back to work and after some fifty hours of concentration came up with an ingenious set of wing racks attached to the wing, eye beams and main spars of the fighters.

A few days later, a flight of P-38's climbed from the coral strip at Makin, each carrying two 1,000-pound bombs, one under each wing. It was the first time a fighter plane had handled such a bomb load in the Pacific.

The Air Force Statistical Control Office, when the Marshalls campaign ended, gravely included the fighters in the bomber category, crediting them with dropping 21.7 tons of bombs — "92.5 per cent on the target." In orthodox operations, they flew 556 sorties, of which only 46 were abortive.

As FLINTLOCK swung into full attacking strength in the closing weeks of December and the early weeks of January, 1944, the tempo of attacks was stepped up. The fighters and dive-bombers were appearing over Mille and Jaluit more and more often; the B-2 5's, reinforced by an additional three squadrons which arrived from Oahu in the middle of January, prowled the lagoons for Jap shipping; the B-24's, pulling the longer missions to the northern Marshalls, were striking now at a gruelling pace. D-Day was less than a month away.

And as our attacks increased, it became evident that the Japanese were reinforcing their air and ground defenses. Ack-ack was heavier and more accurate. Japanese fighters were appearing in larger numbers, and exacted a heavy toll in planes and men.

Some of the battered Liberators and their crews were saved by amazing mixtures of prayer and guts and Yankee resourcefulness. The Texas Belle was one of them.

The target had been Maloelap. For an hour and a half after unloading its bombs, the Belle had fought a running battle with thirty Zekes.

Lieutenant Charles F. Pratte, the Belle's pilot, coaxed and prayed the shot-up airplane four hundred miles back to the Gilberts. His only hope was a landing on one of the Tarawa airstrips. The Belle's hydraulic system was shot out; therefore, no brakes.

Construction on the strip Pratte picked had gone just far enough to accommodate fighter aircraft, and a sizeable crowd was collected to witness the first landing by a Navy fighter. At this point, the Texas Belle came along and stole the show.

With no brakes, and with a field too short even for a healthy bomber, Pratte faced the almost certain prospect of piling up the Liberator on a coral heap at the end of the runway. Or, avoiding that, he could boil down the short strip and into the sea.

To make matters just a little worse, one engine quit as Pratte came down for the landing. He managed to pull up and circle again. Then he got an idea. It turned out to be one of the most original ideas of the whole war.

Going into the down-leg, Pratte called out a series of orders over the intercom. They sounded like crazy orders; but orders, crazy or not, are orders. So the two waist gunners did as they were told. They rigged parachutes to their gun mounts and arranged the packs so that — if everything worked out as the pilot thought it might — the chutes would pop open in the slipstream. The tail-gunner, also following instructions, rigged a chute to his gun mount.

As the wheels of the Texas Belle touched the runway at a speed well over 100 miles an hour, Pratte called out one more order. The gunners yanked at their rip cords and three parachutes simultaneously blossomed open like a series of sea anchors. The Belle was eased to a stop four or five yards from the edge of the ocean.

The stunt drew a special commendation from General Arnold, who, in a letter to General Hale, described the parachute landing as, "unique, so far as I know, in operational history." More important, it became an almost standard method for landing brakeless bombers, first, in the Pacific and, later, all over the world.

Some of them were not so lucky. They were the planes that disappeared over the target and were never again reported, the planes that staggered away from the target and, somewhere on the long journey home, went down at sea.

"Eighteen heavies lost due to combat action," is the way FLINTLOCK operations reports absorbed the losses to Hale's command. But eighteen is a figure, a small figure at that, and it doesn't begin to tell the story of the terrible violence of mid-air explosions, the horror of a thirty-ton airplane diving headlong into the sea with ten men trapped inside, the heart-breaking stories of men who somehow survived the crash landing but whose yellow rafts were never found by Dumbo pilots who never stopped looking for them until all hope was gone. To the men of the ground and air echelons, each one of the eighteen planes lost was a tragedy.

It was a tragedy to the men of the 11th Bomb Group, for instance, when Lieutenant Osborne, with two of his Liberator's engines knocked out, set his plane down on a reef in the northwest part of the lagoon off enemy-held

Majuro. Another pilot, Lieutenant Lundy, stayed with the crippled plane and fought off the two Zeroes which attempted to attack it as it stood in five feet of water. Lundy stayed around as long as he dared, then flew home to report that even though the top hatch of the downed plane was standing open, no member of the crew was seen to emerge.

It was a tragedy to the same group when a control tower operator picked up a Liberator by radar passing 3,000 feet over its home base at Tarawa in the overcast and got no answer to the frantic signals he sent the plane to bring it back. The Liberator flew on and on, into an area where there is no land for more than half a million square miles except the tiny Jap islands of Ocean and Nauru.

The plane, although it was not identified when it flew beyond Tarawa's radar range, was the Galvanized Goose, and out of its tragic flight came one of the most gripping stories of disaster and death and miraculous survival at sea that has come out of the Pacific.

A burst of flak from Kwajalein had knocked out the plane's radio and every instrument it had. Weather had broken up the formation on the way up from Tarawa, so the Galvanized Goose had to try to make it back through the darkness to Tarawa alone. It was an amazing feat of dead reckoning navigation by Lieutenant Dan A. Norris, navigator, which brought the plane back to tiny Tarawa.

"The overcast extended to 11,000 feet," Norris said later, "but above that it was clear. I was able to shoot the stars and get our position. Having no compass, I'd point and say to the pilot, 'Go that way.'

"Sometime after we passed where we thought the island was, we began to run out of gas. We threw everything movable out of the plane and went on to ditch in the dark, with no lights, no altimeter, and a hell of a sea running. I'd say the waves were thirty feet high."

The ditching was disastrous. The Goose ploughed into a swell with a terrible impact and broke up.

"I was knocked out when we hit," Norris said, "so I didn't know how I got out of the plane. Later, I could see how I got out. I just came right out through the skin, which is a hell of a poor way to leave an airplane.

"The plane had broken into four parts but I climbed back onto the biggest section — the waist section — to see if any one was trapped. There were some, all right. The bombardier had had his head cut almost off by his own helmet when it jammed down around the back of his neck. It was an awful sight."

The top turret had fallen on one of the other crewmen, Norris said, pinning him in. "He was dead. By now, it was pretty clear that I had a broken leg so I went overboard again."

Technical Sergeant Glenn O. Howell, ball turret gunner, was lying on the camera hatch in the tail with several other crewmen when the plane hit. The camera hatch sprang open and he landed in the water.

Eight men floundered in the water, groping for the life rafts that floated around in the darkness.

"To make things worse," Norris continued, "we found ourselves in a school of sharks. I wasn't more than ten feet from the pilot, the co-pilot and assistant radio operator when the sharks pulled them under. They were all hurt pretty badly and couldn't have protected themselves with their knives even if they'd thought of them.

"Somebody in the water had some rope and tied the five of us together, then we kept milling around in the big waves trying to find the rafts. We found one finally. It was tough getting aboard because we were all hurt and the waves kept breaking over the raft.

"Later we found four more rafts. After I got aboard, I got sick from all the stuff I'd swallowed.

"Staff Sergeant Jerrold Eis, the engineer, had been knocked out. The radio operator, Technical Sergeant Newton J. Chiafullo and a gunner, Staff Sergeant Ernest H. Despault, rescued him as he floated by, a bad gash over his right eye."

Light brought another terrifying revelation. The water in which the four rafts floated was alive with sharks. The men didn't realize the danger at first; they got scared when the rafts began to leak from rips caused by sharks scraping the bottoms of the rafts as they chased small fish under them.

The emergency equipment aboard the rafts included a pamphlet on sea lore which said sea sharks could be frightened away by a sharp blow on the snouts with a paddle. But these sharks, it developed, hadn't read the book.

"Bopping them on the nose just made them mad," Sergeant Howell, who did the bopping, said. "After the first few bops, when they began to come closer, we just left them alone and prayed."

Lieutenant Norris, taking an inventory of emergency supplies, found that somebody had neglected to check the equipment in the rafts.

"There was only a pint and a half of water," Norris said. The rations were impregnated with sea water.

"But the worst blow of all came when we found we couldn't use the Gibson Girl — the balloon for the aerial wouldn't rise."

The survivors of the Galvanized Goose didn't know it then, but it was just as well that the Gibson Girl was useless. They were floating through the enemy-held Marshalls and a distress signal would probably have resulted in their capture.

"We heard a plane once," Norris said, "on the third day. Our first impulse was to jump up and start yelling because we couldn't see it. Then we could tell that its engines were unsynchronized and whoo-whooing and raising hell just like a Jap Betty. We kept quiet and held our breaths until the noise went away."

On the seventh day, the survivors were picked up by a PBY search plane of the Royal New Zealand Air Force, which discovered them by accident when it was 160 miles off its regular patrol course. They were flown to a seaplane base at Halvo on Florida Island, across the bay from Guadalcanal.

It was a week before the survivors could eat, another week before they could begin a 2,400 mile roundabout hitch-hiking trip back to Tarawa aboard cargo planes.

So alarming was the number of casualties in Liberator groups as the seventy-day assault neared an end, that General Hale ordered daylight missions by the heavies discontinued, and night bombardment operations were attempted.

This method of attack, Hale said later, was less effective, but it "resulted in an immediate reduction of the casualty rate."

But if the Liberator crews found the going a little easier on their night strikes, the Mitchells, whose masthead attacks on shipping and close-to-zero blasting of enemy targets could only be carried out by daylight, were finding the road back from Maloelap tougher and tougher. The target itself was still the hottest in the Marshalls; coming home was even more rugged because they had to run the gauntlet of the alerted Jap fighter bases on the way.

The Japs had apparently done some close figuring. Every time the Mitchells came off the target, the Jap fighters picked them up off the island of Tabal, out of our fighter range. They attacked formation after formation at the same place and the same time.

What they hadn't figured on, however, was the ingenuity, daring, and mathematical genius of a bunch of young fighter pilots from the 46th Fighter Squadron. The pilots figured that by carrying belly tanks and flying home at a reduced speed, which used the minimum of gasoline, they could have three minutes in one spot over the Pacific — the spot where the Japs had been attacking the Mitchells.

On the morning of January 26 — within a week of D-day on Kwajalein — the Mitchells staged what looked like a routine strike on Maloelap. They came off the target hopping the waves. The Zeroes hit them. Same time; same place.

The cocky Jap fighter pilots never knew what happened next. Stacked in flights from 8,000 up to 12,000 feet in the air, the P-40's dropped their belly tanks and streaked down into the battle below.

In 180 wild seconds, the P-40's shot down ten Japs, got three probables, damaged some more, and drove off the rest. Four Japs, trapped between the fighters and bombers, were shot down by the B-25's themselves.

It was the last time a Jap fighter plane was seen during the Marshalls campaign.

Quite suddenly, Japanese resistance collapsed. Ack-ack was almost meager; fighter interception was unknown; Jap reprisal raids on our bases in the Gilberts abruptly ceased.

The Liberators went back to daylight operations and, as D-day approached, the Seventh threw everything it had at the Jap islands. Fighters and dive-bombers bombed and strafed installations and shipping at Jaluit and Mille. In the last week of the assault, four or five enemy atolls were struck simultaneously by every type of Army aircraft known to the Pacific — day and night.

Three days before H-hour, the B-24's started nightly harassment of Roi, Kwajalein, Maloelap and Wotje. The night of January 28, eleven B-24's hovered over Kwajalein from dusk to dawn circling and returning, dropping one or two delayed action bombs on each run — a technique which shattered Jap nerves as well as pillboxes. The same night, and all night, nine planes were over Wotje.

The fighters followed up the next day. For eight hours, during the late afternoon and early evening, they patrolled Mille.

The rising crescendo of the attacks was marred on January 29, within forty-eight hours of the invasion, when a formation of nine B-25's, over Wotje at dusk, were wrongly identified by the Navy, and attacked by a swarm of carrier Hellcats while our own destroyers in the adjacent waters opened up with ack-ack. One of the Mitchells was shot down, two limped home seriously damaged. One crew member was killed and five others injured.

As the hours ran down from D-minus-three to H-hour, the Navy moved in on Kwajalein. For seventy-two hours, a task force lay off the great Jap base, rocking it with the mightiest naval bombardment of the Pacific War to date.

So complete was the Seventh's destruction of Jap planes in the air and on the ground that not a single enemy plane got through to attack the fleet.

Fifteen minutes before the jump off — H-minus-15 in official terminology — while infantrymen of the Seventh Division waited tensely at the rails of invasion ships, six heavy bombers of the Seventh Air Force roared low over Kwajalein, spewing out 2,000-pound atoll busters and 1,000-pounders to crack open Jap ground defenses of the kind which had survived the pre-invasion bombing of Tarawa.

It was the first time the Seventh had used the atoll-buster. One heavy enemy coast-defense gun was blown completely out of its emplacement and hurled end-over-end into the water. As the B-24's went over the island as close to the treetops as it is possible to fly a four-engined plane, the gunners opened up and strafed everything in sight.

As the Liberators swung around after crossing the island, the bomber crews looked down on the line of tiny black squares moving toward the beach — the landing craft of the Seventh Division.

The bombers stayed over the island long enough to watch the craft grate to a stop against the sandy bottom in shallow water, saw the great ramps splash into the water, and saw the men of the infantry swarm down the ramps and run through the surf toward the beach.

Kwajalein fell. Majuro fell. By two o'clock in the afternoon of D-plus one, organized resistance on the islands of Roi and Namur had ceased.

The Marshall Islands were ours.

CHAPTER XVI: "I'LL NEVER GET OUT OF HERE ALIVE"

"KWAJALEIN," SAID PRIVATE FIRST CLASS B. F. SHEPPARD, MEMBER of the Seventh Airforce Airdrome Squadron that landed during the invasion of that island, "looks like one of New York's lower East Side kids with his teeth knocked out!"

The Marshalls stronghold had the same violent effect on everyone who went in on the operations or came down before it was rebuilt by the Aviation Engineers.

Staff Sergeant Bob Price, who came in with the airdrome squadron, wrote from the Jap bastion:

"There is something malignant about Kwajalein. It is alive with legend, dust and flies. There are blue and maroon chunks from saki bottles among the litter and dud ammunition covers the place. Jap cars with steering wheels on the right side are full of holes and lie in squares of blighted taro patches. The Jap railway is a line of torn and curled tracks.

"In the blasted dugouts are pictures of Japanese girls and snapshots of fathers and mothers of dead soldiers. Scattered about are presents that were to be sent home. Old tooth brushes, breath refresher, house slippers and silk socks litter the place.

"Early this evening some tankmen were sitting within sight of their tank eating K rations. Through the silence you could hear the enemy laughing and yelling.

"Suddenly four drunken Japs dashed out of a foxhole, carrying saki bottles in their hands. The officer leading them was cutting the air with his saber. They charged the tank and slashed the sides with their knives.

"Then, laughing drunkenly, they smashed the bottles containing small grenades against the side of the tank. The grenades merely split against the steel and knocked the Japs to the ground.

"The tankmen shot two of the Nips and then began chasing the other two among the battered palms. They finally cornered the Japs against a ruined pillbox and knocked them off.

"The stench of death is everywhere, and swarms of flies come from the bodies of the Jap dead. The flies cling to you with sticky feet, and eating is a job of trying to keep out the insects and dust. Large blow-flies light on your hand as it travels toward your mouth, and there is no way to keep them off. Grit is in your food and your bed."

This Seventh Airdrome Squadron, set up to maintain airfields and planes, came ashore on D-day. But, like many other outfits in the Seventh, it had to do a hundred other jobs before getting around to its own. As the battle raged, with grenades exploding and flame-throwers hissing at Jap pillboxes, the men unloaded tons of equipment, buried the dead, cleared unexploded ammunition, and served as ditch diggers, engineers and labor battalions.

The burial details, which were the worst, lasted two weeks. Men worked in the nude to prevent the stench of death from permeating their scant stock of clothing. They dug into rotten foxholes and tunnels and dodged snipers.

Danger often causes men to do unusual things. An ordnance man in charge of the bomb demolition crew personally handled all the unexploded duds, refusing to let his men touch them because of the danger involved.

"I'll never get out of here alive," he told Price. "One of these damned things will explode before I finish as sure as hell."

"There is a scarcity of everything," Price continued — everything but dust. At the end of each day a man looks like a farmer who has just harrowed his field. The wind and dust, which are worst at noon, abate somewhat in the early evening. Then men come out with their dust-grey towels and take showers in Jap-dug wells. Bath equipment consists of captured barrels, pumps and hose. One group pumps while the others bathe.

"Jap snipers hide in the waste and debris. At night they sneak out, and jeeps turn up with bullet holes in the radiators and guards are killed while walking their posts.

"The battle is won but the hysterical laughter and screams of the remaining Japs still linger over the island.

"There is something malignant in the air at Kwajalein — something that will remain for a long time."

On D-plus-2, while intermittent burst of gunfire still sounded throughout the desolate atoll, Major Herbert T. Brown, St. Paul, Minnesota, commanding officer of the 854th Aviation Engineers, brought a survey party ashore. On the following morning G.I. surveyors began to lay the centerline for the runway. There was a Jap airstrip on the island, but it was so badly pitted with bomb and shell holes and covered with debris that it had to be rebuilt.

One party was busy with transit and chain when a sniper suddenly opened fire on them with an automatic rifle.

"We hit the dirt in a hurry and lay there as the bullets caromed off the strip," said Staff Sergeant Joe LaFlure, Chestertown, New York. "We felt pretty conspicuous lying in the middle of the runway with nothing to hide behind while someone took pot-shots at us. But with no cover, there was nothing you could do but try to make yourself as small as possible."

As LaFlure's group were trying to push through the surface of the strip, other snipers cut loose at a party of ten under Staff Sergeant Charles B. Middlekup, Houston, Texas, working at the edge of the strip.

"Mortar shells were bursting close to us as the infantry went after the Japs," Middlekup said. "This definitely was not peacetime engineering!"

But, when the foot-soldiers finally knocked off the Nips, the engineers went back to work as if nothing had happened.

Despite the unanticipated size of the job and the persistent snipers, the battalion hacked the airstrip out of the smoking debris so quickly that within four days a disabled Navy bomber landed safely, made emergency repairs, and took off again.

In eighteen days the group had completed a hard-surface coral runway that was more that 6,000 feet long, and heavy bomber operations were started.

One of the factors which speeded the project was the adaption of captured equipment by the ingenious engineers.

"We used Jap trucks, tanks, airplanes and artillery shells and all types of salvaged equipment to complete the job," Brown said.

"Battery ignition systems were taken from Jap trucks and used to replace faulty magneto ignition systems on our power rollers. Tractor clutch plates were cut down and fitted to motor graders and trucks. Jap airplane armor plates were used to replace broken dump truck hoists. Machinists cut two-inch thick bases from Jap artillery shell cases and made new bushings, complete with oil grooves, for dump truck transmissions.

"The Japs," he grinned, "helped us to build the base."

There were red faces in higher headquarters one day as a direct result of the ingenuity of these engineers of the 854th. They had virtually completed construction of the runway control tower when higher channels decided that in its present location the tower was a hazard to aircraft — even though Headquarters had originally designated where the tower should be. They ordered the building constructed 25 feet further back from the strip.

The engineers could see no reason for dismantling the 60-foot tower, built of 12 x 12 timbers, and starting all over again 25 feet away. They kept right on with the construction.

Down from Headquarters descended bristling brass-hats, demanding to know why orders had not been obeyed. They were amazed to find the resourceful engineers had completed the tower on the original site and then put it on runners and moved it to the new location.

Brigadier General Robert W. Douglass, Jr., commander of the VII Fighter Command, who was to succeed General Hale as Commanding General of the Seventh on April 1, 1944, issued a commendation to men of the 854th for their work, asserting that: "With nothing but native materials and a minimum of equipment, you transferred a smoking pile of rubble and wreckage into an ideal heavy bombardment base with every facility necessary to carry out major operations against the enemy."

D-day on Kwajalein was scarcely past when our forces pointed toward a new objective — Eniwetok.

Eniwetok, most northerly of the Marshalls, lies nearly 500 miles northeast of Kwajalein and was considered to be such a strong base that, in planning the invasion schedule, it was set up as a separate operation.

Original plans called for a breathing spell to recover from the heavy losses expected at Kwajalein before moving in on Eniwetok. But our losses in the first Marshalls operations had been much less than expected, so the Eniwetok invasion was pushed up.

There was a reason for this tremendous saving in American lives and it set the pattern for all future operations in the Central Pacific. In the Gilberts the all-out bomb assault had lasted only a week before the actual invasion. In the Marshalls it lasted for seventy days and nights.

The Seventh, maintaining around-the-clock schedule in the Marshalls, had flown 1,876 sorties. They had dropped 1,592.7 tons of bombs — 92.5 per cent of which had been on the target. One hundred seventeen enemy planes had been destroyed, 75 probably destroyed and 97 damaged.

On February 4, aboard the USS Rocky Mount, new plans were drawn up for "CATCHPOLE," code name for the Eniwetok operations.

The atoll had been under continuous bombing attacks during the period of the Kwajalein assault and many aerial photographs had been taken. These pictures revealed that above-ground installations on most of the islands in the atoll had been almost completely destroyed. On Engebi Island (in the north crook of the atoll), however, the foxhole and trench systems showed development. It was decided to attack that position before hitting the island of Eniwetok.

Operations Plan No. 4-44-or "CATCHPOLE"-went into action ahead of schedule, and on February 17 landing operations began. On the same day heavy air strikes were made against Tinian and Saipan in the Marianas; Truk, Ponape and Kusaie, in the Carolines; Jaluit, in the Marshalls; and Wake.

During this period the Seventh helped to write history and set a new style of strategy in the Central Pacific — the strategy of keeping by-passed islands neutralized by airpower.

The Central Pacific offensive moved with tremendous speed when it finally started. But there are thousands of islands in the Pacific, and the Japs had occupied all they considered worth taking. To have retaken each of them would have presented a tremendous problem.

This was the main Japanese hope in winning the war — the determination to outlast us and make the war so long and costly that we would pull out and allow her to keep most of her stolen territory. Each bit of coral and jungle was to be fought for to the last ditch.

The enemy calculated that it would take us years to get through the Marshalls-Caroline group by following the "island-hopping" invasion plan. But we had completely bewildered them by taking only the key Gilberts-Marshalls islands and leaving other islands in these groups and the islands of the Carolines in the backwash.

Nauru and Ocean islands, to our rear in the Gilberts, were still occupied by the enemy. The important atolls, of Wotje, Maloelap, Mille, and Jaluit on the eastern flank; Rongelap on the northern; and Likep on the northwestern were Marshalls bases still held by the Japs.

Carolines bases such as Truk, Ponape, Woleai, Yap, Kusaie, Hall, Oroluk, Puluvat, Mokil, Pingelap, Pulawat and Namonuito threatened our west flank.

Wake and Marcus were strong Jap bases to the north and northwest.

The Seventh had a tremendous task. Not only were they supposed to soften up invasion beaches and furnish ground support for our ground forces in the Marshalls, but they were assigned to help maintain the neutralization of the by-passed islands, keep the Jap airfields inoperative, and hit Jap supply ships headed for the islands. Then there was the matter of softening up the Marianas for the next operation.

This job was a series of never-ending missions for the Seventh, now completely surrounded by the enemy. Some of the enemy-held islands in the Gilberts and Marshalls were only a few miles away. Others, such as Truk, Wake and Marcus, presented the old Seventh bugaboo of long distance flights. Many of these bases had airstrips and planes, and Jap bombings were a regular threat.

Each of these islands presented a different problem.

Ocean Island, an oyster-shaped spit of land, is 240 miles southwest of Tarawa. At Nauru, 380 miles southwest of Tarawa, the Japs maintained three phosphate plants and two airstrips — one 4,600 by 500 feet and the other 3,900 by 300 feet.

In the Marshalls we had neutralized 20,000 square miles of Jap-held territory. Maloelap, east of Kwajalein and the most important enemy airbase in the Marshalls-Gilberts group, had two runways of 4,100 by 260 feet and 4,700 by 360 feet. Mille, southeast of Kwajalein, had two runways of more than 3,000 feet and based as many as 18 fighters and 27 bombers at a time. There was also a seaplane anchorage at Port Rhin.

Rongelap, north of Kwajalein, with its 300 square miles of lagoon, was considered a potential Jap fleet and sub base. There were 3,600 feet of runways there.

Wotje, 157 miles east of Kwajalein, was the most active seaplane base in the eastern Marshalls and a strong submarine base. There were two well equipped airfields there, one 3,900 by 300 feet and the other 5,700 by 350 feet.

Jaluit, southeast of Kwajalein, possesses one of the best harbors in the Pacific. The center for submarine operations, the atoll had extensive seaplane facilities at the islands of Enybor and Emidj. The Japs had more than 3,000 feet of runways there.

On our west flank were the Carolines. The most powerful enemy bases there were Truk, Kusaie, Ponape, and Palaus, Yap, Ulithi, and Woleai. These islands were stepping stones to the Philippines.

Kusaie, with over 3,000 feet of runways was 643 miles from Tarawa. We had information that 6,700 laborers who had completed 30 per cent of their work, were fortifying the island.

Ponape, a sub base, seaplane anchorage and possible destroyer base, had runways of 2,300 feet, 320 feet and 4,000 feet.

Ulithi defenses included a seaplane anchorage and runways of more than 3,000 feet.

Wolesi, located halfway between Truk and the Palaus, had seaplane and ship anchorage, a radio station, a weather observatory and runways of 3,050, 3,000 and 2,050 feet.

The greatest problems in distance were presented by Truk, about 1,400 miles from Tarawa and 955 miles from Kwajalein; Marcus about 1,500 miles from the Marshalls and 1,800 miles from Tarawa; and Wake, about 1,200 miles from Tarawa.

Truk, known as the "Gibraltar of the Pacific," was considered the main Jap resistance point in the mid-Pacific and the primary supply base for the entire Jap-mandated area. It consists of 118 islands and islets, about 50 of which are within a great encircling reef.

The enclosed lagoon has a diameter of 33 miles and within this are the larger islands of Moen, Dublon, Tol, Fefan, Uman, Udot, and Falabeguete. The hills overlooking the lagoon, in which the Japs had installed five and six inch guns, gave the atoll more natural defenses than Pearl Harbor.

At the height of its power, there were 70 fleet repair shops in operation there with attending facilities such as small marine railways, one 2500-ton floating dry dock and a repair ship with cranes.

There was a seaplane anchorage with full facilities at Truk. Jap submarines, destroyers and cruisers frequently based there, and air and surface patrol craft continually operated from the atoll with patrol cutters, similar to our PT boats, were often seen as far as 60 miles out. Carriers made frequent use of the facilities and part of the Jap force attacking Midway assembled and set out from Truk.

Memories of the beating they had taken at Midway and in the Gilberts-Marshalls campaigns made the Japs extremely reluctant to risk their Navy against American air power. When we moved into the Marshalls, the Japanese Navy officials got the jitters, and on February 10 the enemy fleet based at Truk steamed out for Palau. There it split into three segments, one going to the Philippines, another part to Singapore, and a third to Yokosuka, Japan. A considerable number of merchant vessels were forced to remain at Truk because of a shortage of fuel and water and high winds which delayed their unloading.

This was the end of Truk as a Jap Navy stronghold. After Febaiary 16, when carrier-based planes sank 30 merchant ships and seven combat ships, no Jap warships (with the exception of the Sixth Submarine Fleet, which was based there) returned to Truk.

Merchant shipping, at the rate of about 20 ships a month, continued to come and go for two more months. The combined Seventh-Navy air attack on April 29-30 completed the destruction of above-ground installations of the Truk naval base. So thorough was the air coverage around the atoll that between the fall of the Marianas and the end of the war no shipping of any kind, with the exception of seven submarines on supply missions, was able to reach Truk.

The mission of the Jap airforce at Truk was to protect the naval base. As far as can be determined, no purely offensive flights were ever launched from this base. Routine searches, in which both land and seaplanes were used, were flown from Truk until June, 1944, after which time there was not sufficient aircraft available.

Enemy shipping had a high priority at this time, but, with the Jap fleet in hiding, hunting was poor. In fact, fighter squadrons were under orders, during continuing strikes against Mille and Jaluit, to destroy even dugouts and canoes.

Men of the 531st were assigned to drop propaganda leaflets from their A-24's. Typical of these messages were those to the isolated Jaluit garrison. It read:

TO THE JALUIT GARRISON

Thousands of your comrades on Attu, Tarawa, and Makin islands are dead and gone from this world because they persisted in a meaningless resistance: They were wiped out by the overwhelming force of American arms.

You on the Jaluit Island are next. You will be bombed daily by many American planes. Further resistance is useless. The result of resistance can only be annihilation. Each of you will be a needless death.

To avoid this, surrender. Make a white cross panel on the ground and show your desire to surrender honorably, and await further instructions to be dropped from an airplane.

There will be no regrets after surrender. Many of your comrades are right now enjoying the kind treatment of Americans and the good California climate.

It will be noted that even in war the inevitable California Chamber of Commerce was busy. But the Japanese diehards, for the most part, refused to be beguiled.

But there were exceptions. One Jap pushed off from Mille in a fishing boat and gave himself up to men on an American destroyer. While the Nip was tossing about in the little craft, an A-24, to show our good intentions, dropped him a packet of food.

On board the destroyer the Jap denied he had surrendered because of the leaflets. He declared that he was an intelligent man and had made up his mind on that score before the leaflets were dropped.

"Did you get the food we dropped you," he was asked.

"Oh, yes," he answered. "And does that salmon stuff stink!"

"He says it stinks!" exclaimed one G.I. in an awed voice. "And that's the stuff we — uh — requisitioned for a change from those damned K rations! And here we've been thinking it was a special treat!"

On February 15, the Seventh hit Ponape. Forty-two heavy bombers dumped 58 tons of bombs on the seaplane base, the airfield, the barracks, machine shops and waterfront areas. Two days later they returned to drop 206 one-hundred-pound bombs on the town and waterfront areas. There were great explosions and fires, and smoke was visible for more than 50 miles.

The attack was continued with incendiary bombs on February 20. Twenty-one planes dropped 840 six-pound gasoline-rubber incendiaries on the thickly concentrated settlement, along with 570 general purpose 100-pounders.

Two days later, thirteen Liberators showered Ponape town with more than 5,000 incendiaries, while nine more B-24's blasted the seaplane base with 54 five-hundred-pound GD's. As the planes turned homeward, the town and waterfront were burning fiercely.

Not a single Jap plane was encountered during all the 176 sorties against Ponape and Kusaie.

All the Japs could do was throw up ack-ack. They did this, frantically but with little accuracy. The Carolines' gun crews had not had the practice we had so helpfully given the Nipponese gunners in the Marshalls. Several of our planes were winged, but not one was lost.

Weather was a bigger adversary and our forecasters had little data to guide the briefing. Flights became split up, part of the planes bombed the alternate target on numerous occasions, and several missions were cancelled, but fortunately none of our planes was forced down.

On February 26, our bombers delivered the finishing stroke at ruined Ponape. Twenty-five B-24's dumped a total of 25 tons, mostly incendiary, on the smoking base.

Ponape, for the time being, was out of circulation.

Reconnaissance photographs showed the overwhelming job which the eleven days of saturation bombing had done. For the first time, it was possible to obtain a clear picture of the effectiveness of the Seventh Air Force bombing, since photographs had been taken before, during, and after the raids, and only a handful of Navy bombs on earlier reconnaissance had "spoiled" our target.

The photos showed almost complete devastation. The first four raids had practically destroyed the town. The southern waterfront section was virtually wiped out.

The radio station was gone. In all, more than 300 buildings of all sizes had been razed, and the seaplane base at Langor Island had been pounded into ruins.

The raids demonstrated for the first time in the Central Pacific, the deadly effectiveness of incendiaries. They gave a preview of what might be expected later when Jap mainland cities were brought within effective bombing range.

A similarly thorough job was done on lesser Kusaie, which was practically demolished in four raids. Nine B-24's first attacked it with nine tons of bombs on D-day, while Eniwetok was being invaded. It was attacked again on February 20-22. Heaviest raid was on February 24, when fifteen tons of bombs were dropped, leaving the entire waterfront burning. Later photos showed twenty-three buildings burned or badly damaged.

Seventh Air Force reports summed up the CATCHPOLE operations thus:

"Photographs and observations of participating crews during this period show that the cumulative damage inflicted on the enemy and his bases was enormous. Practically all buildings and installations above ground on Mille, Wotje, Jaluit and Maloelap were destroyed or seriously damaged. Huge craters show where ammunition dumps were destroyed by direct hits.

"The demoralizing effect on the enemy must have been very great due to his inability to deal effectively with our attacks. The effectiveness of our operations is also attested to by the fact that there was not one enemy plane sighted in the Marshalls during this period.

"Best example of the effectiveness of heavy bombardment was the almost complete destruction of the town of Ponape in five raids without loss to ourselves. Thus, in a period of ten days, a good sized town and one of the Japs' most important bases and supply centers in the Carolines was virtually wiped out.

"This was actually the first time that Seventh AF bombers engaged in strategic bombing, and the results obtained point the way to even greater destruction of the enemy as more important and densely populated areas come within our range."

During the month of the CATCHPOLE Operation our planes flew more than 1,300 sorties and dropped more than 1,200 tons of bombs.

How completely we dominated the air is evidenced by our amazingly small losses — three medium bombers, four dive-bombers and two fighters to anti-aircraft; a heavy bomber and a fighter for operation reasons; one dive-bomber, unknown. Total casualties: thirty-nine men missing. Twenty-one wounded.

One man killed in action.

CHAPTER XVII: THE SEVEN-LEAGUE SEVENTH

WITH THE CLOSE OF THE CATCHPOLE OPERATION, THE SEVENTH went into an all-out "neutralization by bombs" schedule. Endlessly, they pounded the Jap strongholds by-passed in the Gilberts and Marshalls.

Navy and Army bombers reached out farther and farther into the Carolines. The Japs expected we would be preparing an invasion of that group, whose mighty bastions lay across more than 2,000 miles of the Central Pacific. But there again, as so many times before and since, our strategists fooled them. CINCPAC elected merely to keep these intermediate bases neutralized, while we prepared for a tremendous 1,200-mile leap into the Marianas. Such a seven-league undertaking took time.

The Navy began the softening of Saipan, Tinian and Guam on February 22, before CATCHPOLE Operation was formally closed, but it was four months before the landing barges grated on the sandy beaches of the Marianas.

The Seventh Air Force, after the taking of Eniwetok, kept up its steady punishment of Ponape and Kusaie, which the Japs perennially sought to rebuild. Closely coordinating with the Navy, the Seventh renewed its attacks on Wake.

By early March, Air Force bombers were based on Kwajalein, and from that new springboard, our long-ranging bombers joined in the assault on Truk, flying many harrowing missions over the "Gibraltar of the Pacific" during the months which followed.

The first mission from this base was mounted March 15, when 22 B-24's of the 30th Bomber Group took off on a night attack. Storms and engine trouble reduced the size of the final flight, but these were virtually unopposed. Apparently the surprise element was complete, for the huge base was brilliantly lighted and swarming with workers, when our bombers droned into sight.

Searchlights frantically began to probe the skies, and the red ack-ack tracers rose like showers of sparks into the sky, but both were confused and uncoordinated.

Both elements of planes had been assigned specific targets on Dublon and Eton Islands. Our planes scored 100 per cent hits on fuel tanks, and an ammunition dump blew up in a spectacular shower of flames. Only two enemy fighters were seen, and every Liberator returned home safely.

The run to Truk became familiar, but never routine, during the weeks which followed. Alerted enemy fighters and A/A gunners made every strike a hazardous adventure.

No set of missions in the Central Pacific war has produced more stories than those against Truk. One of the most inspiring is the survival of four members of the ten-man crew on one Seventh Air Force Liberator, forced down on their way home due to lack of gasoline. It is a story which illustrates what unbelievable things a man can do when the stakes are life and death.

The Heavy Date was on its way back from a successful bombing mission over Truk. She had dropped her bombs on target after a 6,000-foot dive to avoid enemy searchlights and night fighters, and had emerged unscathed.

"It was after we were well on our way home," later related Lieutenant Elmer T. Pahl, of Lodi, California, the bombardier, "that we knew we did not have enough gasoline to make it, and would have to come down in enemy territory.

"Everyone took it calmly and went about the business of throwing out everything that would lighten the plane. We had a couple of hours to go before the gas ran out, and it made me feel proud to be with them, the way they took it. I don't think there was a man aboard who wasn't sure that he would come through all right.

"Some of them stuffed themselves with K-rations while waiting, but I was too scared to eat. Maybe the others were, too, but if they were, they didn't show it.

"Finally, just about daylight, one engine conked out, and the pilot let us know that we were going down. He kept calling off the altitude as we got closer and closer to the water. I was in the tail, and all I can remember is the spray coming in the window. Then I was in the water, with a broken arm.

"I've done a lot of swimming and I usually get my elbows out of the water when I want to make speed. Once I spotted the life-raft my only idea was to get to it as soon as possible. It wasn't until I got to the side of it that I found I couldn't use one arm. I suppose I was too dazed to notice it before."

None of the four who survived had a clear idea of how they escaped from the plane. Apparently all had been knocked unconscious, reviving when they landed in the water. As a result, the two rafts they had planned to release by hand after the crash remained in the plane, and the two they found were those which came from the sides automatically.

Most critically injured was the pilot, Lieutenant Edwin T. Szezypinski, of Erie, Pa., who had suffered a compound fracture of the left leg and severe lacerations to both legs.

He later remembered only releasing his safety belt, then being in the water, and swimming about fifty yards to a raft. He had to cling to the side of it for more than an hour before he had mustered enough strength to climb in. Alone for three days, he administered first aid to himself, which medics later credited with saving his life and averting amputation of his mangled legs.

Sergeant Ernest Sydlosky, assistant engineer and waist gunner, of Detroit, Mich., had broken a thigh bone. But he too succeeded in swimming to the raft occupied by Bombardier Pahl. Sergeant Harvey Hitt, Twin Falls, Idaho, armorer and nose gunner, the fourth survivor, had escaped serious injury. He got into the raft first and pulled Pahl and Sydlosky aboard.

The three men were confident that other planes in their squadron would report their position, and that rescue would be speedy. During the first day they saw several planes in the distance, but their frantic waving was of no avail.

That night they heard another nearby, but Sydlosky identified it from the sound of its engines as a Jap, and they held their flares. That was the last plane they saw until they were found.

Hitt made a splint for Sydlosky's broken leg from a paddle and the life-raft sail. They spent most of their time bailing water.

By day they baked in the sun, at night shivered in their wet clothing. Real sleep was impossible. Hitt caught a seagull by the legs as it alighted on the raft in the darkness. He plucked it, but there were no customers for the dish, and it was decided to save it for bait. They were just beginning to get hungry.

Next day came rescue.

"The plane that found us came almost straight overhead," said Pahl, "but we weren't taking any chances and let go all but one flare from our Very pistols at it. It circled and dropped a note saying a Dumbo plane would pick us up. They also dropped a packet of badly needed medical supplies. After the plane had gone, we drank the six little cans of water we had been saving, and tried to swallow some hoarded canned K-rations, but they were too salty."

It was almost dusk when the Dumbo arrived and dropped night lights to mark the location of the raft. Then it picked up Szezypinski, who had been spotted floating three miles away.

Another of the repeated sea rescues in which the Army-Navy teamwork clicked occurred during the series of missions the B-25's of the 41st Group began flying against the eastern Carolines late in March.

The medium bombers, which heretofore had confined their strikes to the Marshalls, began ranging out against Ponape. In four days they dropped more than twenty-five tons on Ponape's repair shops, airstrips and barracks areas. On March 26, escorted by Navy Corsairs, they encountered interception for the first time. Fifteen Jap fighters rose to the attack. Four of them were shot down, a fifth probably destroyed. None of our planes was lost.

Again, on March 27, twelve B-2 5's flew to Ponape with an escort of eighteen Corsairs, and again fifteen Jap fighters tried to intercept. This time the Army and Navy gunners did a thorough job. Nine of the Japs were shot down and three more were believed to have been destroyed. One of our bombers was lost.

Returning from one of these missions, a Mitchell developed engine trouble and was forced to land on the water, less than twenty miles from Jap-held Ponape. One member of the crew was killed, another died soon after. Surviving were Lieutenants Henry M. Phillips of Greenville, North Carolina, the pilot; Warren W. Hufstutter, Kearney, Nebraska, co-pilot; Charles J. Glownia, New Britain, Connecticut, navigator-bombardier; and Staff Sergeant Eugene T. Doyle, Morris Plains, New Jersey, radio-gunner.

The four, all veterans of thirty or more missions, were in the water two days. For twenty hours, Mitchells from their squadron flew cover for them, ready to go to their aid in case their raft was attacked.

A Navy Catalina was sent after them, but the water was so rough the plane could not land. Finally a destroyer was summoned and picked them up under the very noses of the Ponape Japs.

Lieutenant Phillips had his twenty-sixth birthday while they were down, but the crew waited to celebrate until they had reached a Seventh AAF rest camp in Honolulu.

"You can't drum up much birthday enthusiasm while you're on a raft surrounded by hundreds of sharks," he said.

On a mission against Nauru another B-25 of the 41st, the Ole Woman, ran into trouble.

"We were flying out of Makin and went in to Nauru to hit gun emplacements," said Lieutenant Marvin B. Watts, pilot. "As we came in over the target I dropped down to 7,000 feet and our bombs went in on the target. The flak was thick and both our engines were hit at once. Another shell burst just outside my compartment.

"The controls were damaged and we plunged downward. I fought for control, gambling on the remote chance that I could level her off before we crashed. We were diving at the rate of 3,500 feet per minute, and it looked like this was really it.

"Just before we hit the water, I was able to bring the plane into a glide and, 20 miles off Nauru, we hit the water.

"Somehow, we managed to get out of the plane before it went down, even though several of the crew were badly injured. There were sharks all about us and they were attracted to Staff Sergeant Gerald Quarles, our tail gunner, who was bleeding profusely from a severed artery. Quarles was almost helpless to defend himself because of a broken leg and injuries to his hip and back.

"Sergeant George M. Dormuth, radio operator, was in the water near Quarles and, although he was also cut and bleeding and had a broken ankle and rib, he went to Quarles' rescue.

"First he splashed water and lunged at the sharks to drive them away from Quarles. Then he towed the gunner to the raft and kicked and splashed at the sharks as we pulled Quarles aboard. Staff Sergeant James L. Jones, engineer and turret gunner, was also losing blood from a bad gash on the left side of his face, but had managed to get aboard.

"The sea was rough and we expected to swamp any minute, but, luckily, a Navy Dumbo plane came to our rescue. The crew sprayed the sharks with bullets and, in spite of high seas, were able to come within 20 yards of our raft. We had finally pulled Dormuth aboard, and they picked us all up."

The Mitchells did a tremendous job during this period. Japanese officials, testifying after the war, said they were the most troublesome of all our planes, because they came in so low that radar was unable to pick them up. High speed of the Mitchells made successful fighter interception difficult. One plane could get away ten shells in approaching a target, and even in a small formation this lay down considerable fire power. They played havoc with Jap shipping and gun emplacements.

Flyers in this theater needed all the innovations and ingenuity possible to overcome the handicaps peculiar to the Pacific.

In Europe our bombers flew comparatively short missions with strong fighter escort and hit targets that were often larger than several atolls combined.

Men of the Seventh were flying missions at this time that averaged 2,431 miles, and hitting pin-point targets on infinitesimal islands. Usually they had to fight their way into and away from a target. They rarely had fighter escort.

On one strike against Maloelap, two B-25's were hit simultaneously by Jap flak and fighter fire. Although in flames, neither Liberator swerved from its place in formation but completed the bomb run before crashing into the sea.

On another strike against the same base, Captain Allan R. Taflinger, Paris, Illinois, pilot of a B-24 of the 26th Squadron, used one of the most daring and ingenious pieces of strategy of the war to trick the Japanese and complete his mission successfully.

He had been assigned a night mission to hit a certain area on the runway at Maloelap, but when he came over the island, there was a complete black-out and it was so dark he couldn't even see the runway — much less the exact spot he was to hit.

He circled low, trying to draw ack-ack fire that might reveal the target, but the Japs refused to fire. Taflinger headed back out to sea — pretending to return to his base.

Then he circled and came back, flying low and heading for what he hoped was the runway. When he was almost on the ground, he boldly switched on his landing lights, and the Japs, thinking it was one of their own planes, turned on the runway lights.

Taflinger then dropped his bombs squarely on the tiny target and returned home.

But luck ran out for this heroic flyer soon afterward, and on April 4 he was lost on a night mission against Truk.

March saw reorganization of the Air Force to fit the fast moving Central Pacific picture. With the air over the Gilberts and Marshall cleared of enemy planes, it was now possible to pull back all units of the VII Fighter Command to Oahu for regrouping, reinforcement, training with new planes, and general reorganization for the Marianas invasion which was brewing. Of this group, only the 704th Signal Aircraft Warning Company remained at Kwajalein.

In the forward area, all Air Force activities were placed under the control of General Landon, Commanding General of the VII Bomber Command, whose headquarters were at Kwajalein. AD VON Headquarters at Tarawa was disbanded and personnel returned to Oahu. Until the Marianas campaign, it was to be strictly a bomber show.

By the first of April the six squadrons of the 11th and 30th Groups moved to Kwajalein, and later that month the 41st Group of B-25's moved from Tarawa and Apemama to Makin.

From March 28-31, the Seventh teamed with the Navy in an attack against the most westerly islands of the Carolines — Palau, Yap, and Woleai.

This thrust by a full-fledged battle fleet carried us nearly 1,200 miles west of Truk, and only 550 miles short of the Jap-held Philippines.

The operation involved a sweeping and daring plan — no less a venture than to put the entire Japanese air force in all the islands east of the Philippines out of operation for the duration of the attack. To achieve this, important Jap air bases for hundreds of miles to the south and east were systematically neutralized.

The Seventh hit Truk from the East and the Thirteenth and Fifth Air Forces joined the attack and hit the Pacific Gibraltar from the South. The Seventh also kept Ponape and Kusaie paralyzed.

Bombers of the Thirteenth took out Kapingamarangi south of Truk. The Fifth struck at Hollandia in New Guinea.

The strikes at Truk from March 29 to April 3 effectively neutralized the Jap stronghold and protected our fleet operating far west of Palau. The Seventh attacked at night and large fires were started on Dublon, Uman, Eten and Moen islands. One hundred and sixty enemy planes were knocked out in the operations and twenty-eight enemy ships were sunk.

At dawn on March 30 the task force struck. Palua, Woleai and Yap shook and shivered under the sledge-hammer blows.

The Japs, unwilling to risk their fleet against the might of the B-24's and our Navy, faced the necessity of pulling their supply lines still further west to the Philippines, leaving all their mid-Pacific garrisons out on the end of a long and fragile limb.

Almost without a break during April, the bombers of the Seventh droned out of Kwajalein to batter Truk, coordinating with the Liberators from the Solomons in the technique of the one-two punch.

One hundred and sixty tons of bombs were dropped on airfields and installations at Moen, Param and Dublon during the week of April 5-12.

On the night of April 13 a score of Seventh bombers soared over Truk in two waves, followed just before dawn by another formation from the Thirteenth.

The Truk run was a perennial adventure and the Seventh encountered a variety of situations. Such as a running "duel" with five Jap searchlights in which the Heaven Can Wait, a B-24 of the 98th Squadron, took part.

"We were one of twenty-three planes scheduled to make individual attacks on various Truk airfields," said Lieutenant Emil Nummi, bombardier of the plane.

"Our plane, piloted by Lieutenant Arthur Suojanen, was assigned to hit the Param airstrip from 8,000 feet, and as we entered the Truk lagoon from Otta Pass, a searchlight from Fefan island began to sweep up on our tail.

As we turned northwest toward Param, the beam caught us. Immediately two others from Dublon Island swung across the sky. Lieutenant Suojanen made a 180-degree turn, heading east and hoping to escape the lights but, instead, we were picked up by two more.

"Bracketed by five searchlights Suojanen pushed the nose down to a 70-degree dive, riding down the cone of light. We dodged right, then left but they still held us. We felt like ducks in a rainbarrel.

"Although nearly blinded by the glare, I was releasing my bombs as fast as I could. I saw them hit on a building area on Fefan. Instantly two searchlights in that area went out."

Suojanen and the co-pilot, Lieutenant Anthony Eckhart, cut the engines and held the plane in the dive. At 4,000 feet, still impaled by three searchlights, they tried to pull her out. The engines were turned back on, but nothing happened.

"I thought those damned engines would never start again," said Nummi, "but finally they caught on with a thundering roar and the plane nosed up and pulled out of the lights and we headed for home."

During the five-minute "duel" both pilots had been too busy to think about bombs. Now they decided to go back and make the run. They notified Nummi, via interphone, to get ready to release his bombs.

"Bombs, hell!" said the bombardier. "I dropped 'em ten minutes ago!"

The Japs hadn't seen the plane come out of the dive. That night "Tokyo Rose" announced:

"One American Liberator was shot down over Truk last night!"

Safe at their base, the crew of Heaven Can Wait chuckled. But the cards were stacked. On May 4, Heaven Can Wait took off from Eniwetok on a mission against Ponape. Trouble developed in the electrical system and the plane and crew were never heard of again.

Those bomber crews went through ordeals that aged men before their time — if they lived. Men of the 27th Squadron tell with grim pride of another mission over Truk when a temporarily blinded pilot brought his plane home with a load of dead and wounded and a 500-pound bomb dangling by its tail half way out the bomb bay doors.

Lieutenant Woodrow W. Waterous, Detroit, Michigan, brought his plane, the A-vailable, over Fefan Island at 10,000 feet. Harried by searchlights and ack-ack fire, Waterous dodged, dived and fish-tailed, as Lieutenant Robert T. Irizarry, New York City, loosed his bombs.

As Waterous headed back to sea the plane was again trapped by searchlights. The A-vailable was down to 6,000 feet when Sergeant Arthur Cristopherson, tail-gunner, spotted the dim outlines of a Jap night-fighter and yelled over the interphone:

"Zero coming in fast at 4:30!"

Sergeant Jack H. Young, Johnson City, Tennessee, right waistgunner, cut loose, but missed as the Jap dived under the plane.

The ball-turret gunner, Sergeant Philip W. Wagner, Mineola, New York, was unable to see the fighter because of fog on the windows of his turret so the Jap had a clear field.

The Zero scored five direct cannon hits, one of which exploded on the canopy bracing just above the co-pilot's seat, and Lieutenant Austin J. Helms, Charlotte, North Carolina, slumped forward over his controls — dead. Waterous was blinded from flying glass — his right eye completely blacked-out and his left eye almost closed. Lieutenant Alex Peck, Milton, Virginia, navigator, was wounded in the left leg by shrapnel.

Finally Staff Sergeant William P. Shelton, Stanley, North Carolina, caught the Zero in his sights and poured a long burst into the fighter's midsection, and the Jap staggered. Technical Sergeant Paul Ragusa, New York City, top-turret gunner and assistant radio operator, then let go at the Zero. The plane burst into flames and plunged into the sea.

With the weight of the co-pilot's body paralyzing the controls, and the throttles jammed wide open, Waterous struggled doggedly to level off the diving plane. It was down to 3,000 feet before he succeeded in straightening it out.

Peck and Regusa finally lifted the body of the co-pilot from the seat and placed it on the flight deck.

The A-vailable was in bad shape. All trim-tab controls, the co-pilot's junction box, and part of the greenhouse were also shot out. The interphone and the radio were dead.

The automatic pilot was ruined, so Waterous, although close to collapse, was forced to remain at the controls. Regusa sat in the co-pilot's seat and gave the pilot regular instrument readings.

It was a five-hour haul back to base and, with the racing engines drinking gasoline and a blind pilot, it looked tough. But the bad breaks were just beginning.

Peck, who hadn't told anyone of his wounds, suddenly collapsed and had to be given first aid by the crew. Now there was no navigator. Black clouds were piling up — threatening a storm!

Shelton relieved Regusa as seeing-eye observer for the pilot and Ragusa went back to try to repair the interphone. On the catwalk he glanced down and saw a 500-pound bomb dangling from the rack.

The engineer yelled for Young and together they lay on the narrow catwalk and cranked open the bomb bay door. There was nothing between them and the ocean but empty spacer

They wrestled with the bomb and finally it was dislodged but, maddeningly, it caught and dangled halfway outside the plane!

Wet with sweat, the two men hung precariously to a strut and managed to lift the nose of the bomb back inside. At last it was secured to a shackle and the heavy doors were cranked shut.

Gas was running low and the plane was rapidly losing altitude. Waterous ordered all movable objects jettisoned. Ammunition, guns, flak suits and even the belly turret went overboard.

It was daylight, but there was nothing to be seen but emptiness. The men sweated out the hours, but without a navigator they could only hope they were on course. Finally, Waterous announced that they'd have to ditch.

"We'll have to go down by nine o'clock," he said.

A few minutes before they were scheduled to go into the sea a speck of land appeared on the horizon. It was Eniwetok!

Then an unseeing pilot nursed her in, using the eyes of Irizarry who had taken the final relief.

The runway came up at them as the bombardier told Waterous to level off. Lower and lower dropped the plane, as Irizarry anxiously called off the instrument readings and the crew braced themselves for a crash landing. But the A-vailable hit the strip, bounced once, and rolled safely in.

Another mission against Truk was completed.

On April 15, General Hale moved to Kwajalein as "COM-AIR-FORWARD," directing the employment of all land-based planes in the forward area. General Douglass, who had become the Seventh's commanding general, turned over the expanding Fighter Command to his deputy, Colonel Ernest "Mickey" Moore.

Two days later the 392nd Bomb Squadron, attached to the 30th Bomb Group, made their first mission against Saipan and Tinian.

Five B-24's, piloted by Lieutenants Gabriel Martin, Jr., Warren G. Myllenbeck, William J. Schneiderhan, Leonard F. Smisson, and Walter L. Crafford, took off from Eniwetok with Navy PB4Y's for a photo recon and bombing strike against Saipan, Tinian and Aguijan islands.

It was a rugged 14 ½ hours' flying schedule, one of the longest strikes made by the Seventh.

This mission involved what General Landon termed "probably the longest combat bomb run in the history of aerial warfare." Ordinarily, planes remain on a bombing run not more than twenty to thirty seconds and, even at top speed, the crews regard themselves as sitting ducks during that critical period of level flight. This time, however, the run lasted ten minutes and was made at slow speed, well within the range of Jap anti-aircraft guns and in the face of rising Zeros and the bright sunshine of high noon.

"The mission was chiefly to obtain photographs and test the feasibility of hitting the Marianas with land-based planes, but bombs were added for good measure," said Lieutenant Schneiderhan, Beaver Creek, Minnesota.

"We flew north and then followed the Jap ferrying lanes south over Saipan, Tinian and Aguijan. We caught the Nips by surprise and I think they mistook our formation for their own planes. We were flying abreast as we went over and were spaced so that the formation covered between eight and nine miles.

"After the first three minutes of the camera run, we came within sight of the huge airfield at the southern tip of Saipan. Each plane had been left free to pick a target of opportunity, and as Nip fighters began to take off, our bombardier, Lieutenant Blair C. Rogers, loosed his bombs on the strip, hoping to block further Jap fighter opposition.

"We were flying with our flaps lowered and our engines throttled down to 140 miles an hour. Our formation was over this target for seven minutes, and as we watched the Jap fighters coming up it seemed like seven years. But by the time they had reached our altitude of 20,000 feet we were leaving the area.

"I brought our plane, the Annie, back into formation as we prepared to meet the Jap fighter attacks.

"The Japs put on quite a show for us but as long as we were in formation they had no stomach for a fight. The Nips did all sorts of slow rolls, snap rolls and other maneuvers, but every time one started to make a pass he cut it short in the middle. There were 25-30 of them.

"The fighters followed us for about an hour and a half before we outdistanced them," Schneiderhan said.

During the photo-bomb run, Lieutenant Smisson's plane and one of the Navy ships developed engine trouble and were forced to drop out of formation. They were ganged by nine of the Japs.

In a running fight that lasted 30 minutes, each of the cripples shot down a fighter and got one probable. The PB4Y and the Liberator both crashed at sea. Sergeant Harley Hines, aboard Smisson's plane, was killed. On April 23, a Navy destroyer picked up the two crews about 350 miles north of Truk.

On April 19 another photo recon plane of the 431st made a similar hazardous camera run over Truk.

The 11th Group had been striking Truk regularly since March 27, without knowing how much damage they had inflicted. A flight of nine Liberators was scheduled for a night bombing mission, so Colonel William J. Holzapfel, commanding officer of the 11th, decided to send a tenth plane along for photographs.

It was a job for a volunteer, since the plane would have to expose itself in straight flight over the target for seven minutes and be over Truk for at least thirty.

Captain Warren S. Rowe had made a previous unsuccessful photo mission and asked for the job.

"When we arrived over the target we found perfect weather," Captain Rowe said. "We were carrying 20 magnesium bombs to illuminate the target.

"We made three runs over the islands of Eten, Moen and Dublon and our bombardier, Lieutenant Julius C. Short, released his photo bombs so as to have a 60 per cent overlay for the photos.

"As I came back for the fourth run, our No. 3 engine went out and we headed home. It is a long drag back to Eniwetok under the best of conditions — with three engines it is really rough.

"To make matters even worse I tried to feather the prop but it wouldn't work. It began to windmill. Then the engine froze and the crankshaft broke, allowing the propeller to rotate dangerously off center, and we began to lose altitude.

"We kept going down and down. Everything that could be cut loose — guns, ammunition, tools and even the camera — was thrown into the sea. Only the film was saved.

"Somehow, we managed to sweat it out and got back. It was a helluva good feeling when we hit the runway at Eniwetok!"

The thirteen photographs obtained proved so excellent that the crew received a special commendation from General Landon.

The 392nd "Pathfinder Squadron," adding to its record of "firsts" over so many Pacific targets, set another record in April: a shuttle bombing mission of more than 4,000 miles!

Seven B-24's of this outfit, teaming with Navy Liberators, took off from Kwajalein for a great triangle route that included Guam and the Carolines.

"It was a funny feeling heading out of our staging base at Eniwetok. There were two full days ahead over the longest route anyone had ever flown on a combat mission. And there were two targets to hit — one of them Guam, which hadn't been touched by our planes during the war.

"There were many things to think about. No one knew how tough the Japs would be over Guam but we had an idea that they would throw the works at us. Then there was a matter of weather. You never knew when a tropical storm would kick up down there. And trying to get through a weather front that tosses a Liberator around like a straw is tough under any circumstances. It was really grim to think that we faced that possibility for 4,000 miles of water flying!

"We staged through Eniwetok and headed for Guam," said Staff Sergeant William H. Sisson, Union City, Georgia, gunner on one of the planes.

"Finally, we came in sight of Guam. It would be a pretty sight under normal circumstances — white cliffs along the coast and green trees — but it didn't look so good when we saw 20-30 maroon, brown, and silver Zekes and Oscars come zooming up to meet us.

"They flew over us and as usual, dropped phosphorus bombs. The bombs threw out weird tails of smoke but none of us were hit. Then we went in on our bomb and photo run and headed out.

"The Nip fighters began to attack us from all sides. For some reason they seemed to pick out our plane and it really kept me jumping. I threw plenty of bursts and knocked down two Japs. The fight lasted forty minutes before they finally had enough and headed back. We shot down two more, got another probable and damaged six during the fight. None of our planes were lost."

The planes went on to Los Negros Island in the Admiralties and he next day headed for Ponape where they showered Langor Island in the Ponape atoll with 100-pounders. Here they met moderate and accurate ack-ack fire but there was no damage to the Liberators. From there the B-24's returned to their base in the Marshalls.

By the end of April, General Douglass announced that the Seventh had bombed Truk twenty times, and had dropped 2,000 tons on enemy bases in the Central Pacific during that month alone — a new record. Bombing had become a big business in the Pacific.

May saw the new Pacific air command swinging into action. Under General Hale's experienced direction as COM-AIR-FORWARD, combined operations of Army, Navy, and Marine land-based planes — heretofore conducted only on a small-scale basis — expanded to new and formidable dimensions.

Pooled under Hale's direction were the ponderous Liberators and the twin-engined Mitchells of the Seventh AAF, the Fourth Marine Air Wing's Dauntless dive-bombers and the Catalinas, and Marines of Fleet Air Wing Two. Officially established May 1, COM-AIR-FORWARD shifted at once into high gear, and was functioning so smoothly that by May 15 it was possible to launch the heaviest attack from land-based planes in the Central Pacific air war to date — a 240-toii bomb air raid on Jaluit.

The little Marshalls atoll by that time had the unhappy distinction of being one of the most heavily bombed targets in the world. That day the surviving Japs must have thought the end of the world had come.

Round-the-clock bombing began at midnight, with harassing strikes continuing throughout the early morning hours. After daylight the attacks were almost continuous, first by the Liberators and Mitchells of the Seventh, then by the Marines and the Navy. They tapered off during the evening. Just after midnight, twenty-four hours after they had begun, the attacks ended.

Throughout the attack, high-ranking officers concerned with planning and directing the Central Pacific air war, circled the island in their planes, studying the tactics, observing results. General Hale himself cruised back and forth with his operations staff for hours, watching the heavies and mediums and attack bombers roar on their precise schedules, each with its pre-determined altitude, its assigned target area.

Hale described the operation:

"The target attack involved a large portion of the atoll, which called for the most accurate of bombing. The heavy bombers made their runs singly, and dropped trains of bombs directly in the center of cocoanut-tree-studded spits of sand which were less than half as wide as the wing span of a Liberator.

"Mitchell bombers and the smaller Dauntless, Corsairs and Hellcats made their runs and returned at tree-top height to strafe Jap installations scattered throughout the cocoanut trees."

All types of bombs were unloaded on the narrow atoll, from 2,000-pound atoll busters to 500-pounders used for pinpointing small targets.

Hale observed the misses as well as the hits, the technique of approaching the bomb run, the evasive action. After the strike, squadron commanders were called into his office. Talking from his personal notes, Hale gave them a critique of the operation.

"Our purpose in this extensive combined operation," he said, "was not merely to put more bombs on this frequently-bombed atoll. We were endeavoring to perfect the already splendid co-ordination between the several commands involved, and to measure the effectiveness of certain types of bombing in this theater.

"The Jaluit attack provided a superb proving ground for the development of air tactics which will prove useful in expanded air operations on the road to Japan."

With but slight interruption, the regular flow of missions continued against the Japs in the Marshalls, the Carolines and the Marianas.

A week later Hale launched another combined attack — the second heaviest in this theater — on Jaluit. The Japs, trying desperately to reduce their heavy losses, had dispersed their personnel and supplies into little concentrations scattered over the atoll. Our bombers ferreted these out one by one, and rained 230 tons on the atoll.

Six days later a two-forked attack was mounted against two distant targets — Wotj e in the Marshalls and Ponape in the Carolines. Following the heavy Marshalls strikes, General Hale declared:

"The Marshalls no longer represent worthwhile targets for heavy bombardment."

Another great act of the Central Pacific drama was ended. The Gilberts and the Marshalls were ours. Already our faces were turned westward. Planes of the joint command were ranging across the ocean, all the way to distant Koror, in the extreme western Carolines. Truk and Ponape were reeling from our blows; Saipan, Tinian and Guam had been hit.

It was a part of the endless pattern of the atoll circuit — a pattern that rock-happy, water-weary men of the Seventh were bred on and died from.

General Hale, standing in the debris of shattered, stinking Kwajalein, had defined it this way:

"To assist naval and ground forces engaged in planning invasions of new islands by softening up the invasion target in extensive pre-assault air campaigns.

"To maintain the neutralization of enemy air bases which have been by-passed."

Men of lesser rank, unfettered by the necessity of couching official pronouncements in military language, were more down-to-earth about the endless road to Tokyo. Staff Sergeant Bob Frederick, a former newspaper man who served as a combat correspondent for the Seventh and went in on most of the invasions summed it up:

"It is a simple process of surrounding yourself with Japs and fighting like hell to keep their guns out of your belly while you get ready for another hop into the middle of a lot more Japs."

One damned island after another. . . .

CHAPTER XVIII: THE MARIANAS

LATE IN MAY 1944 THE GREATEST LONG-RANGE TASK FORCE IN the history of naval warfare began making up in the waters around Hawaii.

The mighty Fifth Fleet, consisting of vessels ranging from tiny destroyer escorts to mammoth carriers, anchored in the narrow, winding channel of Pearl Harbor, once the "graveyard of the United States Navy."

On a twenty-four-hour schedule, endless truck convoys spun through the quiet streets of Hickam Field. The trucks, filled with silent Marines dressed in jungle-green battle dress, eased to a stop before fat, drab transports standing at the Hickam docks.

Into other ships at other docks Infantrymen of the 27th Division, bent under the weight of field packs and combat equipment, trudged quietly into the darkened holds.

The road from Honolulu, glutted with military traffic ranging from jeeps to prime movers, sagged under new and strange weapons.

Big tanks, of a type never before used in the Central Pacific, clanked swiftly out behind the speeding motorcycles and jeeps of Army and Marine military police.

Huge artillery guns, an innovation in the atoll war pattern where machine guns usually furnished the "heavy" support, rumbled toward waiting ships.

At Bellows Field the Seventh was also planning a surprise.

Parked wing-tip to wing-tip, in lines as straight as files of West Point cadets standing at attention, were P-47's of the 318th Fighter Group.

Inspecting the planes were Colonel Lewis M. Sanders, commanding officer of the group, and Major Philip M. Rasmussen.

In the Pearl Harbor tragedy, Sanders, a second lieutenant at the time, had climbed into a P-40 on the wrecked runway at Wheeler Field and knocked an attacking Zero out of the air. Rasmussen, then a lieutenant, had also accounted for a Jap plane in a dogfight over Diamond Head.

Now they were preparing to send 111 fighter planes into action in the Marianas — 73 of them from catapults on the decks of Navy carriers!

On the following morning, 73 of the P-47's were lifted by cranes to the flight decks of the carriers Natoma Bay and Manila Bay. Dubious pilots gathered around the flimsy mechanism which was supposed to propel their fighters from the flight deck. They didn't believe that the small contraption could send them out at the 80-mile-per-hour speed necessary to keep them in the air.

Center of attention in the group were several pilots who had one such previous experience from the carrier Nassau in a small-scale experiment during the Makin operations.

"Those things have more power than you think," said Lieutenant James R. "Stumpy" Snyder of Baltimore, Md., who had been in on the Makin deal. "You get a helluva wallop on the back of your head when they jerk you forward. Anyway," he grinned, "they leave the canopy open in case you go in the drink."

One of the pilots said he wished he'd learned to swim.

Standing to one side of the long lines of Marines, Infantrymen, Artillerymen, Seabees and Aviation Engineers filing into the ships, were small groups of Air Forces men. They were the advance echelon, consisting of operations personnel, clerks, typists and administrative officers.

In their duffle bags were clothing, pencils, stationery and carbon papers ("always make the reports in triplicate").

Some of these men, scheduled to go in with Marine assault waves, carried carbines or .45 pistols. Some, whose supply sergeants were in a good humor at the moment, had jungle knives.

Their combat training, for the most part consisted of a few weeks basic at a plush stateside airbase where often the only guns were those belonging to the MP's.

"Clay pigeons with pencils," was the derisive name they gave themselves.

Then the ships were loaded and the movement was on. Suddenly, Honolulu, which had been jammed with uniforms of every branch of service, was comparatively uncrowded. The waters around Hawaii were suddenly ominously empty as the great snowball started the long, slow roll westward.

The famous "Task Force 58" was underway. It gathered size at Kwajalein, grew larger at Eniwetok, and by the time it was moving into enemy waters was so huge that an ATC pilot, Captain Bob Lubbe, reported that it took his four-engined C-54, flying at a speed well over 150 miles an hour, more than 20 minutes to fly over the striking force!

We had learned very little about the Marianas since Guam had fallen to the Japs in December 1941. Distances had been too great to make regular recon and bombing missions over the islands.

On February 21, Vice Admiral Marc Mitscher had taken Task Force 58 into the Marianas to probe the islands' defenses. For two days, Navy planes had launched bombing attacks against Saipan, Tinian, Rota and Guam.

At the same time, B-24's of the Seventh protected the Navy from the rear by bombing Ponape and Kusaie.

Navy planes, despite fierce aerial and anti-aircraft opposition, had destroyed 135 Jap planes and lost only six. They had also gathered considerable information in this "dry run invasion" test.

Now we were back to put this information to use.

The Saipan job was the most complicated naval maneuver to date, involving intricate coordinated operations of hundreds of ships and thousands of smaller craft. This was the largest long-range fleet in history, and the nearest American base was at Eniwetok, nearly 1,000 miles away.

Mitscher, on June 14, dispatched two task forces, including the carriers Yorktovm, Essex and Hornet, on a strike against Iwo Jima to neutralize that stronghold and prevent enemy planes from hitting our landing troops.

On June 15 we hit Saipan!

For miles, hundreds of ships were deployed close in to the beaches. In the more or less harborless area we knew it would be a problem to move fighting men across the coral reefs — but we were prepared.

Staff Sergeant Robert Price, one of the Air Forces "clay pigeons with pencils," stood at the rail of an invasion ship. Price had gone ashore early on Kwajalein and was destined to land on "every other damned island — including Japan."

"Ahead, and only faintly visible in the gathering dawn, was the 1,500-foot peak of Mount Tapotchau," said Price. "Less than three miles across the channel was the flat, uneven outline of Tinian.

"There was a dead silence. A marine standing next to me dropped an apple overboard and leaned forward to listen to the faint plop as it hit the water.

"From far out at sea came the faint sound of bombardment, and you could taste the powder smoke in the air. Then, as the sun rose out of the mists, the sounds became less muffled and came closer.

"Suddenly the silence split wide open as thousands of big Navy guns opened up simultaneously. In the awful din of the guns, swish of the flame-trailing rockets, and wild hammering of small weapons, the Marines and infantrymen climbed down cargo nets into alligators that clawed their way over the reefs and moved in on the beaches."

The Marines secured beachheads, captured a headland, and fought their way into the village of Charan Kanoa. Then they smashed through enemy tank attacks and seized Agingan Point on the southwest corner of the island.

At the rail of another invasion ship on the west coast of Saipan was Colonel Sanders and a small group of men who were the advance echelon of the 318th Group. They watched Navy planes speed inland and dive low on Aslito Field. Sanders winced as he saw columns of smoke rise from the runway, for it was his job to prepare the field for the seventy-three Thunderbolts aboard the carriers, which were still standing by far out to sea, awaiting orders to send the Seventh fighters into action. Those Navy bomb craters, Sanders thought, weren't going to make it easier.

The Saipan, Tinian and Guam operation, in the beginning, was essentially a Navy-foot-soldier show. Their conquest is a story of Marines of the 4th Division and Infantrymen of the 27th Division fighting their way through the jungles and caves. And it is the saga of carrier pilots from Task Force 58, who in a two-day air battle covering the initial landings, knocked out 402 Jap planes!

For the Seventh, Saipan was where our planes knocked out scores of enemy pockets and the men of the ground echelons, with no previous battle experience, fought off banzai charges, dodged bullets of countless snipers, and survived shellings and Jap air attacks to build the runways from which the Seventh supported the ground offensive and the B-29's launched the strikes that finally knocked Japan out of the war.

Air Forces technicians were scheduled to land as soon as Aslito airstrip was secured. But, unaccountably, many of them found themselves ashore while the field was still a battleground.

On the night of D-plus-2, while the narrow strip on the west side of the island held by the Marines was still rocked with heavy mortar fire, Sergeant Randolph Wood, an armorer from Merriam, Kansas, took a detail of technicians in.

These men were members of a 318th Squadron called the "Bar Flies," a go-to-hell bunch of pilots and maintenance personnel. Lieutenant Colonel

"Swearin' John" Evans, their first commanding officer, had boasted that his boys could "drink more whiskey, raise more hell and keep more women happy than any other blankety-blank squadron in the Air Forces."

Wood and the others didn't feel so "go-to-hell" that night, however. Because Wood couldn't think of anything else to do, he ordered his men to dig in. It was good advice, for the Japs, fighting from caves and strong entrenchments along rugged ridges, were throwing everything they had.

A little further up the beachhead was Sergeant Price, who had picked his way ashore under a continuous stream of fire from Mount Tapotchau.

"We were told to dig in and stay there," said Price. "Besides the Jap mortar and machine gun fire, there was a better than even chance of being shot by a Marine if you showed your head. Those guys weren't taking chances on anything!

"It's hard to imagine anything funny about a beachhead, but all sorts of crazy things happened that first night. Once a can of rations near my foxhole got so hot it exploded with a helluva pop. A huge Marine — he must have weighed 250 pounds — leaped up from the ground and dived into a foxhole already crowded with three others yelling, 'They got me Charley!' That line got to be quite a gag all during the battle.

"Just before morning, a cow somehow wandered down to the beach without being shot. She finally ended up by calmly standing over a foxhole, occupied by Private First Class Romeo Dingle, and obeying a pressing call of nature. Dingle, who was asleep, received a rude awakening.

"That cow," said Price, "gave no more milk."

Colonel Sanders and his advance group were dug in near a sugar refinery. He was waiting for Aslito Field to be secured before making contact with Sergeant Wolfe's detachment.

On the morning of D-plus-3 there was a rumor that Aslito had been taken. Wolfe gathered his men and loaded trucks with equipment brought in the day before, and headed in the general direction of the field only to be turned back. The field had been recaptured by the Japs. On the following day they received word that Aslito was again in our hands.

Wood drove the first piece of Air Forces equipment onto the field — an oil truck.

"I arrived on the following day and was amazed at how well Wood's detachment had things organized," said Sanders. "Hell, there was so much action that you were lucky to stay alive, much less set up equipment!"

Toward dusk of D-plus-5, the party succeeded in moving all but nine big packing cases to the field. They decided to spend the night on the beach with the remaining nine cases and move them in early the next morning, but the unpleasant odors from a dead cow nearby changed their minds. During the night an explosion destroyed the boxes beside which they had planned to sleep.

The same night eighty-five more Bar Flies came in and dug in on the beach. A flood of equipment also arrived and for three days and nights ninety-one men of the squadron didn't sleep. This group, under the direction of Captain Alan Sinauer of White Plains, New York, Squadron Intelligence Officer; and the line chief, Master Sergeant Ray D. Hammer of Los Angeles, California, a mechanical wizard; handled five hundred tons of equipment and managed to have a maintenance section ready for the first planes.

On D-plus-5, the 804th Aviation Engineers came ashore with heavy grading equipment. In a short time they had hacked out a road three quarters of a mile long, running from the beach through a bluff and to the edge of the field. The following day, seven men were able to walk a bulldozer and two graders over the bluff and onto the airfield.

The engineers went on two twelve-hour shifts per day, and by noon on June 22 we had an airstrip of sorts. It was bomb-pitted and split here and there with sharp gullies. And to make things worse, the Japs still controlled the south end. But it was an airstrip — and it was ours at last.

On June 22 the planes of the 19th aboard the Natoma Bay, which was standing by sixty miles off Saipan, prepared to take off.

With flaps down and engines at full speed, Captain Harry E. McAfee of Piedmont, California, commanding officer of the squadron, shot out into space. Apprehensive pilots sighed with relief when he cleared the deck and roared in toward shore. A brief pause and the second plummeted from the carrier. Then the third. In a short time 24 planes had gone in without an accident.

Captain McAfee was the first of our pilots to land on Saipan. The other planes of the 19th came in the following day.

At noon on June 23 the 73rd Squadron planes aboard the Manila Bay were preparing for their take-off. First in line was the flight of Major D. J. Williams, in the Sweet Adeline; and Lieutenants Keith Mattison, in the Azz's Dragon; James Snyder, in the Damn Yankee; and Robert Anderson, in the Little Buckaroo.

Suddenly an alert sounded and four dive-bombing Vals came over at 7,000 feet high dives. Two of the planes headed for the Manila Bay and the other two peeled off and made for the nearby Natoma Bay.

The Vals dived to 700 feet and released their bombs, which threw up geysers of water beside each carrier but caused no damage.

Williams, Mattison, Snyder and Anderson were catapulted off the deck, but the Jap bombers had disappeared by the time they were in the air.

The other thirty-three planes of the 73rd went in on the following day.

All seventy-three planes were catapulted without a mishap, averaging two minutes per launching.

The coming of the fighters added maintenance work to the moving chores of the Bar Flies. And most of the squadron's vital sheet metal equipment, had been lost in an explosion on the beach.

"Use Tojo's tools," said Sergeant Hammer.

So mechanics scoured the airstrip and salvaged abandoned Jap equipment. They found pliers, wrenches and other tools. They dug out an abandoned Jap forge and converted it into a high-speed kitchen range on which to heat canteens of coffee, cans of meat and beans.

Shorthanded and low on equipment, the mechanics worked sixteen to twenty hours a day.

And there was little chance to sleep even when they were off. Nights were filled with the crack of guns as Jap snipers sneaked down from the cave-riddled hills.

To add to the misery of the weary men were the Jap nuisance bombers — "Bed Check Charlies" — which zoomed in to drop anti-personnel bombs.

Ragged nerves faced their first real test in the pre-dawn of June 26. Staff Sergeant Bob Frederick, who was there, tells the story:

"A Jap sabotage party came from the hills. Twenty Nips with fixed bayonets moved in from a cane field at the east end of the runway and marched single-file up the strip. Eight approached from the south and joined the others near the southeast corner.

"Sergeant Frank B. Williams, Staff Sergeant Charles Sweet, Staff Sergeant Arthur Chauvaux, and Sergeant Raymond Murphy, hidden in dirt-filled ammunition boxes on the parking apron, saw the movement and Chauvaux shouted a challenge. It was answered by a grenade which glanced off the pillbox and exploded a few feet away. Simultaneously, a bottle of burning gasoline was thrown under a nearby P-47, the Hed Up 'N Locked, and the plane flamed up.

"The guards saw the Japs jab bayonets in the belly tanks of several Thunderbolts and then take cover under the wings.

"The Bar Flies yelled for reinforcements and opened fire on the Japs.

"Murphy, an assistant crew chief, leaped from cover of the pillbox and raced through a hail of bullets to the plane adjacent to the flaming P-47. He started the engine and taxied to safety.

"More crewmen dashed up to join the fight and Major John Hussey, new commanding officer of the squadron, rushed in with more reinforcements. Gradually the Japs withdrew to the east end of the runway. Regrouping, they circled back along the north side of the strip where they were killed or captured by ground troops coming up to help the airmen.

"The apparent Jap effort to puncture the belly tanks of scores of American planes, fire them with gasoline bottles and escape in the confusion, was frustrated with the loss of only one plane," said Frederick.

But the mechanics were not the only Seventh ground crews who were mixing it with the Japs.

On the same night, three hundred Japs broke through the Infantry lines and overran the field. Men of the 804th Engineers threw down their tools, grabbed rifles and helped wipe out the Japs.

Lieutenant Henry E. McCoy of Sisterville, West Virginia, riding in a jeep, saw two Jap snipers on the runway fleeing for the nearby canefield. McCoy's carbine jammed so he pushed the accelerator down to the floor and ran down one Jap. The other managed to escape. McCoy received a Silver Star for his fast thinking and ingenuity.

On the following night, fast thinking by two more Engineers saved the lives of some of their buddies.

A platoon of Engineers, working under floodlights, were repairing the Jap aviation gas system when a Betty sneaked in and dropped bombs. No one was hurt but several barrels of gasoline burst into flame a few yards from a huge gasoline tank. The drums began to explode, throwing flames and chunks of white-hot metal in all directions.

The men were pinned down and the flames not only threatened to cause a great gasoline explosion but revealed them to the Jap flyers overhead. Vital supplies and building materials were also stored nearby.

Technicians Fifth Grade Loren I. Low and Andrew Hughes, working near by with their bulldozers, quickly raised their big grader blades and charged into the flames. Then the blades cut down into the earth and smashed over the burning drums, smothering the fire with dirt and coral. Within a few minutes the danger was past.

Low and Hughes were awarded Soldier's medals.

Meanwhile, the Navy continued to take a great toll in Jap air and sea power. One June 19th, three hundred Jap planes attacking our task force were destroyed in the greatest Pacific air battle since Midway.

Two days later carrier planes of the U. S. Fifth Fleet hit the elusive Jap Navy in the First Battle of the Philippines Sea, destroying four ships and damaging at least ten more. On June 23 they found the Nip fleet between Luzon and Formosa and sank one carrier, hit three others, and damaged a battleship and cruiser. The following day, five more Jap ships were sunk and seventy-two enemy planes were downed in a series of aerial smashes designed to neutralize Jap air power within range of Saipan.

On June 25, Admiral Nimitz announced that in defense of the Marianas and Bonins, Japan had lost seven hundred and forty-seven planes, thirty ships and thirteen barges in some of the greatest sea-air battles of the war. This helped to eliminate the possibility of a Japanese reinforcement of the Marianas.

Captain McAfee and the other fighter pilots immediately took to the air on night and day shifts, strafing and using general purpose bombs and rockets in support of the advancing ground troops on Saipan.

On one of these missions, Captain John M. O'Hare led one of the many flights that helped clear out stubborn Jap pockets and save the lives of American ground troops.

"In a thicket there was a Jap stronghold that had given our foot soldiers hell," said O'Hare, "so we went in to take a hand. Lieutenants N. R. Thompson, Robert L. Cumpstone, Frank J. Graham and I dived down and hit the pocket with twelve rockets and all our machine guns. Then we circled and gave them a repeat performance.

"A moment later the ground troops moved in and mopped up.

"On another patrol my flight was called in to help out at the Marpi Point air strip. Going in we could see American positions along the south edge of the field. The Japs were in a densely wooded section along the north edge of the strip. Between the two forces was an open runway that exposed our advancing troops to withering fire.

"Twice we wheeled over without firing, pinning down the Japs and acquainting our troops with the attack route. Then we got the signal from the ground to let 'em have it, so we poured our rockets and thousands of bullets into the Nips.

"Then our troops moved in and completed the job."

The Seventh, which had flown the longest combat missions of the war, now began to fly the shortest.

Tinian, less than three miles across the channel and due for invasion, was the base for Jap artillery that proved troublesome to our forces.

Thunderbolt fighters could take off, complete their mission, and return to Saipan and land in 18 minutes. Because the trips were so short, pilots were given credit for only half a mission, no matter how badly shot up the planes were.

On one of these strikes we lost our first Army pilot in the Marianas campaign.

Lieutenant Wayne F. Kobler of Penokee, Kansas, and six other pilots of the 19th Squadron, took off from Saipan on June 27. Their assignment was a rocket mission against the Gurguan Point.

Kobler was killed when he came in low over the target. The Japs set off a buried 500-pound bomb that caught his low-level plane full blast. The War Department named the Number Two strip at Aslito Field in his honor.

Flying the never ending strikes against the Japanese would have been tiring enough, but the 318th pilots spent most of their "rest" periods dodging Jap bombs and sniper fire. Snipers were everywhere.

Even on takeoffs and landings the weary pilots caught hell. Jap snipers, hidden southeast of Isely Field in jungles — and even in discarded oil barrels — cut loose at the Thunderbolts everytime they took off.

By June 26, American troops had reached the top of Mt. Tapotchau, the first Thunderbolt target after the invasion, and captured Kagman Peninsula, to win complete control of Magicienne Bay on the eastern shore. Twice Marines tried to scale Hill 500, a gnarled volcanic peak looking down on southern Saipan. Twice they were thrown back.

The third time they slugged through the hail of Jap fire to win the hill. This was the turning point in the Saipan action.

The battle for Garapan raged on and by June 27 the town was a heap of rubble. Jap soldiers were hiding in the wreckage and the bodies of the dead littered the torn streets. But complete air superiority aided the ground troops.

By June 29th Nafutan ridge (an escarpment that runs 1,550 yards into the sea), was strewn with the bodies of more than 1,000 Jap dead. Enemy resistance ended there.

One of the greatest factors in knocking out Jap positions in buried pillboxes and caves was a new air weapon — the napalm bomb.

In the latter part of June the Navy brought in some napalm powder, but experiments proved that the formula was unsatisfactory. Our technicians tried mixing it with captured Japanese gasoline, but that wasn't satisfactory. Next powder and motor oil were mixed and results were more desirable.

Then they experimented with a mixture of napalm powder, gasoline and oil. It worked very well.

Each plane carried two bombs in belly or fuel tanks (ranging from 75 to 165 gallon capacity) which were detonated on contact with the ground.

"This weapon was first used against Tinian," Colonel Sanders said. "Our planes would come in at altitudes ranging from 25-50 feet and drop the tanks. If one failed to explode other planes in the formation would set it off with tracer bullets.

"The explosion sent out a sheet of liquid fire 300 feet long, 100 feet wide and 50 feet high. Everything in the area was saturated and it penetrated gun positions, foxholes, pillboxes and block houses. It also burned concealing foliage from around trenches, giving our gunners and ground troops a clear shot at the Nips.

"In the early Marianas operations we hit Saipan, Tinian, Guam, Rota, Pagan, and Ascuncion each day. On one of these missions against Ascuncion, which is just north of Pagan, we learned the advantages of the napalm bomb.

"Our target was a weather station, and our planes were loaded with 500-pounders and fire bombs. The six-foot-thick walls of the station stood up under the 500-pounders, but the fire bombs burned out radio instruments.

"The Japs in the Marianas furnished a testing-board for the development of the bomb used by the B-29's to burn so many Japanese cities to the ground," Sanders said.

While American troops and planes rained hell on the Marianas Japs, other American planes smashed enemy troops and installations all the way from the Kurile Islands in the North Pacific to New Guinea and the Solomons to prevent the enemy from reinforcing their garrisons in the Central Pacific.

At the same time the Navy hit Iwo and the Bonins, and B-24's of the 11th Bomb Group neutralized Truk, preventing the Japs on the Pacific Gibraltar from supporting their besieged Marianas forces.

By July 1 American ground forces had captured one-fourth of Garapan. On the following day the ruined city was surrounded on three sides by our forces who had captured heights overlooking Tanapag harbor three miles beyond. On the east coast of the island foot soldiers pushed to within five and a half miles of the island's northern tip, where two smaller air strips were still under Jap control.

On the 4th of July, Garapan and Tanapag with its important harbor was captured. Seven-eighths of Saipan was ours.

In this action, four P-47's, piloted by Captain Robert F. Touhey, Jr., and Lieutenants Robert G. O'Hara, Louis G. Clark and Earl H. Harbour, played a major role in making it possible for the Infantry to break through.

The foot soldiers were being held up by the Japs about two and a half miles northeast of Garapan. The Thunderbolts dived through heavy enemy automatic fire from the ground and made their attack. Shortly afterward they received this message:

"Thanks for making the strafing attack. Results excellent. Troops have driven ahead 200 yards as result."

On another of these missions, Captain Robert T. Viles, and Lieutenants Richard B. Rhody, Henry M. Stampe and Stanley J. Lustic, exhibited marksmanship that would have fitted well in a "Dead-Eye Dick" yarn.

The Marine troops were so close to the Japs that it made firing from the air extremely dangerous, but the Leathernecks directed the P-47's to the pinpoint target. Then the footsoldiers ducked and prayed.

Thirty-two Thunderbolt guns chopped away in a screaming crescendo that ripped the Jap positions to shreds. And they were so close above our own lines that dug-in Marines were showered with empty shells from the P-47 guns!

A few minutes later jubilant ground observers notified 318th Headquarters that the Marines had successfully broken through.

Lieutenant "Smiling" Jack Shoemaker of Portland, Oregon, who flew thirty missions during the Marianas operations, was another Thunderbolt pilot who helped the Marines out of a tough spot.

"The Japs had massed about a thousand reserves in a small valley and the Marines were having a tough time getting at them," said Shoemaker, a flight leader.

"My flight was called in to rough 'em up a bit and we headed over the valley. It was about two miles long and a natural for bombing, so our four planes — each carrying two 500-pounders — went to work.

"Flying the length of the valley we dropped our bombs two at a time, sort of dividing the target into four separate sections. Then we strafed the Nips with our machine guns, making two runs over the valley. The Marines then moved in and completed the job."

The Bar Flies' ground crewmen, who had been through all the action in the early part of the campaign, also got in on the ending.

On the night of June 7, two days before the island was declared secure, the weary crewmen had just climbed out of their foxholes after one of the nightly raids of "Bed Check Charley." Suddenly shells, fired from a Jap big gun on Tinian began bursting all around.

A pattern of fire was laid through the tents by shells timed to go off overhead and hit unprotected men with shrapnel.

A piece of shrapnel cut through one tent and ripped through a helmet, a stack of letters, a mosquito net, six thicknesses of blanket and broke a bottle of Bromo-Seltzer. The helmet fell from a box cutting the back of Staff Sergeant Orrin Madsen of Salt Lake City, Utah.

Casualty rates were miraculous. Only three men were wounded and one, Private Leopold Duhamel, was killed.

Through a continuous twenty-four-hour schedule of snipings, bombings, shellings, and strafings, the Bar Flies kept their planes 99 percent in flying commission. As a result, the pilots were able to fly more than 80 sorties per day. And, in spite of the fact that the flyers sometimes kept their planes in the air eight hours a day, only one ship was out of commission for as long as twenty-four hours!

Shortly before the island was declared secure, on July 9, more than 1,500 laughing, banzai-screaming Japs broke through the American lines. Drunk with fanaticism and fear, the enemy soldiers killed American wounded and took their weapons to turn on our ground troops. They had pushed all the way to the sea before we rallied and wiped them out.

The final phase of operation against organized resistance came after the "secure" signal had been given.

On the northwest shore was a pocket of Jap soldiers and civilians. A public address system was set up and every effort was made to persuade the Saipan natives to surrender. Some came out, only to be shot by Jap soldiers. Finally our ground troops pushed in.

Then they witnessed a dreadful sight.

Terrified Saipan natives killed their wives and children by putting scissors down their throats and opening them! Women threw their babies off the cliff and then followed them to death on the rocks below. Some committed hara-kiri. Some surrendered, but the Japs, with tales of American prisoner torture, had driven scores to their death.

Most of the Jap soldiers, as usual, refused to surrender but fought to the end.

Primary assignment for the Seventh's fighter planes was to protect the island from enemy air attacks. Thunderbolt pilots, however, failed to encounter a single Jap raider during the entire Saipan operations and were kept busy at supporting ground troops.

The Jap raider chores fell to the Sixth Night Fighter Squadron. This group brought the famous P-61 "Black Widows" into action for the first time in the Central Pacific.

Lieutenant Dale F. Haberman encountered the first Jap raider on the night of June 27th.

"I met a dive bombing Kate about 40 miles north of Rota and pulled to within 400 feet before I fired," said Haberman. "Ninety rounds went into him and I plainly saw fire entering his right wing and fuselage. But somehow, just at that time, my cockpit lights were turned on and while I was blinded for a moment, he disappeared. I was certain I got him, but since I didn't see him go down I only got a 'probable' out of it.

"On July 14th, however, I didn't lost sight of the one I hit.

"I was flying at 7,000 feet and found two Jap planes. I could see that one was a twin-engined Betty and the other a small fighter. I closed in to about 1,200 feet of the Betty and cut loose with 134 rounds of 20 mm. fire and saw the plane burst into flames behind the left engine. Then it exploded and crashed to the ground. The fighter got away," Haberman said.

On the night of July 6, the twin-engined Black Widows got two more.

"Lieutenant Francis C. Eaton had shot down one Betty when another began bombing us," Lieutenant Jerome Hansen said.

"Lieutenant William K. Wallace, my observer, and I hopped in our plane and took off, but by the time we got up he was 25 miles away, running for home. I chased him for 70 miles before I caught up. There was a bright moon and he could see us all during the chase.

"Finally I began closing in on his tail and he cut loose at me.

"I ducked away and came in about 100 feet below and 300 feet behind and began firing. His left engine caught fire and it was necessary to pull up and to the right to avoid a collision. I expected him to go down immediately but then the fire began to die.

"Just as I was about to blast him again, he exploded and fell into the ocean."

From June 22 through July 17, the P-47's flew 2,500 sorties totaling more than 4,000 hours. Two hundred and sixty tons of bombs were dropped, 500 rockets and 530,000 rounds of .50 caliber ammunition were fired.

The Japs on Guam received a pounding from carrier-based planes for 17 straight days before the invasion. Battleships moved in close and shelled the islands for four days while other warships hit the island for nine.

Fire from Jap shore batteries gradually grew less and after July 16 stopped altogether. No enemy planes were seen over the island after July 7 when nine enemy fighters, apparently trying to fly to Yap, were shot down.

On July 20, the Third and Fourth Marine Divisions and the 77th Infantry Division stormed ashore. Within fifteen minutes they had raised the flag on the first United States territory recaptured from the Japs in the Central Pacific.

There was little resistance to the landing and in a short time our forces were in control of the beaches on either side of Port Apra where they cut off the Orote Peninsula in the west and then drove to the eastern coast.

The Japanese had withdrawn to such high ground as Mount Barrigada, where they were dug in strongly. Agana, the capital, had been reduced to ruins by the pre-invasion shelling.

As this was going on, Tinian was being prepared for invasion. Thunderbolts, for the first time during the Marianas campaign, were assigned to carry two 1,000-pound bombs apiece, and Major McAfee led a flight of these heavily loaded fighters across the channel.

From Saipan the mechanics could see the planes they had recently serviced make their diving runs on Tinian town. A few seconds later they could see puffs of smoke followed by muffled reverberations as the big bombs went in.

Ninety percent of all bombs were in the target area!

At 6:45 on the morning of July 24th, Major McAfee and another pilot guided the Second and Fourth Marines ashore on Tinian.

Flying at low altitude and in plainly marked planes, the two pilots would fly their directing course. Then they would turn back, coming in over the assault boats, and fly in again so the first waves of troops would know exactly where to land. These pathfinding sweeps were kept up until the Marines, who had done so well on Saipan, landed at their correct beaches.

Tinian, with fewer mountain and forests than Guam or Saipan, was harder for the Japs to defend. Japs without caves and jungles were usually lost.

The Thunderbolts flew continuous strikes from dawn to dusk. Twenty tons of bombs were dropped on the beaches. Ridge areas above the beachheads were bathed with 10,000 gallons of napalm fire that wiped out machine gun, mortar and trench positions.

Lieutenant Shoemaker, who had done a Jap-exterminating job in a Saipan valley, transferred his activities to an enemy ammunition dump on Tinian.

And his job was so successful that he almost eliminated himself!

"I was flying on a low level strafing mission when I spotted a concrete building hidden in a grove of trees," said Shoemaker. "Near the building was what looked like a tarpaulin-covered supply dump, so I went in at 200 feet and started shooting it up.

"Suddenly the damned thing blew up in front of me. I was too close and going too fast to do anything but go right through it.

"I was boosted about 300 feet straight up and was really lucky to get through alive, for observers say the explosion threw debris more than 2,000 feet in the air. There were plenty of rocks and debris in my cowling but no serious damage. That Thunderbolt is a rugged plane!"

For that mission Shoemaker's fellow pilots nicknamed him "Smiling Jack — the Ace of the Base."

On the morning of July 23, Captain E. D. Black, of the "forgotten" 41st Bomber Group, landed on Saipan followed by ten more B-2 5's of that group.

Three days later, Major William K. Pfingst led the twin-engine Mitchells in on a low-level strafing mission to support the Tinian action and then the B-25's joined in the strike against Guam.

On Guam our forces were slugging through the woods and caves. Bloody Sugar Bluff was won on July 26, and on July 28 Orote airport, one of the most important of all objectives on the island, was captured.

The 4700-foot airfield was littered with wrecked Jap bombers and fighters. Seventy-six damaged enemy planes were removed and within six hours after its capture engineers had the runway ready for torpedo bombers.

On July 31st Tinian fell, and Major McAfee, the first to land his P-47 on Saipan, was the first to hit the Tinian strip. Guam was declared secure on August 10.

The entire operations cost us 4,679 killed. Of this total we lost 3,100 on Saipan, 1,289 on Guam and 290 on Tinian.

American bombs and shells killed more than 40,000 Japs!

From June 22 through July 31, weary Seventh AF pilots flew more than 4,500 hours. During this period they flew 762 strafing sorties, 1,322 bombing-strafing sorties, 74 firebomb-strafing sorties and 1,796 combat patrols.

The Japs on the doomed islands were hit with 532 tons of bombs, deluged with 2 1,000 gallons of liquid napalm fire, and riddled with more than 1,700,000 rounds of .50 caliber machine gun bullets.

The P-47's and B-25's played a tremendously important role in the Marianas campaign. For their role in the action they received five commendations from the Marines, Army and Navy.

One of these issued by Lieutenant General Holland M. Smith, of the Marines, and Vice Admiral Kelly Turner, of the Navy, read:

"We send a hearty 'well done' to the men in the Seventh Air Forces who have provided our overhead cover and effectively slashed the enemy on Saipan, Guam and Tinian. All of us have been greatly impressed with your eagerness to do what we have asked you to do.

"When we walk down the Ginza in Tokyo en route to Hirohito's palace, we hope that you will supply the overhead guard for us."

The Marianas, the Marines and the Navy were ours!

CHAPTER XIX: "THE LITTLE GUYS"

WINNING THE MARIANAS WAS ONE THING, TURNING THEM into a springboard for the final B-29 air assault against Japan was something else.

It was the first time men in the Central Pacific, who had played a long engagement in the flat atoll circuit, faced jungles.

From these fever-ridden pest-holes of Saipan and Guam came swarms of malaria-bearing mosquitoes and nightly raids from remnants of the Jap garrisons who came to kill, sabotage and steal.

And these cocoanut-tree morasses were supposed to be turned into heavy bomber bases — a feat which Radio Tokyo scoffed at nightly as an impossibility — and a smooth-functioning advance headquarters base.

From Saipan, Guam and Tinian, correspondents transmitted thousands of words of copy on the pilots "who flew into the sunset to blast and burn Japan out of the war . . ."

But little was written and less published on the men who made these strikes possible — the weary Aviation Engineers, the greasy ground crews, the island-hopping pencil-jockeys, the G. I. medical technicians and scores of other "little" men who made up the Seventh Air Force.

Some of their stories, inscribed in official Army phraseology, were duly recorded (in triplicate of course) by the weary pencil-pushers. But most of these have long since vanished into that mysterious maze known as "Going Through Channels."

So the stories of these men, for the most part, were written with bulldozers and monkey wrenches on the mud of untouched forests and the fuselages of shot-up planes. They were inscribed in the invisible ink of oxygen and morphine administered to thousands of wounded men evacuated from battle fronts by the forgotten enlisted medical technicians.

A few G. I. correspondents, who wrote many of the "glamour" stories regularly mimeographed for, distributed to, and released by Navy-headquartered reporters, saw some of the epics recorded by these little men.

So, fortunately, a few remain.

Staff Sergeant Bob Price, who was there, wrote:

"Today this tableland site on Saipan is covered with an airstrip built by the 805th Engineers in 17 days in an area only a half mile from the battle lines.

"Their surveyors traveled in halftracks, carrying .50 calibre guns in one hand and transits in the other.

"Following them were other engineers with 90 vehicles, 80 pieces of heavy machinery, 37 mm. guns, 1,800 crates and boxes (the total weighing more than 9,000 tons). They made their way over the treacherous roads to the high windswept site that was to be an airfield.

"The men were put on 'two hour call,' which meant that they were subject to order to hold up front line positions while assault troops reform.

"From this beginning, working night and day, the engineers completed an airstrip 5,000 feet long and 300 feet wide. This has a packed-solid 10-inch-thick top and seven and nine-feet fillings were made at both ends of the field.

"During this period they also constructed a tank farm to hold more than 40,000 gallons of gasoline, sealines, distillation units, a control tower, a coral pit that produces 2,000 yards of coral per day, a communications setup, an orderly campsite and a chain of usable roads.

"Such changing of the earth's face appalled the Saipan natives. A family of five, hiding in the hills when the engineers went to work, were captured and brought back. They couldn't believe their eyes.

"They saw the night shift operating the graders, carryalls, tractors, Diesel rollers, trenchers and graders on the spot that had been untouched a short time ago.

"The outfit's 37 mm. guns stood guard against enemy breakthrough or infiltration. Each piece of machinery was mounted with a searchlight that cut the night with a powerful beam.

"Engineers, wearing campaign hats with red engineer cards, rode the big machinery with rifles at arm's reach. There was the scream of brakes, knocking of gears and the slow chatter of generators. Coral flowed from dump trucks; heavy iron blades and rollers crushed it into place. Sea water flooded the field to make the strip compact.

"The native family saw it but still couldn't believe that these strange, masterful giants had won and changed their land in a matter of days. They sat by the runway and jabbered, trying to understand the miracle."

On D-plus-10 the 805th Engineers arrived on Saipan to join the 804th. The 806th and 1878th arrived on D-plus-45 and the 1894th landed 15 days later.

At Guam the 1885th and 1886th arrived on D-plus-10. The 1889th, 1895th, 1887th, 845th and 1899th arrived soon afterwards to be followed by the 1863rd, 1864th, 1868th and 1869th.

Tinian bases were constructed by the Seabees.

On Saipan these groups took part in the construction of Isely Field, Kagman Point Field and Kobler Field. On Guam they joined in the building of North Field, Northwest Field and Depot Field.

All through the Marianas, construction engineers faced deadlines that would have been regarded as impossible under the best peacetime conditions, much less under the wartime handicaps faced by the bulldozer brigades.

Schedules called for completing a B-29 base on Saipan in a little over 90 days.

The Superfortresses, with a gross weight of 135,000 pounds, require runaways at least 8,500 feet long and 200 feet wide — an area almost twice as great as the 150 by 6,000-foot strips used by the Liberators.

At Isely Field the final stage of development called for two parallel B-29 runways with 150-foot shoulders, six miles of taxi-ways, two 300 by 1,950 foot service aprons (each almost as large in area as most fighter strips formerly were), 390,000 square feet of warm-up aprons, and 180 hardstands, each 140 feet in diameter.

For this construction, about 30,000,000 square feet had to be cleared and graded, and about 10,000,000 square feet of this area paved. In addition, the engineers had to provide storage for 188,000 barrels of aviation gasoline and ready tank storage for 40,000 gallons.

In constructing the runways the engineers had little choice of location. For fighter planes and even for ordinary bombers a runway can be shifted slightly out of line from the prevailing winds to avoid such obstructions as ravines or bluffs. But for B-29's the runway must line up with the winds, and ravines must be filled in and bluffs cut down.

Topsoil was never more than a foot above the hard coral rock sub-surface, and over great areas there was no topsoil at all. The rock was too hard to be torn up by medium rooters; the grading job called for heavy rooters augmented by constant dynamite blasting.

And weather was another tough obstacle.

Rains made quagmires of the roads, weakening front springs on 2 ½ and 4-ton trucks. Mud worked its way into the transmissions of all vehicles and choked the steel runners of the half-tracks.

On Guam, deadlines, weather and general conditions were just as bad. And there was even more jungle than on Saipan.

There was heat and sudden, drenching rains. The men worked 12-hour shifts. They lived in the jungle in tents with dirt floors, ate K and C Rations and watched nearby Navy personnel move about in comfortable quonset huts with electric lights and cooling showers.

But, somehow, through it all they were kept going by a sense of humor.

Their attitude about the holed-up Japs, for instance.

The jungles that spelled so much misery for the engineers was a break for the Jap troops that were well organized and lived in well-concealed bivouac areas all over the island.

The fanatic Nips, some who even today are still hiding in the Guam jungles, murdered scores of Americans at work and on sightseeing trips through the island. Yet, because they were Japs, they did a million unpredictable things, and from these eccentricities the engineers drew the stories with which they later welcomed the Johnny-Come-Latelies from Hickam and Hamilton Fields.

Many of these newcomers from the rear echelons, who came down after the fighting was past and Guam had been built into a teeming base, were natural pickings for the veteran engineers.

No one knew the exact origin of these stories and not everyone believed them, but they made the rounds and were excellent fodder with which to greet the flood of newcomers from the rear echelons. Arriving long after the island had been secured and built into a teeming base, the rookies, many of whom arrived armed to the teeth, were ready, willing and even eager to believe that there was a Jap hiding behind every tree and garbage can.

One of the best yarns had to do with one of the squadrons building a runway at North Field. Working near the edge of the jungle one morning, some of the engineers were startled to discover two Japs sitting astride the fence bordering the field.

The Japs, tattered from months of hiding in the jungle, were having a helluva time sidewalk superintending the construction job. They dropped from the fence and scampered off through the jungle when one of the men on a bulldozer reached for his rifle.

On the following day the Japs were back, boldly hanging over the fence with the same fascination people in large cities have for excavating projects. And the engineers, quite pleased to be working for an appreciative audience, kept an eye on them but permitted them to remain.

The Nips, who must have had their own two-man reveille, showed up promptly each morning and stayed throughout most of the day — evidently enjoying the show hugely. It got to a point that the engineers felt a little lonely when their audience would suddenly disappear into the jungle.

One morning the Japs failed to appear and the engineers, consummate hams by now, lost a little of their zing. They brooded but assured themselves that their audience would return the following morning. The Nips, however, never came back, and the engineers never quit speculating over what happened.

The thought that the Japs might have deserted them to watch the Seabees was too horrible to contemplate, so they think their fans were captured or killed and were always a little bitter about it.

Another of the favorite sagas was of the Jap who was a rabid baseball fan. One Brooklyn engineer even vowed that he'd seen the little Nip working at a Japanese restaurant on Flatbush Avenue and remembered seeing him at several games at Ebbets Field before the war.

This Jap turned out for every game played by one engineering squadron and sat on a bare hill overlooking the diamond, alternately cheering the engineers and raising hell with the umpires.

Whenever a decision went against the engineers, the Jap would jump up and scream something which, roughly translated, seemed to mean "Kill the blankety-blank so-and-so."

One day the engineers were playing the Seabees and the game was going on inning after inning with the score tied. Finally an engineer caught a Seabee curve squarely and blasted it down the left field foul line. The umpire took one squint and then called the runner back — foul ball!

This was too much for the Dodger-bred Jap. He jumped to his feet, screaming curses in Japanese, and grabbed a piece of coral. Winding up like a sandlot pitcher, he beaned the umpire and then took off over the hill, followed only by the cheers of the engineer rooting section.

Later a Marine patrol — which the engineers vow was egged on by the Seabees — shot the Jap.

The 854th Engineers on Guam were active participants in numerous Jap shenanigans.

One night a chaplain attached to the outfit was awakened by a noise to find a Jap sitting on his footlocker calmly trying on G. I. shoes. Being unarmed, the chaplain lay quietly while the Nip found a pair that suited his fancy. Then he saw his visitor calmly disappear into the darkness.

On another occasion an 854th Guard, armed with a sub-machinegun, was standing guard while a group was erecting a tank farm. Suddenly he saw a fat chicken come scurrying out of the underbrush and, thinking in terms of a dinner substitute for the eternal spam, cut loose at the fowl. He missed the chicken, but a white flag suddenly appeared from the bushes followed by five gaunt and frightened Nips.

On another morning a Jap soldier climbed up a steep cliff to surrender to an 854th quarrying crew. The engineers were embarrassed when a quick search revealed that they had brought no weapons. The Jap didn't seem to mind, however, and meekly crawled into a jeep to be driven to a stockade maintained by the Island Command.

Jap-taking, as a by-product of engineering, was one thing, but any other form of Jap-hunting, two 854th men learned, was looked upon with an officially jaundiced eye.

One day two of the men of this squadron were invited to visit the ranch of a Guam native. While there, they flushed and killed two Japs. As punishment the commanding officer made the two engineers return to the ranch and bury the bodies.

On Saipan, too, the unpredictable Nips pulled some screwy deals.

Private First Class Bud Nelson told of one of these: "One night while the men were attending a movie, a score or so of the enemy invaded the tent area and made off with as mixed-up a collection of equipment as could be dreamed up by a Section-8 Quartermaster Officer.

"Included in the loot were B-4 bags, officers' dress uniforms (how in God's name dress uniforms were to be used on Saipan I'll never know), Christmas packages, a few pistols, bedding, blankets and a batch of books.

"The books included Ibsen's 'Plays'; E. B. White's 'One Man's Meat'; Thoreau's 'Walden'; Mark Twain's 'Life on the Mississippi'; Gene Fowler's 'Good Night, Sweet Prince'; and Clarence Darrow's 'For the Defense.'

"Evidently the bibliophile from the Rising Sinners took time out to read the titles as he departed and decided that, under the circumstances one text was useless to him. He threw away 'For the Defense.' which was found about 50 yards from the area.

"It was a couple of days later before the Marines and a part of the garrison forces came upon the Jap book-worms, who were rendezvousing in a cove below the area. Most of the stolen property was found there.

"But the amazing part of the story concerns a highly secretive individual in our midst who had been carrying around all sorts of super-secret papers. As a matter of fact he told me his assignment was so secret that they hadn't even told him what it was.

"Anyway, some of those hush-hush papers were included in the loot and when they were recovered it was discovered that the reverse side was covered with Jap writing.

"These were rushed to a translator and Intelligence waited with a palpitating heart while the interpreter deciphered the Jap jottings.

"After reading a few pages the translator threw the copy aside and grinned.

"'This guy was writing a detective story,' he announced. 'A very lousy detective story, I might add.'"

In addition to the mud, forests and Japs, the engineers in the Marianas were faced with another handicap which they found even harder to combat — mosquitoes!

The most extensive epidemic of dengue of the war hit late in the summer. The fever made its appearance soon after the assault but during the first few weeks there were relatively few cases because the rainy season hadn't begun and mosquitoes weren't numerous.

But with the beginning of the rainy season on August 1, fever-bearing mosquitoes became abundant and it was reliably estimated that on Saipan alone, there had been more than 20,000 cases of dengue before the epidemic was brought under control.

Handling this epidemic was a terrific problem because combat operations had left a multitude of insect breeding places in tin cans, shell cases and battle rubble. And men on the island were already engaged in so much other backbreaking work that large-scale assignment to extra details to fight this new foe was impractical. Conditions became so bad that anyone going through the area who hadn't been immunized by a recent attack was almost sure to contract it.

A C-47 transport plane was fitted to carry six 53-gallon drums of DDT and mechanism to spray this deadliest insecticide ever produced. It was the first large-scale use of DDT in the war.

Captain Fredericks M. Wilkes, of the Transport Air Group, was pilot and Lieutenant John L. Maloney was co-pilot. Master Sergeant Robert R. Wells and Staff Sergeant Frank J. Petschar handled the spraying mechanism.

"We'd sweep back and forth over the island at levels from 35 to 50 feet," said Wilkes. "In the first nine days we flew 31 missions and sprayed 8,600 gallons of DDT over a total of 15,650 acres on Saipan. At the same time applications of DDT residual spray was begun in all tents and living quarters of hospitals and AAF and garrison troops."

The epidemic reached a peak on September 15 but by the end of September hospital cases on Saipan had been reduced to 44 and by October 6 they had dropped to 23.

But in spite of epidemics and other major handicaps, the engineers completed their assignments. They didn't always get credit for the things they did. For instance, Navy-released pictures appeared in Life magazine claiming Guam fields as Seabee projects.

The engineers, who fought the Guam jungles, were a little surprised to learn that they hadn't been there.

But Army-Navy administration caprices which gave the credit to somebody else were an old story to the Aviation Engineers. As old as Baker Island.

The 804th Squadron had gone into Baker Island back in 1943 on a practice invasion and prepared the field used to soften up the Gilberts. It was a top-secret operation. The Japs never knew we were there.

Two Marine observers, neither of whom ever got off the boat, came along on these maneuvers. Later, when the story could be released, the amazed engineers read a magazine story that gave the Marines credit for the whole show!

It didn't help morale!

Of all the overlooked "little men" in a forgotten air force in a neglected theater, the enlisted medical technicians stand near the top of the list.

They were a part of the air evacuation teams, consisting of two flight nurses and one male technician, who tended the wounded being evacuated to rear base hospitals in Hawaii and San Francisco.

These technicians of the 809th and 812th Squadrons arrived in time for the Gilberts campaign and remained for the duration. They flew in the big two and four-engined transport planes and, on the long drags from the

Gilberts, Marshalls and Marianas, saved the lives of scores of wounded by administering oxygen, plasma and penicillin in flight.

Later they also flew from Hawaii to Australia to pick up a load of wounded, flew back to Hawaii, and then to San Francisco. More than 7,000 miles — and most of it over water.

These Seventh AF men were called "Pacific Wanderers" and "Vagabonds." These were apt names for these orphans. From the beginning, the single fact that they were men kept them in the shadow of the more glamorous flight nurses.

They were farmed-out to the Air Transport Command, and, like most men on detached service, received few promotions.

But most of them were philosophical about headlines and the other "breaks." After tending so many men whose legs, arms and faces had been shot away, they realized how unimportant headlines can be.

Technicians attended Air Evacuation School at Bowman Field, Kentucky, where they learned the things required of flight nurses, for on regular trips they administered plasma, oxygen, and gave all the other treatments given by nurses. And when the planes went into battle regions they took over completely; women, of course, were not scheduled for flights until an island was secured.

These men flew an average of 350 hours for every three-month period. Army pilots, for a like period, are limited to 300 hours flying time.

The worth of these technicians was never more graphically illustrated than during the Marianas campaign. During the month of July alone, more than 1,500 wounded were evacuated from the strip at Saipan.

"Many of these injured men would have died if they hadn't been rushed to rear base hospitals," said Major Andrew D. Henderson, of Mobile, Alabama, commanding officer of the 809th Squadron.

"Badly wounded men could be rushed back to Hawaii in a short time through the medium of air transportation. There and in San Francisco, in well equipped hospitals, they could be given the best plastic surgery and the most advanced medical treatment in the world."

The first air evacuation plane went into Saipan on D-plus-10.

"When we received orders for this first flight, I called all the men of the 812th together and told them the story," said Major Dominick Lasasso, then commanding officer of the squadron.

"They knew that they would fly down on an unarmed, unescorted plane and land in the middle of a battle. Yet, when I called for a single volunteer, the entire squadron stepped forward. Lots were then drawn and Technician Third Grade Victor Mitchell of St. Louis, Missouri, won."

"Our plane arrived after dark and fighting was still going on all around us," said Mitchell. "All night we were under constant Jap fire and this prevented us from loading and taking off until the following morning.

"This time lapse was unusual, however, for we usually landed, loaded, and were ready to take off in an hour and a half."

These wandering men of the Seventh AF flew under almost constant adverse weather conditions in the unpredictable Central Pacific. They learned more about psychology than most students do in class rooms from handling mentally disturbed men and badly wounded men who, during flights through the sudden tropical storms, had to be "talked-out" of going into shock.

The technicians, especially when working with flight nurses, had to be eternally watchful, for men with battle-shattered minds might suddenly go berserk and do almost anything.

"It was especially difficult when we were carrying a load of badly wounded men and ran into bad weather," said Technician Third Grade Raymond Netzel.

"Everything would be going smoothly and then we'd hit a storm front. The plane might suddenly shoot a couple of thousand feet up or down. Then you'd have to appear nonchalant and kid the patients, for fear could throw a man into shock — and shock can bring death very quickly."

During the campaign these orphans probably learned more about the different branches of service than any other G.I.'s in the Air Forces. They evacuated Army, Navy and Marine personnel of all rank. And they worked in planes flown by pilots of the 7th AF, the Transport Air Group, ATC and Marines.

"Most of them were swell," said Technician Third Grade Raymond Fischer. "Anything necessary for the patients they'd do. On one of my trips from Saipan I had a number of patients with head injuries and for several hours the pilot kept the plane 50 feet above the water so as to not cause discomfort for the injured. The radio operators and co-pilots often came back and assisted us."

Flying unarmed over Jap islands was no cinch, either.

"On one trip out from Tarawa," said Private Ted Newman, first medical technician into Kwajalein, "our pilot, by mistake, flew over Mille. Guns from the ground cut loose at us, and although no one was injured we later found bullets lodged in the life raft in the rear of the plane."

On another flight a C-54 hospital plane, enroute from Tarawa to Canton, lost two engines and had to limp into Canton on the remaining two. The 23 patients and technician were loaded into a Navy PBY and the flight continued.

"But such cases were the exception," said Technician Third Class Myron Lamb, who, at the time, had more flying hours than any other man in the 812th.

"Usually the mechanics of the flight were routine. We took off from Hickam Field, flew to a battle station and picked up our patients. But the trips were never dull, for each patient was entirely different. You had to know exactly when to administer morphine, plasma, sulfa or penicillin. Some men could be kidded out of going into shock. Some guys just wanted to talk and if you were a good audience you could help by just listening."

How well these men covered the Central Pacific was demonstrated in a scene at Saipan where Technician Third Class Foster was preparing to take off with a load of patients for Oahu.

Foster had a cigarette lighter inscribed with a log of the islands to which he had flown on evacuation trips. His list included Saipan, Guam, Leyte, Roi, Guadalcanal, New Guinea, Funafuti, Makin, Kwajalein, Johnston, Christmas, Apamama and Engibi.

"I'm running out of space now," said Foster. "Either I have to get a larger lighter or start carrying two of them around."

Another lost outfit in this theater was the Transport Air Group. They were, in fact, so "lost" that they were never quite sure for whom they were working.

"Hell," said one of the TAG officials, "one day we were taking orders from the Air Forces, the next day we were flying for the Navy, and then the Marines would shoot us an order.

"On August 1, we evacuated 200 casualties from Tinian to Saipan and on August 7 we set up the regular Saipan-Guam air evacuation service. During the first ten days after we moved into Guam we'd evacuated more than 1,500 wounded, and for the month moved 2,083 from that island."

These pilots flew the first cargo planes into every island in the Central Pacific. They also moved some of the most diversified cargo, including new parts for heavy engineering equipment to be used by the Aviation Engineers, anchor chains for Navy ships, blood plasma for the Marines and

— the gem of all — a pre-fabricated latrine that was flown into Saipan, soon after the island was secured, for the private use of a high ranking officer!

When the Bar Flies, which was a typical Seventh AF group as far as living conditions were concerned, came into Saipan, they pitched their puptents in a half-burned field of sugar cane and kafir corn. Down the slope toward the sea were trees and someone told them that there were seacliff caves nearby which were infested with Japs.

Revetments of salmon-pink earth stood around them, giving good protection for infiltrating snipers. There they planted their shelter-halves and dug foxholes right by the front entrance.

By day there were red ants and by night there were huge landcrabs, flying foxes, mosquitoes and lizards.

All building materials had to be salvaged from the half-destroyed Jap farmhouses. The pilots' first ready-room was under a captured Jap tent.

At first the men ate off low crates with K-Ration boxes for seats. Flies and ants were thick and men ate with one hand and fanned flies with the other.

Another good story told by the veterans to newly-arrived personnel had to do with the eating situation.

"Hell, you never had it so good," the old timers would quip when the new men griped at the C-Ration-spam diets. "When we came down on the invasion it was really tough. At first we were kinda particular and took time to pick the ants out of the K-Rations. Then we'd just sort of brush them off and start eating. Then we got to where we'd just eat and let the ants look out for themselves. Finally it reached a point that when the ants started crawling off we'd catch 'em and put them back in the food where they belonged!"

Conditions were more or less the same on Guam and Saipan.

Clerks set up their administrative offices on boxes, and portable typewriters began to pound out reams of "triplicate" copy.

Souvenir hunters had a field day and great heaps of wrecked Jap planes were picked as clean as skeletons in a desert. Samurai swords sold from $100 to $300, Jap flags from five dollars up and a pair of officers' binoculars sold for $40. A 1907 American five-dollar bill, bearing Constance Bennett's signature and taken from a Jap pilot who crashed on the field, brought $25.

Marines did a brisk business in cowbells, lewd Jap postcards, pistols and goodluck charms.

The seemingly inherent American characteristic of souvenir seeking caused the deaths of many men in the Central Pacific.

Three clerks of the Seventh AF, wandering in the hills of Saipan on July 26, escaped this fate but it took one of the strangest accidents of the war to save them. The men involved were Technical Sergeant Albert F. Parsons, a survivor of the Pearl Harbor attack and sergeant major of his fighter group; Corporal Clifford E. Gilham, operations clerk; and Technical Sergeant Ellis E. Shelhamer, a personnel clerk.

"We had a few hours off and were walking along a jungle trail near the top of Mt. Topatchau when we saw someone walking ahead of us," said Parsons.

"Thinking he was one of our group, we yelled. He turned and we saw he was a Jap.

"We fired and saw him go to his knees and then fall behind a boulder. We surrounded the spot and closed in.

"Suddenly all hell broke loose. An American sniper patrol was nearby and they thought we were Japs and cut loose at us with machine guns, automatic rifles, carbines and hand grenades.

"We were in a tough spot for we were pinned down with no way of identifying ourselves.

"Then the damnedest thing happened. A hidden Jap machine crew, also mistaking us for Nips, cut loose at our patrol on the nearby ridge.

"This fire-coverage gave us protection and we got the hell out of there.

"From then on," he said, "we bought our souvenirs from the Marines!"

An informal Jap-hunt, by drivers of the 27th Bombardment Squadron of the 30th Bomb Group, almost got the enlisted personnel involved in trouble. But, it too, had a happy ending.

Staff Sergeant Hudson H. Paddock, Sergeant Glenden R. Burrowes, Corporal Pat R. Deleretta, Private First Class Desmond L. Walker and Private Richard M. Richards were the men who took part.

"For some time we had been missing G. I. equipment from our outfit and we figured that Japs were responsible so we rounded up a patrol to search the woods about 500 yards south of our squadron area," said Burrowes.

"When we got into the wooded area we split up, and as Richards and I walked along we saw a Jap bivouac area. We sneaked up with our guns ready and spotted three Japs in the camp.

"They saw us and ran, refusing to halt when we yelled, so we cut loose and killed two of them. The other was hit but disappeared in the woods.

"We beat the woods for him and a Marine patrol with dogs looked, too, but weren't able to find him.

"The camp contained a rifle, pistol, knives, enough rice to last the three Japs a month, and stolen Marine equipment that included mess kits and canteens."

For this officially frowned-on pastime the men were sternly reprimanded. Then they were called up and decorated!

Staff Sergeant Harry Bozarth, of the 41st Bomb Group, captured four Japanese while visiting a temple on Saipan.

"Special Service was taking a truckload of us on sightseeing tour of the island on our day off and we stopped to look at a ruined Jap temple," said Bozarth.

"I was the first of our group to reach the top of the flight of some 100 steps that reached the temple. The structure had been ruined by the shelling and dead Japs were lying all around.

"Suddenly one of the fellows on the way up yelled that he saw something in the bushes. I whirled and saw a Jap soldier partially hidden behind a clump of bushes.

"I raised my gun but suddenly remembered that there was no shell in the chamber. My hands were shaking and my knees wobbling for I realized that I was a perfect target. I fumbled with the bolt and finally got a shell in the chamber.

"The Jap was only about ten feet away and looking straight into my barrel. As I was about to fire, an officer in our party told me to hold it, so I motioned for the Jap to come out. He came out, hands over his head — followed by three other Japs I hadn't even seen.

"A search of the place revealed enough weapons and ammunition to have given us all a bad time. Why they didn't use them, I'll never know!"

Keeping clean was one of the main problems in the Marianas. One of the pencil-pushers of the 11th Bomb Group on Guam wrote:

"Morale dipped to its lowest ebb when we first arrived here. Everyone worked long and hard and there wasn't too much complaining about having to stand up to eat, sleeping without bedding or mosquito nets, but the shortage of water for drinking and bathing drove you crazy.

"And as soon as we got water and everyone could take a bath morale bounded back."

On Saipan the same conditions existed. From there, another soldier set down these immortal words:

"Water has had the highest priority. For the length of this long battle we have been waiting for rain. The dust has piled up in the roads and the wells and cisterns are running dry.

"Finally the rains came. For a couple of early morning hours the thirsty earth sucked in the water and a cool breeze blew across the plateau.

"Then, in the middle of the heaviest rain, the first two watering wagons seen on this island came up the road, flooding the mud that was already two inches deep.

"We don't know where they got the water. Here we haven't even been able to take showers or wash clothes. Still, they completed their watering project in the midst of a heavy rain.

"There is something grand about War!"

Ingenuity, that saved the lives and added to the comfort to so many Americans at war, helped make the Marianas more livable.

Clerks and mechanics rigged up windmills from salvaged Jap materials and made their own washing machines. This seemingly universal American characteristic also solved the problem of cold drinking water in the humid islands.

Each time the Thunderbolt pilots took off there was a long line of men waiting with canteens. Wrapped in a wet cloth and hung over the cockpit cooling vent, a canteen of the most tepid water, taken to 20,000 feet altitude, could be cooled to stateside taste.

Ingenuity, a sense of humor and a good knowledge of soldier psychology solved many problems. One of the most amusing had to do with the job of flooring tents of a Seventh AF squadron.

Captain Thomas E. Smith, squadron commanding officer, had managed to cadge a load of lumber for this purpose. Ordering the men to put in the floors, he knew, would bring on a siege of grumbling.

So he had the lumber unloaded at the edge of the area and atop the planks he put a sign: "Government Property."

Night came, and nights can be very dark in the Pacific.

Came the dawn and not a scrap of lumber remained. Even the "Government Property" sign was missing.

From the tents came sounds of sawing and hammering. The men were joyfully putting floors in their tents!

The unescapable by-products of war were beginning to catch up with the Marianas, however.

New brass was pouring in from the rear echelons.

A recently arrived general, who had heard legends of "Swearing John" Evans and the Bar Flies, dropped in on the squadron for a closer look at these fabulous men.

A tour of the area collected only two salutes from the men who were in too big a hurry to notice the rank.

"Your men may be 'the blankety-blank best mechanics in the world,' but they're damned sure not the best soldiers," the general is supposed to have complained to Major John Hussey.

Rumor has it that Major Hussey, who is a very brave man, replied:

"Then maybe, sir, we can say that they are the blankety-blank best civilian mechanics in the world!"

CHAPTER XX: FORGOTTEN CORNER

SIX HUNDRED MILES NORTH OF THE EQUATOR, 4OO MILES EAST OF the Philippines, and a million miles from the nearest juke box, there is a forgotten corner of the world called the Palau Islands.

They are a chain of coral and jungle stinkholes which might have been left to wither on the vine but for the fact that they constituted a formidable flanking threat to MacArthur's march back to Bataan.

On September 15th, after a heavy pre-invasion bombardment by a Naval task force which did not draw a single answering volley, the Marines went ashore at Peleliu, smallest and southern-most of the Palau group.

It wasn't, as had been hoped, another Kiska. When the assault troops had gained the beachhead in the false silence, the Japs hidden deep in the caves and dugouts opened fire and touched off a long period of rathole fighting. Two days later, the Army Infantry went ashore at Angaur, north of Peleliu, and had the island secure in two days.

Patau's stay in the headlines was brief. Following the brief announcement of final victory, a heavy cloak of secrecy was thrown over the activities of a group of Seventh Air Force men lent to MacArthur for his campaign to re-establish the Commonwealth of the Philippine Islands.

For a time, the detached Seventh Air Force groups got their orders from a Marine General who headed a task force to neutralize the Northern Palaus. Later MacArthur designated the Bomber Command of the Fifth Air Force to relay his orders to Angaur and Peleliu. And still later, the Thirteenth Air Force assumed tactical supervision of the Seventh's farmed-out units. There is at least one instance where the Air Forces men in the Palau Islands found themselves with a new commanding general twice in one week.

They came to regard themselves, and justifiably so, as bastard outfits.

The pattern was the same. The 1887th Aviation Engineer Battalion, veterans of Kwajalein and Saipan, went ashore at Angaur with the assault troops and began hacking out airstrips while there was still a major battle going on around them.

On D-plus-12, the mechanics and clerks of the ground echelon arrived off Angaur after a 44-day trip around the Central and South Pacific from Hawaii. They went ashore in the late afternoon during a pouring rain. With them were 38 officers and 639 enlisted men of the 13th Service Group who were assigned a camp-site which happened to be in dead center of Angaur's most active sniper area.

There were the usual number of holdout Japs, each with a fanatical compulsion to die for the emperor. Many of them did. The weather on Palau was a little worse than anywhere else in the Pacific. The men who came ashore early had to survive six typhoons, five of them regarded as "baby" winds in view of one three-day blow which wafted huts and tents from the beaches back into the jungle and snapped trees four feet thick which had resisted even the Engineers' powerful bulldozers.

There were swarms of lizards and fleas and flying insects.

There were also huge land crabs about the size of a volleyball, which had a way of dropping over the rim of a foxhole in the middle of the night to land squirming on the face of a sleeping man and send him screaming through the jungle in terror.

Under such circumstances, admittedly the worst in any forward area from Hawaii west, and deprived by rigid censorship of any real sense of participation in a major campaign, the 494th Bombardment Group of the Seventh Air Force and its attached units carried out an aerial assault which earned them a record five-page letter of commendation from General MacArthur after the fall of the Philippines.

Aviation Engineer officials on Angaur had given the 1887th a thirty-day deadline for completion of an air base from which squadrons of heavies could be launched against the Northern Palaus and the Philippines.

The actual work on Angaur's bomber strip could not start in earnest until eleven days after D-day when the battle had moved far enough from the airstrip site to allow the Engineers to bring up their heavy equipment. Advance parties, working under mortar and howitzer fire and not always sure of which way to run as the battle seesawed back and forth over the strip, had already completed their survey.

Trees too formidable for bulldozers had to be dynamited. Landmines, booby traps and unexploded bombs hampered work and stopped pulses.

One bulldozer operator, frustrated and jarred by several attempts to knock over a tree stump, got down from his machine to inspect the obstacle. It proved to be a cache of camouflaged dynamite.

Corporal Dan Cunningham, working on his third airstrip in the Pacific campaign, turned up an unexploded five-hundred-pound bomb with the blade of his caterpillar grader. Half an hour later a land mine blew the treads off the right hand side of his vehicle.

On Peleliu, Seabee Engineers worked in even graver danger. The major and last corner of enemy resistance on the island was a hill overlooking one end of the runway. From caves and tunnels deep in the hill, the Japs fired machine guns, mortars and howitzers at anything that moved on the air strip.

While Peleliu's field was not officially opened until some weeks later, the Engineers regarded the job as somewhat completed twelve days after D-day when a C-47 of the Transport Air Group threaded its way through an artillery barrage and squeezed out a landing to deliver a critical cargo to the stalemated Marines.

The cargo was 5,000 bottles of hydrogen for the Marines' flamethrowers. On one attempt to burn the Japs out of their caves in the hill, the Marines had run out of hydrogen. They brought up artillery to confine the Japs to their caves and sent an emergency request for more hydrogen to Navy headquarters on Guam.

Captain Sam Privitt, pilot of a TAG C-47, and crew took off from Saipan, stopped at Guam to load and tie down the 5,000 bottles of hydrogen and set a course for Palau. They took the shortest route south, flying so close to Jap atolls that Captain Richard C. Bradley, the squadron navigator, kneeling at a window with a pair of binoculars, could see Japs on Yap.

Bradley was thinking what would happen if a Jap patrol plane pinked their slow, fat-bellied and unarmed cargo ship with an incendiary bullet.

"Oh, brother!" he said later. "That hydrogen!"

Privitt's arrival over the airstrip at Peleliu was about as timely as the walk of a peaceful citizen into the middle of a hot gun fight. The crew peering out the plane's window to examine this new damned island, saw fires and explosions wherever they looked. Navy dive-bombers darted at enemy positions around the strip, dropping small, dark objects which struck and burst into flame and smoke. Artillery and mortar shells whumped and swished down the middle of the runway, and Privitt, noted among TAG crews for an ironic sense of humor, wondered how it would be to land with an artillery shell as his wing man. He called the tower and asked for instructions.

"They were rather blunt about it," he said later. "They told me to get the hell over to the other side of the island and stay there,"

For almost an hour, the C-47 flew back and forth over the battle, occasionally bucking and pitching in the wash of a stray shell. Finally, the tower told Privitt the barrage was letting up a little. He was warned to make his approach at less than four hundred feet, the altitude then assigned to artillery shells.

Privitt took the plane out to sea, turned back toward the strip and made landfall again fifty feet off the tree tops. He found himself aimed at the mouth of a big gun which seemed to be blinking at him, hauled his big ship around in the air and sideslipped away from another gun while the bottles of hydrogen strained against the ropes holding them down. After what seemed like a long time to the men being tossed around inside the ship, the wheels touched ground. The plane rolled to a stop a few hundred feet in front of the Jap-held hill. Privitt put his back to the Jap hill and taxied his plane up the runway about as fast as it is possible to fly a plane while it is still on the ground.

Three days later, the same crew led four other transports and their crews back to Palau through weather so bad that, for the first time in TAG history, men were not assigned to the mission but were asked instead to volunteer.

Palau had been hit by a hurricane, and supply ships riding the storm out offshore found it impossible to transfer food to the assault troops.

An attempt had been made to float the rations shoreward on makeshifts but they were capsized in the wild sea and sunk. While every other airplane in the Marianas was being secured to the runway by cables, five TAG transports, manned by volunteer crews and led by Privitt, took off from Guam. In a few minutes, they hit a front so thick that they lost sight of each other and had to fly on instruments. Some of the men in the crews, veterans of rough weather, got sick as the planes dropped hundreds of feet, slewed around sideways and rolled wildly inside the grey blackness on the front.

Just about when most of the crews decided the wings couldn't stand another bounce, the planes broke out into an endless stretch of sunlight and quiet air. The rest of the trip was made comfortably and without incident.

D-plus-thirty had seemed like an impossible deadline to the Aviation Engineers when they came ashore at Anguar. Yet, a little more than two weeks after D-day, two-winged transports were landing and taking off on a completed section of the airstrip, Piper Cubs were using another area and Aviation Engineers were extending the strip and building revetments for the Liberators.

A few days before the deadline, the commanding officers of the Engineer battalions got together and drafted a cablegram to Guam.

"D-plus-thirty met. Ready for next assignment."

It was welcome news to the men of the advance echelons. They had been working with one half of their soldier minds focused on the job at hand, the other half distracted twenty miles to the north where, uncomfortably visible on occasional bright days, were the islands of Koror and Babelthuap, known to hold some thirty-five thousand Japs who might at any moment come down to saw off the limb far out in the Pacific on which a few thousand Americans were perched tenaciously but precariously.

There had been one attempt by a small Japanese force to retake the lost island. Only a few Japs had succeeded in getting ashore and they were quickly dispatched by Marines. There was the constant threat of raids from Jap airstrips in the northern Palaus; and red alerts kept Peleliu and Angaur residents in the foxholes almost all night every night. One Jap formation caused extensive casualties when it approached the island undetected and caught many men above ground. Another alert which proved false was traced to a "Tarzan" picture being shown in a jungle clearing. Tarzan was being pursued up Broadway by police patrol cars with their sirens wide open. A guard in another area heard the sirens and, thinking it was the island air raid warning signal, turned in an alarm which shortly saw the whole island sitting it out in fox-holes.

Real or false, the alerts were jittery experiences, and the men on Angaur and Peleliu had waited nervously for the arrival of the Liberators which, they knew, could help discourage any air or land invasion plans of the Japanese high command in the Northern Palaus.

On the 24th of October, a month and nine days after the initial landing in Palau, the Liberators of the Seventh Air Force's 494th Bomb Group, led by Colonel Laurence B. Kelly, broke cloud coverage over Angaur and began to let down for their landings. It was the end of a spectacular, 5,000-mile mass flight from the Hawaiian Islands.

Seventy-two hours later, and before many of the crews had located their duffle bags in the pile of luggage dumped in the squadron area, Kelly's Cobras, as the 494th came to be known, took off in a heavy overcast to bomb Yap in the Carolines and Koror in the Palaus.

Hours later, while ground crews huddled along the airstrip in the driving rain, the Liberators came back, singly and in groups.

Sergeant Harry J. Seigal, engineer-gunner on the first plane in the lead flight, who like most of the 494th crew members was fresh out of stateside training, reported the first combat mission "less rugged than we expected. The flak was heavy but we didn't meet a single fighter."

Not a plane had been lost. For the Cobras, it was the beginning of good fortune that was to see them through 5,565 combat hours before losing a single plane to enemy action. The record was all the more remarkable because many of their missions were precision bombing strikes against radio stations, bridges, bivouac areas and storage dumps and, to insure maximum bombing accuracy, had to be made at an altitude below ten thousand feet and well within the overlapping zone of automatic weapons and anti-aircraft fire.

There was one five-hundred-pound bomb delivered during one of the Cobras' earliest pin-pointing strikes which must have caused great anguish to high-ranking Japanese officers on Koror, center of Jap Army administration for the Palaus.

A building several stories high with an ornate roof which distinguished it from other buildings in the neighborhood kept showing up in reconnaissance photographs. There always seemed to be a lot of activity around the building and Intelligence officers on Anguar guessed it might be the headquarters of the Palaus' high command.

Major Duncan McKinnon drew the building as his primary target one day and dropped a 500-pound bomb squarely through the roof.

It wasn't until many weeks later that the 494th discovered it had bombed out, not a Japanese general's headquarters, but Koror's largest disorderly house.

One burly Aviation Engineer, Corporal Bill Chevallier, who — like many Pacific Air Forces men — had followed the geisha myth fruitlessly all the way across the Pacific, summed up the feelings of many of his fellow soldiers:

"Jeez," he said, "we always take the wrong damned islands."

But if things were going the way of the 494th in the air, they frequently had the lower hand on the ground. Snipers and infiltrators, some of them hungry and only trying to steal food, and some of them out to kill, made the nights on Palau long and loud.

Such a night was Halloween. It was a perfect night for bombing or infiltration. There had been a storm in the late afternoon and the moon, one night short of being full and more red than orange, reflected the tall cocoanut palms and the blunt outlines of pyramidal tents in the puddles left by the downpour. There was an atmosphere of quiet tenseness as the camp settled down for the night.

By eleven o'clock, everything was quiet in the tent area of the 13th Service Group. A few cardplayers and late letterwriters had gone to bed and the slow drip of water from the tent flaps had stopped. On the fringes of the area a few guards, wet and miserable, walked their posts tiredly sweating out the midnight relief.

In a tent on the swamp and jungle side of the campsite, away from the beach, a soldier got out of bed and pulled on his shoes. More asleep than awake, he walked down the row of pyramidal tents toward the latrine at the end of the company street. A few feet from the latrine, he heard a low-pitched jabbering to his left. He turned and saw a Jap crouching low in the shadow of the last tent.

The soldier, Sergeant Norman Tache, impelled mostly by instinct, raised his hands over his head and began walking slowly toward the Jap. The Jap got to his feet cautiously and walked toward Tache slowly and with his gun pointed at the American's belly.

The distance between them narrowed to a yard. The Jap's gun, which he held in the crook of his arm, was not more than a foot from Tache's belly.

Tache made a dive for the gun and drove his knee into the sniper's groin. Almost soundlessly, they wrestled in the darkness. Tache finally yanked the rifle away from the intruder. He was too close to aim and fire it so he smashed the butt of the rifle sideways into the Jap's head, dove to the ground and began yelling for help.

The sniper took off through the rain puddles, toward the jungle, yelling "no shoot, no shoot."

Tache took careful aim at the fleeing Jap, who was plainly visible in the moonlight, and fired. There was only a dull click; the gun, badly rusted, was jammed.

The Jap headed for the open, dodging the bullets of guards who heard Tache's call for help. Apparently deciding he couldn't make it alive, the Jap turned back abruptly toward the campsite and ran down a row of tents. He tossed a grenade at a tent of sleeping soldiers, pulled the pin of another grenade and held it to his throat. The explosion all but ripped his head off.

The sounds of rifle fire and exploding grenades had awakened every man in the area. Battle-wise because of the almost nightly infiltration attempts, they stayed in the tents, carefully loading their carbines and softly cursing whatever it was that woke them up.

Gradually, quiet again settled over the area. Soldiers hung their rifles up again or placed them cautiously beside their cots.

Most of them were sound asleep when, less than thirty minutes later, a voice in the distance called "Halt!" and a rifle cracked. There was a loud burst of rifle fire and every soldier in the area was suddenly awake and reaching for his rifle.

Down at the Service Group's motor pool, two guards saw three figures emerge from a clump of bushes and trot across a vacant lot. The guards climbed into a command car. Through the rear window they saw the Japs cross the lot, turn around and come back directly in front of the car.

Corporal Stanley P. Caroll challenged them. The three Japs froze in front of the car for a moment and then one of them broke and ran for cover. Corporal Frank F. Pirtle opened fire from the command car. His shots, together with a volley fired by Caroll, dropped the Jap at the edge of the jungle.

The other two Japs broke and began running in circles around the command. Caroll and Pirtle fired again and again, finally sending a volley through the windshield which caught both Japs directly in front of the car.

The two guards climbed down from the truck to make sure the Japs were dead.

By midnight, the guards were relieved and the camp settled down for the third time to sleep through Halloween.

Early in December, when Palau-based Japanese aircraft seemed no longer a threat to American ground forces clinging to their first narrow foothold on the island of Leyte, Kelly's Cobras were ordered into the Philippines campaign.

Their targets, as they spearheaded MacArthur's march back to Bataan, read like playbacks of the tragic radio announcements of early 1942: Clark Field, Grace Park Airdome, Legaspi, Bataan, Cabantuan. The City of Manila. The Island of Corregidor.

Legaspi Airfield on southeast Luzon was the Cobras' first Philippines target.

There was much tension among the crews as they made their way through the darkness for the pre-dawn takeoff of the first mission against the Philippines. They huddled at the waist of the planes as crew chiefs ran up the engines for the last time, smoking and talking in spurts as if to relieve the tension all of them felt.

They had yet to meet an enemy fighter. Koror and Babelthuap, were minor league targets compared to what they could expect in the Philippines. So far, they had been almost too lucky and the streak of good fortune, while it was something to be grateful for, had built up almost excessive tension as the missions mounted. They wondered, as they ground out their cigarettes on the runway and started toward their planes, if this was to be the unlucky mission.

It was raining again when they came back from the target.

Their luck had held. Ack-ack was heavy and accurate. Automatic weapons fire was thick. But not a single hit was scored in the formation. All planes got home safely.

And still there were no Zeroes.

For the next twenty days, the Cobras' luck held as they concentrated on knocking out enemy airpower which could be flown against MacArthur's forces at Leyte. Their primary targets were the aircraft parked in the revetments of the Jap fields at Masbate, Cebu City, Bulan, Lahug, Olan, Bacalod and Carolina.

For ground crews as well as aircrews, the Philippines missions were back-breaking efforts. The target designation, which came from MacArthur's headquarters, usually did not arrive on Angaur until late in the evening the day before a mission.

Ground crews were kept out on the flight line most of the night preparing and loading the planes. Operations and Intelligence men worked through the night under the doubtful lights of eccentric generators which sometimes operated only at twenty-minute stretches. Crews were whistled out of their tents for breakfast at two in the morning — and that meant the KPs had to stay up most of the night. Briefing and takeoff were around four in the morning.

The flights average 14 hours and from 2,300 to 2,500 statute miles, making necessary night takeoffs which added to the hazards of the mission.

Ironically, the first tragedy to overtake the 494th in the air did not come as the result of enemy action.

After a strike at Lahug, when all planes had cleared the target safely, a Liberator named the Bull was plowing home toward Palau, four hundred feet off the water in a driving rainstorm. With no warning, two engines conked out.

There was no time for the pilot, Captain Earl Richards, to prepare the plane and crew for a water landing. He straightened the plane out as best he could and rang the ditching bell. The Liberator smacked into a huge swell and broke up.

Richards, trapped in the pilot's seat, was pulled under with the nose section. He fought free of his safety belt, clawed his way out of the nose and swam to the surface. He managed to haul two wounded men aboard a life raft and they spent that night and most of the next day tossing around in the ocean until a Dumbo rescued them.

Sergeant Bill Devlin, assistant engineer and ball-turret gunner, was standing in the waist of the plane making coffee in a hot cup when the ditching bell rang. The next few minutes are a blind spot in Devlin's otherwise vivid memory of a harrowing experience.

Devlin remembers hearing the ditching bell and then he was clinging to a section of the broken fuselage. He pushed into the water to get at a life raft. He found one but it would not inflate. He located another but it was no better than the first one.

Devlin found himself being carried away from the floating wreckage and grabbed at something which was drifting past him. It was the Gibson Girl, the plane's portable and non-sinkable emergency radio. Devlin threw his feet over one of the life rafts which he had tried to inflate and, with one arm wrapped around the Gibson Girl, tried with the other to paddle back to where the pilot and the injured men floated in a raft. The waves, which were about ten feet high, kept pushing him further away. He shouted but knew it was futile against the sound of the sea. It got dark after a couple of hours.

Devlin wasn't very worried. He was sure a Dumbo would come along before many hours. He clung to the Gibson Girl with his feet in the deflated raft and tried to keep from falling asleep.

During the night, a Dumbo flew over and two Navy ships passed close to Devlin. He shouted until he was hoarse and waved until the motion sank him and filled his lungs with salt water. Then the Dumbo and the ships were out of sight and Devlin was alone again.

As the hours passed, Devlin got more and more drowsy. Once, he was almost asleep when he was jerked awake by something like an electric shock. It probably came from some sort of sting ray.

"I damn near jumped right out of the ocean," he said later.

It was the first time Devlin knew his real predicament. For the rest of the night ("God, it was a long night!") he waited in the darkness for sharks or anything else that would come at him. It was pitch black except when his hand slipped into the water and stirred up a weird phosphorous glow.

Devlin got stung a couple of more times before dawn finally came and with it, a Dumbo and a Navy destroyer.

The Dumbo flew back and forth over Devlin, who was shouting and waving in the water. The plane flew away after awhile and the destroyer disappeared from Devlin's limited horizon.

Devlin thought he would try to open up the Gibson Girl and signal with its radio but was afraid he would sink if he let go of it even for a few minutes. So he tried to make himself believe the Dumbo or the destroyer would come back.

About noon, the destroyer did come back. Devlin clawed at the Gibson Girl and managed to release its small parachute. The destroyer slowed up and began to make a turn toward Devlin. With tremendous happiness he saw some sailors lower a motor-whaleboat into the water. When the launch was about thirty yards away, Devlin saw two sailors in the prow raise their guns and fire into the water alongside him.

When Devlin was safely aboard the destroyer, the Navy men told him that they had killed two sharks swimming around him in circles. It wasn't until then that Devlin remembered that, as he was struggling with the Gibson Girl, he felt something rub against him in the water.

The day before Christmas, on their first strike against Clark Field, Manila, the 494th saw its first airborne enemy fighter aircraft. A Zeke rose as if to meet the formation while it was going in on the target. It drew a few warning bursts from the Liberator gunners, turned tail and flew around outside firing range while the planes bombed the target unmolested.

By Christmas, a little over ninety days after D-day, the island of Angaur had shaken down to an efficient, busy bomber base which, unknown to the world and presumably to the Japanese, was spearheading one of the most publicized military conquests in history.

But Palau remained the most rugged rock in the Pacific. Fungus infections, diarrhea, jaundice, malaria, dengue fever; tropical storms which struck without warning and buried campsites in water and mud; heat that lay over the island like a shimmering tide; and the most damnable boredom a Pacific soldier was ever called upon to endure, made Palau tough to survive.

It had been that way on D-day. It had improved only a little at the end of six months.

In the month of November, there was an outbreak of the GIs (the military equivalent of diarrhea). One hundred and forty-nine cases in the 13th Service Group alone required medical attention; roughly, about one man in every five was affected. In March, when diarrhea was thought to be under permanent control, there was another outbreak which was traced to contaminated food.

In December, jaundice broke out. And every day soldiers were reporting to sick call with fungus infections of the feet, hands and ears. The infections, which resist medical treatment in tropical climates, persisted for a long time.

Although Palau was only a little over six hundred miles south of Guam, a comparatively short interval of water in Pacific logistics, it was, as far as supplies were concerned, on a direct line to nowhere.

Movies, which had always ranked right after mail in the matter of morale, were infrequent and not always entertaining. One of the pictures which toured Angaur's outdoor theatres as late as February, 1944, was made in 1926 and starred Fanny Brice. In the same month, the serving of apples and oranges for a few days at breakfast was considered sufficiently important for entry in the Group history.

The beer ration, which had long since come to be regarded as the enlisted man's last civilized privilege — only officers were allowed whiskey rations — was being distributed in January at the rate of one can to each man every second day. Even on the remotest outposts, it was a scant ration.

Nor was the supply shortage limited to items which might be regarded as important only to a soldier's morale. At one point in the assault on the Philippines, the 13th Service Group's ammunition dump was down to ten 100-pound general purpose bombs. The termination of the 494th missions from Angaur in April was a timely reprieve for aircrews who might have been faced with enforced idleness while luckier crews flew their quota of missions and went home; the group ran out of engine replacements and as far back as Hawaii, no new ones were available.

Women, well, there were none — white or otherwise. While flight nurses and USO entertainers occasionally passed through places like Kwajalein and Guam, and could be regarded from a respectful distance by enlisted men, it was not until April, more than seven months after the islands were taken, that a white woman appeared in the Palaus. It was, as might be expected, a public holiday when the USO show "Girl Crazy" arrived with seven women in the cast — all of them white.

Christmas, while it promised nothing special to the air and ground crews on Angaur, had been planned as a day of rest. But late on Christmas Eve the word came through that there would be a mission to Maclabat, an airbase adjacent to Clark Field outside Manila.

It turned out to be quite a Christmas.

Twenty-five Liberators of the 494th went over the target with an escort of P-38's provided by the Fifth Air Force. They met eighty Zeroes carrying phosphorus bombs and ran into enough flak, as one returning pilot said, "to equip every officer and enlisted man in the Army with an iron seat in his pants."

The action over the target was wild. Twenty-five of the Zeroes, coming in high and out of the sun, were ambushed by the P-38's and shot down. Fifteen Zeroes in another flight got through. Seven of them were knocked down by Cobra gunners shooting at their first live targets.

Considering the fact that fifteen fighters got close enough to the Liberators to get themselves shot down, it was something of a miracle that not a single bullet hole was found in any one of the B-24's.

A few planes were nicked by flak but the damage was very slight. The most surprised man in the group, when the Liberators all returned safely and unscarred, was the flak officer, Captain John Schermmerhorn. He had warned the crews that they could expect to meet the concentrated fire of 99 heavy guns at Maclabat.

Kelly's Cobras, fresh from the States when they entered the Palau and Philippines campaigns, were running into gun defenses several times as great as any encountered by the units of the Seventh AAF in the fourteen months since it had taken the offensive in the Gilberts.

Clark Field, the largest enemy air depot outside Japan and a frequent 494th target, was one of the most bitterly defended areas in the entire Pacific theatre. On one particular day, Clark showed defense by 86 heavy guns, 402 medium weapons and more than 180 machine guns. To make the going a little tougher, prevailing winds frequently forced formations to make their bombing runs to Clark over the city of Manila, carrying them within easy range of an unknown number of big guns.

It was at Clark Field, on their first mission after the Christmas Day strike, that Kelly's outfit lost its first airplane to the enemy.

There was an overcast over Clark as the formation approached. Bombing was visual, so they let down below ten thousand feet for a clear view of the target area.

Crews in the first planes to go across Clark said they were pretty sure their luck had run out when they saw the hundreds of black smoke puffs in the air ahead of them; more anti-aircraft bursts than they had ever encountered. It wasn't tracking fire as it had been before; it was ahead of them and it was exactly on their flight level.

There is nothing so inflexible as a bombing run. The planes moved into the field of flying steel as though drawn on strings. As the lead planes bored into it, three hundred bursts were counted in and around the formation.

Sitting in as co-pilot on one of the Liberators, the Group's Deputy Commander, Lieutenant Colonel Lyle Halstead, happened to be looking at the plane ahead of him when he saw a small, black puff of smoke suddenly take form on the leading edge of the wing between the plane's No. 3 and No. 4 engines. Almost at the same time, the entire wing parted from the fuselage and there was an explosion which showered the other planes with debris.

A big section of the wing from the exploded plane sailed back and smashed into the windshield in front of Halstead. Chunks of aluminum and parts of an engine plowed into the plane piloted by Lieutenant Joe Dubinsky, which was already sieved by flak.

Riding away from the target, the tailgunners in the last elements reported they saw three parachutes far below them. Two were furled. The third was unfurled and appeared to be on fire.

It was a new thing to Kelly's Cobras, this loss of a plane and its crew, new and tragic enough so that there is more than just a formal listing of their names in the official history of the Philippines air campaign.

The historian wrote: "Major Rowe, Lieutenant Winnan and the crew of '684' were men whose qualities we had tried, admired and respected.

"We shall not see their like again."

It was the end of 5,565 consecutive hours of flying without a single combat loss.

Those early missions to Clark, although they produced no more casualties, held more than their share of narrow escapes. On the same mission which cost the group its first loss, a Zero pressed home his attack on Captain Raymond Yeoman's plane so close that his propeller clipped a foot and a half from the right wing.

The next day over Clark, a single ack-ack burst scored 36 holes in the Black Cat, flown by Captain Ed Strum. The burst gave the Group its first Purple Heart when shrapnel wounded Sturm's tail gunner, Sergeant Max Burton.

On the same mission, 19 pieces of flak tore into the Liberator on which Staff Sergeant Elbert Lindley was top-turret gunner. Lindley was tracking an enemy fighter which was fortunately out of range when a piece of shrapnel passed between his body and his left arm and knocked the gun controls out of his hand.

About the same time, in a plane directly behind Lindley, Staff Sergeant James R. Cox was looking out the waist window watching the hits scored by the lead planes. He was holding a water jug in his left hand.

There was a sharp cracking sound and Cox saw water pouring down the left leg of his flight coveralls. There wasn't a water jug in his hand — only the handle. Something dropped to the floor in front of Cox and he picked it up. It was a two-inch piece of shrapnel which had come up through the floor, shattered the water jug and spent itself against the ceiling of the plane.

January, notable to ground crews on Angaur as the month when the first mattresses arrived on the island and wood for tent flooring was doled out, saw the 494th reaching deeper into the Philippines as MacArthur's forces, on the ninth of the month, landed at Lingayen Gulf on Luzon.

As American troops moved to within thirty miles of the City of Manila, the Island of Corregidor became a target for the 494th Bombardment Group on the far away island of Angaur.

There was a point in almost every Pacific air campaign where bomber crews knew they were over the hump and the enemy's ability to resist a strike from the air had broken. In the Gilberts and the Marshalls, Japanese opposition above targets marked for invasion had grown tougher and tougher and then, suddenly, there were no more Zeroes and very little anti-aircraft fire.

It was at Corregidor that Jap defenses in the Northern Philippines folded up.

Because Corregidor was the guardian fortress of Manila Bay, and because there is no way to bomb a one-mile-square target without flying directly over its guns, the first missions were expected to bring heavy casualties. But the planes met only scattered fire, most of it badly aimed.

Then after the 494th teamed with bombers of the 5th and 13th Air Forces in a one-day assault on January 23rd which saw high altitude precision bombing refined to the extent that squadrons were briefed for specific gun emplacements, the anti-aircraft fire on Corregidor ceased altogether.

For the rest of the month, the 494th concentrated on Corregidor and its companion island of Caballo in Manila Bay, powdering the surface with demolition bombs to get at the underground defenses while MacArthur's men took Clark Field and moved through the outskirts of Manila.

D-day on Corregidor was to have been a special day for Kelly's Cobras. Morale had soared when word came from MacArthur's headquarters that 500 wrecked Japanese aircraft had been found at Clark Field, where the Cobras' primary target had always been parked aircraft. It soared even higher when Kelly called his men together and told them they would fly to Corregidor a few minutes ahead of the invading troops.

D-day on Corregidor was February 16th.

And, on February 16th, a storm front, impenetrable and insurmountable, too vast to fly around, too low to fly under, stood squarely between Angaur and the Philippine Islands.

Angry, and with bitter hatred for a rock which was too far from everything except bad weather, pilots, navigators, gunners, ground men who had taken care of the planes before and after every mission, Intelligence officers and everybody else on Angaur collected around radios and listened to news accounts of how a fleet of C-47's swarmed up Manila Bay and spilled 1,999 American Parachutists onto Corregidor Island.

For the rest of the month, as ground forces continued mopping up and General of the Armies Douglas MacArthur re-established the Commonwealth of the Philippines, weather restricted Kelly's Cobras to shakedown missions against the Northern Palaus.

It was during this period, after twenty strikes against Koror without a single combat casualty, that the 494th lost its first plane and crew to enemy action in the Northern Palaus. A Liberator took a direct flak hit which blew off the right wing and sent the fuselage and left wing hurling down on fire with the crew trapped inside.

While the Philippines campaign had virtually ended, there was still Mindanao, south of the retaken islands and originally planned as the Philippines invasion site. Through March and April, the Cobras flew in support of the guerilla army. San Rogue, Cebu City, Bunawan, Cabatan, Davao and, finally, Zamboanga on the southern tip of Mindanao, were the targets.

For the most part, the missions to Mindanao were as nearly routine as it is possible for a combat mission to be. The Cobras never saw a fighter in the air — reassuring proof of the Intelligence division's statement, at the beginning of the campaign, that there were not more than half a dozen Jap fighter aircraft on all of Mindanao.

Occasionally, there was a memorable mission. In a strike at Ising Town, near the Davao Penal Colony, a string of Cobra bombs blew up in the middle of an enemy encampment and killed 300 Japs. On a medium altitude mission over the City of Cebu on Cebu Island, aircrews had the satisfaction of watching most of the buildings crumble to the ground as 97 per cent of the bombs hit dead center. They came back asking for more targets like that one.

At times, it got pretty boring. On the 12th of March, while Captain McMahan was flying a lonely photo mission over Central Mindanao, he spotted two trucks moving along a road between the towns of Maker and Buluan. Obeying an impulse which all four-engine pilots have at one time felt, McMahan put his Liberator in a steep dive, leveled off and came up the road behind the trucks with all forward guns firing.

The result, as entered in official Intelligence reports which called McMahan's strafing job "a highlight of the Mindanao campaign," was:

"Quite a few Japs caught up on a year's calisthenics."

But the Cobras' most memorable mission to Mindanao was one which was never entered in the official reports. No bombs were dropped. No guns were fired.

To anybody who didn't have a personal stake in the mission — and that would have excluded everybody on the island of Angaur — the mission would have looked like a routine flight to deliver supplies.

Early on a morning in March, two C-87 Liberator-transports, loaded far beyond the weight limit at which aircraft manufacturers wash their hands of the whole thing, took off from Angaur and set a course toward Mindanao. Everything removable, including some emergency survival equipment, had been thrown out to make way for parapacks which bulged with United States Army uniforms, medical kits, howitzer shells, small arms ammunition, guns and a hundred other items which were never officially checked out on supply records — including $750.00 in cash. The planes crossed the Philippines Sea and circled over a designated spot on the Jap-held Island of Mindanao.

There they emptied their parapacks into a clearing in the jungle, waggled their wings in a final, friendly salute and flew uneventfully back to Angaur.

The flight of the C-87's, routine as it appeared to be, ended in a dramatic way the magnificent adventure of eleven men who flew toward Mindanao one morning in a Liberator called I'll Get By.

CHAPTER XXI: "WHAT WONDERFUL PEOPLE"

FINALLY, EVERYTHING WAS QUIET.

Technical Sergeant Floyd Swain felt the wind tugging at the legs of his flight coveralls as he hung in the parachute harness and watched the green jungle move slowly up to meet him.

Floating downward in the parachutes near him, and close enough for Swain to recognize their faces, were the three men who had gone out of the plane just ahead of him: the tail gunner, the radio operator and the ball turret gunner.

Higher up, and spread out over seven miles of calm sky, Swain counted six more parachutes.

Far below him and a couple of miles away, Swain located the eleventh parachute. He knew that could only be the pilot, Lieutenant Lampe, who had stayed with the blazing plane long enough to give everybody else a chance to get out. Lampe had finally jumped when the I'll Get By was at the bottom of her crazy loop and less than twenty-five hundred feet off the ground.

Swain was thinking how quiet it was now and how damn lucky they had all been when something whistled past his face.

He looked down and saw Japanese soldiers firing up at him. They were inside a bare area in the jungle which was closed in by a high wooden fence. Other Japs jumped on motorcycles and sped out of the gate onto a road which wound through the jungle in the direction of the other falling crew members. Still other Japs scurried around below Swain organizing the chase.

Inside that fence, Swain knew, was the Davao Penal Colony.

Five long minutes ago, the eleven men of the crew of I'll Get By had been at their stations inside the Liberator and the Davao Penal Colony had been simply the orientation point for a strike against a camouflaged Jap bivouac area near the prison and on the outskirts of Ising Town. Captain Julian Penrose, a squadron navigator who had been to the same target once before, rode along in the nose turret of the I'll Get By to be sure the 24 planes of the 494th Group got their fragmentation bombs on the target, which was small and hard to find.

The I'll Get By's bombs had just cleared the bomb bay when the crew felt a sudden jolt and, almost instantly, the plane was in flames. The tail gunner, Staff Sergeant Lawrence Murphy, dived through the photography hatch. Staff Sergeant Ermiddio Fortunato, the ball gunner, followed him. Swain went through next and the radio operator, Technical Sergeant Paul Cantu, tumbled out after him.

The I'll Get By dived thirty degrees to the left and then, with only two engines turning over, climbed straight up into a loop. Four crew members dived from the catwalk through the open bomb bay doors and another dropped down through the nose hatch as the plane began its climb. The bombardier, Lieutenant Smith, knocked to the catwalk and pinned there by centrifugal force, rolled off into space as the I'll Get By was poised ten thousand feet in the air at the top of her loop.

The pilot, Lieutenant John Lampe, stayed with the plane all the way around and jumped when it was at the bottom of its loop.

Lampe's parachute had boomed open just as the I'll Get By went into the jungle in a red roar.

Then there had been the quick interval of quiet as the crew, spread out over seven miles of sky, began drifting slowly down. The feeling of safety was less than momentary; it ended abruptly for each man as he heard bullets whizzing past him and saw that he was drifting toward the Davao Penal Colony.

Swain's parachute was falling straight toward the inner courtyard of the prison. He tugged at the shroud lines; somewhere he had heard that you could spill some of the air out of a chute and change its course that way. But it didn't work for Swain. He began swinging back and forth in the harness and saw that the arc of his body was growing wider as the Japs grew bigger and their bullets came closer.

About a hundred feet above the courtyard, Swain saw he had time for one more swing. He hurled himself forward, swung back and hit the ground about thirty feet outside the prison fence.

Swain freed himself from the parachute while he was still lying on the ground, got up and tried to run down a path which he saw led away from the stockade. His left leg caved in under him and Swain discovered he had broken his ankle when he hit the ground. He got up again and half-crawled, half-hobbled down the path; his only thought was to put distance between himself and the Japs.

Swain had crawled around a bend and was lying on the path resting his ankle when he heard footsteps running down the path behind him. He felt for his .45 but remembered, even as he reached for it, that he had left it in the plane. He got to his knees and began crawling as fast as he could.

The footsteps kept gaining on Swain so he stopped crawling and turned to face whoever was chasing him.

It was a little Filipino boy. He came around a bend in the path into Swain's view and stopped a few yards from him. He looked gravely down at the injured man for a moment and asked:

"You come America?"

Swain nodded. The boy gestured in the direction of the Davao prison and said, simply, "Jap." Then he pointed into the jungle in the opposite direction and said, "Quick." He helped Swain to his feet, placed an arm around his waist and they hobbled down the path together with the barefooted youngster acting as a crutch.

It was about ten minutes later, after the boy had led Swain through a maze of twisting and turning paths, moving always away from the prison stockade, that they heard something crashing through the jungle ahead of them. They hobbled off the path and burrowed into the underbrush.

It turned out to be Technical Sergeant Paul Cantu, the radio operator, who had jumped through the plane's photography hatch behind Swain. He had landed half a mile away in a clearing and had been running down back paths ever since.

The Filipino boy again took charge. He hid Swain in the jungle and went off down the path leading Cantu. Thirty minutes later, the boy, Cantu and six Filipino men came back with a rude litter. Working fast and without saying a word, they bundled Swain into it and started at a trot through the jungle paths.

In a little while they came to a native village in a clearing. The people of the settlement crowded around Swain, nodding and smiling and touching his Sergeant's stripes. The women brought fruit and sweet potatoes and Cantu, who noticed that the natives were ragged and emaciated, guessed it was probably all the food they had.

There was a consultation going on between the men who had carried Swain in and some of the villagers. Presently, one of the men detached himself from the group and walked over to Swain. With many gestures and an occasional word of English he told Swain that everybody in the area had watched the eleven men as they parachuted from the plane and that members of the guerilla army and Filipino civilians who supported the underground were out looking for the other men.

The grim contest lasted for more than a week, with Jap patrols combing the jungles for the fliers while guerillas, Filipino civilians and children drifted like shadows through the underbrush trying to reach the men before the Japs found them.

The native told Swain the Filipinos would try to take the two Americans to the guerilla headquarters and presently a new crew picked up the litter and set out through the jungle.

Swain and Cantu were the only two men from the crew of the I'll Get By who had landed in a clearing. The others parachuted into the jungle, some of them landing in tree tops more than a hundred feet high. Getting to the ground was a problem most of them solved by sliding down the thick trailing vines.

A few minutes after the Filipino boy located Swain, civilians had found Fortunato. He had dropped through the photography hatch just ahead of Swain and landed in the jungle about a mile from the prison. Staff Sergeant Robert E. Gorman, the assistant engineer who dove through the bomb bay as the I'll Get By began climbing straight up, wasn't so lucky. He landed several miles away from Davao, deep in the jungle, out of reach of the Filipino guerillas and civilians closing invisibly and protectively around the men who fell nearest to the prison. Gorman set out in the direction of Leyte, nearly two hundred miles away, and wandered four days and nights before he encountered a Filipino civilian. Like the other rescued crew members, he was passed from hand to hand through the Mindanao jungles.

The bombardier, Lieutenant James E. Smith, who cleared the I'll Get By when it was at the top of its loop, came down in a tree. He freed himself from his parachute, slid to the ground and found himself in the middle of a swamp where the vines, trees, logs and tangled undergrowth were so thick that he could never see more than five or six feet ahead of him. As he started to pick his way through the massed undergrowth, he heard a loud, raucous noise above him and, looking up, saw a bird about the size of a buzzard with a vivid red head. Smith saw more of the birds in trees around him; they did not follow him but they cried out loudly every time he took a step so that he was pursued through the jungle by their betraying voices.

Smith's worst ordeal was the leeches which hooked onto his face from the underside of leaves as he pushed through the jungle. He picked them out of the wound on his face caused when he struck a stanchion on the way out of the plane, but there were so many of them, and they clung so tenaciously to the bleeding wound, that he finally gave up and let the things stay.

Smith wandered vaguely in the direction where the Intelligence officer who had briefed the mission in Angaur told the crew there was a guerilla Army headquarters. Two hours had passed when he heard something else moving through the jungle near him.

Risking capture, Smith called out "Hello!" A man staggered into view and Smith saw, with tremendous relief, that it was Staff Sergeant Foster Derr, nose gunner, who had gone out the forward hatch door after telling the pilot the plane was on fire. Derr had landed somewhere in the jungle and was wandering around hopelessly lost when, miraculously, his erratic path had crossed Smith's. They continued north together until it grew dark and then sat with their backs against the base of a tree. They spent a wakeful night fighting off clouds of mosquitoes and trying to close their ears and minds to the weird jungle noises. When they were most drowsy, they would be jerked awake by a shrill wail which sounded like the cry of a lost child. (Later, they were told the sound came from jungle frogs.) Several times during the night they thought they heard voices and people moving near them.

Anxious to put an end to the longest night of their lives, Smith and Derr started north again in the first grey light of dawn. They were hungry and their bodies were covered with insect bites. Their hands, torn and bleeding from clawing their way through the jungles, became infected and swollen. All that day, the men moved slowly north; their only food a single bite of a red jungle fruit about the size of an apple — which was promptly spat out because it was so bitter.

At dusk, Smith and Derr came upon a river and lay down on its bank to wait out the night. In the morning, they set out again, following the dark brown water as it moved slowly northward.

Sometime around noon, Derr, who had been walking ahead of Smith to protect his cut face from the tree branches, stopped and pointed ahead wordlessly. On the top of a hill which commanded the area Smith saw a small shack with a dozen men sitting around it. Smith and Derr crouched on the river bank trying to decide whether to approach the men or turn back into the jungle.

Suddenly something moved behind them and Smith, turning quickly, pulled out his .45. It was a small boy who stood on the river bank smiling at the two men. Completely disregarding Smith's gun, the boy walked up to him and said, "You wait here." Then he trotted up the hill toward the men sitting around the shack.

Smith and Derr wanted to run but knew they wouldn't last five minutes before they were found. Resigned to whatever was going to happen to them next, they stood close together on the river bank and watched the men come running down the hill with their rifles ready. As the men got closer, Smith and Derr saw that they wore floppy hats, ragged pants, torn shirts and had no shoes. Then, as the men came to within thirty yards of them, Derr grabbed Smith's arm and pointed at the gun carried by a man running a little ahead of the others.

It was an American Army rifle.

What followed is perhaps the most fantastic single incident of the extraordinary saga of the crew of the I'll Get By. Smith told the story later, repeating it over and over again in detail as though trying to make himself believe it really could have happened to two American airmen, trapped and lost deep in Japanese territory two hundred miles from the nearest Allied base at Leyte and four hundred miles across the sea from Angaur.

"One little guy came up ahead of the rest and looked us over," Smith said. "I noticed he was wearing homemade Sergeant's stripes. He had started to take my gun when his eyes fell on the Lieutenant's bars on my flight jacket. He stepped back from me and shouted something over his shoulder in Tagalog.

"The damnedest thing happened then. Those ragged little guys swung into line on the river bank. It happened quickly and effortlessly. One moment they were just milling around watching us; the next they were standing rigidly in a line so straight you could have swung a transit line down their top chest buttons — if they had had any buttons.

"Then this incredible little squad leader, who had been facing his men and watching them sternly, did an about face, shouted another order and there — in that God-forsaken jungle — those ragged, barefooted little men snapped to and presented arms."

Smith and Derr, after they had accepted the salute and had shaken hands all around, were taken to a guerilla company headquarters where they were fed and their body sores were treated. Then they were moved further back into the jungles to a battalion headquarters and finally to a divisional headquarters — a mountain stronghold where, as the days went by, other rescued members of the crew were brought in. As they arrived, their names, the date they were found and the important details of their rescue were shortwaved in code to Angaur over a powerful radio which had been delivered to the guerillas by an American submarine.

Lieutenant David Rolfe, the co-pilot, and Lieutenant Wesley Co well, the navigator, who had jumped through the open bomb bay together but landed several miles apart in the jungle, were picked up separately on the third day. Both had bad luck.

Co well came down in the jungle and found himself hanging in the top of a tree ten feet from the nearest vine. He swung back and forth in his chute until he was able to grab the vine and held it between his knees while he freed himself from the chute. Then, as he tightened his grip on the vine and turned to get his escape kit out of the parachute, the vine carried him out of reach. He swung back and forth for a while trying to reach the dangling chute but finally gave up and slid to the ground. His only equipment was a compass and a pair of fingernail clippers.

On his third day in the jungle Co well came upon a small-gauge railroad and walked along it until he saw two men patrolling the track ahead of him. He hid until they came close enough so that he could see they were carrying U. S. Army carbines and then stepped out and hailed them. They saluted him and led him to safety.

Rolfe, the co-pilot, was the only man in the crew who contracted malaria. He had managed to extricate his escape kit from his parachute tangled in a tree top but somehow lost his atabrine tablets. Struggling through the jungle on his first day, Rolfe heard what sounded like the baying of hounds. Sure that the Japs were following him with bloodhounds, he ran and doubled back through the swamps trying to break his scent, but the barking followed wherever he went.

On the third day, delirious from malaria, Rolfe wandered into a small clearing. A woman, nude from the waist up, came out of the hut in the center of the clearing with two children at her side. While Rolfe and the woman were staring at each other, the woman's husband entered the clearing from the jungle. The natives were members of a jungle tribe which is almost extinct, and although they could speak no English, Rolfe, by the use of sign language managed to tell them who he was. They gave him a few sweet potatoes and some water and fixed a bed for him in their hut.

The next day, the native man disappeared into the jungle and in a little while returned with an old man who showed Rolfe a worn and dirty piece of paper, signed by a guerilla leader and saying that the man who carried it was trustworthy. The old fellow led Rolfe to a guerilla outpost and eventually he turned up at the divisional headquarters and joined the rest of the crew.

"The guerillas got quite a laugh out of my story about the Jap bloodhounds," Rolfe said. "It seems the baying sounds came from a species of dwarf deer which bark like dogs."

Lampe, the pilot, was picked up by a guerilla patrol on his fifth day in the jungle. He had managed to keep his escape kit and some emergency rations and was a little better off than the other crew members when he was found.

Oddly enough, the only man still unaccounted for was the squadron navigator, Captain Julian Penrose, who was not a regular member of the crew of I'll Get By and who, but for an unlucky chance, might have ridden in any one of the other 23 Liberators which got home safely from the mission over Mindanao. With the great compulsion to live which was typical of the American soldier, Penrose wandered in the jungle for eight days with nothing to eat and armed only with a small pocket knife.

Penrose had been sitting in the nose turret of the plane when a Jap 37 millimeter shell exploded against the No. 2 engine. He dropped through the nose turret and landed about forty feet up in a mahogany tree. He was about halfway down, picking his way from limb to limb, when he slipped and fell.

He was knocked out; for how long he never knew. When he came to, his head ringing and his body aching and bruised, he started through the jungle in a northeasterly direction. Leeches gradually covered his legs and ulcerous sores broke out on his body as the jungle slowly ripped his uniform from his body. Twice during the eight days Penrose heard patrols moving close to him and hid in the underbrush; he assumed that they must be Japanese.

Light-headed and wobbly from lack of food, Penrose staggered onto a railroad track sometime during his eighth day in the jungle. He sat down between the tracks because it was dry there and he knew he could go no further. He had been sitting there for some time when two men walked down the tracks toward him.

Penrose was squatted between the railroad tracks, too weak to get to his feet, when the two men stepped up to him briskly and saluted. One of them asked, in clear English:

"Captain Penrose, Sir?"

"All I could think of," Penrose said later, "running over and over in my mind, was the expression, 'Doctor Livingston, I presume.'"

"I started laughing like crazy."

On the morning of March first, ten days after they had parachuted from their crippled Liberator, the eleven men said good-bye to the guerillas and boarded a Navy PBY which, after an exchange of coded messages between guerilla headquarters and Angaur, landed at a designated spot in the Gulf of Mindanao.

"Saying good-bye to the guerillas was the hardest thing I ever had to do," said Lieutenant Rolfe. "What wonderful people they were."

Swain, who perhaps had come closest to capture by the Japanese said — like the other ten men — that he had tried to thank the guerillas but "they kept insisting it was some sort of honor to rescue us."

"At first," Swain said, "we couldn't understand why they treated us like kings. They risked their necks for us and we were certainly grateful enough for that. But they went even further. They fed us chicken and rice every day when we knew that they didn't have a damned thing themselves. They made Rolfe use the last of their atabrine for his malaria. They used up the only bandages they had dressing our sores and cuts."

Two days after the last man of the crew was found, the eleven Americans, through an experience more moving and impressive than even the details of their own rescues, finally understood why the Filipinos regarded themselves as the honored ones. It occurred late in the morning of February 27th when a mob of whooping and cheering guerillas surged out of the radio shack and quickly formed ranks around the American fliers.

"There was a lot of yelling that we didn't understand," said Sergeant Gorman. "Then it got very quiet and an old non-com stepped forward and began talking to us. He was so choked up we couldn't make out much of what he was saying, but we finally understood that Corregidor had been taken. Gradually, the old soldier got control over himself and said:

"'Many of us fought at Corregidor. This means the Philippines are free. You Americans did not forget. You gave us back our country. On behalf of our countrymen we thank you. Tell all your countrymen we thank them.'

"Then another man stepped forward with some kind of a banjo," Gorman continued. "The guerillas stood at attention and saluted us while he played the Star Spangled Banner and the Philippines national anthem. There was no sound except the music, and nothing moved except the hands of the man playing the banjo. The guerillas stood at attention, holding their salute all through the music.

"We hardly knew what to do. We returned the salute, all of us with tears in our eyes. We knew that we didn't deserve the tribute, but we knew that, to the Filipino guerillas, we symbolized the Americans who went down in the fight for the Philippines.

"We stood at attention and wished to God we had taken basic training seriously so we could really do honor to the occasion."

On March 2nd, after a roundabout journey in the Navy PBY, the crew of I'll Get By returned to Angaur. A few minutes after landing they were told that the rest of their combat mission had been cancelled; as soldiers who had escaped from enemy territory they could legally be executed as spies if they fell into the hands of the Japs. With a speed rare in Army administration, they were hustled out of the Pacific theater.

Intelligence officers, trying to draft detailed reports of the survival of the crew of I'll Get By while their stateside orders were being cut, had a great deal of trouble locating the eleven men. Through most of the day and night, they were out making calls on ordnance colonels, supply sergeants, flight surgeons, mess sergeants and everybody else (including a General and an Admiral) who had access to supplies.

The aviation engineers, when they heard about the airstrip a handful of Filipinos were cutting through the jungle in preparation for the Allied invasion of Mindanao — with three wheelbarrows and a dozen shovels for heavy equipment — began losing a number of tools. Nobody cared that the tools turned up in a stack of Army equipment in front of Lieutenant Lampe's tent.

Although the sick book entries at medical dispensaries on Angaur show a sharp decline during the month of March, a great amount of medical supplies suddenly and inexplicably disappeared. Guards at ammunition dumps began walking their posts on one side only at prearranged times. Supply sergeants, mess sergeants, and colonels reputed to be stern military conformists, got stiff necks from looking the other way as shoes, rations, carbines, pistols, howitzer shells, Army uniforms and dozens of expendable and non-expendable supply items joined the growing mountain in front of Lampe's tent. Seven hundred and fifty dollars in cash was collected from the squadron mates of the eleven rescued men. As the idea snowballed through the Marine, infantry and artillery outfits on the island, it became obvious that it would be necessary to schedule not one, but two, Liberator-transports to a practice navigation run over Mindanao.

And so it was that the two cargo planes appeared above the divisional headquarters of the Filipino guerilla Army in Mindanao on a day in March and circled while crews parachuted more than twenty tons of equipment to the same courtyard where eleven American fliers had stood awkwardly at attention and heard an old Filipino soldier say, through his own tears:

"You Americans did not forget."

CHAPTER XXII: "I'M SORRY WE WRECKED YOUR PLANE, SERGEANT"

THERE WERE NO FAMOUS PILOTS AND NO FAMOUS AIRPLANES IN the Seventh Air Force; famous, that is, outside the coral and jungle confines of the 5,000-mile chain of islands which comprised the Seventh's air command.

The Seventh Air Force had produced no Gabreskis or Bongs. Too often, the Jap fighters were out of range of the Army land-based fighter pilots.

Although the Seventh's bombers consistently flew the longest missions in the world against the smallest targets, there was no Memphis Belle touring Stateside defense factories to tell the story of the men of the Seventh. For a long time, they didn't have an airplane or crew which could be spared from the pressing business of war against the Japanese to fly a publicity mission to the States.

They had come rather close to it once with a Liberator named the Bolivar, which flew 186,000 combat miles against twelve Japanese islands from Funafuti to Iwo to complete eighty-one missions and drop 405,000 pounds of bombs. The Bolivar, at the outset of a bond-selling tour which might have given the forgotten Seventh the kind of publicity that was going to other air forces, crashed to an ignominious and untimely end in full view of several thousand Consolidated aircraft workers at Downey, California. The Consolidated plant was the first and only stop on the aborted bond tour.

But there were men and airplanes famous all through the islands of the Central Pacific for accomplishments worthy of remembrance in a theater where the fantastic was commonplace.

Planes like the Texas Belle which, months after it made its parachute landing on Tarawa, was still being talked about in chow lines as far west as Angaur.

And men like Technical Sergeant Guillermo Abrego, a B-24 flight engineer who, after the rest of his crew had parachuted from a disabled bomber 200 miles off Marcus, and without an hour's flight training, piloted and navigated the shot-up plane 600 miles home to Tinian, only to miss winning one of the greatest gambles of the war when he picked an airstrip only partially completed and crashed to his death.

There was one airplane which achieved everlasting fame among the men of the Seventh for a mission and a crash landing so fantastic that the thousands of men who saw the plane come in on Saipan could never fully believe what they saw.

The airplane was the Chambermaid. So remarkable was its flight home from Iwo, and so devastating its crash landing, that it was the subject of a lengthy and detailed report in the New Yorker Magazine written by a Seventh Air Force man, Sergeant Roger Angell. It was, for the tiny and forgotten Seventh, quite a burst of acclaim.

It is a complete aside, but perhaps interesting to note here that even a few thousand words in a national magazine were not accomplished without some backstage wrangling.

Trouble of a kind developed when a Navy censor, sitting in the plush safety of an air-conditioned office at Pearl Harbor, deleted a line in Sergeant Angell's story which said that Lieutenant Robert Doscher, an observer aboard the Chambermaid, "took down his pants" to dress a wound. The Navy man substituted, in place of this earthy reportage, the Nice-Nellie phrase of "removed his trousers."

The Air Forces Public Relations Officer, Lieutenant Colonel Dickson Hartwell, blew a fuse. He argued that the phrase in question constituted honest reporting — that men stopped removing their trousers when they left the comparative security and modern plumbing contrivances of places like Pearl Harbor and, at outposts like Saipan, began taking down their pants.

The matter was at a stalemate for several days, with Colonel Hartwell taking the stand that the Navy was empowered to censor press copy for military security only and that deletions such as the one in question gave censors authority to judge according to their literary whims.

The Navy won out. The censor produced an obscure directive which, according to Navy interpretation, gave the censor the power to blue-pencil copy "of questionable taste." As a gesture of good sportsmanship, the censor finally compromised and permitted Sergeant Angell and the New Yorker Magazine to say that Lieutenant Doscher "removed his coveralls."

It may seem pointless to review the argument here. But, minor as the incident appears to be, the Navy man's preoccupation with meaningless details is indicative of a common attitude among lesser administrative officers, Air Forces as well as Navy, which threatened to add days and weeks and perhaps months to V-J Day.

For purposes of complete honesty in this report of the Chambermaid's flight, Lieutenant Doscher will, at the proper moment, take down his pants.

The Chambermaid took off from Saipan early on a morning in September as part of a formation of B-24's going north to Iwo Jima in tight formation through bad weather.

For the plane, which the crew privately called the House of Bourbon after their cocker mascot, Burma Bourbon, it was the thirty-fifth mission. The Liberator had seen one crew safely through its quota of combat missions. The present crew, with only six missions behind them, were comparative newcomers to combat.

The flight north was uneventful except for bad weather which forced the formation to detour constantly.

Fifteen minutes before Iwo was sighted, the crew of the Chambermaid discovered a flight of eight Jap pursuit planes far below them.

"That was unusual," said Lieutenant William V. Core, the pilot. "But Iwo had a reputation for being the most unpredictable target in the Pacific anyhow."

Even more unusual was the fact that the Japs began making long passes at the formation from below. Usually, the Jap fighters held their attack until our planes came out of their bombing runs and broke formation to evade flak.

One of the Zeroes was hit by fire from the B-24's and blew up. Then, as the Liberators came over the target, the Jap fighters dropped back to let the anti-aircraft do its work.

Lieutenant Core, who had made three previous trips over Iwo but "never saw the damned place," gave the Chambermaid's controls to his co-pilot, Lieutenant Glen W. Beatty.

Leaning forward in his seat, Core saw red and white flashes appear all over the island. It made him feel that every Jap down there was firing at his personally.

Lieutenant Melvin K. Harms, the bombardier, released his load over the Chambermaids specific target, the installations and storage areas around the airstrip.

Standing over the open bomb bay, Lieutenant Doscher, an Intelligence officer flying that day as observer, and Lieutenant Clarence Wasser, the navigator, watched the bombs curl down toward the island and score 100 per cent hits in the target area.

Then, as the Chambermaid picked up speed and began evasive action, Doscher and the navigator went forward to the flight deck.

Wasser was standing on the flight deck with one hand on the pilot's seat and the other on the co-pilot's, when the saga of the Chambermaid began.

About twenty-five seconds after bombs away, while Core was calling out the positions of Jap fighters which jumped the formation while flak was still breaking around it, Sergeant Milton E. Howard, the nose gunner, called and asked why his turret had stopped.

A few seconds later, Staff Sergeant George S. Shahein said that something was leaking into his turret. Whatever it was so thick he couldn't see a thing.

It was the first that Core knew the Chambermaid had been hit by flak. Harms, who left his place in the bombardier's cage to investigate, found that the Chambermaid had taken a direct flak hit on the nose. Some hydraulic lines had been severed; the fluid spread quickly through the plane and leaked down into the ball turret.

"It was a hell of a mess," Core said. "I knew then that we were in a bad way. One turret wasn't working; the other was useless because the gunner couldn't see anything."

Two Japs came in on the disabled Chambermaid, one high at ten-thirty, the other at two o'clock. Core watched them both but called out the one at ten-thirty because it was closest.

The plane at two o'clock did a half roll, dropped a phosphorous bomb and came in on the Chambermaid, smoke trailing from his wing guns.

There was a dull explosion behind the co-pilot's head.

Core saw a hole in the roof of the pilot's compartment. Bits of aluminum and glass showered the flight deck. Core, who didn't know that Richards had been standing behind him only inches from where the shell exploded, saw no visible damage and figured that, so far, the Chambermaid had been lucky.

The fighter at ten-thirty was still coming in, so Core kept calling him out to the gunners.

About half a minute after the shell exploded, Beatty, the co-pilot, reached around and felt his back, which had begun to hurt. His hand came away covered with blood.

Beatty turned in his seat to let Core have a look at him. The pilot saw there was a hole in his uniform with a lot of blood around it. Beatty, although nobody knew it then, had been wounded by a piece of aluminum from the plane which had been driven into his back when the shell exploded over his head. Beatty wanted to keep on flying but Core took the controls from him.

Core then discovered just how badly the Chambermaid had been hit. The throttle controlling the No. 1 engine was loose and waggled back and forth; number two throttle was jammed. Both engines were running at a speed which would use up a lot of gas. The No. 4 engine was throwing oil, and Core was sure it would be only a matter of minutes before that engine would be of no further use.

At that point, Core gave up all chances of getting home and wondered if he could set the Chambermaid down at sea on one engine; it looked as though that was all he would soon have.

Core checked the airspeed and called the flight leader, Captain Robert Valentine, to ask for protection against the Zeroes beginning to crowd the crippled plane. Four planes boxed the Chambermaid in, one above, one below and one on each wing. They adjusted their airspeed to Core's and pooled their firepower to fight off the Japs trying to get at the cripple.

The damage to the Chambermaid, bad as it seemed to Core, was far greater than he knew.

Harms, coming back from his position in the nose of the Chambermaid to check the damage to the rest of the plane, found Staff Sergeant Ted Richards, the radio operator and top turret gunner, and Wasser, the navigator, lying on the flight deck in their own blood.

Apparently, the exploding shell had blown Wasser through the narrow opening in the pilot's compartment and back onto the flight deck.

A freezing wind whipped through the plane and, where the top turret had been, there was now a great round hole. A second shell had exploded in the turret, blowing the dome out into the slipstream, where it careened back and tore a hole in the leading edge of the right vertical stabilizer.

Both men were in a bad way. Forty-three pieces of shrapnel from the shell which had exploded near the co-pilot had gone into Wasser's right arm and shoulder, and a burst of machine-gun bullets from the same Jap had also hit him. Three bullets had gone through the right hand, two through his shoulders.

That Richards was even still alive was something of a miracle, since the shell which blew out his turret exploded only about three feet from his head. He was bleeding badly from his face. His windpipe was severed. His left knee, right leg, neck, and shoulders were punctured with bits of glass and shrapnel.

Harms pulled Wasser to his feet and half-carried him along the catwalk, a steel beam about a foot wide which runs over the bomb bay. Harms was afraid that Wasser would slip from his grasp and fall into the bomb bay. Although the doors were closed, Harms knew they might not support Wasser's weight if he fell.

It was a slow, agonizing journey made all the more dangerous by the hydraulic fluid which oozed along the catwalk and made it as slippery and untenable as a cake of ice. Harms got Wasser safely over the catwalk and laid him down in the waist. He pulled the leather sleeve out of Wasser's flying jacket, tied a tourniquet around his arm and sprinkled his other wounds with sulpha.

The waist gunner and engineer, Staff Sergeant Michael Verescak, made his way forward to Richards, lying on the flight deck. Verescak gave Richards an injection of morphine and began bandaging his wounds.

Most of the crew of the Chambermaid was now assembled in the waist. The ball turret gunners, their weapons useless anyhow, were helping with the wounded. Lieutenant Doscher made his way over the catwalk, borrowed a bottle of iodine, took down his pants and, with Shahein's help, dressed a deep wound in his right thigh caused by the shell that had exploded in the flight deck.

Harms, bandaging Wasser in the waist of the plane, saw Verescak run and slide over the slippery catwalk to the waist gun. He began firing.

Surely, Harms thought, this was the end. Verescak's lone gun couldn't beat off the Zeroes.

Actually, there were no Zeroes. The Chambermaid had finally passed out of fighter range and the Japs had turned for home. Verescak, bandaging Richards on the flight deck, got furious at what the Japs had done and was firing the waist gun in sheer rage.

Beatty, the co-pilot, presently came back into the waist to have his wounds dressed, and Core called back over the intercom for Staff Sergeant Robert E. Martin, the left waist gunner.

Martin, a slight, freckled youngster who looked more like a Boy Scout troop leader than the gunner of a combat bomber, was — like many enlisted aircrew members — a frustrated pilot. Two thirds of the way through Cadet Training, when he had piled up 150 hours of flying, Martin was rejected for "lack of flying ability."

Back in the States, during transitional training, Core had allowed Martin to sit in occasionally as co-pilot with the idea that someday his ability might come in handy. This, surely, was the day.

Martin moved into Beatty's seat, took the control column and began flying the Chambermaid with Core.

The pilot, greatly relieved to know that the Chambermaid was finally out of Jap fighter range, turned his full attention to the disabled engines.

He now had full control only over the No. 3 engine; and although its cowling was peppered with shrapnel, it was functioning smoothly. He had no throttle control over the No. 1 and 2 engines. Every few minutes, No. 2 would "hunt" or go wild, speed up, and cause the plane to vibrate wildly until it threatened to fall apart in the air. Engine No. 4 was throwing oil and smoking badly.

Every hour, just about on the hour, the No. 4 engine would burst into flames, burn for about thirty seconds until it consumed the surface oil and then go out.

Every rule Core knew about mechanics said that the engine should have burned out right after the oil went. But it kept on smoking and burning and running without oil hour after hour.

Unless Core could find a way to cut down the propeller speeds on the No. 1 and 2 engines, the Chambermaid would consume her last ounce of gas far short of Saipan.

Core tried the No. 1 engine first. After a lot of experimenting, he found that he could slow down the prop by feeding it air from the turbo-charger, an instrument normally used to feed oxygen to engines in the thin air of the stratosphere.

Core slowed down the No. 2 engine by a totally unorthodox use of the feathering button, a device usually employed to hold the propeller of a useless engine motionless against the wing by changing its pitch. Without the feathering device, the propeller windmills and can tear itself out of the nacelle.

Core would hit the feathering button of the No. 2 engine, wait until the propeller slowed down almost to a stall and then pull out the button. He kept changing the setting of the supercharger to keep the port and starboard engines running somewhere near the same speed.

Every little while, Core turned in his seat and winked at Richards, lying on the flight deck behind the pilot's seat. Richards, unable to speak because of his severed wind pipe, grinned and winked back.

While Core kept manipulating the engines, Martin steered the bomber along the heading for Saipan. The Chambermaid lumbered along at 140 miles an hour, fifteen miles above the speed at which a Liberator stalls out.

Despite Core's efforts, the engines were eating gas at an alarming rate. Worse, the Chambermaid was settling toward the water at the rate of 40 feet per minute.

The unwounded members of the crew in the waist began throwing things out the windows. The machine guns were taken from their mounts and thrown into the sea. Ammunition belts, flak suits, and extra radio coils were tossed out. They tried to unbolt the lower gun turret but the wrench they were using, the only one aboard, got slippery from hydraulic fluid and fell overboard.

Except for Harms and Shahein, who remained in the waist to take care of Wasser, the rest of the crew made its way forward to the flight deck to help balance the plane, which was moving through the rough weather and bucking violently.

Core, up to this time, had been concerned only with keeping the Chambermaid in the air and had given no thought to the possibility of reaching Saipan; the chances had seemed too remote.

Now, as the hours passed, Core began to hope that the Chambermaid might hold together and the fuel might last until they reached the island.

The new hope gave Core something else to worry about. With the hydraulic system out of commission, the brakeless plane would overrun the landing strip and crash. Bailing out over Saipan, the safer course however risky it was, was out of the question because of the wounded men aboard.

Verescak worked his way to the Chambermaid's bashed-in nose and tried to repair the damaged hydraulic lines. He patched up one line, taped a hole in another and poured hydraulic from the emergency tanks into the system. The taped hole opened and most of the fluid was lost.

Core called the flight leader, Captain Valentine, and told him his predicament. Valentine remembered the parachute brakes used first by the Texas Belle at Tarawa and told Core to rig three chutes in the same way.

Five hours from the moment the Chambermaid was hit over Iwo Jima, Saipan appeared on the horizon.

It was growing dusk as the Chambermaid and her four escorts made landfall. Three of the planes left the formation to land at other fields; Valentine stayed with the Chambermaid and led it toward the airstrip.

Core couldn't get through to the control tower, so communications between the Chambermaid and the ground had to be carried on through Valentine.

While Sergeant Martin flew the crippled bomber, Core went back into the plane to prepare it for the landing.

Three parachutes were rigged, one at each waist mount and one from the tail gunner's position. Corporal Robert C. Harriff, the tail gunner, volunteered for the suicidal task of remaining in the tail — the most dangerous spot in the bomber during a bad landing — to pop the pilot chute on signal from Core.

With the hydraulic system useless, the Chambermaid's heavy landing gear could only be lowered by an emergency hand crank. Verescak tested the cables by tugging at them with his full weight. They seemed to hold, so Core ordered the wheels cranked down.

The right wheel went down and locked. The cable controlling the left wheel snapped; the wheel remained locked in its well.

To the wounded and unwounded men aboard the Chambermaid, who had come six hundred impossible miles and five endless hours to within a few thousand feet and less than five minutes of safety, that was the end. They wanted to cry.

It would have been difficult enough to land the Chambermaid without brakes and with most of her instruments shot out. It would have been dangerous, but still possible, to slide the thirty-ton bomber in on its belly.

But now the Chambermaid faced the most impossible landing of all: one wheel up and one wheel down. The very best Core could hope for was a bad crash.

Verescak made one last attempt to repair the severed hydraulic lines. With a pair of pliers, he tried to pinch the tubing together at the main break. The hole was too big. Then he held his hand over the break while Core tried to get the wheel down. The fluid squirted through Verescak's fingers.

Core went back to the controls and tried to dislodge the wheel by slamming and skidding the Chambermaid around in the air. It was no use.

Verescak and Shahein, working in the cramped space of the nose, managed to kick the nose wheel down into place. It couldn't help much, but it might help Core to keep the plane from falling off its supporting wheel onto the wing; a ground loop would probably finish the Chambermaid and everybody aboard.

Core called Valentine and told him the new development aboard the Chambermaid. Valentine could do nothing but call the tower and order the right side of the runway cleared for a crash landing.

Core ordered everybody back into the waist except Sergeant Martin, who remained as co-pilot.

Verescak and Shahein carried Richards from the flight deck back to the catwalk. Verescak led the way across, holding Richards' left leg straight as he could. Richards hopped and slid along the beam on his right leg while Shahein held him from behind. They got Richards into the waist and laid him down beside Wasser.

It seemed to take a long time to clear the runway. The double row of field lights marking the strip grew sharper and brighter as darkness settled. Core could make out the dim outlines of planes being towed across to the left side of the runway.

Ambulances and a crash truck came out from under the control tower, moved down the runway and waited with motors running.

The unwounded men aboard the Chambermaid got down on the floor and arranged themselves around Richards, Wasser, Beatty, and Dorcher, facing the wounded so their own bodies would help cushion them against the shock of the crash.

Two men braced themselves near the parachutes attached to the gun mounts.

Core and Martin strapped themselves in.

Then Core called Valentine and said simply, "Coming in!"

The Chambermaid came in high and straight. Martin pumped the flaps down by hand. Core switched on the landing lights; one of them had been shot out, too. Martin cut the No. 1 engine. Core braced his full weight against the left rudder.

The Chambermaid touched the ground.

It hit the runway at 105 miles an hour and swerved sharply to the right. Martin cut the power with the master switch. The chutes popped open and slowed the plane a little but failed to halt its wild plunge over the field lights and off the runway.

The Chambermaid teetered level for a moment and then lost its balance. The right wing dug into the ground and the massive propeller of the No. 1

engine snapped off and skidded down the runway trailing a shower of sparks.

The wild plane plowed onward toward a jeep trailer fitted with a rack of floodlights. There was a slight jar and the floodlights showered into the air.

Core saw the whole left side of the instrument panel caving in toward him. He got two thirds of the way out of his seat and was held there by his safety belt.

With a great, grinding roar, the Chambermaid plowed a hundred yards through dirt and gravel, crashed sideways into a revetment and stopped.

And then everything was quiet.

There was no sound in the crumpled and broken mass of steel and aluminum. Nothing but the faint, far away hiss of flames eating at an engine.

Core and Martin sat motionless in the wreckage of the cockpit. They were trying to make themselves believe that it was all over, that they were on the ground and still alive.

Core thought vaguely of the fire in the No. 1 engine. He decided it would die out.

Core and Martin unstrapped themselves, broke a window and squirmed out of the wreckage. They ran around to the waist of the plane.

Some of the men were already out of the wreckage. The others were crawling through great gaps in the fuselage.

Harms began to count the crew and suddenly remembered he hadn't seen Harriff, the tail gunner. He ran toward the back of the plane. There was something hanging from the gun mount; it looked like a man's body. It turned out to be the parachute Harriff had opened.

It was a couple of minutes before Harms found the tail gunner. He had jumped from the plane and was wandering around dazedly in the crowd which had gathered to see the Chambermaid come in.

Every man was cut or bruised in the crash, but nobody was seriously hurt. The wounded men were not much worse off than they had been before the landing.

The ambulances came up and the medics started putting the wounded men on stretchers.

Beatty, the co-pilot, lying on a stretcher and waiting to be lifted into an ambulance, saw the Chambermaid's crew chief in the crowd.

Beatty felt sorry for the crew chief. He had taken care of the Chambermaid before and after every one of her missions.

There was nothing the crew chief could do now to fix the Chambermaid. Her fuselage was broken in half behind the bomb bay. Her nose was buckled in, and her wings were all but torn off. Parts of her were strewn along the path she had plowed up coming in.

As Beatty was being lifted into the ambulance, he saw the crew chief walk slowly toward the wreckage and called out after him:

"I'm sorry we wrecked your plane, Sergeant."

CHAPTER XXII: ASSAULT ON IWO

FROM THE TIME THE 30TH BOMBER GROUP HIT IWO JIMA ON August 10, 1944, until the invasion of that stronghold on February 19, 1945, the flyers and ground crews of the Seventh had little time for rest. No other plane returned after such a beating as was received by the Chambermaid, but some of the things that happened to that fabulous Liberator also happened to scores of other planes during this period. And it was the endless task of the ground crewmen to patch and rebuild, and the job of the airmen to take the battered, war-weary planes back into action.

Headquarters of the 30th arrived at Saipan on August 4 and set up near Isely Field in a frame building formerly occupied by the Jap Army. Three days later, the 38th Squadron arrived from Kwajalein and on the following day the 819th moved in. The two squadrons flew their first mission against Iwo on August 10.

Iwo Jima was the most unpredictable target in the Pacific. One day there would be meager and inaccurate anti-aircraft fire and no fighter opposition. The Seventh would deluge the island with bombs and return to Saipan unopposed. Then, on the next mission, all hell and would break loose. Jap ack-ack would be deadly, and enemy fighters would swarm the formation.

On the second mission, flown by Liberators of the 30th on August 14, we learned how tough the Japs could be. Thirteen B-24's, carrying 500-pound bombs, headed for the Jap airstrip and dropped 147 bombs.

A plane of the 38th Squadron received three direct hits. Fire broke out on the command deck and Sergeant Bernard Temple, combat photographer, extinguished the flames with his hands and body. The craft managed to get back but there were 150 holes for the ground crewmen to repair.

Not so fortunate was a plane of the 819th, piloted by Lieutenant James R. Mosher of Minneapolis, Minnesota. Private First Class Kealer Harbin, Tulsa, Oklahoma, assistant radio operator on the Liberator, tells the story:

"As we dropped our bombs on the target and headed out, I spotted a Zeke coming in at 5 o'clock and yelled over the intercom phone, but he dived past our tail before any of us could fire," said Harbin.

"Suddenly, Zekes were all around us and three phosphorus bombs burst directly in front of the nose of our plane. Everyone was firing and I heard Corporal John Gaydzik yell, 'Yahoo! I got the bastard!'

"Then a 20 mm. shell tore into the cockpit and exploded, riddling our co-pilot, Lieutenant Jack H. Davis, with shell fragments. Captain Carey A. Stone, flight surgeon, who had come along to observe combat conditions, tried to give Lieutenant Davis first aid but it was no use. Davis was dead."

The manual controls were hit and the plane shot upward several thousand feet. Lieutenant Mosher was hit in the right arm, face and body, but managed to switch to automatic pilot and use the trim tabs to level her off. Oil pressure for the No. 2 engine was dropping rapidly, so Mosher feathered the prop. The No. 3 engine was running away and No. 4 was stuck at 2,400 rpm's. By jockeying his throttles, the wounded pilot was able to obtain a fairly even distribution of power.

"Lieutenant Harold Puckett, our navigator, and Staff Sergeant Thomas G. Clancy, the radio operator, came up and removed the body of Lieutenant Davis to the flight deck," Harbin said. "Then Lieutenant Mosher's flight jacket was cut off and his wounds were treated with sulfanilamide powder.

"At first we were unable to contact other planes in our flight because our radio was damaged. Finally we managed to repair the radio to a degree, but it kept cutting out. We notified the others we were in trouble and two of the planes dropped down to fly cover but their prop-wash almost threw our crippled plane out of control. Fortunately, Mosher managed to straighten her out again.

"Lieutenant Puckett surveyed the damage and discovered that machine gun bullets had entered the box that held the rudder, aileron, and one set of elevator controls. All the cables had been cut and were entangled in a hopeless mess.

"Staff Sergeant Bernard J. Mistretta, the engineer, and Puckett went to work on the broken cables, with Mosher manipulating the controls to identify the rudder cables. Then he held the controls in neutral position while Puckett and Mistretta spliced the ends. Lieutenant Mosher tested the controls and felt them catch, but, not wanting to put any strain on them until the landing, switched back to automatic pilot.

"Captain Stone, who had been standing at the entrance of the pilot's compartment, had been knocked against the upper turret when we were hit. The jar had dazed him and he was bleeding from cuts on the head, but, noticing that Lieutenant Mosher was shivering with cold, the surgeon offered him his fleece-lined jacket. The pilot refused to accept it. Stone also tried to get Mosher to take some sulfanilamide tablets but those were also refused because Mosher was afraid that the powerful drug might impair his sight and reflexes.

"The three hours that it took us to get back seemed centuries, but at last we spotted Saipan.

"We came in at 11,000 feet and Mosher told Lieutenant Puckett to ask us if we wanted to bail out or stay with the plane and risk a crash landing. All of us decided to stay."

Mosher changed over from automatic pilot and the plane immediately began to slip off on one wing. By using trim tabs and automatic pilot, he was able to right the plane, but then it slipped off on the other wing. Again he managed to straighten out, but again it slipped. This time the plane went into a flat spin. Mosher tried his rudder controls, cut the power of the engines on the right wing and gunned the engines on the left, but the downward spiral continued.

"You'd better get the hell out of here," he yelled.

Captain Stone, fastening his parachute in the bomb bay, had secured his left leg strap and was fumbling with the right when the doors suddenly opened and he went hurtling out. When his chute opened, his left arm and leg were wrenched.

Puckett and at least two other crew members also went out while the others stayed with the plane. Stone, as he floated toward the water, saw two more parachutes open.

When the flight surgeon hit the water, he slipped out of the parachute harness and inflated his life vest. He hung on to the parachute, which was floating, and it supported him. A P-47 fighter plane threw out a life raft but it was damaged and wouldn't inflate properly; so Stone secured the cans of drinking water from the raft and put them inside his flying suit.

Two hours later he was picked up by a Navy patrol boat.

"I was knocked out when we hit and regained consciousness under water," said Harbin. "When I came to the surface, I saw the plane about fifty feet away. The two wing rafts had automatically inflated and I swam over and released them.

"Only Lieutenant Mosher was in sight and we assisted each other aboard a raft. None of the others could be seen and we guessed that they'd gone down with the plane.

"Finally we were picked up by a Navy crash boat. Again we looked for the others but no one could be found. Sergeant Mistretta was picked up by a patrol boat but died on the way to the hospital.

"We were lucky to be alive. It was really a rough deal," he said.

Iwo was rough enough, but the Seventh, following the same strategy that had upset the entire combat plans of the Japanese, also continued to hit by-passed islands and neutralize flanking threats in the Carolines.

During August, the 27th Squadron hit distant Yap four times. The 11th, from Kwajalein, and the B-25's of the 41st, from Makin, kept Truk, Nauru and by-passed Marshalls targets off balance.

On September 3, the 30th Group flew its first four-squadron mission in the history of the group.

Forty-one planes of the 38th, 819th, 392nd and 27th Squadrons hit Iwo on a daylight mission and dropped 96 tons of bombs on the island. Seventy-four percent of the bombs landed in the target area.

On this strike Lieutenant Richard E. McBride of Dallas, Texas, bombardier on the 38th Squadron's Dottie Anne, lived through his worst moments of the war.

"Our plane developed mechanical trouble just five minutes off Minami Rock and we were forced to bail out," said Lieutenant McBride. "Fortunately, we managed to get back over one of our destroyers before we were forced to jump.

"As soon as I was clear of the plane, I yanked my ripcord but nothing happened. I yanked again, this time with both hands, and the ripcord wire pulled out. I remembered staring at it and at the unopened parachute on my chest. There is no describing the terror I felt when I saw that ripcord in my hand.

"I could see the ocean rushing up at me as I somersaulted through the air. I tore at the chute pack with both hands, and I still don't know how I managed it, but somehow I pulled open the fasteners. The spring popped and the silk opened.

"I had fallen so far before the thing finally opened, that the jar tore my shoes off my feet."

McBride and all the others of the crew, with the exception of Technical Sergeant Richard L. Williams, the engineer, were rescued. Williams, who couldn't swim, was drowned.

On the following day, the 819th began to investigate Marcus, northeast of Saipan.

Captain Nathan G. Mehaffey flew the reconnaissance mission to try to discover any shipping around the island. Bombs were dropped, but before the crew returned safely to Saipan, they had discovered one of the greatest hotbeds of anti-aircraft fire in the Pacific.

"On some of the islands bomb-happy Japs threw ack-ack wildly and with little accuracy, but not on Marcus," said Captain Mehaffey. "That target was hell. The Nips there were deadly with their flak and their fire control was the best we encountered. Since the island was small, they threw up a pattern that was almost impossible to penetrate."

Marcus remained tough to the end — even when the war and the headlines had moved to Okinawa, some 1,200 miles nearer Japan.

Ingenuity, a factor that played such an important role in all our victories in the Pacific, helped save another Liberator from a crash landing during one of these September strikes.

Bullets from a Jap fighter plane severed the hydraulic tubes in the left wing of the Pistol Packirt Mama on a mission over Iwo Jima.

Technical Sergeant Philip A. Brodziak of Rockaway, New Jersey, engineer on the plane, grabbed a pair of pliers and stopped the flow of the hydraulic brake fluid by pinching the tube shut.

Coming into the landing field and realizing that not enough fluid remained to operate the flaps and brakes for a safe landing, he added three cans of fruit juice and a jug of water from the crew's flight rations.

When Pistol Packin' Mama hit the landing strip, the flaps came down, aided by the force of the landing, and the brakes had just enough pressure to keep the plane from rolling off the end of the runway.

The Seventh flew more than 120 long overwater missions during September and not a single plane was lost in aerial combat with the enemy. The flyers and ground crews weren't working in vain!

During October the pounding was stepped up. On October 1, Liberators hit shipping at Chichi Jima and on the following day the 392nd Squadron got 100-percent hits on runways at Marcus. On October 3, a destroyer and large cargo ship were bombed off Iwo Jima and on the same day the 819th returned to Marcus and dropped 500-pound bombs on the runways.

On October 6, the 392nd and 819th Squadrons hit air installations on Marcus and on the following day the 27th attacked two ships off the eastern shore of Marcus and the revetment areas on the island.

Again on October 11-12, the 27th returned to this flak-hell to hit dispersal and torpedo storehouse areas and drop 500-pounders.

On October 13, the Liberators went southwest to hit Yap in the Carolines. Lieutenants Odie R. Green, Andrew Patrick and Peter C. Mourtsen attacked the bridge connecting Ramung and Yap and the Gillifitz and Buloul areas.

Green and Patrick, along with two other Liberators, returned to Yap on October 19, striking at the same bridge and the Tabunifi town shore installations. From 9,000 feet, 100-pound bombs were dropped and at least two hit directly on the bridge. An oil fire was started on shore which sent smoke 4,000 feet in the air.

For weeks the 318th Fighter Group had been planning the first long range escort mission from Saipan to Iwo Jima. Gas consumption tests had been made in which P-47's and Liberators flew to Soral Island, in the Carolines, a total distance of 1,207.5 miles.

On October 21, ten P-47's from the 19th Squadron and ten from the 73rd prepared for the longest fighter strike entirely over water of the war — a total distance of some 1,500 miles.

"We had attached wing and belly tanks to the planes," said Colonel Sanders, "and for the mission we had picked some of our most experienced pilots, men who had seen months of action over Saipan, Tinian, Guam, Rota, Pagan and other targets.

"Plans called for us to escort thirty-two Liberators, with the 73rd flying 5,000 feet above the bombers and the 19th just above the B-24's.

"On earlier missions the Jap fighters had followed our bombers out at least as far as Minami Island. There we were to pick them up after they dropped their bombs.

"Everything worked with the exception of our plans for the Jap fighters. For some reason the Zekes turned back before they reached our rendezvous and only a twin-engine Nick followed the Liberators to where we waited. He was shot down by Captain Charles W. Tennant of the 19th. The flying time for the mission was 6 hours and 38 minutes."

On this strike a Liberator of the 392nd Squadron, piloted by Lieutenant Robert L. Barnsley, was lost when the plane was rammed by a Zeke. Over the target the Jap fighter suddenly dived into the B-24, tearing off the bomber's entire tail assembly and sending the Liberator plunging into the sea where it exploded. None of the crew were saved.

The 11th Bomb Group now added its strength to the air war against the unhappy Japs in the Volcanoes-Bonins area and also ranged out against Marcus, Woleai and Yap.

The ground echelon of the group left Kwajalein on October 11 and the air units left four days later. Most of the units arrived on Guam on October 21, and on the same day the 431st Squadron hit Yap with 100-pound fragmentation bombs.

During October the 30th Group flew 336 sorties, including 16 against Marcus, 182 against Iwo Jima, 63 against Chichi Jima, 42 against Haha Jima, 21 against Pagan and 12 against Yap. The group's four squadrons dropped 458 tons of bombs during the month, with shipping still the priority target.

The Japs were frantically trying to reinforce their beleaguered garrisons, and on November 3 our Liberators attacked enemy transports attempting to move reinforcements and supplies into the Bonins.

At Chichi Jima the bombers caught and blasted eleven Jap vessels, including two destroyers, one large, one medium and four small transports. Another large transport was attacked off Haha Jima, south of Chichi, and the airstrip at Iwo was blasted. Two Jap planes were destroyed and another was possibly destroyed on the Iwo strike.

On one of these Iwo missions a steel gas tank cap probably saved the lives of some of the crew of the Upstairs Maid. Technical Sergeant James R. Smiley, Wilson, North Carolina, engineer, tells the story:

"Over the target a Jap fighter zoomed in and cut loose at us," said Smiley. "A 20 mm. shell came tearing into our wing gas tank but, luckily, it was deflected by the gas tank cap and we missed a possible explosion.

"On the same pass, however, the Jap hit a hydraulic cylinder and put the hydraulic system out of commission.

"When we reached Saipan, so much of the hydraulic fluid had drained out that we lacked sufficient pressure to lower the landing gear. We tried to crank it down by hand but the cable broke. We were racing against time, as our gasoline was almost exhausted. Finally one wheel came down and the other halfway down and we gambled on a landing. Luckily, we made it without a crash. I still have that gas tank cap," he grinned.

Luck took a deciding hand in many games of chance in which flyers of the Seventh gambled their lives and planes against the enemy, the largest water theater in the world, and the crazy weather of the Central Pacific. Rarely, however, did it hold so many hands with any one pilot as it did with Lieutenant Woodrow Waterous of the 27th Squadron. And whether it was good or bad depends entirely on how you look at it.

Over Wake, in April, Waterous had two engines shot out by anti-aircraft fire. In May, fragments of a phosphorus bomb hit his horizontal stabilizer over Guam. In June, he flew the famous "blind" mission from Truk.

On September 11, his plane was damaged by flak over Iwo, and on September 25, a round of 20 mm. fire from a Jap fighter killed his navigator and filled his cap full of holes. Six days later his plane was again hit on an Iwo mission.

Lieutenant Waterous sweated-out his luck, however, and the end of the long trail came on November 5 when he was ordered back to the mainland for reassignment.

The 11th again threw its weight into the Iwo-pounding marathon when fifteen planes of the 26th and 431st Squadrons hit runways and dispersal areas on that island on November 11.

Three Zekes and a twin-engine plane intercepted the formation six minutes before the target, but the gunners of the Liberators drove them off. The B-24's dropped 463 bombs and ninety percent fell in the target area. Three explosions occurred and black smoke could be seen 20 miles away from the target.

On the same day, luck again took a hand in a plane piloted by Lieutenant Leland A. Bates, of the 98th Squadron.

"Just as we got our bombs away, a Jap 75 mm. shell entered our open bomb bay doors at station 6, grazed to the right of the ball turret, and finally went out the right-waist window," said Bates.

"Staff Sergeant Frank E. Cincinello, our ball-turret gunner, was dazed, and Staff Sergeant Howard F. Dalton, our right-waist gunner, was knocked down by the concussion. If the shell had exploded inside, as it was due to, both probably would have been killed.

"The nose of our plane was damaged by fragments from a 120 mm. gun, and shell fragments also entered the bombardier's compartment, tearing a large hole in the right nose turret ammunition box. The fabric in the back of the flak suit worn by our tail gunner, Staff Sergeant Edgar R. Glass, was torn. We were really lucky to come out of that alive!"

Liberator gunners rarely had an opportunity for strafing practice, since the usual mission was from high altitude. On November 21, however, a bomber piloted by Lieutenant Roger Kline, of the 98th Squadron, went down so low that the gunners could use the old "whites of their eyes" technique.

Lieutenant Kline's plane was one of fifteen en route to a daylight strike against enemy shipping in the Bonin-Volcano area. Just north of Haha Jima the formation began to climb, but Kline's plane began to act up.

At 9,000 feet one of his turbo-superchargers was fluctuating so he decided to leave the formation and hit Kitamura Town on Haha Jima.

"We went down to 800 feet and then leveled out for the bomb run," Kline said. "We dropped delayed action 500-pound bombs and saw two of them land among small craft near the pier at the north end of Kitamura Town. The other two hit in the main street of the town."

"Then we dropped down to 50 feet and Sergeant Lawrence E. Smith, Staff Sergeant Alphonse J. Boehm, Staff Sergeant Harry F. Bisnett and Sergeant Peter G. Eowan strafed the town and automatic weapon positions on top of the cliff.

"We were so low that we could see the Japs running around, and as we went over the town we saw a Nip carpenter working on the roof of a house. When he saw us, he fell off the roof and dived under the floor of the house. He was the most startled-looking guy you ever saw."

Speedy P-38 Lightnings had been delivered to Saipan in the middle of November and P-47 fighter pilots, with no previous training in the new twin-engine fighters, were assigned to fly them. The versatile pilots tuned up for their first mission, with four or five hours' training over Saipan.

On November 22 they flew an escort mission over Truk.

Although the Pacific Gibraltar had been given no rest from bombings and was more than 75 percent neutralized, it suddenly came to life and eight Truk-based Zekes strafed an American convoy. This was the signal for the P-38's to strike.

Twenty-six Lightnings of the 19th, 73rd, and 33rd Fighter Squadrons joined a like number of B-24's for the mission. The bombers were flying at 17,000 feet and the Lightnings directly above them at 23,000 feet when they reached the reef surrounding the Truk atoll.

The Liberators continued south toward the target while the Lightnings skirted the reef to close the trap on the eight Zekes. A single-engine float plane came up to intercept the bombers.

It was the first time we had used land-based fighters over Truk and the enemy was completely caught off guard. When the Japs circled for the attack, the P-38's came diving out of the sun.

"I spotted a Zeke about 500 feet below and dived on him, firing as I came in," said Major De Jack Williams of Long Beach, California, squadron commander of the 19th. "I fired four bursts, the last from about 400 feet astern of the Nip, and he seemed to stop in midair — almost as if in surprise. Then his tail section was shot away and he rolled over and plunged into the sea."

Lieutenant Boone N. Ruff, Joplin, Missouri, another 19th pilot, spotted two more Zekes flying parallel and to the right of the bombers.

"Just as I dived, one of them broke off to attack the B-24's," Lieutenant Ruff said. "I headed him off and the surprised Jap immediately climbed. I followed and in about three minutes I caught him over Ozen Island. When I was within 600 feet of his tail I fired and he began to burn on the left side. Then he exploded and crashed into the sea.

Captain Tennant, of the 19th, who had shot down a Nick on the first fighter-escorted mission to Iwo, and Flight Officer James E. Spaulding, Bakersfield, California, dived at two Zekes and fired at one that was making a pass at a Liberator. The Jap went into a cloud and disappeared.

Then someone reported a float plane near the water. Tennant and Spaulding went down to investigate but failed to find him. They did, however, locate a Jap surface boat inside the reef of Uliperu Island. They strafed him amidships and saw smoke coming from the superstructure when they withdrew.

Another enemy fighter, making a pass at a B-24, found himself looking into the guns of Major John J. Hussey.

"The astonished Nip pulled sharply to the left but I stayed on his tail," Hussey said. "Fire from my 20 mm. cannon hit his left wing root, tearing away the wing. He plunged smoking into the Pacific and exploded."

Captain Winston H. Park of Flint, Michigan, and Lieutenant Joseph G. Sullivan, Washington, D. C, spotted another at about 10,000 feet just north of Moen Island.

"We both took after him," said Lieutenant Sullivan. "He doubled back but we were riding his tail and cut loose. He went down into the sea."

Veterans of the 11th Bomb Group were now occupied in one of the top-secret projects of the war.

As a part of the campaign to keep troops and supplies from reaching the Bonins-Volcanoes area, a new 1,000-pound mine was brought into use. Originally a Navy project, the assignment to fill the waters around those islands with the new explosive was turned over to the Seventh Air Force.

This was an extremely risky project, for it meant flying at virtual wave-top level within easy range of shore batteries and Jap fighter planes. And the Liberators were carrying explosives that they had heard were twice as powerful as their ordinary bomb!

One Liberator tangled with one of these mines in a way that will never be forgotten by the crew.

Corporal Bud Nelson tells the story:

"Three Liberators took off at 4 o'clock on the morning of November 29 and headed for Chichi Jima," Nelson said. "An hour out from the target we dropped down close to the water and felt our way into Chichi.

"When we passed Haha Jima we rose to 1,000 feet and headed between the two hills on the island.

"The Japs began firing first and from 600 feet the flashes from the grey cliffs on either side of the valley seemed right in our faces. Our gunners fired back.

"Of necessity, our formation was exceedingly close, with our plane, piloted by Captain Phil Kroh, flying lead. Lieutenant R. L. Strong's plane was flying about 25 feet out and 75 feet to the rear of us and Lieutenant Herb Robinson was flying about 100 feet above Strong and about 50 feet behind him.

"As we plunged downward, just before we were over the bank that marked our target area, Robinson's Liberator suddenly lifted and brushed the wing-tip of Strong's ship. This put a dent in Bombardier Lieutenant Ernest Miles' nose compartment just as he released his mine.

"As the two planes broke away one of the mines sailed into Strong's plane and lodged between the waist hatch and the tail. A gaping hole in the top of the fuselage, six feet long and three feet wide, outlined the path of the projectile.

"Strong thought they had been hit by flak and when Corporal Vince Sutter yelled over the intercom that they had a bomb in their laps, he told Sutter that this was no time for joking and to get the hell off the line.

"But it wasn't a joke to Sutter. He later told me that when the mine came crashing through he just couldn't believe it. Sutter was busy strafing Japs at the time but he looked at the mine out of the corner of his eye a half dozen times. Then he and Corporal Al Newell were hit by the same thought at the same time. The damned thing might explode at any second!

"They couldn't budge it by hand so they yanked the barrels out of their guns and used them for levers. They said they didn't really get scared until they had pushed the mine out of the plane.

"Everyone returned to Saipan safely, but I doubt whether any of those guys sleep well — even now," Nelson said.

Missing sleep wasn't an inconvenience shared solely by shot-up flight crews. During November the Japs raided Saipan frequently, keeping weary ground crews and clerks diving in foxholes and fighting fires. The Nips were desperately trying to destroy the new B-29's that were hitting the Jap mainland. The enemy however, paid a heavy price.

The most brazen attack came on Thanksgiving Day, while our B-29's were hitting Japan for the first time.

"There had been pork chops for dinner that day but our boys had been on duty during the regular meal period and by the time we got to the mess hall there was nothing left but spam," said Corporal Lawrence Morton, Corry, Pennsylvania, member of a crash crew.

"Some of the fellows were grumbling about a Thanksgiving dinner of spam when we heard the raid signal and had to tear out of the mess hall.

"Four Zekes were over the field and we saw two of them shot down. The others strafed the area, proceeded to another field and then returned. They were plenty close. One was shot down on the runway and the other smacked into the ocean nearby."

During November, the 30th dispatched a total of 349 sorties. Five hundred eighty-nine tons of bombs were aimed at shipping in the Chichi and Haha Jima areas, and 354 tons were dropped on Iwo Jima. Truk received 47 tons. Woleai took 27 tons and Ani Jima 11 tons.

When the B-29 Superforts arrived in the Marianas the heat was on for the Japs.

With Japan feeling the pressure of recent losses in the Palaus, Philippines, and Marianas, and with Radio Tokyo jittering from Superfort attacks on the Jap mainland, the battle from the Marianas north to the Bonins and Volcanoes was stepped up in intensity. The B-24's, in spite of interceptors, flak, and phosphorus bombs, bombs which sometimes explode in the path of their own falling bombs, were pressing home attacks on selective targets.

The Japs, in addition to their phosphorus bombs, were now using phosphorus anti-aircraft shells. On a December 1 mission against Iwo, a B-24 was hit by one of these fiery missiles.

"About twenty seconds after our formation started on the bomb run, our bombardier, Lieutenant Wilfred A. Bloom, called me on the intercom and told me to hold the plane steady," said Lieutenant Frank W. Johnson, the pilot.

"As Bloom was getting ready to get his bombs away, a white phosphorus shell burst about 50 feet in front and a few feet below our plane. Bloom was knocked back against the wall by the concussion.

"After recovering his balance, Bloom toggled his bombs and saw them go in on the target. Then he called me and told me he was wounded.

"Our navigator, Lieutenant Norman H. Truscott, rushed up to give him first aid and discovered that Bloom had been hit in the left shoulder by a pellet of white phosphorus and partially blinded by fragments of glass from the broken bombardier's window.

"All the way back to Saipan Bloom suffered like hell. When we landed he was rushed to the hospital and given treatment. Then it was easy to understand why there was so much pain.

"When the pellet was removed from his shoulder, it was still smoking!"

The P-38 Lightnings and P-61 Black Widow night fighters of the 318th Fighter Group were important factors in the December action of the Seventh.

On December 6, pilots and aircraft of the 318th were formed into a group known as the "Lightning Provisional." This outfit had 26 P-38's. During the month they flew more than 500 hours, including three missions to Iwo Jima and one to Truk. These strikes averaged 1,500 miles each and there was only one accident — a minor taxiing mishap.

The night fighters shot down four Jap planes which were trying to knock out more B-29's.

Marianas-based flyers and ground crews were often sent cursing to foxholes by the Jap night raiders, but it was nothing in comparison to the Seventh-induced neuralgia given the unfortunate Japs crouching in the caves and foxholes of Iwo Jima.

These strikes, called "snooper" missions, were a combination tactical and psychological weapon that served the double purpose of knocking out Jap planes that might otherwise be raiding the Marianas bases of the B-29's and Liberators, and of giving the Japs a series of sleepless nights.

A snooper plane flew alone. Around five o'clock in the afternoon the Liberators took off singly and at forty-five-minute intervals from Guam and Saipan. And every forty-five minutes throughout the night a B-24 would roar in over Iwo and deposit a full load of fragmentation bombs. To make certain the strikes were on a clockwork basis, pilots were instructed to increase or decrease their air speed so that the timetable never varied.

"The Nips usually sent up a single fighter plane," said Staff Sergeant Jeremiah O'Leary, a snooper veteran. "The ship would fly alongside us, blinking its lights on and off but staying just out of range of our guns. Why they did this we never knew, but my guess is that it was to give our altitude to the ground batteries. But none of the night fighters ever made a pass at our planes and more often than not there was no ack-ack, so it was always a mystery to me."

Staff Sergeant Mac Harris thought it was a decoy job. "They probably wanted us to fire at the fighter so the ground gun crews could spot us," he said.

Even Captain Theodore S. Stevens, the Intelligence officer who briefed many of the missions before the take-off, was puzzled by the Jap's antics.

"Why the ack-ack was so meager, especially when they had our planes in range with their lights, is something I can't explain," he confessed. "They knew when we were coming and they sometimes had planes there to intercept us but they never pressed home an attack at night. The only answer I know is that they were Japs, and Japs are not very smart."

Despite the lack of interception and ack-ack at night, many of the flyers preferred daylight runs.

"We had little opposition at night," said Sergeant O'Leary, "but I preferred day missions. There was a terrific feeling of loneliness in the darkness with no other planes around you. It was just you against anything the Japs wanted to throw at you. There was no more naked feeling in the world than to be caught in those lights and not to be able to evade them. It seemed that the whole Jap garrison must have their fingers on their gun triggers and were preparing to blast away at you."

Technical Sergeant George Simmons echoed O'Leary's sentiments. "In our first snooper mission over Iwo we dropped our bombs and I thought we were through with our work, but was I wrong! Just as our frag bombs burst on the target we were caught in lights from every direction.

"We dived and tried other evasive action but still couldn't manage to shake them. Finally we got out of range without being hit with anything harder than a beam of light, but it was a helluva feeling while we were there."

All-night bombings made the dispersal areas dangerous parking spots for the Jap bombers that were preparing for missions against the Marianas.

"After hitting the foxholes during the Nip raids those all-night-every-night shuttle missions were a lot of satisfaction, and in a short time after we got them going regularly the Jap raids fell off to almost nothing," said O'Leary.

But Iwo Jima wasn't through — even if its offensive power was almost completely neutralized.

The B-24's had been hitting the island since August. Now the P-38's of Colonel Sanders' fighters accompanied the Liberators by day and the snoopers hit by night. The sulphurous pork-chop was deluged, but each time the Seventh returned, the tenacious Nips had not only made their blasted airstrips operational but were now working on a third strip. And no matter how many anti-aircraft batteries were knocked out, there always seemed to be just as many added.

December marked the beginning of the air campaign that was maintained without letup for seventy-two days — the longest sustained aerial offensive in history.

On December 7, the third anniversary of the Pearl Harbor attack, Iwo Jima got the works. The 30th and the 11th, the 318th Fighter Group, teamed with the Navy and a large force of B-29's to hit Iwo.

Eighty-nine B-24's, the largest number of Seventh bombers ever to appear over any one target on the same day, were included on the strike. Twenty-eight P-38 Lightnings escorted B-29's on the missions, and P-47's also joined the show.

Thirty minutes before the giant Superforts hit, fighters swept in over the island.

The Overcast was heavy that day but the planes fought through the thick weather and dropped 2,396 five-hundred-pound bombs. The Japs, stunned by the terrific bomb barrage, stayed in their holes and failed to send up a single fighter. Only two inaccurate flak bursts were seen during the entire strike and all our planes returned safely.

One of the few "advantages" the Japs received from the around-the-clock bombings was that their ground crews were getting plenty of marksmanship practice.

The Patriotic Patty , a veteran B-24, felt the results of this eye-sharpening on a strike over the Volcano stronghold at this time.

"I had just loosed my bombs when three flak bursts hit us," said Lieutenant Robert Bemiss, bombardier. "Our hydraulic system was knocked out, the gas lines punctured, and forty electric plugs were cut —

making gun turrets and electric flying suits useless. Gas streamed out the fuel lines. One spark would have been the end of all of us on the plane.

"Overhead Jap fighters were dropping phosphorus bombs. One engine was knocked out and the supercharger on another was severely damaged but, fortunately for us, it didn't quit.

"All of us were working frantically plugging the fuel line leaks with pencils, whittled plugs from the tail section bannister, handkerchiefs and anything loose that would fit.

"But it was like trying to plug a sieve. Five hundred gallons of gasoline swamped the plane. Corporal Lyle E. Leber passed out from the fumes. Back in the tail gunner's position, Corporal Ralph King was drenched with gasoline but managed to breathe through the shrapnel holes in his plexiglass.

"Jap planes followed us for half an hour, but not knowing our condition, failed to attack. If they had, it would have been tough, for, with the plane flooded with gasoline, fear of sparks would have kept us from firing.

"We finally limped back and cranked down the landing gear by hand. Because we had no brakes, King attached two parachutes to his guns. Then, as we hit the runway, he yanked the ripcords.

"The jolt yanked out the guns and knocked King unconscious but it stopped the plane before we went off the strip."

Uncertain weather and distance, the two greatest scourges of the Central Pacific, were even tougher than the Japs.

Ice was one of the worst curses. About three times each month, during this time, the northwesterly monsoons shoved the polar front down from the Bonins and Volcanoes, and the freezing level was at about 10,000 feet. The ice caused drag and loss of climb, encrusted airfoils, lessened speed, and made the planes hard to control. It often forced them to turn back or drop below bombing level.

On a strike against Chichi Jima, a B-24 piloted by Lieutenant James H. Graham, flying at 18,000 feet, began picking up ice on the turret and leading edges. He dropped to 9,000 feet.

Other planes in the formation were forced by ice to return to base and finally Graham discovered that his was the lead plane and was expected to guide the way over the target. When the Liberator was over the mark and Flight Officer Robert H. Graham, the bombardier, prepared to release his bombs, he discovered that his bombsight was frozen out of commission.

Undaunted, Graham sighted over his right big toe and dropped his bombs. Crews in other planes saw them fall directly on the target!

The Liberators now received another assignment — "spotter" service for the Navy.

This job consisted of carrying Navy fire-control experts to spot task-force shelling and correct inaccuracies through constant plane-to-ship radio communications. This involved the dangerous task of having the Liberators hover at low level over Jap installations for periods of an hour and a half, virtually at the mercy of Jap guns.

On December 27th, Liberators piloted by Major Tom Peddy, Captain Boris Kutner, and Lieutenants Ray Lester and Bob Hadsall, Arthur Knudson, and Don Painter, of the 819th Squadron, accompanied by P-38 Lightnings, joined with the Navy for this venture.

The Liberators, after dropping their frag bombs on the targets, circled and crossed the island at heights ranging from 500 to 5,000 feet. Then the spotters on the planes called the shots and corrected the range of the naval guns that shattered the island with artillery fire from point-blank range of 3,000 yards. The harbor, the barracks area, gun installations, ammunition and fuel dumps, airstrips and taxiways — everything of military value — was shelled.

Sporadically, as the bombers came within range, the Japs cut loose with bursts of 7.7 and small-arms weapons. Sometimes the enemy, risking exposure of their heavier weapons positions, threw up flak, driven to desperation by the heavy barrage. Then the spotters would direct naval shelling to the area and the flak fire would stop.

Kneeling at the plane's waist, with microphone in one hand and grid map in the other, Navy officers listened for their ship gunnery officers' salvo and watched bursts as the shells struck the island. Then they corrected inaccuracies of as little as 30 yards, and usually the following salvo would box in the target like a mortar barrage. Innumerable fires and visible signs of destruction at every inhabitable part of Iwo attested to the success of this liaison between the Seventh and the Navy.

Fighter planes of the Seventh on many occasions flew escort for shot-up Liberators, beating off Jap planes that would have ganged the crippled bombers.

On January 5, a B-24 reserved the usual procedure and flew escort for a damaged Lightning. Over Iwo that day the P-38's and Liberators came in for the attack. Lieutenant Fred Erbele took his Lightning down to 300 feet and strafed enemy gun installations.

Suddenly a 20 mm. shell hit his left engine, tearing off the prop governor, but Erbele held his course and threw tracers at the gun positions. He tried in vain to feather the damaged engine, then turned it off, letting the prop windmill. The falling plane was almost on the ground before he could pull it out of the dive.

Then an explosive shell hit his right wing, and flames streaked back to the tail assembly, and the control surfaces on the wing froze. With speed down to 150 miles an hour, the P-38 was a juicy plum for Jap picking.

Luckily, Erbele's left engine caught on again and he was able to put the battered Lightning into a climb and got up to 5,000 feet.

The damaged left engine was heating; so he cut it off again. A foot-square hole was in the plane's trailing edge as Erbele, protected by Lieutenant Joseph G. Sullivan, his wingman, reached the other planes in the formation.

For the entire group to have flown at Erbele's maximum of 135 miles an hour would have been fatal; so the others returned to base, leaving Sullivan and two B-24's to fly cover for the battered Lightning.

After 300 miles, the slow flying was exhausting Sullivan's gasoline and he was ordered to head for Saipan. One of the Liberators went along to navigate and the other remained with Erbele.

Usually a B-24 is no match in speed for the speedy P-38's, but this time the situation was reversed and the bomber, time after time, was forced to circle and return. Finally, by lowering his flaps, he was able to stay with the fighter.

Long after the other planes had landed, Erbele and his escort were still limping toward home. Vibrations from the windmilling prop shook the fighter and threw the instruments into a turmoil.

It really looked tough when they hit a storm front. Erbele was drenched with rain but luckily they suddenly broke out of the clouds and met a life-raft team of P-47's.

Then with Saipan in sight and twenty minutes' gas supply remaining, he waved his faithful Liberator escort on and followed the P-47's in.

With the invasion of Iwo close at hand the versatile Seventh took another new assignment — that of shooting pre-invasion closeup pictures of invasion beaches and island defenses.

First of these 1,600 miles missions was flown by Captain Edward S. Taylor, commanding officer of the reconnaissance squadron; Captain Bennie P. Bearden and Lieutenants Lloyd Q. Mettes and Leo F. Wilkinson in gun-stripped P-38's converted to recon planes.

Despite heavy ack-ack and Jap fighter interception, the ships came in 50 feet above the ground at 300 miles an hour, clicking off three 5-by-5 inch photos per second.

Most elaborate of the missions followed, with twelve armed P-38's and four B-29's flying escort for five of these recon planes.

The formation hit Iwo at noon. Flying abreast with the Lightnings when they reached the target, were Captain Bearden and Lieutenant Don J. Howard. Over the center of the island, Lieutenant Charles E. Decker, also in the formation, was shot down in flames. Lieutenant Marshall E. Mullens flew in just north of the island and made his camera run down the east coast. Nearly an hour later Lieutenant Alfred A. Wootten, escorted by three B-29's and four P-38's, photographed the west coast.

Lieutenant Mullens raced across the center of the island and almost collided with a Jap bomber taking off from the airstrip.

It was a tough assignment for the flyers of the unarmed recon planes. Going in at tree-top altitude, they had to depend on speed, maneuverability and surprise to get through fire from the 50 anti-aircraft guns and more than 150 automatic weapons plus small arms fire.

But the risks paid off, for the Seventh provided 1,170 negatives from which 17,170 photographs of Iwo were made. These pictures furnished information that made possible the destruction of scores of guns which would have cost the lives of many more Marine, Navy and Air Forces personnel during the invasion.

Iwo was being softened for the kill on a 24-hour schedule in the greatest pre-invasion bombing of the war. But we were paying a price in planes and men.

One of the crews to die was the famous Texas Belle unit — the men who had first used parachutes to stop a brakeless plane.

Lieutenant Charles F. Pratte, of the 42nd Squadron, who had piloted the Texas Belle on the mission over Maloelap made his last flight on January 22.

Flying on a mine-laying mission against Chichi Jima, Lieutenant Pratte and his crew, including Lieutenant Paul E. Vinroot, co-pilot; Lieutenant Randolph H. Ball, navigator; Richard J. Meagher, bombardier; Technical

Sergeant William H. Mashaw, engineer; Technical Sergeant Arthur T. Maloney, gunner, and Staff Sergeant William J. Farrell, gunner, took off from Saipan and were never heard of again.

The 30th Group also suffered losses. Lieutenant Donald E. Painter's Liberator was hit by flak over Iwo and forced to ditch. All crew members were lost.

On January 24, another 30th plane, piloted by Lieutenant James B. Fagan, was damaged by anti-aircraft fire over Iwo and crash-landed in the water between Saipan and Tinian. Three of the crew were never found.

Again, on January 27, the 392nd Squadron ran into trouble over this island. Just as the lead plane, piloted by Lieutenant Herbert O. Broemer, was to releases its bombs, a 75 mm. shell smashed into the left side of the fuselage to the rear of the nose turret. The shell burst inside the cockpit, completely wrecking the instrument panel and damaging the hydraulic system. Broemer, Lieutenant William M. Smith, the co-pilot, and Lieutenant John W. Donnelly, the navigator, were seriously injured. The plane went out of control, banking sharply. Broemer was stunned, but managed to grab the controls before the B-24 crashed. Then he headed back for Saipan.

Smith was too badly injured to be of any assistance. Broemer's right arm was useless and his right eye was full of glass. With only one hand he was unable to work the throttle; so the engineer handled that. The radio operator furnished eyes and called off readings on the air speed indicator.

When they came into Saipan, the damaged landing gear could not be lowered and the suffering pilot was forced to circle the strip for twenty-five minutes before the crew could get the wheels down. Then he brought it in safely.

In February the pounding of doomed Iwo was stepped up to fever pitch and "every available aircraft in the Pacific" was assigned to hit the island on February 1.

Again the "stinking pork chop" rocked with blasts and 819th Squadron dropped 55-gallon drums of deadly napalm. The liquid fire cleaned out a wooded section concealing important buildings.

The P-38 Lightnings, which flew a total of 237 sorties against the island, teamed with the Liberators on February 15, on another all-out strike against Iwo.

Taking off from Saipan at 7:15 in the morning, the fighters reached Iwo just before noon. Major De Jack Williams caught sight of two Zekes at

14,000 feet and a third at 7,000. The Lightnings went into a mutual support formation and Williams got on the tail of one of the Japs. But, as he closed in for the kill, he saw a Zeke on the tail of another P-38. Williams broke away to aid his companion but the Jap fighter took off for the shelter of the island.

Lieutenant Victor C. Besche saw another Zeke head out to sea and followed him. He closed in to 250 feet and saw his tracers rip into the plane. The Zeke disappeared from sight.

Then, after driving away the fighters, the P~38's escorted the Liberators over the target and returned to base.

On another of these missions, Lieutenant James Hewitt, pilot of the B-24 Evasive Action, worked the same stratagem that Captain Allan R. Taflinger used against the Japs at Maloelap.

On a search for Jap shipping in the Bonins area, Lieutenant Hewitt had covered his assigned area without spotting a Jap vessel and had headed for his secondary target — the airstrip at Iwo Jima.

As he passed Kito Iwo Jima, just north of Iwo, he saw a light and went down to investigate. It turned out to be a beacon. The Japs were not expecting enemy planes but apparently some of their own were due.

Hewitt put the Evasive Action into a gradual dive as though coming in for a landing, and the Japs, thinking it was one of their own planes, didn't fire. Hewitt flew down the center of the runway and the bombs hit squarely in the target. The Japs were caught flatfooted and the Evasive Action was away before a single shot was fired.

On the 16th the Seventh joined with the Navy to begin the final pounding of the gun positions and invasion beaches. Six battleships, supported by cruisers and destroyers, steamed into range of the island and rained heavy shells on military installations revealed by Seventh recon planes. On one of these strikes, Staff Sergeant Leonard A. Merz, a Liberator gunner, "teamed" with the Navy to wipe out a gun position.

"We went in low for strafing and I spotted an automatic weapon," said Merz. "I could tell from the flashes that it was firing at our formation. I cut loose at it and could see my tracers going in.

"Then, as I set my sights again, the whole thing vanished in a terrific explosion as a big Navy shell got a direct hit.

"The Navy and I did all right!"

As the Marines stood by waiting for the signal to hit the beaches, the Seventh increased its tempo even more. On February 17 the Seventh struck again, dropping bombs from 5,000 feet and strafing airfields, parked planes, gun positions and buildings.

On February 19, while hundreds of ships steamed in to join the battle wagons already pounding Iwo, the Seventh struck again. Flying below 5,000 feet, the air fleet joined the sea fleet in deluging the island with bombs and shells.

The Marines, under the command of Major General Harry Schmidt, hit the beaches, and on what should have been a "dead" island, met one of the most withering fires ever encountered by troops anywhere, as desperate Japs emerged from underground tunnels and shelters and cut loose from deeply embedded steel pillboxes.

Moving in with the Marines was a Seventh Air Force aircraft warning unit, a group assigned to go in and set up a warning outfit that would be able to give the Marines advance notice of enemy air raids.

Some of these men, such as Staff Sergeant Ted La Varta and Staff Sergeant Jack Fowler, had been in the original unit which had flashed the famous "disregarded warning" signal when the Jap planes came in on Pearl Harbor. Others had hit the invasion beaches of Saipan and Tinian.

With all these months of service, they had expected to be returned to the mainland for reassignment but, instead, they were sent on the toughest assignment of the war.

First Army man on Iwo was Sergeant Walter Matuszowski, who went in with the Fifth Marine Division.

"I was assigned to pick out the site for our installation," said Matuszowski, "but on H-hour-plus-3 I was dug in 10 yards from the water's edge, a bullet crease in my helmet, and lucky to be alive."

For seventeen hours Matuszowski was the only one of his unit ashore; then three more of the unit volunteered to bring in two truckloads of radio equipment.

Technician-5 Richard N. Kimmons, one of this trio, described the action to Private First Class Alan K. Hartman:

"It was five o'clock in the morning when we came in and still dark. The waves were higher than hell and mortar fire was heavier than at H-hour.

"Our LCM's grounded on the beach and then backed off before we were able to get our trucks on shore. Our wheels could get no traction in the wet sand and, with shells bursting all around, we finally managed to get a tractor and drag them out of the water.

"The trucks were hit twice by mortar fire, but, fortunately, the equipment wasn't ruined. Two hours later the rest of our advance party zigzagged ashore and dug in on the beach.

"For hours we took everything both sides could offer, including terrific explosions when our own beach parties were forced to blow up wrecked landing craft only a few yards from us in order to clear the beach for traffic. Late in the afternoon we crawled through a small draw in the volcanic terrace toward the CP.

"There we dug in around a bomb crater, but around midnight one of our road-repairing bulldozers forced us to move. Two hours later the general hell of mortar and artillery fire was increased by eight tremendous explosions when the Japs hit an ammunition dump 100 yards south of us.

"At dawn our detachment went to work on a makeshift warning system. By mid-afternoon, laboring under constant shellfire, we had hooked up a large siren near the Fifth Division CP, right in the front lines. The setup was completed just in time, too, for on D-plus-2 the Japs made their first raid.

"Fortunately our hastily erected system worked and we were able to sound an alert in sufficient time to avoid a surprise."

By D-plus-4, the day the Marines raised the flag on Mount Suribachi, the group finally set up headquarters near a rations dump. But the Marines soon made this one of the most hazardous spots on the island by storing munitions and high octane gasoline all around them.

"My crew went on for the nightshift and at two o'clock in the morning the Japs began to shell the area," Staff Sergeant Denver St. Claire told Hartman.

"Four men were in the radio dugout, maintaining contact with the Information Center. Along with our unit they kept right on sending in plots as we became the center of a flaming inferno.

"After an hour of this, I sent all but two of our men into the already crowded radio dugout and the rest of us tried to stick it out, but the camouflage net around us caught fire.

"We headed for an abandoned foxhole, donned gas masks, and were sweating it out when Information Center ordered a red flash because of approaching Jap planes. The fellows in the radio dugout managed to pull out all the stops on the big siren and the island was alerted. I tried to crawl out and help, but an explosion blew me back into the foxhole.

"All around us drums of gasoline, flames, smoke-pots and ammunition were exploding. Men in near-by foxholes tried to crawl out and make a break but were mistaken for Jap snipers and fired on.

"The food dump caught fire and the air was filled with exploding cans of spaghetti and beef. Then smoke shells went off and Information Center was forced to go off the air until the men donned gas masks.

"The radio men managed to keep alive only by splashing their clothing with water and putting wet rags on their faces. Just as they set off the all-clear siren, the flames swept over the control wires, but the siren sounded long enough to inform everyone that the Jap planes were gone.

"But we were still pinned down until five o'clock in the morning when the fire finally burned out. When a detail from our outfit came looking for us they thought they were on a burial assignment, but all our crew walked out to meet them."

On D-plus-6 this unit was operational, although the main business still was that of sandbagging the position and dodging sniper and mortar fire. Meanwhile other sections of the warning group were coming ashore.

One of these, under Lieutenant George M. Goldberg, had hit the beach on D-plus-4 with the 4th Marines. In the confusion of landing, their personal gear was loaded on Marine trucks and taken to the north end of the island. It was retrieved by a party that was pinned down by shellfire on the way back.

They were still under fire while setting up the equipment and the Japs managed to knock out one of their motors, but an auxiliary motor was installed and seven hours after they landed they were on the air.

A third group, which consisted of six trucks carrying control units, came in on D-plus-3 day. To these men, however, Iwo was an old story, for most of the personnel had come in on the first day and served on the front lines as volunteer stretcher bearers.

Gradually the units integrated and formed the intricate network that became the modern aircraft warning system.

For twenty-six days the fighting on Iwo raged. The Japs, who had received the greatest baptism of fire in history, held on tenaciously and had to be burned and dug out of their holes like rats. Scores were buried alive in caves in Mt. Suribachi.

Life was a hell of choking volcanic sand that covered clothing and food and fouled firearms. Sleep came only when complete weariness made it possible to ignore mortar fire and banzai charges.

Yet, in spite of all this, aviation engineers moved in and cut out airstrips. Clerks, mechanics and cooks of the Seventh — men who had never seen combat before — cleared the Jap strips of wrecked Zeros, Zekes, and Bettys.

Gradually the island was converted into a base through which the B-29 Superforts staged many of the final attacks that ended the war.

With the operations against Iwo completed, the 30th Bomb Group, which had played such a major part in the whole campaign, began to break up. Many of the veteran flyers were transferred to the 11th on Guam, and the VII Bomber Command Headquarters and Headquarters Squadron at Saipan.

The remainder of the group prepared to move back to Oahu to be reassigned to Army Air Forces, Pacific Ocean Areas.

But, on February 26, Lieutenant General Millard F. Harmon, Commanding General of AAFPOA, was lost on a routine flight.

His plane, a C-87, had radioed two positions back to the base and a third had come through garbled. Then there was silence.

The 30th was called in to assist in the greatest search of its kind ever undertaken. B-24's, C-46's, C-47's, C-54's, OA-10AS's, B-25's and PB4Y-2's were among the aircraft employed.

Flying at altitudes ranging from 1,500 feet to practically sea level, the Iwo-weary flyers combed the empty Pacific for twenty-one days. A total of 123 sorties were flown by the 30th Group alone, resulting in a total flying time of 1,181.3 flying hours.

Almost everything imaginable was reported during this time-flares, life rafts, sea markers, wreckage, orange boxes, lights, Jap submarines, and even a pair of khaki trousers floating in the water. All were duly evaluated and investigated. The empty, greedy Pacific, which made no distinction between private and general, had taken another victim on its already crowded sacrificial altar of war!

Iwo was ours! The barren, sand-choked island was teeming with American airpower. Airfields were springing to life beneath the tireless hands of the Aviation Engineers and the Seabees.

In March and April many new units moved in. Stationed there were the Seventh Fighter Command, the 15th Fighter Group, the 21st Fighter Group Headquarters, the 45th Fighter Group and the 548th and 549th Night Fighter Squadrons.

New names, new planes, new men! The tiny Seventh, the infinitesimal air force that did so much with so little for so long, was beginning to lose its identity in the giant machine that was beginning to take shape. The war-weary B-24's were beginning to wind up their job!

CHAPTER XXIV: BANZAI AT IWO

IN THE LATE AFTERNOON OF MARCH 27, TWO MEN CLIMBED DOWN stiffly from a C-47 transport plane which had just landed on Iwo Jima. They began walking across the runway toward the operations tent.

The two men were Lieutenant Herbert Bowden and Staff Sergeant Tom Hall. Like all people arriving on Iwo for the first time, they noticed the thin wisps of yellow steam rising from the ground and felt the soles of their heavy GI shoes grow warm and then almost hot as they trudged over the ashy surface of the volcanic island.

Bowden, who had been pleasant and talkative on the long plane ride up from Guam, suddenly grew silent.

Hall, filled with the excitement of a newcomer to overseas service, was aware of a peculiar thing happening to himself.

He had found it hard, during the flight from Guam, to focus on the young Lieutenant who sat next to him talking enthusiastically of his plan to open an advertising agency in New York after the war. His mind had been a whirling kaleidoscope of islands, coral runways, water, endless clouds and churning propellors which, in less than two weeks, had carried him almost seven thousand miles from California.

Then, as Sergeant Hall walked his first hundred yards on the island of Iwo Jima, the whirling stopped abruptly and his senses came suddenly, sharply into focus.

Iwo was like that.

"Iwo hit you in the face and kept hitting you," one Air Forces man said. "Iwo was the end of the world."

Iwo had hit Lieutenant Bowden and Sergeant Hall the way it hit the Marines who came ashore a month and ten days before; the way it hit the thousands of men who had arrived since D-Day.

Iwo was high-pitched-frantic. It boiled with the noise of men and bulldozers and airplanes. But it was grim and silent and desolate.

On Guam, Bowden and Hall had talked enthusiastically of their assignment. Working for the Intelligence section, they were to handle part of the work necessary to carry out the first Seventh Air Force fighter escort mission over Japan, now less than ten days away. It was a choice assignment.

On Iwo, they talked quietly and dispassionately of the work they could accomplish the next day and, when it grew dark, made their way to the separate quarters assigned them.

Iwo Jima hit Sergeant Hall again while he was putting up his canvas cot.

The men around him, crew chiefs and mechanics, talked of little except the queer sounds that filtered through the ground at night — the muffled clanging of subterranean digging coming from the deep caves where an unknown number of Japs still held out.

Hall noticed that the men around him kept their knives and carbines handy and wished he hadn't replaced his own gun with a portable typewriter before he left Guam.

Exhausted as he was, it took Hall a long time to fall asleep; he was nagged with an uneasy feeling of impending tragedy.

"Iwo was always like that," one man said. "If something violent wasn't happening at the moment, there was a dread sense that it was about to happen."

There is no coherent account of exactly what happened on Iwo Jima on the night of March 27. There are individual accounts of terrible violence; the babbled, shocked words of the dying; the signs of mortal combat which persisted for a long time.

It was sometime in the early hours before dawn when the distant sounds of gunfire awoke Sergeant Hall. He jerked upright on his cot.

"It's nothing," a voice near him said. "Probably just a couple of guards shooting at each other. Happens almost every night."

The sounds grew louder, closer. Hall, trained as a combat infantryman before he transferred to the air forces, recognized the bursts of grenades and small mortars.

"Jesus!" somebody in the tent yelled. "That's right in our area."

In a flash, the tent was empty. Hall, stumbling over cots and duffle bags in his rush toward the door, glimpsed men darting through the moonlight toward a road at the end of the company area.

Two men seemed to be helping another man who, clad only in shorts, stumbled and limped between them. There was blood all over the man's shorts.

As Hall reached the door, he saw an Army carbine hanging from a nail. He reached for it and then remembered that its owner might come running back for it at a critical moment.

Hall reached the end of the company street behind the group he had been following and dove to the ground after them, burrowing with his arms and legs into the layers of ash.

Over and over again a man next to him was saying hysterically: "The bastards! The dirty bastards! Hundreds of 'em. Hundreds of 'em!"

Hall's body shook uncontrollably with fear. His arm, flailing in the ash, came to rest for a moment against the body of a husky major dug in next to him. The major's body was quivering with spasms of terror; his flight coveralls were wet with the sweat of honest fear. Sergeant Hall was no longer ashamed.

By now, the Japs were everywhere, running from tent to tent, slitting the canvas with swords, tossing grenades through the openings, pouring rifle and machine gun fire into the tents; shouting, laughing, screaming, "Banzai!"

Under a truck parked on a rise of ground a few yards from where Sergeant Hall had taken cover, there were half a dozen pilots pinned down by rifle fire. One of them was Lieutenant Joseph Coons, a twenty-one-year-old fighter pilot who was one of the few people awake when the attack started. Coons, scheduled for a pre-dawn patrol mission, had climbed into the truck and was waiting for it to start for the airstrip when a grenade, probably the signal that launched the attack, went off. He dove under the truck.

"It was pretty dark," Coons said, "but I could make out a small party of Japs a short distance away. I emptied my .45 in their direction, but I don't think I hit any of them.

"Japs seemed to come right up out of the ground. In the bivouac area, we could see them milling around the tents, cutting the canvas with swords or lifting the flaps and throwing grenades inside."

Coons grabbed a rifle just as a Jap raised up from a hole between the truck and the company street. They both fired at the same time. The Jap toppled over; his bullet went wide of Coons and killed another officer in a nearby foxhole. Another Jap got up and started toward the man who had been mortally hit. Coons dropped him with one shot.

Crawling down the incline toward a foxhole, Coons could see into a crater near the bivouac area. He called back for a grenade and flipped it into the crater. Seconds went by before the grenade exploded, and Japs poured from the hole. Coons and the men behind him cut them down.

It was clear that this was no desperate infiltration by a few crazed Japs. It was a carefully planned attack carried out by hundreds of Japs, timed for the critical interval when most of the Marines had been withdrawn and the infantry was on its way in. Its specific purpose seemed to be the decimation of the fighter pilots who, the Japs must have known, were soon going to Tokyo.

The attack carried into every part of the Fighter Command area. As the Japs struck and fled, they discarded their own guns for American weapons and used them with deadly effectiveness.

Most men were caught fast asleep by the raid. A few, awakened by the first sounds of gunfire, managed to get to some kind of cover before the Japs moved in. Most of the pilots were armed only with .45 pistols; some men had army carbines.

Many had no weapons. One armed pilot who apparently decided to risk a sprint up the company street, gained the door of his tent as a Jap was slashing at the canvas with his sword. The Jap whirled and struck the pilot across the head with his saber.

The pilot grabbed his attacker and wrestled him to the ground. Locked in mortal combat, the pilot and the Jap rolled over and over in the ash until the American got his hands around the Jap's throat. He choked him to death.

A group of cooks, caught without weapons when six Japs stormed their kitchen, seized trays, pots and pans, carving knives and everything that wasn't nailed down and drove the Japs out.

The night before the attack, there had been an alert. Three Air Forces men, Technical Sergeant Philip Jean (later reported missing in action), Technical Sergeant Albert L. Stein, and Sergeant S. T. Coker, Jr., had made a deal with some Marines to borrow two BAR's and some ML's. They were the only adequate combat weapons in the Fighter Command area when the attack opened.

At the sound of the first fire, the men in Jean's tent dove for their foxhole. In the gathering dawn, they could see Japs working over adjourning areas. Jean and Stein crawled out of their foxhole and began to snake through the ash toward a ridge behind the tent area.

Two Japs suddenly popped out of a hole. One of them raised his arm; there was a grenade in his fist. Jean whirled and poured a stream of BAR fire into the Jap. The Jap fell back into the hole and his exploding grenade killed his companion.

The two Americans gained the ridge, which looked clear of Japs. Jean left Stein on guard with the BAR and, armed only with a .45, moved on into an adjoining tent area. As he stepped around the corner of a tent, he almost stumbled over two wounded Japs crawling for cover. One of them started to raise his rifle. Jean grabbed it by the muzzle, swung it around and blew off its owner's head. His .45 took care of the second Jap.

A few Marines, attracted by the sounds of battle, began to arrive with BAR's and machine guns.

A big, hulking Marine Major, running into the area from the road, came upon Sergeant Hall and the half-dozen Air Forces officers still frozen in their shallow holes.

"Three or four Japs still in there," the Marine Officer said to the men. "We can organize a skirmish line and clean them out. Let's go!"

"We jumped up and followed the Marine down the company street," said Sergeant Hall. "I felt silly as hell; I still didn't have a gun."

Hall picked up a carbine from the ground just as some Japs at the end of the street opened fire on the group. He ducked behind a big steel can filled with water. A Jap, apparently concealed in a nearby tent, began lobbing grenades. The grenades exploded on the other side of the barrel and Hall made himself very small. It was pretty clear to him that the Marine's estimate of "three or four Japs" was in error.

"Three hundred was closer to it," Hall said. "I was lying behind the barrel when a Jap got out of a hole not fifty yards away. I got a perfect bead on him and squeezed the trigger.

"That damned carbine didn't go off."

Somebody else, one of the officers who had been dug in with Hall at the end of the street, got the Jap with his .45.

"That Marine guy was magnificent," Hall said. "He came running from behind a tent, crouched over pouring BAR fire into the crater where the Japs were holed up. Then, quite calmly, he began pegging grenades into that hole."

The enemy seemed to be concentrated in a pocket-shaped area like a flat V. A call went out for volunteers to clean out the pocket and Technical Sergeant Philip Jean and another man armed with a BAR stepped forward.

Jean crawled into the nearest arm of the V, past a pillbox which had been knocked out. Around the corner of a tent, some Japs had set up a knee mortar and Jean could hear them chattering. He stepped quietly around the corner of the tent and opened fire. He poured out one clip, then a second. Halfway through the third, his gun jammed. It wasn't until then that he realized he was alone. The other man's BAR had jammed; he wasn't able to get off a single round. Jean's fifty rounds accounted for eight Japs dead and three probables.

As Jean's fire ceased, Stein, armed only with a .45, walked cautiously forward toward the exact center of the V, where there were still plenty of Japs. Just behind the pile of Japs killed by Jean's BAR fire, a Jap jumped from a hole, a grenade in each hand. Stein stopped him with two bullets in the head. Just to be sure, he emptied the rest of the clip into the Jap, explaining, later:

"I didn't think the government would mind wasting the ammo."

Sergeant Coker, from the same tent as Jean and Stein, was moving up the area about the same time. A Jap got up from behind a bush and started to run. Coker shot him down. Another Jap got up from under a pile of bodies in a gulch, a grenade in his upraised hand. Coker shot him through the head.

In the first, faint gray of dawn, the Army moved up with flame-throwing tanks. For a moment, it looked as though the battle would end quickly. But the tanks could not be used; too many Air Forces men were still trapped in their tents.

In one tent, the fighter pilots had rolled from their cots and flattened themselves on the floor. Some Japs piled into a crater just outside the tent and the pilots could hear them talking and yelling. They tossed grenades at the tent where the flyers were, but the grenades either went off into the air or rolled down the canvas and exploded outside the tent. Then they raked the tent with rifle fire.

Captain R. B. Kessler, one of the men in the tent, heard the sound of ripping canvas. He crawled closer to the door and saw a Jap officer about fifteen feet away, swinging his saber like an axe to rip open the adjoining tent and screaming "Banzai!" at the top of his voice. Kessler took a chance of tipping off his position and fired. The Jap officer fell backward, dead.

One pilot was trapped in the tent which the enemy seized as a command post.

All through the battle, while Japs moved in and out of the tent in a continuous stream, the pilot lay behind an upturned cot, terrified even to move his foot which stuck out in plain sight for fear the Japs would hear the sound.

Trapped in another tent was a group of enlisted men who had slept through the first sounds of gunfire and were awakened by the sounds of Japs talking just outside.

The men in the tent slid quietly out of bed and lay on the floor — all except Sergeant Harry Hamilton, a sound sleeper.

Fully aware of what was happening, the men on the floor wisely refrained from waking up Hamilton. The slightest sound would have drawn fire.

There was a slight, ripping sound and a Jap bayonet was thrust into the tent. It struck a wooden box. The bayonet was withdrawn and plunged into the tent at another spot. Again, it hit a box. It ripped through the tent a third time, waggling in thin air two feet above the nose of Staff Sergeant Ernest Huth.

For awhile the Japs seemed to think it was a supply tent. Hamilton slept on.

Apparently the Japs decided to make sure. A saber ripped an opening in the canvas and a grenade hissed through the hole, rolled across the long, narrow tent and stopped under a packing box. The explosion blew Hamilton out of bed. He woke up on the dirt floor with his head ringing. Near him lay a man with a bad leg wound. Hamilton crawled to the man and applied a tourniquet which doctors later said saved his life.

A hail of bullets crashed through the tent at waist height. Outside, Japs were crawling under the outstretched tent ropes, brushing against the canvas sides. The firing receded for a moment and then moved closer again. Rifle barrels appeared through holes at the north and south ends of the tent and raked the double row of cots. One man was mortally wounded; another lay groaning.

The Japs began firing in the direction from which the groaning could be heard.

"There wasn't time to be gentle," Hamilton said later. "I gagged the man, applied a tourniquet and made my way to the south end of the tent."

Hamilton could see a wounded Jap lying outside the door, with two other Japs talking to him. Hamilton raised his carbine silently, took careful aim and pressed the trigger. Nothing happened. The weapon had jammed. He grabbed another carbine and pressed the trigger. It was jammed.

"Son-of-a-Bitch!" Hamilton shouted.

The form in the doorway stirred. "Don't swear like that," the dying Jap said in a flawless English. "It isn't nice."

The other two Japs were under cover now so Hamilton moved back to the center of the tent and cut a small hole in the canvas near the ground. There were seven Japs in a foxhole between Hamilton's tent and the one adjacent. Hamilton couldn't fire without endangering the men in the other tent.

On the other side of the tent, Hamilton got his sights on a Jap rifleman. Suddenly a Jap officer popped to his knees; there was a potato-masher grenade in his upraised hand. Hamilton whirled and fired. The officer doubled up, still clutching the grenade. It exploded and blew his face open. The other Japanese soldier guffawed.

A rifleman rose to half crouch, laughing hysterically, digging the ground with his bayonet and brandishing a grenade.

Staff Sergeant Milton Hlebof hit him first. The Jap flinched and laughed.

Corporal Frank B. McCollum raised his carbine and shot eight bullets into the Jap's chest. Blood gushed from the man's wounds and a great, spreading stain of red appeared on the Jap's tunic. Still, he roared with laughter, dug at the ground with his bayonet and brandished the grenade.

Hamilton slid to an opening and fired two shots into the Jap's chest. He was rewarded with a gale of wild laughter.

Carefully, Hamilton trained his rifle sights on the bridge of the Jap's nose. Deliberately, he squeezed the trigger.

"The bullet drilled him between the eyes," Hamilton said. "He collapsed like a rag."

"He didn't laugh any more."

"Somehow," said Sergeant Robert Fredericks, combat correspondent from whose written report much of this account is taken, "in spite of the battle, in spite of the awful bloodiness, the sun came up over Iwo Jima on the morning of March 28."

The battle was over. The Jap attacking force had been cut to pieces, although mopping-up operations continued until noon. Jap bodies, 333 of them, sprawled over a wide area of the northwest corner of the island. Eighteen were captured alive. Tents were spattered and soaked with blood.

It wasn't all Japanese blood. Forty-four officers and enlisted men of the VII Fighter Command and attached units were killed in action. Eighty-eight were wounded.

Shocked and haggard, Sergeant Tom Hall sat limply on his cot as the sun came up and the sounds of gunfire died down on the morning of the twenty-eighth. He supposed that, despite the awful bloodiness and the terrible stench of the dead, the war would go on. Probably, the first fighter escort mission to Japan would come off on schedule.

Hall pulled himself erect and, picking his way around the bodies sprawled in grotesque attitudes all through the area, made his way to the tent where he had left Lieutenant Bowden the night before.

A pilot who sat on the edge of a cot with his head in his hands looked surprised when Hall asked about Bowden. He seemed to have forgotten there was an extra man in the tent that night.

Suddenly, Hall knew.

He turned and walked quickly out of the tent and forced himself to look into a crater where a body lay. The man's face was shot away, but he was a huge man; Bowden was slender.

Hall ran to another foxhole and again made himself look. There were two dead men in this one; both were Japanese.

The beads of sweat traced thin, white lines in the ashy grime on Hall's brow. His hands were wet.

He began to run from foxhole to foxhole.

It was a long time before Sergeant Hall could talk about it.

"I found him finally," he said, slowly. "He was at the bottom of a foxhole. At first, it looked like he was just resting there."

A flight surgeon told Hall that the end had come swiftly. The bullet had gone through Lieutenant Bowden's head.

CHAPTER XXV: THE MUSTANGS GET THOSE BASTARDS

REVENGE IS A FUTILE BATTLE CRY. IT WAS A WORD THAT THE men who fought the war in the air over the Pacific, and the men on the ground who supported the air war, used only rarely and then with careful reservation.

It was hard to hate an enemy you couldn't see. Hard to hate a Japanese soldier two miles or more below you through the overcast. Hard for the men on the ground to hate the enemy in a theater where a mechanic or a clerk conceivably could spend three years at forward bases and never see a live Jap.

It was when HE was ten or twelve thousand feet overhead that you began hating. And even then you really didn't begin hating him until the split-second when you knew his shrapnel had found you.

Or the split-second when the Zero went away under the wing and flame began to grow where there had been an engine.

It was when the war got personal that you really hated the enemy — when it was he against you.

But even then, if you used the word revenge at all, you said it casually, coldly; as matter-of-factly as you might have made the statement that on the morning of April 7, 119 Mustangs of the VII Fighter Command took off from the island of Iwo Jima and flew to the Japanese Empire.

It was ten days after the Japs had come out of the caves to kill or wound 132 men of the Seventh. It was forty months to the day after the Japs had come out of a peaceful sky to bomb and strafe the old Hawaiian Air Force, from whose charred remains the Seventh was built.

The first fighter mission to Japan was one of the few combat air actions of the Pacific where it could be said honestly that the men who did the fighting were motivated by revenge.

The war, on the night of March 27, had become very personal to the Mustang pilots of the VII Fighter Command.

The Japs must have known it was coming. For weeks the B-29's, at night as well as in the daytime, had been meeting interception in greater and greater numbers over the Japanese Empire.

The flak was bad. B-29 crews shrugged it off and went on into the target. The lucky ones, at the end of the bomb run, had only to sweat out shot-out engines and dwindling gas supplies.

It was the Kamikaze which took the greatest toll in planes, men, and morale. The Jap fighters who tore the big bombers in half, cleaved off wings, sheared off vertical stabilizers or exploded the B-29's in suicide collisions.

It had begun happening on one of the early raids over Tokyo, when a Jap fighter plummeted into the midsection of a B-29 and broke it in half. At first, pilots though it was a crazy accident, one of those things which could overtake an unlucky crew.

But as the weeks went by, it became more and more apparent that the crashes were deliberate tactics against which the B-29 crews were all but defenseless. Gunners had to knock down oncoming fighters to avoid collision, for the pilot of a crippled fighter could still retain sufficient control to jam his hurtling plane into a Superfort.

It was a grim, ruthless kind of war which took an alarming toll in planes and lives and threatened to collapse B-29 operations. Superforts were running into clouds of Jap fighters often numbering more than three hundred. Sometimes, the B-29's stood off more than 600 attacks on single formations, in running battles lasting forty-five minutes or more.

So alarmed were the generals and admirals on Guam that they clamped a tight censorship on all press releases about the Kamikaze. They argued that to let the American public know what was happening was to admit to the Jap that he had finally devised a weapon for which we had no sure defense.

There was only one possible answer: fighter-escort for the B-29's. Fast, maneuverable fighters which could knock the Zeroes down before they got at the Superforts.

So the Japs knew it had to happen. The B-29's crews, tired and dispirited, summed it up in one sentence: "Wait till the Mustangs get those bastards."

Saturday, April 7, 1945, was the pay-off day. It was the day the fighter pilots would settle a personal grudge; the day they would begin to exact a terrible revenge for the crews of the B-29's; the pay-off blow for the men on the ground who had carried the war forward six thousand miles over coral and water to bring Tokyo within flying radius of the Seventh Air Force.

When the pilots assembled on the evening of April 6 for their preliminary briefing, the banzai attack was still the main topic of conversation. Most of the men still carried carbines or pistols. Their uniforms were a hodge-podge of everything from standard gear to helmets. Marine fatigues and long-billed flight caps were a common uniform.

Not all the conversation was serious. The mail had arrived late that afternoon and the latest strips of "Terry and the Pirates" were passed around. In one corner, Lieutenant Henry L. Koke, who wore a battered campaign hat he had picked up from a cavalry outfit in the Southwest Pacific, was being ribbed about how Snake Tumblin, whom Koke resembled, had crashed in the latest episode of "Terry."

Koke and the men who ribbed him didn't know that the next day he would make a landing so lucky that even Milton Caniff, creator of "Terry," would have rejected it as improbable.

Second Lieutenant Garland R. Cottle was disgusted with his mail because his family thought he was still in the Marianas. Like everyone else, he found it hard to believe that they didn't know he was about to start on the first fighter mission over Tokyo. Over in a corner, Captain Thomas W. Lewis tried to relax in a collapsible chair as the Group dentist, Captain Mario Pieri, worked on one of his teeth. Lieutenant Albert V. Davis helped Pieri by holding a flashlight trained on Lewis' mouth.

Captain Harry C. Crim, a squadron commander and P-38 veteran from North Africa, was telling some pilots what to do in case they had to ditch and wanted to call the Navy. "If you're in distress," he said, "just tell them in plain English what's wrong and what you're going to do."

As Flight Surgeon Captain George Hart handed out benzedrine tablets for the flight next day, the generator engine sputtered and died, plunging the tent into darkness. "That's my engine over Tokyo," somebody groaned.

The generator picked up and the lights went back on. A pilot told Second Lieutenant Robert V. Merklein: "You'd better make a good landing if you have to come in on a Tokyo airfield."

"I'll come in with wheels up," Merklein said. "I figure I won't be leaving again soon."

"Hell, they'll probably make you a flight instructor," was the answer.

The briefing was quick and to the point. Operations Officer Major Dewitt S. Spain, wounded in<the shoulder during the banzai attack, conducted the briefing. Major James Crawford told the men what opposition they might

encounter over Japan. He wrote on the maps with ease, despite a bandaged right hand, which was still crippled from a grenade wound.

The pilots were given strip maps to carry with them the next day. Technical Sergeant Elliott Ball, Staff Sergeant Jerry Ferragallo and Private Jack Lent wrote additional data on the maps as they passed them out. The briefing didn't take long. After it was over, the pilots broke up and headed for their cots. It was going to be a tough mission, this first one, and they knew it.

The operation was under way before the P-51's were airborne the next morning. Two large fleets of Superforts were flying north from the Marianas. One of these was headed for Nagoya. The other, numbering more than a hundred planes and including three navigational B-29's, was to pick up its escort of P-51's at a predetermined rendezvous. The target was the Nakajima aircraft plant in the Musashino district of Tokyo.

Despite a slight overcast, the Mustangs rendezvoused with the Superforts on schedule and the fleet headed for Japan. The fighter pilots were tense. For three years and four months, the Seventh had waited for this day. Each pilot felt he had a personal debt to pay the Japs. They intended to pay it with interest.

The '51's hadn't picked the wrong day. The Japs were up and waiting — an initial force of between 110 and 125 of them. As the bombers made landfall, they met a light shower of flak, which increased as the planes approached the target, shortly before 11 A.M.

The first Jap pursuit strikes were made at the bombers, not the fighters. Watching for their blisters, B-29 gunners saw the first Zeke rise to attack and a Mustang break off to engage it. The Japs attacked singly, as the Mustangs, flying in teams, intercepted. Most of the Jap attacks came during the bomb run and immediately afterwards.

Major James F. Vande Hey, who led the first flight of Mustangs, got one of the early kills. "We pulled off, making a head-on run to the bombers," he said. "I saw this Dinah [twin-engined recon]. We went after him, diving down to 10,000 feet. Part of his cowling flew off when I fired a long burst into him. When last I saw him he was smoking. My wingman, Lieutenant Doug Moore, fired and hit him, too."

Lieutenant E. L. Bright got one kill and two probables. "I got a Zeke going in," he reported. "I guess I saw about fifty fighters. The ones I saw were just sitting ducks. You just drove up behind them and pulled the trigger. The twin-engined ship I hit had both engines burning. Then I hit a

Tony broadside. When I broke off, he was smoking badly and pieces were flying off. I made at least five passes."

Captain Tehon Markham and another pilot saw a Myrt (single-engine recon) and chased it until they realized it was trying to draw them away from the bombers. "As I turned to go back to the bombers, I saw two Nicks," Markham said, "They were at 17,000 — about 1,000 feet below me. I dived on one and hit his right wing. He was smoking as I went by."

Over the target, the action got wilder. The air suddenly seemed full of Jap parachutes. The B-29 gunners were knocking down a lot of planes, and the P-51's were doing their share, too. The Japs were attacking from above and ahead now, some of them diving out of the sun. Other planes circled and dropped phosphorus bombs among the Superforts. Most of them were inaccurate. One fighter swooped in on a '29, clipped the No. 3 engine and caromed crazily off the tail, taking the top of the vertical stabilizer with him. The bomber staggered but miraculously kept on flying.

Captain Robert W. Moore, using the old "turkey-shoot" maneuver, got two kills within forty-five seconds. "I was escorting the bombers and watching one that was on fire," he said. "I saw four Hamps above him in a loose string. The bomber exploded but I turned my flight into the Hamps anyway and joined their formation as number five man. I closed in fast on number four, gave him a short burst from about 600 feet and he exploded behind the cockpit.

"Then I gave my plane full throttle and closed on the number three man. I caught him at the bottom of their lazy eight (a long, slow climb and dive maneuver the Japs were using for good visibility above the '29's) and gave him about a three-second burst that hit his engine and cowling.

"Then I looked up for the number two man and saw the leader of the formation turning into me. I told the flight to give it full throttle and dive away. I headed straight for the deck and looked back over my shoulder to see the number three man burning badly. I left the other two Hamps and rejoined the bombers."

Major Gilmer Snipers, who had one kill, said: "I saw about three passes on the bombers. The Japs started their runs above them. But we were in their way and they'd break out. They didn't seem very eager to go in. I fired at two that pulled straight up. I came in on the tail of another and saw pieces fly off and fire trail from his wings. I pulled up, turned left and got on the tail of another. I fired one burst, and he went down about 2,000 feet and bailed out."

Captain Crim, an ex-P-38 pilot, got a Tony and a Nick. "I hit the Tony twice," he said. "On my first pass his engine caught fire, and on my second, his right wing fell off. The Nick was hit in the left engine and fire covered the whole left wing. He went down and crashed."

High score of the day was turned in by Major James B. Tapp, a flight leader and squadron-operations officer, who on later missions, became the Mustang group's first ace. He was over the target twenty minutes and accounted for a Tony, an Oscar, and a Tojo. "As we came in, we saw a Nick approaching from high altitude," he said. "We gave chase. I fired a long burst into the fuselage and both engines, but he wouldn't burn. As we broke off and pulled back to escort position, there was a small explosion in his right engine and lots of pieces flew off the plane. Then we saw a Tony climbing ahead of us at high speed. We opened up our engines and caught him in his climb. I closed in and fired. The first hits started a fire and he exploded, and a wing blew off as I went by. We got back in position again and saw a Dinah making a front-quarter run on the bombers. I fired a burst at him at 90 degrees, but he had too much speed.

"I got back in formation in time to observe a disabled B-29 trying to make the coast. He was at 14,000 feet and I gave him cover. An Oscar started a pass and we intercepted him. I fired a long burst into the fuselage and knocked the canopy and windshield off. Pieces of the shield hit my ship. The plane went into an uncontrolled spiral and we followed him down and watched him crash and explode. We pulled back up to cover the damaged '29 and saw four Zekes and two Tojos. We cut loose on one and saw our incendiary bullets hit his engine and cockpit. We closed in and blew part of his left wing off and he went into a spin. By that time, my wingman was running short of gas and we had to head home."

Swearing out the gas supply was the worst problem for most of the returning fighter pilots. Lieutenant Frank L. Ayres, who flew top cover, was among the last to leave. Two hundred miles north of Iwo, he sighted an American destroyer below and, realizing his fuel wouldn't last, decided that this was the end of the line. "I rolled the ship over on its back," he said, "and dropped out. After hitting the water I was about 1,000 yards from the destroyer."

Lieutenant Koke, the pilot with the cavalry hat, was separated from the other Mustangs on the way home; He got a heading by radio from a '29 navigator. When he ran out of gas he had no idea where he was. He hadn't been sure of his bearing and Iwo was a tiny spot on a huge piece of ocean.

But there was no future in staying with his plane. He jettisoned his canopy and prepared to bail. He hesitated momentarily as his plane descended through the clouds.

Koke looked hopelessly down and was amazed to see Iwo directly below him. He hastily changed his plans and brought the Mustang in for a dead-stick landing.

Back in Fighter Command Headquarters, interrogation came first. It became clear that the pilots had run into almost every kind of interception the Japs could muster. Nicks and Tojos were the most numerous, but Irvings, Oscars, Tonys, Zekes, Jacks, Myrts, Marys, Dinahs, and Hamps were also seen. About 450 individual attacks were counted. As the fighter pilots gathered to compare notes, the most confused man on Iwo was Lieutenant Charles C. Heil. The more he heard about the mission, the less familiar it sounded.

"Where were you all?" he kept asking. Eventually it all got straightened out and he found, to his embarrassment, that he was the first fighter pilot to fly over Nagoya. He had missed the rendezvous and had met the Nagoya force instead. "B-29's all over the sky and not one damned '51," he said. He went along to Nagoya, thinking he was with an individual flight of Tokyo bombers.

Over the target Heil's engine began sputtering, but the Superfort radioed him: "Don't worry; we'll take care of you." And the B-29's escorted their lonely escort most of the way home.

"So far," Heil said, "nobody has been mad at me."

The fighter pilots smoked, drank tomato juice, and discussed the mission as intelligence officers added the score. It was an impressive total, especially for a first mission. Twenty-one enemy planes were destroyed, six were probably destroyed and ten were damaged by the Mustangs. And later, when the Superforts' tally of fifty destroyed, twenty-four probably destroyed and thirty-four damaged was added, the operation had cost the Japs 145 planes shot down or damaged.

More important, the target had been bombed with only light losses. Three B-29's were lost and two P-5i's, one of them Lieutenant Ayres'.

But of this first mission, the best summary came, not from Iwo, but from a B-29 gunner in the Marianas. Sergeant Burdell C. Hanson, whose Superfort was nicked by bullets, summed it up simply:

"The Mustangs were knocking Japs down all over the sky. For awhile there during the fight there were Japs parachuting down all around us. I'll never forget it."

CHAPTER XXVI: THE LAST DAMNED ISLAND

OKINAWA WAS DIFFERENT.

It was the last island. It was the end of a forty-month trail of atolls, jimas and shimas over which the tiny but versatile Seventh had plodded, island by damned island, until, finally, it found itself living on the doorstep to Japan.

And the Air Forces men, who thought they had seen everything in the way of Pacific islands, were finding life on a doorstep confusing indeed. One of them, Staff Sergeant Bob Price, a veteran of 42 months and 26 islands with the Seventh, at a loss for some way to define how different was this last island — where D-day was L-day — said, resignedly:

"Okinawa was screwy. It was the screwiest damned place in the Pacific."

The initial landing on April 1, Easter Sunday, coming shortly after bloody Iwo Jima, was expected to be the costliest in Pacific battle history. Instead, the beachhead was almost bloodless. Kerama Retto, a group of tiny islands twenty-five miles southwest of Okinawa, invaded a week before the major operation got under way, was literally undefended. Only Ie Shima, an outlying atoll ten miles off the northwest Okinawa coast, conformed to the Pacific invasion pattern. A 700-foot crag on Ie, somewhat similar in outline to Mt. Suribachi on Iwo, proved tough to take. Seven thousand land mines planted on the five-mile island slowed the assault and caused heavy casualties.

Only 365 miles south of Japan and our first venture into the Jap homeland, Okinawa was expected to be the best developed and most heavily fortified island in the Pacific. It turned out to be a place where the Japs used horses to haul their artillery over rutted ox paths.

At Saipan, Peleliu, Angaur, Kwajalein, Iwo, some of the bitterest fighting had centered around the airstrips. On Okinawa, from whose airstrips even short-range planes could be flown against the Jap home empire, the infantry had captured the enemy's two most important airfields, Yontan and Kadena, in the first two and a half hours of fighting.

And on the other islands, the Japs had come back, singly and by the hundreds in repeated banzai charges that saw airstrips change hands several times before they finally settled down to American ownership.

On Okinawa, they came back only once.

"And that was screwy too," said Sergeant Price. "It was sort of an aerial banzai; a crazy thing. Five Jap bombers loaded with suicide troops tried to crashland on Yontan one night."

At Okinawa too, there was a weapon without precedent in the history of war — the Japanese Baka Bomb. But for all its grim threat of a bomb aimed right down to the second of explosion by a suicide pilot, it was a weapon that didn't quite come off. Its weird legend of a white-robed pilot who flew into a glorious and loud death with a hangover from a last, wonderful night on earth when he attended his own funeral and was feted as a hero, made it, as one Air Forces man, Private First Class Alan Hartman, said, "a weapon that was almost too fantastic to be feared."

And at Okinawa there was the Kamikaze. Apparently at a desperate measure to sink every ton of Allied shipping that entered the anchorage, the Japanese high command unleashed its corps of suicide pilots. These desperate pilots came out of the sun and out of the moon in death dives that ended only when they had blown themselves and their bombs up against a ship or had been shot into the water. The Navy, when the Okinawa campaign ended, had suffered its worst losses of the Pacific campaign — 334 ships sunk or damaged and 10,000 men wounded or killed.

There was no defense against the Kamikaze pilot short of blowing him up in the air.

"The son of a bitch dives straight at you, and what are you going to do about it?"

That was the way one Air Forces man who survived four days of unremitting suicide attacks summed up the average soldier's grim resignation to the awful finality of the Kamikaze's dive.

A week before the Easter Sunday invasion of Okinawa proper, small units of the Tenth Army and Marines went ashore on the Kerama Retto, a small group of islands 25 miles southeast of Okinawa.

Out of Kerama Retto came one of the most cockeyed Air Forces invasion experiences of the Pacific war.

An orphan detachment of nine Air Forces weather men were sandwiched between the 10th Army, the Navy and Marines during the landing and sent ashore to do a job which nobody except the nine men and a few generals seemed to know much about.

Their assignment was to take observations on the upper air and relay to the anti-aircraft and heavy artillery the details of density, humidity, wind direction and temperature. Their findings were supposed to make it possible for heavy artillery set up on Kerama Retto to support the invasion of Okinawa, twenty-five miles away. When somebody got the bright idea of using weather men as artillery spotters, the experts in big guns had said: "With their information we can theoretically knock out a pyramidal tent at 20,000 yards."

The Infantrymen and the Marines, confused by the presence in the assault waves of nine Air Forces men wearing baseball caps instead of steel helmets, promptly named the weather detachment "Poyser's Ball Club," after the officer in charge, Lieutenant Joe Poyser.

A little later, when the ground troops saw the men in baseball caps running around the beach collecting their massive equipment, they were re-named The Rover Boys of Kerama Retto.

The morning after the landing on Kerama Retto the nine men had assembled all their equipment on the beach. They had borrowed a cat to haul the twelve-ton equipment trailer and the five-ton generator trailer off the LSM.

"We were pretty pleased with ourselves for getting organized so fast," Poyser said. "Then we discovered we had to get that equipment to the top of a 230-foot hill which went up at a forty-degree angle. The only thing going up it when we landed was a cow-path."

Poyser happened to mention his troubles to a Navy Officer he had met on the beach.

"The guy apologized to us for not having a road up the hill. He offered to put one in right away but we said it would be all right if he had in it by noon the next day. Funny thing — he did."

When they had reached the top of the hill with their massive equipment, the Rover Boys were on what remained the outer perimeter of the American lines. But they could look down into the Okinawa anchorage where hundreds of ships were moving up to the invasion. The climate on Kerama Retto was pleasant and, all in all, the Rover Boys thought it was a fine place.

For a few minutes during the first night they spent on the hill, it looked as though they might be in for a tough campaign. Things had been fairly quiet from midnight on, but Sergeant Joe Dorlaque, a technician, couldn't get to sleep. He kept his gun cocked and near him and was wondering what the password for the night was when he heard something moving down a ravine outside the tent. He shouted "Halt!" a couple of times but whatever it was kept right on coming. Dorlaque's tentmate, Warrant Officer Irving Newton, woke up to see Dorlaque on his knees, staring through the mosquito bar over his cot into the enormous face of a boar hog.

"That was the biggest damned animal I've ever seen," Dorlaque said later. "I got out of bed and threw a stick at him but he just stood there making noises at me. Finally, I got sore and ran right at him. He ran out of the tent and I chased him up a gully, stumbling over things in the darkness. All the while, I could hear Newton laughing like crazy."

The boar, which disappeared behind Japanese lines, was the first of many false alarms for the Rover Boys.

"Every night," Dorlaque said, "the Japs would land on the other side of the island and we'd have a scare. But the Infantry or Marines always wiped them out."

As it turned out, they had a lot more trouble with their own equipment than with Japs. The technicians, Dorlaque and Corporal Clyde Wendelken, found that hundreds of small parts in their equipment had been jarred out of order on the boat trip.

"Look at that damned thing," Dorlaque said to Poyser when he was trying to put a generator in order. "There must be five thousand plugs, and there's something wrong with every one of 'em."

It was serious trouble. Their first three days of collecting information had been called the most critical and they had little more than twenty-four hours to get the equipment in working order for their first mission on the night of L-minus-I on nearby Okinawa. They went on 16-hour shifts.

By deadline day, they were pretty tired and disgusted. Dorlaque forgot about the sign on the equipment which warned "contact with operating potentials will cause death." In his frantic hurry Dorlaque got careless and grabbed a 10,000-volt charge of electricity.

"The jolt knocked him clear across the trailer," Wendelken said. "He was almost out but we gave him a slug of rum and wrapped him in blankets. It scared hell out of us, but an hour later he was back on his feet and helping us."

By 5:30 that afternoon, two hours before the deadline, there were still twelve bugs in the set. Thirty minutes later the set was operating at peak efficiency. The technicians went to bed, and Staff Sergeant Keith Davidson, Sergeant Bob Supple, Corporal Ralph Rossi, Sergeant Henry Chester and Warrant Officer Newton began sending their weather finding by radio to the Field Artillery, Antiaircraft, Army and Marine aircraft. At

10:30 the 155 millimeter long guns on Kerama Retto began their long-range bombardment of Okinawa.

The next morning, a couple of Rover Boys watched the invasion of Okinawa from comfortable positions in a latrine on the hill overlooking the anchorage.

"Somehow," said Lieutenant Poyser, "the whole thing seemed like we had been brought along only as spectators."

With the orphaned unit operating full time and making six weather balloon runs a day, invasion day — because it was Easter Sunday — seemed like a good time for a celebration. The Rover Boys had a big dinner of baked liberated chicken, mashed potatoes, corn, string beans, hot bread, butter and custard pudding, cooked by Warrant Officer Newton. The potatoes and butter had been brought ashore from the LSM which took the Rover Boys to Kerama Retto; the bread was cadged from an Infantry mess and the custard pudding was made from the eggs of a friendly Okinawa Plymouth Rock named Roberta. The main course was Roberta herself.

As the battle for Okinawa moved inland, the Rover Boy's only contact with its progress was in the radio reports they got from the Navy. The nearest thing to a battle hazard for the Rover Boys was the ticklish job of getting their balloons off the ground at night. The Infantrymen had orders to shoot anything that moved and only the Rover Boys' vast amount of luck, plus their sublime detachment, kept them from being shot as they wandered around the outer perimeter at night launching their weather balloons.

Somehow, again nobody got shot when the Rover Boys looted an abandoned enemy quartermaster building and began wearing Jap uniforms around the front lines. A Colonel, after very nearly shooting at one of them, gave Poyser and his men what was probably the most monumental chewing out in Army history.

The Rover Boys, who liked the warmth of the Jap shirts and the snug fit of the pants, were quite indignant about it.

April 4th was Warrant Officer Newton's birthday — time for another party. It was about the time, too, that Newton thought his wife might be having their baby; so the Rover Boys broke out a bottle of Scotch, several fifths of rum and plenty of beer. The party was going along nicely when somebody remembered it was time for the first night balloon run.

"We had a little trouble getting the things off the ground that night," Poyser said, "but nobody fouled up and the reports got out all right."

This fabulous interlude in the middle of an invasion might have gone on until the end of the battle for Okinawa — and the Rover Boys would have liked that — but they ran out of caustic soda for their balloons. They went back to the beach and asked the Navy to move them to Okinawa. The Navy agreed and told them to be on the beach the next morning at eight. That seemed a little early for the Rover Boys and Poyser asked the Navy if they couldn't make it nine. The Navy insisted on eight. So promptly at eight the next morning the Rover Boys were waiting on the beach.

"Four days later," Poyser said bitterly, "they sent a boat in to pick us up."

The four days, however, were not unpleasant. The Rover Boys had quite a bit of fresh meat which they had obtained from the Navy in exchange for a useless Jap suicide boat and Joe Dorlaque still had the watch business which he started on the hill.

"Of course," Dorlaque said thoughtfully, "I never repaired a watch before, but I learned an awful lot the first few days."

Okinawa was as screwy as that.

There was no pattern to the battle for Okinawa. If the beach head had been mercifully bloodless, it was more than made up for by the bitter and costly battle that started when the assault troops had cut the island in half and were pushing their way north and south to force the Japs to the extreme ends of the island. When the battle finally ended, our casualties had mounted to 45,000.

In every other Pacific invasion, the Air Forces advance echelons, which had come in aboard troopships and LSTs behind the assault forces, had encountered little trouble until they were on land. The convoyed journeys from Hawaii and other far-flung ports had always been monotonous but rarely were dangerous. There were frequent submarine alerts, and occasionally an enemy fighter got through to attack a crowded troopship but, for the most part, the trips had always been uneventful.

It was different at Okinawa. As the invasion ships moved toward the Ryukyus anchorage, the monotony of the long water journeys was put to a sudden and often disastrous end by Japanese suicide pilots. For many men who had survived every other kind of fantastic battle experience, the Kamikaze was the most bewildering and terrifying experience of the war. It was, as one man said, like being surrounded every minute of the day and night by a forest fire. It enveloped a lot of Air Forces men and turned routine assignments into Purple Heart details.

Such an assignment was the one drawn by eight Aviation Engineers, a Lieutenant and seven enlisted men, who were sent ashore to unload some of their battalion's supplies and heavy equipment. The routine assignment turned out to be four days of unremitting Kamikaze attacks during which the eight men saw some of their friends killed, a square block of tents leveled by a suicide's explosives, and a field hospital full of wounded men blasted into bloody canvas fragments by a Kamikaze.

The Japanese had reached back a thousand years to the so-called Divine Wind that wrecked the ships of the Mongol invaders for the name they planted on their special attack or suicide corps. The symbol of their macabre assignment was a cherry blossom painted on the Baka Bomb or the fuselage of a suicide plane.

The Kamikaze candidates, reportedly a privileged and carefully chosen class but actually the sad and dumb sacks of the Japanese Army Air Force, were told that a suicide pilot was "a beautiful soldier who has fallen like the cherry blossoms in the spring."

The eight Aviation Engineers assigned to unload the battalion's equipment were split up the first night they went to work. Three of the men remained on the beach to receive the equipment, the others went out to the ship to get the heavy equipment out of the hold and on board an LST. Both groups were Kamikaze targets within twenty-four hours.

Early in the evening, the overcast cleared and Okinawa lay naked and gleaming in the moonlight. Ashore, Technician-3 Tommy Pruitt, Staff Sergeant Henry Spect and Technician-5 Richard Young were in shallow foxholes along the beach when it grew dark and the attacks began. Jap planes bombed and strafed Yontan airfield. Every hour, almost on the hour, a wave of enemy planes moved slowly over the island at high altitude. Searchlights swung back and forth over the sky and a shower of tracers from automatic weapons and big guns climbed after the Jap bombers.

"Just about the time we'd get settled, the ack-ack would start going and the bombs would fall again," said Pruitt.

About midnight, as the intervals between attacks lessened, a Jap plane suddenly detached itself from a formation high over the island and dived straight down on the beach. It crashed and exploded about fifty yards from Pruitt and Spect.

Thin, red-haired Pruitt was crouched under a truck when the Kamikaze exploded.

"It hit in the middle of a temporary hospital where they had dengue patients and men wounded in other raids," he said. "The tents were set afire and there were pieces of aluminum flying around. I climbed up the bluff to help dig out the dead and wounded.

"We dug out one shelter where there were still five men alive; they were hysterical when we finally got to them."

Young, in a foxhole a little further up the beach, saw the plane coming down toward the beach.

"The guns kept firing at it all the way down," he said, "but it never wavered. I was praying it wouldn't hit when I saw the explosion and knew it had landed in the Navy hospital. There was a lot of fire but even above that awful din I could hear the screams of the wounded.

"I never want to hear anything like that again."

Spect, who had climbed the bluff behind Pruitt, arrived too late to help.

"The thing I remember about it," he said, was something that had happened earlier in the evening. One of the ships out in the harbor had been hit by a Kamikaze, and there was a man on the beach who thought his brother was on board. I guess he went a little crazy. They had to give him some morphine to quiet him down; then they took him up to the hospital.

"I got up there as soon as I could after the bomb exploded on the hospital. There were 26 people killed — one was the fellow they had brought up from the beach."

Out on the ship the five other members of the unloading party had spent a sleepless night on the deck. There had been an alert early in the evening and all night the ship sat quietly at anchor, concealed by the stifling smoke screen from smudge pots which the Navy placed in the harbor on the theory that a Kamikaze couldn't hit what he couldn't see.

At 5:30 in the morning, the last all clear had sounded and the men went below to wash up and have breakfast. They were coming up through the hatch when the alert sounded, and before anybody could move, a Zero which had banked out of formation as though it was going to turn away, dived suddenly toward the ship.

"You must stand there. You can't do anything," said Lieutenant Malvin Chewning, in charge of the unloading detail.

Sergeant Alex Vacchio couldn't move either. "Some guys were hollering to duck," he said. "I just stood there — my legs wouldn't move."

The Kamikaze came toward the ship's stern, straight and swift as a bullet, ringed by a cloud of red tracers from the guns of other ships in the harbor. A hundred yards from the stern, while the men stood riveted to the deck, the Kamikaze was hit and burst into flame.

"It missed the stern kingpost by not more than four feet and plunged into the ocean about 75 yards from the rail," and Private First Class Richard McFarland, another man who just stood there and watched the plane come toward him.

In a few minutes, while the wreckage of the plane burned on the water, McDonald saw the dead Jap pilot bob to the surface with his parachute strapped to his back.

"... A beautiful soldier who has fallen like the cherry blossoms in the spring . . ."

McDonald, looking at the dead Jap, simply remarked: "Well, there goes another one of the bastards."

It rained most of the day. There were several alerts and some light bombing but the eight-man detail had moved most of the heavy equipment ashore by evening. Seven of them remained ashore and survived a long night of jumping into muddy foxholes every few minutes until they finally got disgusted and just stayed in the foxholes. They were still in the mud the next morning when they saw a Jap Betty, chased by four Navy Corsairs, sweep across the island and dive toward their ship out in the harbor.

Pruitt was standing on the deck talking to two men of the ship's company when he saw the Kamikaze coming.

"I fell flat on my face," he said. "The plane hit the mast and her two five-hundred-pound bombs exploded in the air. The only thing I saw was the body of a gunner fly through the air and hit the deck near me. There was a gas explosion and a lot of fire up around the gun tub. The two men I had been talking to ducked down beside me. Both of them were badly wounded. I don't know what saved me."

Pruitt climbed up into the gun tub, where fire fighters were trying to extinguish the blazing wreckage of the Jap bomber. The gunner whose body had landed near Pruitt on the deck had been sitting with his legs strapped to his gun and all that was left in the tub were the stumps of his legs.

"The thing that hit me hardest," Pruitt said, "was that I knew the gunner who was blown out of his turret. He was one of the friendliest fellows you could meet.

"He was always talking about his wife, and the day before he was killed, he received 22 letters from her. That night he cracked open a bottle of whiskey — and you know how hard it is to get here — and insisted we all have a drink with him."

As the long weeks of the battle for Okinawa passed, the danger of the Kamikaze diminished, although the fury and determination of its pilots continued to the end of the war, when an occasional die-hard Jap somehow got through the fighter patrol and survived the ack-ack to crash deliberately somewhere on the crowded island.

"At least," said Sergeant Price in evaluating this last damned island, "Okinawa had very few snipers. Once in awhile, some Air Forces man standing guard, who probably didn't know which end of his carbine was up, would open fire on something that didn't answer a challenge and discover to his everlasting amazement, that he had killed one of the Emperor's soldiers.

It was the absence of snipers in any appreciable numbers which made it possible for aviation engineers to make operational in a record time the four Japanese airstrips on Okinawa and Ie Shima. Yontan airstrip, which carried the brunt of traffic during the early months of the campaign, was a good example.

The history of Yontan's development as an American property started on the night of L-day, about twelve hours after the first American had come ashore, when an Air Forces Colonel walked the length of the airfield — alone and unmolested. A few hundred yards to one side of the strip, the Marines were skirmishing with the first Japs they had met since they gained the beach.

The Air Forces officer was Colonel Jack Bentley, Air Liaison Officer for the Tenth Army and one-time military attache to the Italian Government ("until they kicked me out").

Bentley, who has been flying so long he feels uncomfortable on any piece of land where there is no place to set a plane down, found Yontan checkerboarded with Navy shellholes. He also found grass growing on the runway, a condition which appalled him.

On L-plus-1, Bentley commandeered a Navy bulldozer, appropriated a junior officer and two enlisted men and got to work filling the craters. Before the first Aviation Engineers came ashore in the evening, Bentley had wired the Navy that Yontan was ready to receive carrier pilots looking for a place to land.

The Aviation Engineers, unhampered by the sniper opposition they had encountered on every other island, began chopping down a hill which restricted Yontan to short-range planes. By the second day, they were completing 1,000-gallon aviation gas farms, hardstands and roads. Four days later, a four-engined C-54 transport flew up from Guam and landed easily on Yontan to evacuate the first wounded.

Okinawa's other major airstrips, at Kadena, Naha and on Ie Shima, were as quickly operational, although the hundreds of land mines which the Japs had buried around the two airstrips on Ie Shima slowed construction and caused casualities.

It was a new experience to veteran Pacific Aviation Engineer battalions; this unopposed construction of airstrips. So it was a startling surprise, but consistent with the fantastic kind of warfare conducted at Okinawa, when, at about 9: 30 on the night of May 24, five Jap twin-engine Sallys loaded with suicide troops attempted to crashland on Yontan.

Only one plane succeeded in getting to the ground; the rest were exploded a few hundred feet in the air. Jap troops, heavily armed with machine guns, grenades and a crude weapon apparently made for the occasion, poured out of the one bomber which landed and began running toward the aircraft standing in the revetments. Some of them were shot down by Marines and by Air Forces tower men, but others got to the planes with charges of dynamite wired to broomsticks which had rubber suction attachments and looked like ordinary household bathroom plungers.

The Japs, under cover of darkness and the confusion, were able to jam the plungers home against the parked airplanes and set off the dynamite charges. They destroyed seven planes before their entire force was wiped out.

By the end of June, nobody could have made a soldier on Okinawa believe that in a few weeks a B-29 named the Enola Gay would take off from Tinian in the Marianas and fly Japan out of the war, and the rest of the world into a new era, with a single bomb.

On Okinawa, Ie Shima and Kerama Retto, it was no secret to most soldiers that they were getting ready for another push. The final push — the last, long jump into Japan. Most men knew the date: November first. And the place: the southwestern shore of Kyushu Island. The codeword: Operation OLYMPIC.

Within sixty days of the time it was officially called secure, Okinawa had become the little England of the Pacific war. All through the day and night, fighters and bombers of every type — some of them going into combat for the first time — were fanning out from Okinawa to hit targets on the China coast, in Southern Japan and on the remaining islands between the Ryukyus and Kyushu.

And that was to have been only the beginning. Lieutenant General Jimmy Doolittle, a few hours after he had stood in the pelting rain to raise the American flag over a tiny encampment on Okinawa which was the headquarters of the New Eighth Air Force, told a group of war correspondents that "the day will come — and very soon now — when 5,000 American planes will hit the Japanese mainland in a single day."

The job of airstrip construction, which had only just begun, was to have been the biggest aviation engineering project ever attempted. Its statistics were startling. Lieutenant Colonel J. E. Morris, Engineering Officer at Guam Air Depot before he came to Okinawa, estimated that the latest American unsinkable aircraft carrier would have 25 miles of paved airstrips. The hardstands, taxiways and service aprons feeding the strips would have, Morris said, a paved area equal to four hundred miles of two-lane highway — a cross-country distance from Boston to Richmond, Virginia. The smallest field planned would have handled double the traffic of LaGuardia Field. About five and a half million truckloads of coral and earth had to be removed; if dumped in one spot the haulage would have built a cone-shaped mountain one mile high and 2,000 feet across.

Hundreds of miles of highways had to be built. Okinawa's road system under the Japanese was a series of narrow, wandering and unpaved paths which, during the heavy rains in the Ryukyus area, turned to muddy booby traps for the prime-movers, trucks, weapons carriers and jeeps which moved bumper-to-bumper up and down and across the island.

Okinawa's lack of roads was one of the factors which caused General Doolittle to say, when he was comparing the job that had to be done on Okinawa to the one completed in England:

"There, we had everything; here, we have to start from scratch."

A veteran Aviation Engineer, appalled at the endless chain of supply convoys which steamed into the Okinawa anchorage to dump mountains of equipment on the beaches, and thinking of Kwajalein where the engineers had to depend on captured Japanese equipment and their own genius for adaptation, said:

"There, we had to start from scratch. Here, we have everything."

Suddenly, and so suddenly that the men who had sweated their way across the stinking coral atolls were left bewildered and unbelieving, the

Pacific war had exploded from an almost anonymous back alley scrap into a full-blown onslaught to which most of the world had turned its full attention.

There were many changes. Some of them, like the constant flow of new equipment, were welcome. Some were confusing and some were downright demoralizing.

There were changes which brought to the Pacific some of the glamour — if it can be called that — of the European Air War. The United States Army Strategic Air Forces moved over from London and established headquarters on Guam with General Carl "Tooey" Spaatz in command. The Eighth Air Force and its Commanding General, Jimmy Doolittle, had set up its headquarters on Okinawa. Holzapple's Circus, a hot-flying Mediterranean outfit and the vanguard of the redeployed European air forces, landed their brand-new A-26's on the airstrip at Naha.

To Okinawa also, to this mammoth unsinkable carrier which supported the greatest show of flying force in the war against the Japanese, came the tiny Seventh Air Force. It was picked up bodily, planes, tugs and filing cabinets, from its AAFPOA command and moved to Okinawa. Its bombardment and fighter groups were dispersed as leaves before a hurricane.

The transplanting of the Seventh was, as one Air Forces combat correspondent, Corporal Dick Dugan, said, "like nothing more than the physical rerouting of the Southern Railway from its run through the red hills of Alabama to the Pennsylvania's main road-bed from Washington to New York."

Up from Palau came Kelly's Cobras to park their beat-up, 80-mission airplanes next to the brand new B-24M's on Yontan airstrip. In the same move, the Eleventh Bomb Group, which had flown its last Central Pacific missions against a target called Marcus Island (a spot which nobody except the men who had to fly over it seemed to care about), flew up from Guam. The B-25's of the 41st Bomb Group, whose mission logs went back as far as Makin Island, sat down on Kadena airfield and parked in revetments next to shiny, new B-25's which, it was rumored, could launch torpedoes as well as drop bombs.

The bombardment groups of the Seventh, which, with the exception of the B-29's in the Marianas, had always been the only Air Force flying groups on their islands, found themselves sharing airstrips and tents with the planes and pilots of two other Air Forces, the Fifth and Thirteenth. All three were lumped under one sprawling air command under the direction of General Douglas MacArthur and his air chief, General George Kenney.

From Saipan to the island of Ie Shima, off the northwest corner of Okinawa, came the P-47's of the 318th Fighter Group. With them still was Colonel Lewis M. Sanders who, as Second Lieutenant Sanders, had shot down one of the first Japanese planes of the war over Diamond Head on December 7th.

The 318th found itself in the anomalous position of belonging still to the AAFPOA headquarters, 1,800 miles away on Guam, but attached to the 301st Fighter Wing which was under the operational control of the Air Defense Command at Okinawa. This, in turn, functioned under the Navy strategically and under the Army defensively.

The official doubletalk, translated very freely, involved for the pilots some missions on which they took their orders from the Navy, others on which they were directed by Army ground defense officers and still other missions where they just said, "Oh, the hell with it," and went out and shot down some Japanese planes. The chain of changing commands brought about an administrative situation so muddled that, as Colonel Sanders said, "nobody knew where to send the reports in triplicate."

For the men of the transplanted Seventh, the quick changeover to war on a huge scale was bewildering. There were still men in the scattered Seventh who had been on duty in Hawaii on Monday morning, December 8, 1941, when the Seventh had started with fifteen operational airplanes. There were men on Okinawa who were on hand in November 1943 when the Seventh had grown to adulthood as Hale's Handful. By now, they had come to regard the air war in the Pacific as their own private battle.

Now, the war belonged to a lot of other people and it was a new kind of war. Where it was impossible for crew chiefs at Makin, Tarawa and Kwajalein to get a new relief tube for a bomber, they now found themselves with more replacement parts than they needed. Where sixty airplanes put in the air from Marshall bases had been a maximum effort, there were now huge air armadas moving in and out of single airstrips on Okinawa. From Hawaii to Saipan, a handful of colonels and a couple of generals had run the air war. Now, ATC transports landing on Yontan were disgorging more Pentagon generals and colonels with briefcases than there were privates and corporals with duffle bags coming off the LSTs in the old days.

There were still other changes wrought by this suddenly grown-up war. They are unimportant now; they had a very personal importance then. One by one, the units of the Seventh, dispersed to the far corners of the huge, throbbing military installation that was Okinawa, began to feel the ill-wind of this new way of fighting.

For the flying and non-flying members of the 318th Fighter Group, the blow fell the morning Group Memo 18 was posted.

"Chin whiskers," commanded Group Memo 18, "will be removed."

Group Memo 18 was demoralizing to the 318th; they took a fierce pride in looking like the Dead End Kids of the otherwise resplendent Army Air Forces.

The ill-wind traveled far and fast. It reached even the 13th Service Group which had come out of Angaur to find itself happily encamped in a pine thicket on the terraced crest of a mountain on Okinawa which overlooked the East China Sea. With obvious reluctance, the Group's First Sergeant had finally bowed to a new military era. He called his men together one morning.

"Military courtesy," the Sergeant said, "has suffered considerably up to now and it's time something's done about it. Like the Colonel, for instance. The Colonel really should be saluted. No one is expected to go out of his way to throw one, but it would be nice if the Colonel got a salute, at least first thing when he appears in the morning. Lieutenant colonels and majors also should be saluted occasionally.

"Captains and lieutenants," the Sergeant said, "will just have to get along as best they can under the present setup, but the practice of looking the other way when they approach should be done with more tact.

"And, finally," the Sergeant concluded, "there is the matter of our speech with officers. It has been suggested by higher command that we slowly, gradually work the word 'Sir' back into our vocabulary."

"It'll pass," said one of the men standing in the disconsolate group around the First Sergeant. "It always does."

But somehow they all knew that this time it wouldn't pass. Okinawa, this last damned island, was not at all like the others.

CHAPTER XXVII: Target-Japan!

OKINAWA HAD PACE. IT WAS A PACE THAT, COMPARED TO THE depressing, lethargic atmosphere of the other islands, was like the triumphant sound of a bugle breaking into a funeral dirge.

It was gaudy and showy and noisy. The pilots, the eager, green fledglings fresh from the States, and the veterans, leathery and shriveled from the endless days in the sun, were as hot and cocky as they had been in the days when they were flying spectacular cadet air shows at places like Randolph and Kelly.

It was the moving picture kind of flying. The B-25's of the 41st Bomb Group, which never before had had a permanent air-base large enough for formation flying, were roaring back from the target to Kadena airfield dressed tightly on each other's wing-tips, peeling out spectacularly into the traffic pattern and hitting the airstrip with a quick smoking WHUMP every thirty seconds.

Even the tired, beat-up Liberators of Kelly's Cobras and the 11th Bomb Group, their fuselages still crusted with the coral and mud of the Marianas and the Palaus, took on a new life. Always, they had straggled back from the target singly and in small groups, minutes, and sometimes hours apart. Now they came by the hundreds in flying wedges and buzzed Yontan with the impudence of P-38's.

To Kelly's Cobras, veterans of the Palaus and Philippines campaigns but comparative newcomers to the Seventh, went the honor of putting the first Army Liberators over Japan from Okinawa.

Less than twenty-four hours after the air echelon of this group arrived on Okinawa, and when only forty-eight of their planes were on the island, the aircrews were called out for a strike. Their target was Omura airfield, a major Jap airbase in Kyushu.

There was need for hurry. The Navy planned to return to the Tokyo area around the middle of July and wanted the twenty-six major Jap airfields known to be in southern Kyushu destroyed or neutralized so that their striking force could move in close and operate with the minimum opposition.

The takeoff broke all known Seventh Air Force Liberator records. Only forty-eight minutes elapsed between the takeoff of the first plane and the last — a plane a minute.

One Liberator developed engine trouble, dropped out of the formation after it reached the Jap mainland and bombed a secondary target. The other forty-seven swept over Omura at medium altitude in javelin formation and spewed out 192,000 pounds of fragmentation bombs. Fifty percent landed on the exact target, the Jap airfield's east dispersal area. There was a big explosion on the railroad track running through the airfield.

Twenty miles from the target on the way home, the jubilant aircrews saw a column of gray-black smoke standing 8,000 feet in the air.

The first Liberator mission to the Japanese mainland, which the Seventh had sweated out for forty months over five thousand miles of coral and jungle islands from Hawaii to Okinawa, was finished before the forty-eight aircrews of Kelly's Cobras had time to be awed or frightened by their distinction.

Ack-ack was moderate and inaccurate. There was one casualty. A flight engineer, Technical Sergeant Donald Leddy, was wounded in the left hand by flak.

A few days later, while the crews were still shaking their heads in pleased disbelief, they were caught up again in the quick pace of Okinawa. With other transplanted units of the Seventh, the Cobras flew a mission new to the Pacific — a large scale multiple attack in which four types of bombers and fighters from two air forces, the Fifth and Seventh, participated.

The target was the Jap's sprawling airbase at Kiangwan on the outskirts of Shanghai.

Technical Sergeant Robert Speer, an Air Forces weather observer at Guadalcanal and a former newspaper man who reverted to combat reporter at Okinawa, flew in one of the first planes across the target. His report, written while he was still bug-eyed from the unprecedented show of air power, would have sounded like a jet-propelled flight of literary fancy in an earlier Pacific era. But it was accurate in both fact and feeling.

"It was the works," Speer wrote. "It was full of zoom and buzz and Hell's Angels, and someday the movies will probably do it with Enrol Flynn."

The takeoff had been impressive. Veteran Seventh Air Force planes like Liquidator and the Dragon Lady waddled through Yontan's intricate system of taxiways toward the takeoff point behind bright, shiny, new Liberators of the B-24M class.

There were new planes with old names. Planes like Bolivar the Second, a replacement for the original Bolivar which had crashed at Downey,

California, on the first stop of a projected bond tour. There were planes so new that they had no names at all.

Squadron after squadron, group after group, lifted from Yontan, and flew through a piney valley toward the East China Sea and the rally point.

From the watery approaches of the Chinese coast to Shanghai is a short distance but, as Speer reported: "It was an exciting few minutes. Gunners and bombardiers and pilots gawked and pointed and shouted comments about new and exotic names — names that went back to fifth grade geography lessons and Saturday afternoon Fu Manchu movie serials. The East China Sea. The Yellow Sea, The Yangtze River.

"Then somebody called out Shanghai and from there on it was strictly business — and the business was the biggest raid of the war on Shanghai.

"The big Liberators wheeled over the city and came in over the airbase at Kiangwan from different directions, on different levels, at different times.

"The 11th Group swept through the ack-ack and got 90 tons of bombs away. Kelly's Cobras dumped 92 tons.

"Two big groups of Liberators from the Fifth Air Force flew in from another approach. Behind and below them were 60 B-25's of both Air Forces.

"Riding herd above the bombers were eighty Thunderbolts, cocky, pushy and spoiling for a fight.

"And along with the mob were two dozen wicked-looking A-26 attack-bombers of Holzapple's Circus, throwing their muscles around at medium altitude.

"There were a few Jap fighters," Speer stated. "But they turned tail when the Thunderbolts pointed their noses at them.

"Ack-ack was thick and two planes of Kelly's Cobras were hit hard. One spiraled crazily down and dropped out of sight through the clouds. The other faltered and fell, but recovered and staggered out to sea for a crash landing which seven men survived.

"And through it all, Chinese gathered on rooftops across the old city to watch the smoke and flame billow up from the Jap airbase.

"Dammit," Speer exulted, when he had exhausted non-censorable prose, "it was a bitch."

The first missions of Seventh Air Force outfits to the Japanese mainland were as deceptive and anticlimactic as the first missions and long-range strikes against Maloelap and Truk. Anticlimactic because they were almost too successful. Deceptive because they couldn't be counted typical missions to Japan. The opposition grew with each raid.

To the 41st Bombardment Group went the distinction of flying the first medium bombers over Japan since Jimmy Doolittle's spectacular raid in April of 1942.

"They deserved the honor. They were always the most forlorn, demoralized group in the Seventh Air Force," said Sergeant Bob Price, who had lived with the outfit twenty months before at Apemama.

"As far back as fourteen months before the 41st came to Okinawa, there were pilots who had completed more than fifty missions and who still had no hope of going home. Liberator pilots at that time were being relieved from combat at the end of thirty missions. The B-25 men never had a combat quota and had nothing more to look forward to than the disheartening assurance that the law of combat averages would sooner or later overtake even the best and the luckiest pilots."

A long time before Okinawa, First Sergeant Paul DeBrule had called the 41st "The Want To Go Home Outfit." The name had stuck.

The pilots of the 41st, when word of the mission to Japan flew around Kadena airstrip, found it a little hard to believe. The target, the very name of Kyushu, was frightening.

"Hey, Curly," one of the crew chiefs said to Major N. V. Woods, who was to lead the mission, "you know what? The last man who held your job made Lieutenant General."

Corporal Ted Manross, an assistant crew chief who had taken care of the Mitchells after their low-level sweeps over Nauru, shipping strikes in the Marshalls, and strafing missions over the jungles of Guam, was a little breathless about it.

"This is pretty terrific," he said. "After all, we'll be the first Army mediums off Okinawa hitting Japan!"

The excitement began to show the night before the mission. The air around Kadena was heavy with choking coral dust stirred up by speeding ordnance trucks, gasoline tankers, jeeps. Out on the line, the armorers worked until long after dark to the welcome blare from a truckload of musicians moving up and down the alert line.

Late that night, after Technical Sergeant Billie Earnhart had checked the fourteen forward-firing guns of Major Wood's plane, he stepped around in front of it and patted it on the fuselage.

"It's ready to give them hell," he said. "The first time in three years."

Up in the living area, in the open spot where movies usually were shown, the pilots were being briefed for the mission. They were told they were heading for rough flak country, rougher than anything they had ever before encountered.

They were told to expect 20 percent casualties!

At 3:30 the next morning, the aircrews were whistled out into the darkness. After breakfast, the half-ton trucks, filled with crew chiefs and crew members, began moving out of squadron areas toward the flight line.

Each man picked up his parachute and walked to where his plane was parked. They stood around the planes, talking and smoking excitedly. Finally, an order traveled down the line and the ground crews began walking the props through while the combat men climbed into the Mitchells.

It was getting light as the first plane, its tail lights blinking and its wing lights pointed down at the runway, cleared the strip and began climbing. By the time the sun was up, the Mitchells were gone.

From Kadena airstrip to the assigned target, Chiran airfield in Southern Kyushu, is not more than 400 miles — a short distance for pilots and crews who had known the long, tough road to Maloelap. But there was much tension and, as the formation flew north, the minutes were endless. Crew members checked their weapons over and over, navigators double-checked and double-checked the heading, engineers listened nervously for the first sounds of troubled engines.

All eyes anxiously watched for enemy fighters.

Finally the Mitchells roared over the Southern Kyushu coastline and broke up into two formations to approach the target from different directions.

"The target was socked in solid when we got there," said Captain James B. Crump, co-pilot of the lead plane. "There were a helluva lot of clouds.

"We knew it was dangerous but we decided to circle until we could see the target. Dammit, we hadn't bombed and sweated our way twenty months from Apemama to be cheated of our first mission against Japan.

"We took about fifteen minutes making a big circle. I guess everybody was pretty scared. We kept watching the clouds, expecting the Zeros to jump us any minute."

The clouds broke and the Mitchells knifed down to 7,000 feet and roared over the target, toggling their fragmentation bombs in unison on signal from the lead bombardier.

"We got away fast," Crump said, "as fast as those planes would take us out of there."

Back at Kadena, the ground crews had been sitting restlessly in the shadows of bomber wings around the airstrip. It had been a long, hard and hot sweat.

In the middle of the morning, the planes came back. They roared over the field wingtip-to-wingtip and began turning into the traffic pattern. A crew chief, who had been counting them in, bawled "They all made it!" and suddenly the airstrip was alive with running, shouting men.

Curly Woods, first man over the target and first man down, was shaking his head incredulously when he dropped through his plane's hatch to the ground.

"You won't believe it," he said to the men swarming around him, "It was a pushover.

"Forty flak bursts over the target. Forty — that was all.

"Two Zeros, up high over the target. They never even made a pass at us.

"Nobody got hurt. Nobody."

Lieutenant T. J. Williams, who had long since surrendered the last hair on his head to the Pacific sun, grabbed at somebody's offer of a cigarette when he got out of his plane.

"God, that was a cinch," he said to the crowd around him. Then, correcting himself, "No, I'll take that back. I sweated more today than I ever did on those missions from Makin. I think I sweated more today than any other day of my life."

On the tiny island of Ie Shima, out on the tip of the AAF spearhead in the Ryukyus, just as it had been a year before and 1,500 miles away at Saipan, was the 318th Fighter Group.

Six months before, the 318th had been the only fighter outfit in combat in a Central and Western Pacific area five times the size of the United States — 16,000,000 square miles. Their Thunderbolts had been old then, very old — each having flown an average distance of five times around the world.

Now, 325 miles and ninety minutes regular flying time from Japan, the 318th was a trifle confused. Their P-47's — there were less than one hundred of them — were all scrambled up on East Field with P-47's of two other Air Forces, with P-51's, P-61's, P-38's and even Marine Corsairs. Their planes were brand new P-47N's which they had flown more than

5,000 miles from Hawaii to Ie Shima in the longest shuttle mission of single-engine aircraft in Air Force history.

Lieutenants Richard H. Anderson and Donald E. Kennedy nosed their Thunderbolts down from 14,000 to 1,200 feet and broke out of the clouds over Southern Amami O Shima, a Jap base roughly halfway between Okinawa and Kyushu. Neither wore a beard (Chin whiskers will be removed: Group Memo 18) and neither dreamed of playing a major role in the new kind of war waged by the Pacific AAF, which had grown overnight into a disciplined, organized giant. They were just riding along, in Lieutenant Anderson's words, "fat, dumb and happy."

They thought the thirty planes bearing down on them from the north were Marine Corsairs.

They were flying directly beneath the last fighter in the thirty-plane southbound formation when the truth came home. Anderson and Kennedy were not among friends. The "Corsairs" were thirty Japanese Zekes.

Anderson and Kennedy attacked.

Jettisoning his bombs into the water, Anderson streaked up to the left and rear of the Japs. He was still slightly below and 2,000 feet out to the side when the last Zeke winged over to meet him. They went for each other in a head-on rush, firing. In the last split-second before collision, the Jap pulled up. Anderson gave the Jap a final burst as his belly flashed overhead. Flames streaked back from the Zeke's engine and swallowed the fuselage.

Up ahead, another Zeke crossed from right to left in front of the Thunderbolts. Kennedy went after him in a level, side approach and opened fire at 1,500 feet, his bullets leading the enemy by two and a half lengths. Jap and tracers collided and there was a flaming explosion.

Anderson and Kennedy rejoined and closed at full throttle on two more Zekes trailing the Jap formation in a loose V. Anderson sent the one to the right flaming into the water with a 30-degree deflection shot. He moved up on the lead Zeke, on which Kennedy had already fired, and had to push over hard to avoid a collision.

The Zeke, its pilot apparently dead, flashed past Anderson and went into a shallow dive to the waves. Another Jap curved left in a diving turn and exploded as Kennedy's bullets splashed the big red ball on his fuselage.

Once more the Americans reformed. They eased back on their throttles and closed deliberately on two more trailing Zckes. Anderson opened fire and one of the Jap fighters dropped its nose toward the water and fell straight down, trailing heavy black smoke. The Jap was finished, but

Kennedy crossed over and gave the falling plane an extra burst. It exploded.

Kennedy then turned his stream of bullets into the next Jap, who split-S'd into the water.

Anderson closed fast on another Jap and became the 318th's first pilot to qualify as an ace by shooting down five planes. The Zeke, burning from nose to tail, cart-wheeled into the sea.

In four minutes, Anderson and Kennedy, outnumbered 15 to 1 when they turned back to attack the thirty Zekes, had destroyed eight of them. There was only one Zeke still in sight; the others had fled into the clouds.

Kennedy remained in the upper air as overhead cover for Anderson, who nosed down after the lone Zeke. Throttled back and hugging the base of the clouds 500 feet over the running Jap, Anderson eased up, then popped out directly behind his prey. It was a sure thing and Anderson pressed the trigger.

The Jap flew on. Anderson was out of ammunition.

All over the Okinawa area that morning the sea was splotched with burning, exploding Zekes, Oscars, Vals, Nates, Tonys. The Thunderbolt formation was turned back from a bombing strike over Kyushu by bad weather. Teamed with other P-47's on combat air patrol around Okinawa, they had occupied the morning pouring out 34,558 rounds of ,50 caliber ammunition and burning 15,550 gallons of gasoline to break up Kamikaze attacks on American shipping in the Ryukyus anchorage.

When the 318th had settled back to its coral strip for lunch, its pilots had set a world's record for a single fighter group in a single action. In four hours, they had shot down thirty-four Japanese planes!

It was a long way from Saipan and Makin and Midway. Always, the Thunderbolt pilots had hunted the Jap pilots, from 40,000 feet down to the deck, over the flat coral spits of the Gilberts, over the hilly jungle of the Marianas, or in the foggy air over Iwo.

They had met only a few. Their first enemy plane was Colonel Sanders', shot down over Diamond Head on December 7th. The long Makin campaign brought their total to six.

At Saipan, the record had inched up to forty-eight enemy aircraft destroyed. Most of them had been brought into the 318th's firing range by such unorthodox measures as were taken when the P-47 pilots borrowed P-38's and flew north to Iwo.

Forty-eight kills, distributed among the pilots of five squadrons assigned or attached to the 318th, was not an impressive showing for forty months of war. In the Southwest Pacific, one man, Major Dick Bong, shot down forty planes. Over on Iwo, the Mustang pilots, in combat less than a month, had beaten the 318th in the race to produce the Seventh's first fighter ace. A lanky, twenty-four-year-old Mustang pilot, Major James B. Tapp, had shot down his fifth Jap on his fourth mission over Japan.

Then, in four hours of action near Okinawa on the morning of May 25th, the 318th had destroyed thirty-four planes.

A kill made by Lieutenant William Spencer the day before the turkey shoot over Japan brought the 3i8th's Ryukyus-Kyushu score to thirty-five.

It was only the beginning. In the final days before the AAF was to swarm over Japan on a scale dwarfing the achievements of any single group, the 318th got its chance. It knocked down Japs with machine-gun bullets, rockets — even with a blast of prop wash.

May 26th was a good day for the 318th. It bagged a pair of Jap dive bombers north of Okinawa. May 27 was a quiet day. May 28 was not. Twenty-four Thunderbolts, taking off in small flights at intervals during the day, had gone north to Kyushu.

Captain John E. Vogt led his four-plane flight over Kanoya at 16,000 feet in mid-afternoon. He could see two airfields below, a barrage balloon floating over a factory district, and 28 Zekes boring in from the northwest with a 4,000-foot altitude advantage.

The four Thunderbolts attacked.

Vogt and his men dropped their external gas tanks and climbed. They gained slowly on the Japs until, at 28,000 feet, they had a 1,000-foot altitude advantage. The four Americans leveled off over the west coast of Kagoshima Bay, flanked on the east by the 28 Japs who had split their mass formation into seven flights of four planes each. Vogt turned to intercept the lead Jap flight. One by one, the Japs in front of him pitched out of formation and dived for the deck. Vogt and his wingman, Lieutenant Philip La Rochelle, plunged down after them.

A black, shiny Zeke with red roundels loomed in Vogt's gunsight. The American's bullets stitched the black left wing and worked over and up toward the cockpit canopy. There was a trail of flames and then an explosion. Vogt swung left and plastered the wingroots and belly of a second Zeke which burst into flames.

Vogt and La Rochelle, momentarily alone, went back up to 28,000 feet and skidded down on the rear of three more Zekes. La Rochelle hopped the Jap on the extreme left and sent him down; Vogt swung a long burst from left to right. Both Japs flamed.

Again the Thunderbolts reached for the ceiling, then dove as they spotted four more Japs. They saw their bullets lace one of the Japs in the center of the flight as two outside Zekes whipped around in a maneuver that would have put them on the tails of the Thunderbolts. Vogt and La Rochelle got out of there fast, then swept back after three more Zekes.

Two of the Japs came up to meet them, firing. Vogt traded tracers with the lead Jap. The Jap's tracers sped past Vogt's wing; Vogt's tracers punched through the Jap's wing and canopy. The Jap flipped over on his back and fell out of sight, smoking. La Rochelle's bullets chewed into the fuselage of the other Jap, who also went down smoking. There was no time to see whether they crashed.

The third Jap had raced up and away from the fight. Now he dived back toward the P-47's. Vogt and La Rochelle nosed up to meet his rush. Neither side would give away in the race toward collision. The Jap opened fire at 2,000 feet. Vogt held his fire until he was 1,500 feet from the Jap. They were 200 feet apart, still firing point-blank, when the Jap exploded. Vogt rammed the stick against his stomach and snapped up and to the right, dodging the debris.

The surviving Japs had seen enough. They ran away.

Vogt had bagged five and a probable. La Rochelle, whose primary job as wingman was to protect his flight leader's tail, had downed one and a probable. Together, they had damaged a ninth.

"On missions of this nature," Vogt wrote into his report that night, "recommend that at least twenty planes be assigned."

The 318th Thunderbolts, on May 28th, had done a solid day's work. The 24 planes which had ranged Japan at intervals in eight-plane formations, had encountered 48 Japanese fighters. Ten Thunderbolt pilots had scored 17 confirmed kills, four probables, two damaged. By evening, the 318th had two new fighter aces, Captain Vogt and Lieutenant Stanley Lustic, who had picked two Japs off a fellow pilot's tail to bring his total to six — one off Saipan, three north of Okinawa and two over Kyushu.

The 318th's score, for five days of the Ryukyus-Kyushu campaign, stood at 54 to 0. They had yet to lose a plane to the Japs over Okinawa or Japan.

Bad weather held the 318th to three Japanese kills during the next ten days. It lost its first pilot, Lieutenant Irving Albert, who failed to pull out when he dived on a wave-skimming Jap fighter. Then, on June 6th, clearing skies sent 32 Thunderbolts on another rampage over Kyushu. Their assignment was to attack ground targets. Four planes swept down on Kanoya Air Field. Six others rocketed and strafed Kagoshima Air Field, skimmed the trees to Byu, scattering 50 Japs at work on the south end of the runway. Then they raced on to Ibusuki Seaplane base to leave a twin-engine flying boat burning on the water.

On the June 6th mission, Captain Judge E. Wolfe became the first Army pilot in the Pacific to pick off an enemy plane with a rocket.

Wolfe, who had downed two Jap Bettys while flying a borrowed P-38 over Iwo in February, was leading a patrol flight at 21,000 feet over Kyushu. He spotted seven Zekes coming at his flight with a 4,000-foot altitude advantage. Two rockets were fixed to the wings of his Thunderbolt and Wolfe was reluctant to jettison them. He decided to see how they worked out as air-to-air weapons.

Closing to within a thousand feet of the onrushing Japs, he salvoed his rockets at the lead Zeke.

"He disintegrated," Wolfe reported later. "Hell, I was just as surprised as he was."

Wolfe spotted another Zeke ahead and flew through the debris of his rocket-kill to explode his second plane in less than a minute. Above him, Thunderbolts shot down two more Zekes. The rest fled.

Four more Thunderbolt pilots in another formation scored victories that day over Japan. Back at Ie Shima, Lieutenant Colonel Harry E. McAfee, the first Army pilot to land on Saipan and Tinian, flushed a Jap bomber and shot it into the East China Sea.

Sixty-six to one.

On June 8th, a large formation of Japanese planes came down to Ie Shima for what was undoubtedly planned as a retaliation raid. In the wildest melee of the Okinawa campaign, the 318th scorched the waters around Ie Shima with the burning wreckage of thirteen Japanese planes.

Seventy-nine to one.

At dawn on June 9th, heckler met heckler over Amami O Shima and Captain Roy A. Jacobson brought the 3i8th's Ryukyus-Kyushu score to an even 80 to one. Jacobson and his wingman, Lieutenant George W. Trumbour, were flying home after a night nuisance raid to touch off the sirens in Southern Japan and drive the Japs out of bed. A Jap dive bomber was heading north after a similar night's work over Okinawa. They met at the halfway point, Amami O Shima. Jacobson opened fire at 1,500 feet. The Jap faltered, flamed and fell.

With its handful of insolent the 318th was outfighting the enemy from Okinawa to Central Kyushu, goading the Japs into an all-out defensive effort which came on June 10th. Thirty-five Thunderbolts flew north that morning to protect Navy photographic Liberators. They ran into 134 Zekes, Jacks, Tonys, Tojos and Georges, all fast, single-engine fighters.

Few Thunderbolts were free to carry the battle to the Japs. Most held their defensive screen to discourage the major attack on the photo planes and destroy the few fighters who did attempt to break through.

Only eight of the escorting P-47's got a crack at the Japs. But the eight handed the Japs a lacing which left the wreckage of 17 planes sprinkled over a twenty-mile area north of Kagoshima Wan.

There was pandemonium in the briefing tent that night as the pilots tried to describe the wildest rat race they had ever seen. Some of the pilots were still laughing about Lieutenant John Brunner's tense few minutes shortly after he had shot down his first Jap. Brunner was going toward the deck, as fast as his Thunderbolt would take him, bucking and weaving and looking nervously back over his shoulder when he called into his radio:

"I've got five Jacks on my tail. Anybody who wants 'em can have 'em."

Seated at the side of a harassed Intelligence officer, Captain Wolfe, whose last four planes had brought his total to nine and established him as the Group's ace, was giving a routine summary of the mission when Lieutenant Bob Stone walked in.

Stone was the last man to land. He sat down, pushed back his long-billed flight cap and said:

"You guys aren't going to believe me."

Stone had shot down two Zekes when he heard Captain Wolfe call out 50 enemy fighters. He climbed for altitude. But his induction system had been damaged on takeoff and he couldn't develop full power in the rarefied air. It was no go up there, but Stone saw a lone George far below that looked ripe for picking.

He was maneuvering to the attack when he discovered 25 Japs streaking down on his tail. There was nothing to do but run for it. Stone nosed down and went from 28,000 feet to the deck in one long screaming dive.

He pulled out ten feet off the bushes and streaked across country with two Japs on his tail, the rest of the pack strung out behind. Most of the time, the belly of his Thunderbolt was less than three feet off the ground. The two leading Japs were within 300 feet of his tail. Tracers whipped around Stone but he hadn't been hit.

A low hummock had appeared before him and Stone nosed up to hurdle it. Then he was flashing past startled Jap faces on the runway of Nittagahara Air Field. A twin-engine Betty just leaving the Jap strip loomed squarely in Stone's path.

He swerved left to avoid the Betty and at that moment became the 318th's fifth ace.

The blast of Stone's prop wash caught the two Japs behind him. They crashed together and, still together, plunged into the Betty.

"There was a hell of an explosion," Stone said. "The last time I looked back at the runway, it was covered with chunks of burning airplanes."

The rest of the Japs hung on, but Stone hedgehopped up the coast and finally shook them.

To Major John J. Hussey, a squadron commander, went the honor of shooting down the 3i8th's 100th enemy plane in 18 days.

Hussey scored two kills and a probable to pace the licking which seven Thunderbolts handed 30 Jap fighters near Miyakonojo, Kyushu. The score went to 102 when Lieutenants Thomas Martin and Lloyd Millet each accounted for a Jap plane.

It stayed at 102 for ten days. The Japs made a few feeble gestures over Ie at night. Black Widows attached to the 318th mortally stung three of them.

On June 22nd, Japs tried the daytime air over Ie and ran into an aerial buzz saw of Thunderbolts and Marine Corsairs.

Over Kikai Shima, north of Okinawa, Lieutenant William H. Mathis got two Zekes to become the 318th's six fighter ace. Major Charles W. Tennent flamed another.

The score including planes downed by the 548th Night Fighter Squadron attached to the 318th on Ie, was 116 Japanese planes shot down in eighteen days.

On Wednesday morning, August 8, 1945, a flight of eight 318th Thunderbolts were 10,000 feet over Southern Japan on their way home from bombing airfields on Shikoku.

Lieutenant John Brunner, flying the lead plane, had just checked his watch — it was exactly 10:40 a.m. — and was peering through his canopy for enemy fighters when he was blinded by a quick white glare which pierced the overcast with the intensity of a thousand suns.

The flash was momentary. Brunner, as did the other seven pilots, thought that one of the planes in the formation had exploded. He was looking over his shoulder, counting the planes strung out behind him, when he saw — forty miles to the east — a great bubble of flame and smoke.

While Brunner watched, the ball of fire catapulted itself 40,000 feet in the air and began to take the form of a huge tapering cloud, miles across and greyish white at the top, black and purple at its narrow, twisting base.

The cloud hovered at 60,000 feet over the Japanese city of Nagasaki.

And the eight pilots knew, for the first time, why the sectional maps used by their briefing officers had ruled out Nagasaki as a target not to be bombed "until further notice."

CHAPTER XXVIII: THE SUN ALSO SETS

A FEW MINUTES AFTER NINE O'CLOCK ON THE MORNING OF August 19, 1945, a formation of P-38 fighter planes lifted from the runway on Ie Shima, circled once over the East China sea, and set a course straight toward Japan.

There were many men on hand to witness the take-off. Early in the morning, long before the sun was up, they had begun to collect around the airstrip. The earliest arrivals were huddled in small groups under the wings of parked aircraft, for in a little while it promised to be very hot in the places where there was nothing to cast a merciful shadow to block off the glaring sun.

And it might be a long, fruitless wait — the way it was yesterday when the same men sat or stood along the airstrip for eight hours, waiting with the quiet endurance of men long accustomed to sweating out something that might never happen.

This, the nineteenth day of August, was their third day of waiting; of hurrying to the airstrip with the first streak of morning light, of leaving it only a few minutes for noon chow — and sometimes not leaving at all — until the sun went down and it grew dark and it was hopeless to wait any longer.

By 11 o'clock, the airstrip, the revetments and the roads leading to the field overflowed with a solid mass of sun and atabrine-colored American faces. Gasoline tankers, prime movers, bulldozers, command cars and jeeps were turned into impromptu grandstands and wheeled as close to the two white crosses freshly painted on the runway as the military police would permit.

At noon, a colonel from Ie Shima's island command headquarters estimated that, of the 60,000 men garrisoned on the five-mile island, wore than 55,000 were concentrated around the 7,000-foot landing strip.

Sprinkled in the throng, anonymous spectators to an historic event they felt they hand played a major part in bringing about, were small groups of Seventh Air Force men.

On the west side of the strip, pressed against the rope barrier which the MP's had hastily strung along the edge of the strip, were Lieutenant

Colonel Harry McAfee, Captain Marsden Dupuy and Lieutenant Robert George, of the 318th Fighter Group. Dupuy and George, more than 70 missions and 40 months ago, had flown together at Makin Island.

McAfee, the first Army pilot to land on Saipan and Tinian, had been appointed group commander of the 318th when Colonel Sanders, shortly before the first atomic bomb was dropped, had been ordered back to Hawaii for reassignment.

It had been McAfee's unpleasant job to tell his men why the P-38's of the Fifth Air Force had been chosen to replace the P-47's of the Seventh Air Force for this, the most memorable fighter mission of the war.

Ironically, it was a simple matter of aircraft recognition. The snub-nosed P-47's, in flight at least, resembled the Jap Tojo or Jack. The peace, if it really was to be peace, could not be jeopardized. So, the twin-engine, double-boomed P-38's, easily distinguishable from all other friendly and enemy aircraft, had been selected to rendezvous with the Japanese bombers off Southern Kyushu and escort them safely to Ie Shima.

The bitterness, the cheated feeling of the P-47 men had lessened when they learned that the Fifth Air Force men making the flight were themselves veterans of 42 months continuous combat in the Southwest Pacific.

There were other Seventh Air Force men present that day on Ie: Sergeant Bob Price, veteran of 42 months and 26 islands from Hawaii west; Sergeant Bob Frederick, who had gone ashore at Saipan with the Barflies a few weeks after arriving in Hawaii from the States, and who had lived with the fighter group ever since.

There were Seventh Air Force Aviation Engineers, who had paved the aerial road of conquest from Kwajalein to Okinawa. There were truckdrivers, crewchiefs, clerks. They were a very small part of the crowd of 5th, 13th and 8th Air Forces men, the Marines, artillerymen, infantrymen, the veterans, the newcomers whose bunktags, in the parlance of the Pacific, "hadn't stopped swinging."

Shortly after 11 o'clock, there was a commotion at the seaward end of the airstrip and one by one the 55,000 faces turned to the northern horizon. They saw only a lone P-38 which had aborted far short of the rendezvous point.

It was another of the endless false alarms — as misleading as had been the evasive Japanese peace commitments beamed to MacArthur in Manila.

"They aren't coming," said a man standing near Colonel McAfee. "They haven't got any white paint to paint the Bettys like MacArthur told them to."

"Hell," said McAfee, "maybe they just don't have a Betty left up there."

Then, suddenly impressed with the likelihood of so disastrous a situation, he added: "God, wouldn't that be awful!"

It was a quiet, almost wordless crowd. They had vented all their excitement and emotion the night shortly after the second atomic bomb had been loosed on Japan, when suddenly, unbelievably, the war was over.

It wasn't true of course. But the first report of the Jap offer to capitulate, coming while most men on Okinawa and Ie Shima were being told to expect a gas attack in retaliation for the atomic bomb, had set off the wildest, loudest celebration in the Pacific.

For an insane half hour, the sky around Ryukyus was split open with the indescribable sound of pistol and rifle bullets, artillery shells, rockets, anti-aircraft bursts, fired without direction and fired only for the sake of making noise. They were the only means for celebration the men on Okinawa and Ie Shima had at their disposal. The false peace casualties were 13 men killed and more than 200 wounded.

Whatever hopes they had for a quick end after that wild night had died during the five jittery days that followed. Days of rumor and counter-rumor, of staring tensely at radios which yielded only the news that there was no news. Days — and nights too — when there was still the sound overhead of American planes going out to combat. And Japanese planes coming in.

All through the long, hot morning of August 19, the rumors traveled from group to group and from man to man

The Japs weren't going to surrender to us; we were going to surrender to them

It was a Jap trick — a sort of psychological booby trap contrived to throw us off guard while an enormous enemy fleet, hidden until now, sailed on Hawaii.

A few minutes after noon, a Marine radar operator sitting in a paneled truck on the northern tip of Okinawa saw a disturbance on the oscilloscope screen. Whatever caused it was 120 miles north of Ie Shima, moving toward the island with a speed that caused the pip to flare wildly up and down.

At thirty minutes past noon, from far out to sea there was the heavy drone of many airplane engines. The 55,000 men on Ie Shima shaded their eyes and looked to the north. The men who had been sitting or lying down got quickly to their feet.

Just breaking the horizon was a fleet of P-38's. As the planes sped closer, the men on Ie could make out two larger, plum-shaped planes locked in the center of the fighter formation.

As the planes sped closer, the P-38's swung off course and began to orbit the island.

The two larger planes held a course straight toward the island.

Then the first Jap bomber, painted white and with five green crosses (one under each wing, one on either side and one on the upper tail fin), moved across the island of Ie Shima.

Except for the movement of eyes and the slow turning of heads as the Jap Betty passed overhead, the men gathered below were motionless and silent.

The second enemy plane flew over the island.

Three times the white Bettys circled and passed over the island, perhaps making certain of the white crosses painted on the runway below, perhaps waiting for the landing signal, perhaps hesitant.

Then the Japs flew out to sea, and still restricted to the immediate area of Ie Shima by the circling P-38's, began to turn toward the runway.

The first Betty touched its wheels cautiously to the coral and began rolling down the runway past the incredible number of suntanned, expressionless American faces.

As the plane flashed by, Lieutenant Bob George turned to Colonel McAfee.

"For three years I've been meeting up with Bettys," he said, "but this is the first time I've ever been damn glad to see one. Wonderful, isn't it?"

McAfee wasn't listening. He was staring apprehensively at the second bomber, which had sideslipped toward the landing strip at a crazy angle with its nose dropped far below the safe landing attitude. McAfee was thinking how disastrous it would be if the plane crashed on the strip, or, worse, if it ploughed into the closely-packed spectators.

The Jap pilot recovered at the last moment and bounced into a landing so sloppy that McAfee silently cursed him.

As the plane rolled past McAfee, he noticed for the first time the great, ugly splotches of brown showing through the white paint. To the end, the Japs had done things badly.

As the Bettys moved slowly back up the airstrip behind the "Follow Me" jeep which had sped out to meet them, a hatch above the pilot's compartment was pushed open and a Japanese head was thrust into the open.

"So that's what they look like," one man said. And then, aware of the critical stares of the men around him, he added, self-consciously, "I've never seen one before."

The Jap was wearing a leather flying helmet with fur earlaps turned up and, as he pulled off his flying goggles, the men at the edge of the strip saw he was wearing thick, horn-rimmed glasses. The Jap, apparently the co-pilot, signaled the jeep's course to the pilot below by banging on the fuselage with his open hand.

That, and the unsynchronized burbling of the Betty's engines, were the only sounds disturbing the spontaneous silence.

The two planes halted about 100 feet from a C-54 Skymaster parked toward the seaward end of the strip — the transfer ship which was to carry the surrender delegation to MacArthur's headquarters in Manila.

For a few moments, nothing happened. The military police, in rigid files on the east and west sides of the strip, stood stiffly at parade rest, the sun flashing from their bayonets. The men massed behind them were motionless and silent.

Then, a small hatch in the side of one of the Bettys was pushed open. An Army Lieutenant, wearing an interpreter's armband, walked across the strip to the open hatch and talked into the airplane.

A thin man — tall for a Japanese — squeezed through the narrow opening and dropped to the runway. He wore a sports coat, a shirt open at the collar, tan shorts, white, knee-length stockings and white shoes. Heavy glasses and a small black mustache gave his face a rather quizzical expression.

The man took a few tentative steps forward and then, apparently noticing for the first time the mass of staring, silent Americans, halted in his tracks.

Through the same small door, and an identical opening in the second Betty, 14 Japanese Army and Navy Officers and a second civilian made their way to the ground.

Most of them were short and round and wore horn-rimmed glasses under their peaked hats. All except the two civilians trailed great samurai swords from their left hips. A few carried harakiri knives.

The 16 Japs lined up under the broad wing of the transfer plane — their eyes cast resolutely down.

The 55,000 Americans looked on entranced, each man aware of his presence at an historic spectacle, but experiencing the soldier's ancient inability to regard himself as a participant in the drama of war.

One of them expressed in a soldier's simple terms the familiar, detached attitude of the spectator which each man was consciously experiencing:

"It's like a dream," he said to no one in particular. "Like looking on something from another world."

Ie Shima's spectators to the first tangible evidence of final capitulation, the same men who had staged the Pacific's rowdiest, wildest victory celebration five days before, had not been briefed on their conduct before the enemy's generals and admirals.

The silence, the motionless staring as bit by bit the peace began to unfold, were spontaneous — the unanticipated reaction of men who had not expected to see this thing happen during their own lifetimes.

Staff Sergeant Bob Price, who had worked his way closer to the Japs than most American soldiers were permitted, noticed that the uniforms of the high-ranking enemy officers were a cheap, sleazy green cotton. The leather boots and belts looked artificial. Most of the Japs carried their lunches wrapped in white paper and small tins filled with pastry. Price thought they looked strange and lonely, as if they had gotten all dressed up to impress us and it didn't quite come off.

"Or then again," Price said, "perhaps there is nothing in the Jap military code which tells a man what to wear to a surrender."

The Japanese aircrewmen, when they rolled out of the Bettys after the peace delegation, made a flashier but more comical impression. They wore gleaming, mahogany-colored leather flying jackets with hoods lined with white fur and knee-length flying boots. Dwarfed by the American interpreters around them, who wore rumpled khaki uniforms, the Jap crewmen looked like small, oriental versions of the Graustark soldier.

Standing 20 feet away from the Japanese officials now lined up under the Skymaster's wings, and towering over them even at that distance, Brigadier General Frederick H. Smith, an early fighter pilot in the Pacific, delivered brief instructions. He told the delegation it would proceed at once to Manila. He offered to house the Jap aircrewmen on Ie Shima until the delegation returned from Manila. The Japs listened without looking up from the runway, and with their heads turned slightly away from the

American General. Lieutenant General Kawabe Takashiro, leader of the Jap delegation, nodded grudgingly as Smith finished talking.

There was an awkward moment as the Jap emissaries, ready to board the Skymaster, looked around for their baggage. Takashiro, after pondering the problem in surrender protocol for a few moments, said something over his shoulder to a lower-ranking officer, who — in the ancient custom of all the world's armies — passed the problem on down the line.

Watching the Jap pilots and enlisted men shuttling back and forth between the Bettys and the Skymaster with the delegation's luggage, Lieutenant Bob George was trying to make the spectacle fit into a pattern which for him had started at Makin Island and ended here on Ie Shima more than 70 missions later.

The tiny, spit-and-polish, comic opera soldiers, struggling awkwardly under the weight of baggage as they scurried back and forth like brown beetles, looked not at all like the enemy — the ruthless, might aggressor who, early in 1942, was steamrolling unopposed through the Pacific.

The pilot was staring at the phenomenon, trying to bring into focus whatever it was that left him with no sensation of proximity to the enemy, when a Jap crewman inside the lead Betty moved to a glass blister opposite him.

The fighter pilot, staring at the Jap, felt the cold impact, the quick downward plunge of his stomach familiar to American airmen about to engage the enemy in combat. The spectacle on Ie Shima assumed its place in the pattern.

Somehow the Jap crewman, hunched over behind the glass blister and peering momentarily through the glass at the Americans, was a familiar enemy.

Their baggage finally assembled, and the delicate protocol problem settled in a manner which caused broad grins among the high-ranking American officers present, the 16 Japs queued up before the flight of landing steps wheeled up to the Skymaster.

A grizzled crew chief, noting the dispatch cases and portable typewriters of the two Jap junior officers at the end of the line, said derisively: "A couple of lousy T-5 clerks."

The Japs began climbing the long steep flight of steps. Each Jap officer was periled at every step by the samurai sword which clanged against the wooden framework and became entangled between his legs.

Standing close to the plane, Staff Sergeant Bob Price said.

"I'm praying. It would be hell if one of them slipped. It would be an international incident."

The Japs, to Price's great relief, made it safely, and the plane's big steel doors were slammed shut.

The transfer plane wheeled slowly down the runway past the white crosses. Then it parked at an angle for a few moments while the pilot revved up its four engines, and came back up the runway gathering speed. At 28 minutes past one o'clock, the plane pulled itself into the air.

The 55,000 Americans on Ie Shima, still entranced and silent, watched the Skymaster out of sight and then turned their attention to the two Bettys and the nine Jap crewmen left on the island. Through an interpreter, the Japs were directed to move their planes into revetments.

And in so doing, the Jap crewmen suffered further an ignominy which, to the American pilots, crewchiefs and line mechanics, was a sweeter remembrance than the submission of the Jap generals and admirals. The landing gear of the lead Betty, as the plane was being wheeled into a revetment, broke through the coral surface. The tire went almost out of sight.

The Americans pressed as close to the disabled Bettys as the MP's would allow and, smiling openly, looked on as the Japs, sweltering in their high-altitude flying suits, struggled with the embedded landing gear. Nobody said a word. Nobody offered to help.

Finally, the Japs freed their plane and were rounded up and placed in command cars. The pilot of the lead Betty was led to a command car which had a provocative Varga girl painted on its side. He sat on the back seat with his possessions, wrapped in a bright silk scarf, placed beside him. With the white fur earlaps of his leather helmet turned up, the Jap pilot looked, to Sergeant Bob Frederick, "like a bewildered rabbit."

The procession of command cars and MPs' jeeps had started to bore through the crowd when the Jap pilot remembered something. He ran back to the lead Betty, climbed inside and in a few moments came back to the command car carrying three wilted bouquets — roses, pinks and larkspurs.

A technical sergeant Nisei interpreter from Honolulu asked the pilot in perfect Japanese why the flowers. The pilot answered, in just as perfect English, "Just because."

Then the Jap aircrews were gone and the only tangible evidence still remaining on the airstrip of the peace which had been so long in coming were the two Bettys, closely guarded by military police, and the flight of landing steps the Japs had climbed for the last lap of their ignominious journey.

For a long time, nobody moved from the airstrip. The men sat or stood just as they had all through the morning, talking quietly or not talking at all. Some lingered near the Bettys, as though reluctant to take leave of the visible reassurance that this dream was not false like all their other dreams of peace. A few men lingered near the landing platform, examining it with careful glances but not noticing that it was the exact companion of dozens of other landing platforms at places like Hickam Field, Johnston Island, Kwajalein, Saipan.

Finally, as the sun — which looked that day like a bright, midwest harvest sun — was halfway down the sky, the men began drifting away from the airstrip. Some of them went to their tents to write letters which had been thought out and mentally written over and over again in that other lifetime before the morning of August 19. Others remembered there was a beer ration that day and it was the first time within the memory of any veteran that many men had to be reminded of it.

Still others lay back on their cots, staring wordlessly at the canvas ceiling.

Hours after the Skymaster had flown the Japanese delegation off the island, a formation of P-47's from the 318th Fighter Group, which had been out on combat air patrol, came out of the setting sun and began letting down into the landing pattern.

Sitting under the wing of a parked Thunderbolt, where they had been talking quietly all afternoon, Colonel McAfee, Captain Dupuy and Lieutenant George watched the planes as, one by one, they landed and rolled to the end of the strip.

They watched the last plane as it turned off the airstrip and heard, as from a great distance, the quick gasp of its engine as the propeller turned over for the last time.

Then the airstrip was long and empty and quiet. The three men got slowly to their feet and began walking back toward their tents.

As they trudged along in the evening freshness, McAfee looked around the island and out over the Pacific as though he was seeing it all for the first, or perhaps the last time.

Far out to sea there was a tapering path of orange light — dark and diluted with the greenish-blue of the sea where the whitecaps began to move shoreward, stronger, brighter where it stretched beyond the tumbling horizon.

The sun had set.

A NOTE TO THE READER

WE HOPED YOU LOVED THIS BOOK. IF YOU DID, PLEASE LEAVE A REVIEW ON AMAZON TO LET EVERYONE ELSE KNOW WHAT YOU THOUGHT.

WE WOULD ALSO LIKE TO THANK OUR SPONSORS **WWW.DIGITALHISTORYBOOKS.COM** WHO MADE THE PUBLICATION OF THIS BOOK POSSIBLE.

WWW.DIGITALHISTORYBOOKS.COM PROVIDES A WEEKLY NEWSLETTER OF THE BEST DEALS IN HISTORY AND HISTORICAL FICTION.

SIGN UP TO THEIR NEWLSETTER TO FIND OUT MORE ABOUT THEIR LATEST DEALS.

Made in the USA
Coppell, TX
19 April 2021